How to Use Your Words – Neubearbeitung

Lensing
Wörterbücher

Carin Pollmann-Laverentz · Friedrich Pollmann

Lernwörterbuch in Sachgruppen

How to Use Your Words

Neubearbeitung

Lensing Wörterbücher

Sprachliche Beratung: Rosemary Carter-Dangloff und Timothy Sodmann

Gedruckt auf chlorfrei gebleichtem Papier

ISBN 3-559-**23300**-3

Herstellung: Ernst Knoth GmbH, Melle

Printed in Germany

Druck A 6 5 4 3 / Jahr 1996 95 94 93

Die letzte Zahl bezeichnet das Jahr des Druckes. Alle Drucke der Serie A sind gegenüber der Auflage 1/1990 unverändert und daher im Unterricht parallel verwendbar.

Inhalt

The order in our world – Die Ordnung in unserer Welt

Zur Einführung

Die Zielsetzung des Lernwörterbuches

Mit *How to Use Your Words* wurde 1982 ein „Lernwörterbuch in Sachgruppen" vorgelegt, das den englischen Wortschatz in Wort- und Kollokationsfeldern darbietet, die auf ein geordnetes, in sich widerspruchfreies, horizontal und vertikal gegliedertes Gefüge von Schlüsselwörtern bzw. -vorstellungen bezogen sind. Auf die Bedeutung von Wort- und Kollokationsfeldern für den Erwerb fremdsprachlicher Fertigkeiten, aber auch von außersprachlichen Gliederungsgefügen für das Lernen, Behalten und Anwenden ist in der methodisch-didaktischen Fachliteratur schon vor längerer Zeit hingewiesen worden. Seit einigen Jahren ist zu beobachten, daß die damals formulierten Einsichten zunehmend in der Praxis des Fremdsprachenunterrichts umgesetzt werden. Dafür das richtige Arbeitsmittel in der Hand des Schülers und Lehrers bereitzustellen, war und ist die Zielsetzung des „Lernwörterbuches in Sachgruppen". An den bewährten Prinzipien von *How to Use Your Words* ist deshalb auch in der Neubearbeitung festgehalten worden.

Die Gliederung

Die Wort- und Kollokationsfelder des Lernwörterbuches sind drei Gruppen zugeordnet: den 201 fortlaufend numerierten Sachbereichen und den 38 Sachgebieten, die wiederum zu 6 Hauptgruppen zusammentreten. Nach dem Prinzip der sich vergrößernden Perspektive spiegelt diese Ordnung eine mögliche, lernerleichternde Betrachtungsweise des „Menschen in und mit der Welt" wider, deren formale Ausprägung sich an der Theorie der sozialen Systeme Talcott Parsons orientiert.

Der Aufbau eines Sachbereiches

Die meisten Sachbereiche sind dreispaltig angelegt. In der **linken Spalte** erscheint das Einzelwort zusammen mit der phonetischen Umschrift, Hinweisen zum britischen (*BE*) bzw. amerikanischen (*AE*) Sprachgebrauch, ggf. mit unregelmäßigen Pluralformen und den Formen der unregelmäßigen Verben. Es ist in dreifacher Weise mit dem übrigen Wortmaterial des jeweiligen Sachbereichs vernetzt.

a) Es ist Kernwort (*headword, node*) der in der rechten Spalte aufgelisteten Kollokationen und festeren Wortverbindungen.
b) Mit den bedeutungsverwandten Wörtern derselben Wortklasse im Sachbereich bildet es Wortfelder.
c) Als Teil einer Wortabfolge repräsentiert es ein Element eines lernerleichternden Ordnungsprinzips, z.B. eines zeitlichen Ablaufs oder eines räumlichen Nebeneinander.

Die **mittlere Spalte** dient der Bedeutungserschließung. Mit den deutschen Entsprechungen werden die Bedeutungen eines Wortes innerhalb eines Sachbereiches erfaßt. So tritt (*to*) *see* mit der Bedeutung „sehen" im Sachbereich *14 sight* im Sachgebiet

senses, mit der Bedeutung „verstehen" dagegen im Sachbereich *38 understanding, knowledge* im Sachgebiet *mental life* auf. Der Zugang zu den einzelnen Bedeutungen eines Wortes kann über das alphabetische Wörterverzeichnis am Ende des Buches gewonnen werden.
Die **rechte Spalte** erfüllt zwei Funktionen. Zum einen ergänzt sie die Einträge der linken Spalte um damit zusammengesetzte bzw. durch Anfügen von Vor- bzw. Nachsilben gebildete Wörter (*compounds* bzw. *derivatives*), falls diese nicht als gesonderte Einträge erscheinen. Zum anderen zeigt sie das Einzelwort in seinen konventionellen Verbindungen mit anderen Wörtern, meist in der Form von Kollokationen (*collocations*), auch in festen Verbindungen (*fixed phrases*) und idiomatischen Ausdrücken (*idioms*), gelegentlich auch eingebettet in einem Satz.

Zum Einsatz des Lernwörterbuches im Unterricht

Der auf die oben beschriebene Weise erreichten vertikalen und horizontalen Verflechtung des Wortmaterials entspricht grundsätzlich eine Wortschatzarbeit, die nicht chronologisch von einem Sachbereich des Lernwörterbuches zum nächsten fortschreitet, sondern die unterschiedlichen inhaltlichen Aspekte des Unterrichts über die im Gliederungsgefüge enthaltenen Schlüsselwörter mit den zugeordneten Wort- und Kollokationsfeldern verknüpft und diese in kontinuierlicher, auf die Inhalte des Unterrichts bezogener Sprech- und Schreibübung schrittweise verfügbar macht.

Zur phonetischen Umschrift

Von vielen Benutzern ist angeregt worden, den Einträgen die Lautschrift beizugeben. Die Angabe der Aussprache und Betonung orientiert sich an der 14. Auflage des *English Pronouncing Dictionary* von Jones/Gimson (Dent, 1977). Einige, besonders mehrwortige, Einträge, die dort nicht belegt sind, wurden so gewissenhaft wie möglich recherchiert und unter Beratung geschulter *native speakers* gesetzt.

1. Lautzeichen (*phonetic symbols*)

[ɪ]	s**i**t	[iː]	s**ee**	[eɪ]	n**a**me
[ʌ]	b**u**t	[ɑː]	**a**sk	[aɪ]	t**i**me
[ɒ]	b**o**x	[ɔː]	br**oa**d	[ɔɪ]	b**oy**
[ʊ]	l**oo**k	[uː]	m**oo**n	[əʊ]	**o**ld
[e]	g**e**t	[ɜː]	s**ir**	[aʊ]	m**ou**se
[æ]	f**a**t			[ɪə]	h**ere**
[ə]	**a**nother			[eə]	th**ere**
				[ʊə]	s**ure**
[s]	**s**on	[z]	ha**s**	[l]	**l**ike
[ʃ]	**sh**e	[ʒ]	lei**s**ure	[m]	**m**an
[tʃ]	**ch**alk	[dʒ]	lar**ge**	[n]	**n**ose
[θ]	**th**ick	[ð]	**th**ey	[ŋ]	si**ng**
[f]	**f**an	[v]	**v**an	[r]	**r**un
[p]	**p**ig	[b]	**b**ig	[h]	**h**and
[t]	**t**o	[d]	**d**o	[j]	**y**ear
[k]	**c**ar	[g]	**g**ood	[w]	**w**ind

2. Das Zeichen * (*asterisk*)
Es steht für das vor anlautendem Vokal des Folgewortes gesprochene, sonst stumme auslautende "r" (*linking-r*).

3. Betonungszeichen.
ˈ = Hauptbetonung (*primary stress*); ˌ = Nebenbetonung (*secondary stress*).

4. Der Bogen ‿
Ein besonderes Merkmal der englischen Aussprache ist die Verbindung einzelner Wörter einer Äußerung (*link-up*). Sie wird üblicherweise durch einen Bogen angedeutet. In *How to Use Your Words* ist der Bogen bei aufeinanderfolgenden Wörtern dann gesetzt worden, wenn eine getrennte Aussprache besonders störend wirken würde. Das ist z.B. immer bei auslautendem *-t* bzw. *-d* vor anlautendem Vokal der Fall. Ein in anderen Fällen fehlender Bogen darf aber nicht so gedeutet werden, daß die Regeln des *link-up* außer Kraft gesetzt wären.

5. Der Gedankenstrich (*dash*) –
In der rechten Spalte ersetzt er die phonetische Umschrift des Stichwortes der linken Spalte, wenn dieses als Bestandteil eines mehrwortigen Ausdrucks auftritt. Eine dann davon abweichende bzw. beim einsilbigen Stichwort nicht vorhandene Betonung wird beim Gedankenstrich gesetzt.
Wenn gelegentlich in der linken Spalte eine Kollokation (z.B. *lose one's life*) statt eines Stichworts erscheint, so steht der Gedankenstrich für das Einzelwort, das Betonungszeichen für seine Betonung in der Kollokation.

6. Der Bindestrich (*hyphen*) -
Er ersetzt eine bereits vorher gegebene phonetische Umschrift eines Stichwortes der linken Spalte, wenn es als Bestandteil eines neuen Wortes in der rechten Spalte erscheint. Eine dann davon abweichende bzw. beim einsilbigen Stichwort nicht vorhandene Betonung wird beim Bindestrich gesetzt.

Die neuen Wörter

Die neubearbeitete Fassung von *How to Use Your Words* enthält ca. 800 zusätzliche Wörter mit ihren Kollokationen, die durch Vergleich mit den Wortlisten neuerer Lehrwerke ermittelt wurden. Damit wurde eine feinere Abstimmung auf das Wortschatzangebot der Lehrwerke erreicht und der Gebrauchswert für die Unterrichtspraxis erhöht.
Neue Wörter, die heute immer wichtiger werden, wurden ebenfalls ergänzt, z.B. zu den Themen „Umweltschutz" (im Sachbereich 172) und „Computer" (im Sachbereich 67).

Abkürzungen

sing.	singular	Singular, Einzahl
pl.	plural	Plural, Mehrzahl
v.	verb	Verb, Zeitwort
pred.	only predicative	nur prädikativ (bei Adjektiven)
attrib.	only attributive	nur attributiv (bei Adjektiven)
adj.	adjective	Adjektiv, Eigenschaftswort
sb	somebody	jemand
sth	something	etwas
form.	formal	formal (Sprachebene)
inform.	informal	nicht formal (Sprachebene)
BE	British English	Britisches Englisch
AE	American English	Amerikanisches Englisch
hist.	historical	historisch (Fachbegriff)
med.	medicinical	medizinisch (Fachbegriff)
mil.	military	militärisch (Fachbegriff)

Zeichen

~	– Wiedergabe des Eintrags, pro Wort eine Tilde; wird der erste Buchstabe im Gegensatz zum Stichwort groß geschrieben (etwa am Satzanfang), so erscheint er vor der Tilde
/	– der Schrägstrich trennt einzelne Beispiele, Redewendungen oder Strukturen
→	– Verweis auf einen Sachbereich (eine Nummer) oder ein Sachgebiet (mehrere Nummern)
=	– bedeutungsgleich
(+ ...)	– Ergänzung mit ... möglich
(or: ...)	– Austausch durch ... bei anderer Bedeutung möglich

Ourselves – Wir selbst

Man – der Mensch

Man – der Mensch 1

man [mæn] (*sing.* only)	der Mensch, die Menschheit	the rights of ~
mankind [mæn'kaınd]	die Menschheit	all ~ / the history of ~
humanity [hju:'mænətı]	die (gesamte) Menschheit	The H-bomb is a danger to ~.
human ['hju:mən]	menschlich	the ~ race / a ~ being / ~ nature / To err is ~.
race [reıs]	Rasse	the white ~ / **racial** ['reıʃl] hatred (or: discrimination)
people ['pi:pl]	Volk	the ~s of Asia / a brave ~
tribe [traib]	Stamm	American Indian ~s
people ['pi:pl] (*sing.* only)	Leute	the ~ of America (or: this town) are ... / a lot of ~
individual [ˌındı'vıdʒʊəl]	Einzelwesen, Individuum, einzeln	the ~ in society / ~ interests
person ['pɜ:sn]	Person	The police have questioned four ~s. / a **personal** ['pɜ:snl] question / **Personally** ['pɜ:snəlı], I don't believe him.
somebody ['sʌmbədı] = **someone** ['sʌmwʌn]	jemand	here's ~ at the door.
anybody ['enıˌbɒdı] = **anyone** ['enıwʌn]	jemand (in Fragen oder Verneinungen); jeder (beliebige)	Is there ~ else here? / I can't see ~ at all. / A~ could do that!
nobody ['nəʊbədı] = **no one** ['nəʊ wʌn]	niemand	N~ (= ~ ~) is perfect.
one [wʌn]	man	O~ can't always win.
you [ju:]	man, du	Y~ never can tell!
they [ðeı]	man, sie	T~ say life is short, but ...

Person – Person

2 Sex – Geschlecht

sex [seks]	Geschlecht	candidates of both ~es / the fair ~
male [meɪl]	männlich	a ~ child
female ['fiːmeɪl]	weiblich	of the ~ sex / **female worker** (Arbeiterin)
boy [bɔɪ]	Junge	a young ~ of 13
girl [gɜːl]	Mädchen	a ~ of 12
man [mæn] (*pl.* men [men])	Mann	a young ~ of 22 / an old ~
woman ['wʊmən] (*pl.* women ['wɪmɪn])	Frau	a young ~ / an old ~ / a **woman doctor** (Ärztin) / a **woman teacher** (Lehrerin)
gentleman ['dʒentlmən] (*pl.* gentlemen)	Herr	behave like a ~ / '**Gentlemen** ['-mən]!' („Meine Herren!") / be **gentlemanly** ['dʒentlmənlɪ]
lady ['leɪdɪ]	Dame, Frau (als Titel, als respektvolle Anrede)	She is a ~! / behave like a ~ / '**Ladies and Gentlemen**!' („Meine Damen und Herren!") / be **ladylike** ['leɪdɪlaɪk] / **My Lady** / **Lady** Alice Smith
sir [sɜː*]	Herr (als Titel, als respektvolle Anrede)	'Yes, **Sir**.' / **Sir** Winston Churchill / Dear **Sir** (or: **Sirs**) (in Briefen)
madam ['mædəm]	gnädige Frau	'Can I help you, ~?' / Dear **Madam** (in Briefen)
fellow ['feləʊ] (*inform.*) = **chap** [tʃæp] (*inform.*) = **guy** [gaɪ] (*inform.*)	Bursche, Kerl	a fine (or: nice/clever/jolly good) ~ / Poor ~!

3 Name – Name

name [neɪm]	Name, (be)nennen	What's your ~? / know (or: call) sb by ~ / know sb by ~ only / be **named** [-d] **after** (= **for**, *AE*) sb
Christian name ['krɪstjən neɪm] = **first name** ['fɜːst neɪm] = **forename** ['fɔːneɪm] (*form.*)	Vorname	What is your ~ ~?

surname ['sɜ:neɪm] = **family name** ['fæməlɪ 'neɪm] = **last name** [læst 'neɪm] (*AE*)	Nachname	Write your ~ here.
Mr ['mɪstə] = **Mr.** [–]	Herr	~ Smith
Mrs ['mɪsɪz] = **Mrs.** [–]	Frau	~ Smith / ~ Richard Smith
Miss [mɪs]	Fräulein	~ Smith
Ms[1] [məz]	Frau	~ Smith
maiden name ['meɪdn neɪm]	Mädchenname	Mrs White's ~ ~ was Black.
née [neɪ]	geborene, geb.	Jane Brown, ~ Green
nickname ['nɪkneɪm]	Spitzname	George's ~ is Cakesy.
call [kɔ:l]	nennen, rufen	They ~ him Cakesy. / He is ~ed Cakesy. / ~ sb by his first name
introduce [ˌɪntrə'dju:s]	vorstellen	Tom, may I ~ you to Jane? / I ~ed them.
meet (met, met) [mi:t, met, –]	kennenlernen	I'd like you to ~ Jane. / Please, ~ Jane.
How do you do? [ˌhaʊdjʊ'du:]	Angenehm!	
sign [saɪn]	unterschreiben	~ one's name / ~ a letter / put one's **signature** ['sɪgnətʃə*] to a letter

Age – Alter 4

birth [bɜ:θ]	Geburt	date and place of ~ (*form.*) / give ~ to a boy
birthday ['bɜ:θdeɪ]	Geburtstag	When is your ~? / want sth for one's next ~ / on my 40th ~
born [bɔ:n]	geboren	When were you ~? / be ~ in London
baby ['beɪbɪ]	Baby	be expecting a ~ / a newborn ~ / She had her ~ in October. / a **baby-sitter** ['beɪbɪˌsɪtə*]
child [tʃaɪld] (*pl.* children ['tʃɪldrən])	Kind	a small ~ / We have two **children**.
childhood ['tʃaɪldhʊd]	Kindheit	have (or: spend) a happy ~ / in one's ~ / do sth from (= since) ~
kid [kɪd] (*inform.*)	Kind	school ~s
young [jʌŋ]	jung	a ~ child / my **younger** ['jʌŋgə*] brother

[1] A woman who does not wish to use either Mrs or Miss with her name chooses the form Ms.

youth [juːθ]	Jugendlicher; Jugend	two ~s of 17 / in my ~ / the ~ of Europe
adult ['ædʌlt]	Erwachsene(r)	for ~s only / Children 10p, ~s 25p
grow (grew, grown) [grəʊ, gruː, grəʊn]	wachsen	~ fast / **grow out** [ˌgrəʊ 'aʊt] of one's T-shirt / not ~ much
grow (grew, grown) **up** [ˌ– 'ʌp]	aufwachsen, erwachsen werden	~ ~ in China (or: in a large family) / His children have **grown up**.
grown-up [ˌgrəʊn'ʌp] ['grəʊnʌp]	groß, erwachsen, Erwachsener	his ~ sons / for **grown-ups** only (mainly used by children)
grow (grew, grown) **old** [ˌ– 'əʊld]	alt werden	He has grown ~.
age [eɪdʒ]	Alter,	What's your ~? / What ~ are you? / be 12 years of ~ / at the ~ of 20 / Their ~s are 14 and 12 / When I was your ~, …
	altern	~ fast (or: a lot)
of age [əv 'eɪdʒ]	volljährig	come (or: be) ~ ~
in one's twenties [ɪn wʌnz 'twentiːz]	in den Zwanzigern	be ~ ~ ~
middle-aged [ˌmɪdl'eɪdʒd]	mittleren Alters	a ~ man
aged [eɪdʒd] ['eɪdʒɪd]	im Alter von; alt, betagt	a boy ~ 10 / be ~ 10 years / homes for **the aged** [ðɪ 'eɪdʒɪd]
the elderly [ðɪ 'eldəlɪ]	ältere Menschen	
senior citizen [ˌsiːnɪə 'sɪtɪzn]	ältere Mitbürgerin, älterer Mitbürger	
old [əʊld]	alt	How ~ are you? / be 20 years ~ / a ten-year-~ boy / the problems of **old age** [əʊld 'eɪdʒ] (das Alter) / the young and **the old** [ðɪ 'əʊld]
elder ['eldə*]	älter (meist von Geschwistern)	one's ~ brother (or: son) / He was **the elder** [ðɪ 'eldə*] of the two.
eldest ['eldɪst]	älteste(r)	one's ~ sister
elderly ['eldəlɪ]	älter	an ~ lady

5 Life – Leben

(→ 180 Exist)

life [laɪf]	Leben,	Is there any ~ on other planets? / be tired of ~ / show no sign of ~ / daily (or: public / private / town / country) ~ / the American **way of life** [ˌweɪ‿əv 'laɪf]

	das Leben (des Einzelnen)	lead (or: live) a(n) exciting (or: quiet / simple) ~ / enjoy one's ~ / spend all one's ~ doing sth / in all one's ~ / Many people lost their **lives** [laɪvz].
lifetime ['laɪftaɪm]	Leben, (auf) Lebenszeit	once in a ~ / a ~
lifespan ['laɪfspæn]	Lebensdauer, Lebenserwartung	The average ~ of a dog is 12 years.
lifelong ['laɪflɒŋ]	auf Lebenszeit, für's Leben	a ~ friend
live [lɪv]	leben;	~ a long life / ~ on £60 a month / **the living** [ðə 'lɪvɪŋ] and the dead
([laɪv] *attrib. adj.*)	lebendig, lebend	a ~ mouse / a ~ show (= a show that was not recorded)
living ['lɪvɪŋ]	Lebens-, Lebensunterhalt	~ conditions (or: standard) / earn one's ~
alive [ə'laɪv] (*pred. adj.*)	lebendig, lebend	be still (or: very much) ~ / stay ~
survive [sə'vaɪv]	überleben	~ an accident / be the only **survivor** [-ə*] / sb's **survival** [-l] is a wonder / the **survival** of the fittest (Darwin)

Death – Tod

6

death [deθ]	Tod, Todesfall	die a natural ~ / a sudden (or: tragic) ~ / sb's ~ is a blow to one / the third ~ in the family this year
dead [ded]	tot	He has been ~ since 1975. / **the dead** of World War II / a **deadly** ['-lɪ] disease / be **deadly pale** (totenblaß)
mortal ['mɔːtl]	tödlich, sterblich	receive a ~ wound / be ~ly wounded / Man is ~. / the **immortal** [ɪ'mɔːtl] works of Shakespeare
fatal ['feɪtl]	tödlich	a ~ accident (or: illness)
die [daɪ]	sterben	~ a natural death / ~ of hunger (or: old age) / ~ from a wound / ~ in an accident / ~ by drowning
drown [draʊn]	ertrinken; ertränken	death by **drowning** ['-ɪŋ] ~ a cat
be drowned [draʊnd]	ertrinken	He fell from the bridge and **was drowned** (= and **drowned**).
kill [kɪl]	töten	~ sb (or: oneself)
be (was, been) **killed** [– '–] = **get** (got, got) **killed** [– '–]	getötet werden	~ ~ in an accident

suicide ['sjʊɪsaɪd]	Selbstmord	commit ~
lose (lost, lost) **one's life** [ˌ– – '–]	sein Leben verlieren	Many people **lost their lives** ['laɪvz].
take (took, taken) **one's** (+ **own**) **life** [ˌ– – ('–) '–]	sich das Leben nehmen	She **took her (+ own) life**.
lifeless ['laɪflɪs]	leblos	sb's ~ body
late [leɪt]	verstorben	our (or: the) ~ president
body ['bɒdɪ]	Leiche	
corpse [kɔːps] (*med.*)	Leiche	examine a ~
coffin ['kɒfɪn]	Sarg	carry a ~ / lay a body in a ~
bury ['berɪ]	begraben, beerdigen	~ sb / be **buried** [-d] in one's hometown / The **burial** [-əl] will take place tomorrow.
funeral ['fjuːnərəl]	Bestattung, Beerdigung, Trauer-	Are you going to his ~? / attend sb's ~ / a **funeral procession** [ˌ– prə'seʃn] The **funeral service** [ˌ– 'sɜːvɪs] (Trauergottesdienst) will be at St Michael's.
cemetery ['semɪtrɪ]	Friedhof	a war ~
churchyard [ˌtʃɜːtʃ'jɑːd] = **graveyard** ['greɪvjɑːd]	Friedhof, Kirchhof	be buried in the village ~
grave [greɪv]	Grab	dig a ~ / a **gravestone** ['-stəʊn]
tomb [tuːm]	Grabmal	erect a ~
wreath [riːθ]	Kranz	lay a ~ at (or: on) sb's grave (or: tomb)
mourn [mɔːn]	(be)trauern	~ for sb / ~ over sb's death / ~ the death of sb / be in (+ deep) **mourning** ['--]
will [wɪl]	(letzter) Wille, Testament	make a (or: one's) ~
leave (left, left) [liːv, left, –]	hinterlassen	The old lady **left** everything to her dog.
heir [eə*]	Erbe	be ~ to the throne / be ~ to great wealth
heiress ['eərɪs]	Erbin	
inherit [ɪn'herɪt]	erben	~ a title (or: fortune) / claim (beanspruchen) an **inheritance** [-əns]

Body – Körper

Figure – Figur, Gestalt 7

short [ʃɔːt]	klein	a ~ woman (or: man / boy) / be ~
small [smɔːl]	klein, schmächtig	a ~ child (or: man)
little [lɪtl]	klein (oft gefühlsbetont)	a good ~ girl / an energetic ~ woman
tiny ['taɪnɪ]	winzig	a ~ baby
tall [tɔːl]	groß, hochgewachsen	a ~ man / How ~ are you? / be 6 ft ~
big [bɪg]	groß (und breit)	a ~ boy / a ~ man and a small man
large [lɑːdʒ]	groß und breit	have ~ feet / a ~ man / his ~ body
huge [hjuːdʒ]	gewaltig, sehr groß	have ~ hands / a ~ man
height [haɪt]	Körpergröße	What's your ~? / be of medium ~ (von mittlerer Größe)
thin [θɪn]	dünn	be rather ~ / a long, ~ neck
slight [slaɪt]	dünn, schmächtig	his ~ body
slender ['slendə*]	schlank	a ~ young girl
slim [slɪm]	schlank	a ~ young girl / be **slimming** ['--]
fat [fæt]	dick	be (or: get / become / grow) ~ / a ~ man
weigh [weɪ]	wiegen	He ~s 13 stone. / lose (or: put on) **weight** [weɪt] / be **overweight** [ˌəʊvə'weɪt]
stout [staʊt]	beleibt, stämmig	a ~ figure
broad-shouldered [ˌbrɔːd'ʃəʊldəd]	breitschultrig	a ~ policeman
figure ['fɪgə*]	Gestalt, Figur	have a lovely (or: good / fine) ~ / see a dark ~

Head, hair – Kopf, Haar 8

(→ 139 Bathroom, hygiene)

head [hed]	Kopf	from ~ to toe
hair [heə*]	Haar(e)	have fine ~ / a **grey-haired** ['greɪheəd] (*attrib.*) / [ˌ-'-] (*pred.*) gentleman
fair [feə*]	hell, blond	have ~ hair / a **fair-haired** ['feəheəd] (*attrib.*) / [ˌ-'-] (*pred.*) girl
blond = blonde [blɒnd]	blond, Blondine	be ~ / be a ~
curl [kɜːl]	Locke	have golden ~s / have **curly** ['-ɪ] hair
wave [weɪv]	Welle	have a natural ~ in one's hair / have **wavy** ['-ɪ] hair

parting ['pɑ:tɪŋ] (*BE*) = **part** [pɑ:rt] (*AE*)	Scheitel	wear the ~ in the middle
part [pɑ:t]	scheiteln	~ one's hair in the middle (or: on the side)
bald [bɔ:ld]	kahl	have a ~ head / be ~
beard [bɪəd]	Bart	grow a ~ / a **bearded** ['-ɪd] young man
moustache [mə'stɑ:ʃ] (*BE*) = **mustache** ['mʌstæ:ʃ] (*AE*)	Schnurrbart	have a long ~
shave [ʃeɪv]	(sich) rasieren	~ every morning
hairdresser ['heəˌdresə*]	(Damen-)Friseur	go to the ~'s
hairstyle ['heəstaɪl]	Frisur	a new ~
hairdo ['heədu:] (*inform.*)	Frisur (einer Frau)	have a new ~ / change one's ~
barber ['bɑ:bə*]	Herrenfriseur	go to the ~'s
cut (cut, cut) [kʌt, kʌt, –]	schneiden	~ sb's hair / have one's hair ~ / have a **hair-cut** ['heəkʌt]
set (set, set) [set, set, –]	legen	have one's hair ~
do (did, done) **one's hair** [ˌdu: wʌnz 'heə*]	frisieren	**have** (or: **get**) **one's hair done**

9 Face, looks – Gesicht, Aussehen

(→ 46 Facial expression, gesture)

face [feɪs]	Gesicht	have a long (or: round / oval) ~
features ['fi:tʃəz]	Gesichtszüge	sb's ~ are hard (or: even / regular)
expression [ɪk'spreʃn]	(Gesichts-)Ausdruck	have a funny ~ on one's face
look [lʊk]	aussehen	~ marvellous
good-looking [ˌgʊd'lʊkɪŋ]	gutaussehend	a ~ young man
handsome ['hænsəm]	gutaussehend (über Jungen oder Männer gesagt)	a ~ boy / have a ~ face
pretty ['prɪtɪ]	hübsch	a ~ girl / have a ~ face
beautiful ['bju:təfʊl]	schön (über Mädchen, Frauen, Babys gesagt)	a ~ woman / have a ~ face / have ~ eyes
attractive [ə'træktɪv]	anziehend	an ~ woman
cute [kju:t] (*inform., AE*)	nett, niedlich	a ~ little girl

ugly ['ʌglɪ]	häßlich	be (or: look) ~ / have an ~ face / an ~ man
complexion [kəm'plekʃn]	Gesichtsfarbe, Teint	have a fresh (or: fair / dark / rosy / pale) ~
ruddy ['rʌdɪ]	rosig, rot, gerötet	have a ~ complexion / have ~ cheeks
pale [peɪl]	blaß	be (or: turn) ~ / have a ~ face (or: complexion)
tan [tæn]	Sonnenbräune, braun werden	get a good ~ / lose one's ~ quickly / have a **tanned** [-d] face
sunburn ['sʌnbɜ:n]	Sonnenbrand	get a bad ~
sunburnt ['sʌnbɜ:nt]	sonnenverbrannt, sonnengebräunt	get badly ~ / have a ~ face
freckle ['frekl]	Sommersprosse	have ~s all over one's face / have a **freckled** [-d] face
wrinkle ['rɪŋkl]	Runzel, Falte	have lots of ~s on one's face / a **wrinkled** [-d] face
make-up ['meɪkʌp]	Schminke	wear ~

Parts of the face – Teile des Gesichts 10

(→ 14 Sight; 15 Hearing; 16 Smell; 17 Taste; 30 At the dentist's; 47 Voice)

forehead ['fɒrɪd]	Stirn	have a high (or: low) ~
brow [braʊ] = **eye-brow** ['aɪbraʊ]	Augenbraue	have bushy ~s
eye [aɪ]	Auge	have blue ~s / a blue-**eyed** [-d] baby / The boxer had a **black eye** (blaues Auge).
eyelid ['aɪlɪd]	Augenlid	
eyelashes ['aɪlæʃɪz]	Wimpern	
pupil ['pju:pl]	Pupille	sb's ~s grow larger (or: smaller)
tear [tɪə*]	Träne	be in ~s / burst into ~s
nose [nəʊz]	Nase	have a long (or: flat / hooked [Haken-]) ~ / blow (or: wipe) one's ~ / one's ~ is running
nostril ['nɒstrəl]	Nasenloch	
cheek [tʃi:k]	Wange	have hollow (or: chubby / pale / red) ~s / have high **cheekbones** ['-bəʊnz]
mouth [maʊθ]	Mund	a wide ~ / Don't speak when your ~ is full. / eat three **mouthfuls** ['-fʊlz] of peanuts / open (or: wipe) one's ~
lip [lɪp]	Lippe	red ~s
upper lip ['ʌpə lɪp]	Oberlippe	a thin ~ ~
lower lip ['ləʊə lɪp]	Unterlippe	a thick ~ ~

tooth [tu:θ] (*pl.* teeth [ti:θ])	Zahn	have one's own **teeth** / **milk teeth** ['mɪlk ti:θ] / a **toothless** ['tu:θlɪs] old man
set of teeth [ˌset əv 'ti:θ]	Gebiß	have a fine ~ ~ ~ / have (or: wear) a ~ ~ false ~
gums [gʌmz]	Zahnfleisch	Chewing gum is good for the ~.
tongue [tʌŋ]	Zunge	put out one's ~ / the tip of one's ~
chin [tʃɪn]	Kinn	have a double ~ / be **double-chinned** [ˌdʌbl'tʃɪnd]
jaw [dʒɔ:]	Kiefer	a broken ~
upper jaw ['ʌpə dʒɔ:]	Oberkiefer	
lower jaw ['ləʊə dʒɔ:]	Unterkiefer	
ear [ɪə*]	Ohr	have protruding (abstehend) ~s / box sb's ~s

11 Trunk – Rumpf

(→ 23 Eat, drink, digest; 13 Organs and their functions)

neck [nek]	Hals, Nacken, Genick	have a scarf round one's ~ / have a long (or: stiff) ~ / break one's ~
throat [θrəʊt]	Kehle	a bone sticks in one's ~ / have a sore ~ (Halsschmerzen)
chest [tʃest]	Brust	have a broad (or: narrow / weak) ~ / have pains in the ~ / be **narrow-chested** [ˌnærəʊ'tʃestɪd]
breast [brest]	Brust	a woman's ~s / a baby at his mother's ~ / give a baby the ~ / The old soldier had a ~ full of decorations.
bosom ['bʊzəm]	Busen	press a child to one's ~
shoulder ['ʃəʊldə*]	Schulter	have narrow (or: round / broad) ~s
armpit ['ɑ:mpɪt]	Achselhöhle	
back [bæk]	Rücken	have a straight (or: crooked ['krʊkɪd] / bent) ~ / stand with one's ~ to sb (or: sth) / stand ~ to ~
waist [weɪst]	Taille	have a slim ~ / wear a belt around one's ~ / **waist-high** [ˌ-'haɪ] / **waist-deep** [ˌ-'di:p]
stomach ['stʌmək]	Bauch, Magen	a pain in the ~
bowels ['baʊəlz]	Eingeweide, Gedärm	
belly ['belɪ] (*inform.*)	Bauch, Magen	a pain in the ~
tummy ['tʌmɪ] (*inform.*)	Bauch, Magen	a pain in the ~
hip [hɪp]	Hüfte	have broad (or: narrow) ~s / be **narrow-hipped** [ˌnærəʊ'-t]

lap [læp]	Schoß	take sb on (= onto) one's ~ / put one's hand in one's ~
seat [si:t] = **behind** [bɪ'haɪnd] = **bottom** ['bɒtəm]	Gesäß	fall on one's ~ / get a smack (Klaps) on one's ~
buttock ['bʌtək] (*med.*)	Gesäßbacke	get an injection in the left ~

Limbs – Gliedmaßen

(→ 46 Facial expressions, gesture) 12

arm [ɑ:m]	Arm	a broken ~
upper arm ['ʌpər‿ɑ:m]	Oberarm	
forearm ['fɔ:rɑ:m]	Unterarm	
elbow ['elbəʊ]	Ellenbogen	Don't put your ~s on the table when you eat.
wrist [rɪst]	Handgelenk	wear a watch on one's ~
hand [hænd]	Hand	have large ~s / be **left-handed** [ˌleft-'hændɪd] / made by ~ (= **handmade** [ˌ-'meɪd])
palm of the hand ['pɑ:m – – ˌ–]	Handteller	
back of the hand ['bæk – – ˌ–]	Handrücken	
fist [fɪst]	Faust	clench (ballen) one's ~
knuckle ['nʌkl]	Knöchel	
finger ['fɪŋgə*]	Finger	
forefinger ['fɔ:fɪŋgə*] = **index finger** ['ɪndeks ˌ–]	Zeigefinger	
middle finger ['mɪdl ˌ–]	Mittelfinger	
ring finger ['rɪŋ ˌ–]	Ringfinger	
little finger ['lɪtl ˌ–]	kleiner Finger	
thumb [θʌm]	Daumen	
fingernail ['fɪŋgəneɪl]	Fingernagel	cut one's ~s / have long (or: short) ~s
leg [leg]	Bein	have short (or: long) ~s / a **long-legged** [ˌ-'legd] girl / **bow-legged** [ˌbəʊ'legd] (O-beinig)
knee [ni:]	Knie	rounded ~s
shin [ʃɪn] = **shinbone** ['ʃɪnbəʊn]	Schienbein	a kick on (= in) the ~
calf ['kɑ:f] (*pl.* calves ['kɑ:vz])	Wade	

ankle ['æŋkl]	Fußgelenk	
foot [fʊt] (*pl.* feet [fi:t])	Fuß	big **feet** / sit at sb's **feet** / go **barefoot** ['beəfʊt] / **flat-footed** [ˌflæt'fʊtɪd] (plattfüßig) / leave muddy **footprints** ['fʊtprɪnts] on the floor
heel [hi:l]	Ferse	run with sb at (= on) one's ~s
sole [səʊl]	Fußsohle	
toe [təʊ]	Zeh(e)	big ~ / **toe-nails** ['təʊneɪlz]

13 Organs and their functions – Organe und ihre Funktionen

(→ 14 –18 Senses; 23 Eat, drink, digest)

Skeleton – Skelett

skeleton ['skəlɪtn]	Skelett	the human ~ / He is like a ~ (abgemagert bis auf's ~).
bone [bəʊn]	Knochen	She is all skin and ~s. / be wet to the ~s / feel sth in one's ~s / a **bony** ['bəʊnɪ] figure
skull [skʌl]	Schädel, Totenkopf	have a thick ~
spine [spaɪn]	Wirbelsäule, Rückgrat	a bent ~ / **spinal column** [ˌspaɪnl 'kɒləm] (= spine)
rib [rɪb]	Rippe	poke sb in the ~s
joint [dʒɔɪnt]	Gelenk	stiff ~s / **finger-joint** ['fɪngə-]

Muscles – Muskeln

muscle ['mʌsl]	Muskel	exercise one's ~s / develop one's ~s / the arm ~s / Every ~ was tense (angespannt). / **muscular** ['mʌskjʊlə*]
flesh [fleʃ]	Fleisch (von Mensch und Tier)	soft (or: firm) ~ / **fleshy** ['-ɪ] arms

Nerves – Nerven

nerve [nɜ:v]	Nerv	suffer from bad (or: weak) ~s / get on sb's ~s
nervous ['nɜ:vəs]	nervös	be very ~ about (= over) sth / have a **nervous breakdown** [ˌ– 'breɪkdaʊn]
strain [streɪn]	Anspannung	The ~ on her nerves had been too great.
brain [breɪn]	Gehirn	The ~ is the centre of the nervous system.

Skin – Haut

skin [skɪn]	Haut	have greasy (fettig) (or: dry) ~ / have a fair ~ / a **dark-skinned** ['dɑːkskɪnd] boy
perspire [pə'spaɪə*] (*form.*)	schwitzen	I'm **perspiring** all over. / be wet (or: covered) with **perspiration** [ˌpɜːspə'reɪʃn] / have **beads** [biːdz] **of perspiration** on one's forehead
sweat [swet]	schwitzen, Schweiß	~ in the heat / ~ with fear ~ is pouring (or: running) down one's forehead / be dripping (or: running) with ~ / be (or: wake up) in cold ~
goose-pimples ['guːspɪmplz]	Gänsehaut	arms covered with ~
spots [spɒts]	Pickel	a face covered with ~

Heart – Herz

heart [hɑːt]	Herz	have a strong (or: sound / weak) ~ / hear one's ~ beating (or: pounding / throbbing / hammering)
circulation [ˌsɜːkjʊ'leɪʃn]	Kreislauf	have good (or: poor) ~
heartbeat ['hɑːtbiːt]	Herzschlag	listen to sb's ~ / count 80 ~s (= **beats** [biːts]) a minute
blood [blʌd]	Blut	~ circulates (or: flows) / sb's **blood-pressure** ['-ˌpreʃə*] is high (or: low)
blood type ['blʌd taɪp]= **blood group** ['blʌd gruːp]	Blutgruppe	
pulse [pʌlz]	Puls	feel (or: take / measure) sb's ~
vein [veɪn]	Vene	feel the blood pulsing through one's ~s
artery ['ɑːtərɪ]	Schlagader, Arterie	

Lungs – Lunge

lung [lʌŋ]	Lungenflügel	breathe with only one ~
lungs [lʌŋz]	Lunge	have good (or: strong) ~
windpipe ['wɪndpaɪp]	Luftröhre	Some food stuck in his ~.

breathe [briːð]	atmen	~ in (+ fresh air) / ~ out / ~ deeply (or: hard / evenly) / ~ through the nose (or: mouth) / even **breathing** ['briːðɪŋ] (Atmen)
breath [breθ]	Atem, Atemzug	take (= draw) a deep (or: long) ~ / hold one's ~ / catch one's ~ (nach Luft schnappen) / be out of ~ / have bad ~ / be (or: get) **breathless** ['-lɪs] / lose one's ~
blow (blew, blown) [bləʊ, bluː, bləʊn]	blasen	~ a candle out
pant [pænt]	keuchen, hecheln	After running ten miles he stopped and ~ed for breath.
gasp [gɑːsp]	keuchen, (nach Luft) schnappen	When they pulled him out of the water, he ~ed for breath.
choke [tʃəʊk]	ersticken, (er)würgen	The smoke almost **choked** [-'-t] me. / I **choked** and started coughing. / ~ sb / ~ on a fish-bone

Other organs – andere Organe

liver	['lɪvə*]	Leber
kidney	['kɪdnɪ]	Niere
bladder	['blædə*]	Blase
sexual organs	['seksjʊəl 'ɔːgənz]	Geschlechtsorgane
sense organs	['sens 'ɔːgənz]	Sinnesorgane

Senses – Sinne

14 Sight – Sehvermögen

(→ 10 Parts of the face)

eye [aɪ]	Auge (als Sinnesorgan)	have good (or: keen / poor / bad / weak) ~s / be able to see with the naked ~
sight [saɪt] = **eyesight** ['aɪsaɪt]	Gesichtssinn, Sehvermögen	sb's ~ is good (or: bad / poor / dim) have good ~ / lose one's ~
long-sighted [ˌlɒŋ'saɪtɪd]= **far-sighted** [ˌfɑː'saɪtɪd]	weitsichtig	
short-sighted [ˌʃɔːt'saɪtɪd]= **near-sighted** [ˌnɪə'saɪtɪd]	kurzsichtig	

blind [blaɪnd]	blind,	be (or: get / become) ~ (+ in one eye) / be ~ from birth / be **colour-blind** ['kʌlə-] / Help **the blind**!
	blenden	a **blinding** light / The dazzling light ~ed him.
glasses ['glɑːsɪz] = *AE* also: **eye-glasses** ['aɪglɑːsɪz] = **spectacles** ['spektəklz] = **specs** [speks] (*inform.*)	Brille	wear (or: need) ~ / put on (or: take off) one's ~ / a **pair of glasses** [ˌpeər‿əv –]
contact lenses ['kɒntækt 'lenzɪz]	Kontaktlinsen	wear ~ ~
binoculars [bɪ'nɒkjʊləz*]	Fernglas	watch sth through one's ~ / a **pair of binoculars** [ˌpeər‿əv –]
torch [tɔːtʃ] (*BE*)	Taschenlampe; Fackel	
flashlight ['flæʃlaɪt] (*AE*)	Taschenlampe	
see (saw, seen) [siː, sɔː, siːn]	sehen	~ sth (or: sb) / ~ clearly (or: distinctly / indistinctly) / ~ sth dimly (verschwommen)
look [lʊk]	schauen, gucken,	Look! / ~ at sb (or: sth) / ~ another way / ~ around / ~ sb straight in the eye
	Blick	have (or: take) a ~ at sb (or: sth) / give sb a(n) long (or: angry) ~
sight [saɪt]	erblicken, sichten, (An-)Blick	~ land / at first ~ / know sb by ~ / at the ~ of sb (or: sth)
glance [glɑːns]	(flüchtig) blicken, Blick	~ at sb (or: sth) / ~ over a letter / take a ~ at sb (or: sth) / see sth at a ~ / see sth at the first ~
glimpse [glɪmps]	(flüchtig) blicken, Blick	~ at sb (or: sth) / catch a ~ of sb (or: sth) (nur flüchtig zu sehen bekommen)
peep [piːp]	lugen, hervorschauen	~ into (or: out of / at) sth / ~ from behind sth
stare [steə*]	starren, stieren, große Augen machen	~ at sb (or: sth) / ~ into the distance / ~ with (= in) surprise
gaze [geɪz]	starren, unverwandt anschauen	~ at sb (or: sth) (+ in disbelief / in astonishment)
watch [wɒtʃ]	beobachten	~ sb (or: sth) (+ closely / carefully) / ~ TV / ~ a film / ~ sb doing sth
observe [əb'zɜːv]	beobachten	~ sb (or: sth) (+ keenly [scharf]) / ~ that sb does sth / be a good (or: keen) **observer** [-ə*]

view [vjuː]	(genau) ansehen	~ a building before buying it
inspect [ɪn'spekt]	untersuchen	~ a factory (or: soldiers) / give sth a thorough **inspection** [ɪn'spekʃn]
examine [ɪg'zæmɪn]	genau ansehen, untersuchen	~ sth carefully (or: closely) / ~ a patient
survey [sə'veɪ]	untersuchen (um etwas in seinem Wert abzuschätzen);	~ a house before buying it
	überblicken	~ the town from the tower
look for ['lʊk fə]	suchen	~ ~ sb (or: sth) (+ all over the place)
search [sɜːtʃ]	gründlich (durch-) suchen,	~ a thief (or: room) (+ for sth) / ~ for sth / ~ (+ through) one's pockets for sth / look around **searchingly** ['-ɪŋlɪ] / '**Search and you shall find**.' (Bible)
	Suche	be (or: go) in ~ of sb (or: sth) / after a long ~
seek (sought, sought) [siːk, sɔːt, –] (*form.*)	suchen	
find (found, found) [faɪnd, faʊnd, –]	finden	~ sb (or: sth) / ~ sth for sb / ~ one's way
spy [spaɪ]	erspähen	~ sb in the crowd / ~ for the enemy
distinguish [dɪ'stɪŋgwɪʃ]	ausmachen	~ sb (or: sth) at a great distance
discover [dɪ'skʌvə*]	entdecken	~ sb (or: sth) somewhere
notice ['nəʊtɪs]	bemerken, beachten	~ sb (or: sth) / ~ that ... / ~ sb doing sth / take (+ no) ~ of sb (or: sth)
eye [aɪ]	Auge (als Sehvermögen),	turn one's ~s to sth (or: sb) / take one's ~s off sb (or: sth) / keep an ~ on sb (or: sth) / have a good ~ for sth
	beäugen	~ sb curiously (neugierig) (or: with suspicion)
catch (caught, caught) **sb's eye** [kætʃ, kɔːt, –; ˌ– – 'aɪ]	Aufmerksamkeit auf sich lenken (indem man zu jemandem hinschaut),	try to ~ the teacher's ~
	ins Auge springen	The pretty girl **caught his eye**.
look [lʊk]	(nach etwas) aussehen	~ ill (or: young / friendly) / ~ like sb / ~ one's age / It ~s like rain. / It ~s as if it is going to rain. / They ~ as if they are going to fight.
conspicuous [kən'spɪkjʊəs]	auffällig sichtbar	

In sight, out of sight – in Sichtweite, außer Sichtweite

sight [saɪt]	Sicht, Sichtweite	be in ~ / come in (= into) ~ / be (or: stay / get / pass) out of ~ / be in ~ of the lake
view [vjuː]	Sicht, Schau, Aussicht	be in full ~ / come in (= into) ~ / pass from ~ / There's a good ~ from here. / sth is on ~ (zur Schau)
appear [ə'pɪə*]	(er)scheinen	~ suddenly / ~ on the horizon
visible ['vɪzəbl]	sichtbar	be (or: become) ~ (+ to sb) / be **visibly** ['-ɪ] nervous / be **invisible** [ɪn'-] to the naked eye
disappear [ˌdɪsə'pɪə*]	verschwinden	~ from a place / ~ for good (für immer)
vanish ['vænɪʃ]	verschwinden	~ from sight / ~ completely
show [ʃəʊ]	zeigen, zu sehen sein,	~ sth (+ to sb) / ~ that ... / sth is **showing** ['ʃəʊɪŋ]
	Schau	be on ~ / a **flower show** ['flaʊə –]
hide (hid, hidden) [haɪd, hɪd, 'hɪdn]	(sich) verstecken	~ sth (+ in / on / under / behind) / ~ sth from sb / ~ (+ away) from sb / **hiding place** ['haɪdɪŋ pleɪs]

Colour, light – Farbe, Licht

colour ['kʌlə*] (*BE*) = **color** [-r] (*AE*)	Farbe,	What ~ is your car? / What's the ~ of your car? / a **colourful** [-'-fʊl] dress
	buntmalen	~ a picture
coloured ['kʌləd] (*BE*) = **colored** [-rd] (*AE*)	farbig	~ people / ~ Easter-eggs / **single-coloured** ['sɪŋglˌ-] / **multi-coloured** ['mʌltɪˌ-]
red [red]	rot	
blood-red [ˌblʌd'red]	blutrot	
brick-red [ˌbrɪk'red]	ziegelrot	
redden ['redn]	sich röten	sb's face ~s
reddish ['redɪʃ]	rötlich	
redness ['rednɪs]	Röte	
scarlet ['skɑːlət]	scharlachrot	
pink [pɪŋk]	blaßrot, rosa	~ carnations (Nelken) / **pinkish** ['pɪŋkɪʃ]
purple ['pɜːpl]	purpurn, purpurrot	~ robes of a cardinal
blue [bluː]	blau	a ~ sky / the ~ ocean / **sky-blue** ['skaɪ-] (*attrib.*) / [ˌskaɪ'-] (*pred.*) / **bluish** ['bluːɪʃ]
green [griːn]	grün	~ grass / **greenish** ['griːnɪʃ]
brown [braʊn]	braun	

yellow ['jeləʊ]	gelb	
orange ['ɒrɪndʒ]	orange	
grey [greɪ] (*BE*) = **gray** [–] (*AE*)	grau	
black [blæk]	schwarz	a very ~ night / **pitch-black** [ˌpɪtʃ'-] (pechschwarz) darkness
white [waɪt]	weiß	~ snow / **snow-white** [ˌsnəʊ'-] / sb's hair has **whitened** ['-ənd]
gold [gəʊld]	Gold, golden	the ~ of the autumn leaves / ~ paint
golden ['gəʊldən]	golden	a ~ sunset / ~ hair
silver ['sɪlvə*]	silber(n)	~ clouds / a **silver-haired** [ˌsɪlvə'heəd] old man / the **silvery** [-rɪ] moon
tone [təʊn]	Farbton	in various ~s of brown / in warm (or: brown) ~s
shade [ʃeɪd]	Farbstufe, Schattierung;	Pink and purple are different ~s of red.
	Schatten	sit (or: be / stay / keep) in the ~ / a **shady** ['-ɪ] place
shadow ['ʃædəʊ]	Schatten	a ~ falls on sth / sth throws (or: casts) a ~ (+ on sth) / a **shadowy** [-'-ɪ] place
dark [dɑːk]	dunkel, düster	~ green / in ~ colours / a ~ shade of blue / It's getting ~. / the **darkness** ['-nɪs] of the night
darken ['dɑːkən]	dunkel werden, verdunkeln	The sky ~ed. / sb's face ~s
gloomy ['gluːmɪ]	düster	a ~ picture
dim [dɪm]	düster, trübe	the ~ light of a candle
dull [dʌl]	trübe, stumpf, matt	~ colours / a ~ light
deep [diːp]	tief, satt	the ~ blue of the ocean
rich [rɪtʃ]	kräftig, satt	the ~ green of the pastures
bright [braɪt]	lebhaft, bunt	~ colours / ~ dresses
pale [peɪl]	blaß	a ~ blue sky / ~ colours
light [laɪt]	hell,	~ blue / in ~ colours / a **light-coloured** ['-ˌkʌləd] dress
	Licht	work by the ~ of a candle / **moonlight** ['muːn-] / in broad **daylight** ['deɪ-] / switch on (or: off) the ~
light (lit, lit) [laɪt, lɪt, –]	anzünden;	~ a candle (or: cigarette)
	erhellen, erleuchten	A candle ~s (+ up) the room.
lighted ['laɪtɪd]	angezündet	a ~ cigarette (or: match)
lit [lɪt]	angezündet;	The match is ~.
	erleuchtet	The restaurant is ~ by candles.
ray [reɪ]	(starker) Strahl	the ~s of the sun / **sunrays** ['sʌnreɪz]

bright [braɪt]	hell, leuchtend	a ~ light / ~ colours
brilliant ['brɪljənt]	strahlend, glänzend, funkelnd	the ~ sunshine / ~ jewels / a ~ red
shine (shone, shone) [ʃaɪn, ʃɒn, –]	scheinen, leuchten, glänzen	The sun (or: moon / lamp / light) is ~ing (+ brightly). / ~ (+ down) on sb / ~ into sth / His shoes were **shining** ['-ɪŋ] (= **shiny** ['-ɪ]).
sunshine ['sʌnʃaɪn]	Sonnenschein	in the (+ bright) ~
moonshine ['mu:nʃaɪn]	Mondschein	
glow [gləʊ]	glühen,	a ~ing sunset / A cigarette ~ed in the dark.
	Glut	a warm ~
glare [gleə*]	(blendend) strahlen,	the **glaring** ['-rɪŋ] sun
	(blendender) Strahl	the ~ of the sun
gleam [gli:m]	strahlen, (auf-)leuchten,	cat's eyes ~ in the dark / furniture ~s
	Strahlen, (Auf-) Leuchten	the red ~ of firelight / the ~ of distant car lights
glitter ['glɪtə*]	glitzern, funkeln,	stars (or: diamonds / Christmas trees) ~ / ~ing stars
	Glitzern, Funkeln	the ~ of the Christmas tree decorations (or: diamonds) / a ~ in one's eyes
sparkle ['spɑ:kl]	glitzern, funkeln,	stars (or: diamonds / Christmas trees) ~ / ~ing stars
	Glitzern, Funkeln	the ~ of a diamond
dazzle ['dæzl]	blenden	~d by the lights of a car
twinkle ['twɪnkl]	glitzern, funkeln,	stars (or: diamonds / distant lights) ~ / ~ing stars
	Glitzern, Funkeln	the ~ing of a diamond
glisten ['glɪsn]	glitzern, schimmern	eyes ~ing with tears
flash [flæʃ]	(auf)blitzen, Blitz	a light (or: lightning) ~es (+ across the sky) / a ~ of lightning / ~es of light
reflect [rɪ'flekt]	(sich) spiegeln, widerspiegeln	be ~ed in the water (or: mirror) / the **reflection** [rɪ'flekʃn] of sth in the water

15 Hearing – Hören

(→ 10 Parts of the face; 47 Voice)

ear [ɪə*]	Ohr	have a good (or: quick / keen / sharp) ~ / prick up one's ~s (*inform.*) (die Ohren spitzen) / be **all ears** [ɔːl‿'ɪəz] / be **within** (or: **out of**) **earshot** ['ɪəʃɒt] (Hörweite) / It goes in one ~ and out the other.
hear (heard, heard) [hɪə*, hɜːd, –]	hören	~ well / ~ sth (+ well / distinctly / indistinctly)
hear (heard, heard) **about** [ˌ– (r)‿ə'baʊt]	hören über, hören von	~ ~ sth / ~ ~ sb doing sth / ~ quite a lot ~ sb
hear (heard, heard) **of** ['hɪər‿əv]	hören von (hören, daß es jmd. oder etwas gibt)	I've **heard of** them (+ but I don't know them personally).
hearing ['hɪərɪŋ]	Gehör	sb's ~ is good (or: bad / poor) / be **hard of hearing** [ˌhɑːd‿əv –] (schwerhörig)
overhear (overheard, overheard) [ˌəʊvə'hɪə, ˌ-'hɜːd, –]	zufällig (mit)hören, (be)lauschen	~ a conversation / ~ one's name
listen ['lɪsn]	zuhören	be ~ing / L~! / ~ to sb (or: sth) / ~ attentively (or: intently / with one ear / with half an ear) / ~ to the radio / have many **listeners** ['-əz]
listen for ['lɪsn fə*]	auf etwas lauschen	~ ~ the phone (or: a car / footsteps)
sound [saʊnd]	(er)klingen, sich anhören;	~ like sth / ~ as if ... / sb ~s tired / The trumpet ~ed.
	Klang, Geräusch	the ~ of music (or: a car being started) / hear ~s of laughter
loud [laʊd]	laut	hear a ~ noise / be ~ / talk (or: laugh) ~ly / knock ~ly on sth
noise ['nɔɪz]	Geräusch,	make (or: hear) a ~ (or: ~s) / make no ~ (or: ~s)
	Lärm	Don't make such a (= so much) ~! / Stop that ~! / What a ~! / an awful (or: a terrible) ~ / traffic ~ / the ~ of traffic
noisy ['nɔɪzɪ]	laut, lärmend	be ~ / ~ children / It's very ~ here. / do sth **noisily** [-lɪ]
ring (rang, rung) [rɪŋ, ræŋ, rʌŋ]	läuten, klingeln,	~ the bell (or: at the door / for sb) / The bell (or: telephone) is ~ing.
	Läuten, Klingeln;	hear a ~ at the door
	(er)tönen, (er)schallen	sb's words ~ through the house (or: in one's ears)

bang [bæŋ]	knallen, donnern	~ a door (or: window) (+ shut) / ~ sth (or: one's fist) on the table / a door (or: window / lid) ~s
deaf [def]	taub	be ~ on (= in) one ear / a **deafening** ['defnɪŋ] noise / **the deaf** (= **deaf** people)
crash [kræʃ]	krachen, mit lautem Krach stürzen,	a tree (or: plate / cupboard) ~es down (+ to the ground) / ~ through a window
	Krach;	hear the ~ of breaking glass / a loud ~ / a ~ of thunder
	schlagen, knallen	He ~ed his fist (or: the book) on the table.
roar [rɔː*]	brüllen, heulen,	wind ~s / a car (or: an engine) ~s / a car (or: the traffic) ~s past (or: along) / the ~ing of the sea
	Getöse, Heulen, Brüllen	the ~ of an angry lion / the ~ of an engine (or: the wind and waves)
knock [nɒk]	klopfen,	~ at the door (or: on the window)
	Klopfen	hear a ~ (= **knocking** ['-ɪŋ]) at the door
rattle ['rætl]	rütteln, klappern	The wind ~s the windows. / ~ in the wind / An old car (or: bike) ~s along the road. / a ~ing bike
crack [kræk]	knallen,	~ a whip (Peitsche) / A whip ~s.
	Knallen;	hear the ~ of a whip
	knacken	dry twigs ~ing under one's feet / hear a ~ing noise in the bushes
clatter ['klætə*]	scheppern, Geschepper	hear the ~ of metal plates
rustle ['rʌsl]	rascheln (lassen),	paper (or: silk) ~s / leaves ~ / mice ~ in the straw / ~ a newspaper
	Rascheln	hear a ~ of leaves
echo ['ekəʊ]	widerhallen, Echo	a room ~es with the sound of ...
quiet ['kwaɪət]	ruhig, leise,	Be ~! / a ~ evening / ~ music / a ~ voice / do sth ~ly
	Stille	in the ~ of the night
soft [sɒft]	sanft, weich	~ music / a ~ whisper (or: murmur)
silent ['saɪlənt]	still	be (+ absolutely) ~ / the ~ hours of the night
silence ['saɪləns]	Stille	break into (or: shatter / disturb / interrupt) the ~

16 Smell – Geruchssinn

(→ 10 Parts of the face)

smell (smelt, smelt, *BE* [smel, smelt, –] / smelled, smelled, *AE* [-d, -d])	riechen,	~ sth / sth ~s good (or: sweet / nice / pleasant / fresh / bad / nasty / old / disgusting / spoilt) / sth ~s of (or: like) sth
	Geruch;	sth has a strong (or: faint / characteristic / good) ~ / sth spreads (or: gives off) a ~ / a ~ spreads throughout a place / Have (or: Take) a ~ of this! (Riech' mal daran!)
	schnuppern	The dog is ~ing (+ at) the package.
sniff [snɪf]	schnuppern, schnüffeln	~ sea air / ~ at a rose (or: bottle) / The dog ~ed the ground.
odour ['əʊdə*] (*BE*) = **odor** [-r] (*AE*)	Duft, Geruch	smell (or: spread) an ~ of sth
scent [sent]	Geruch, Duft,	sth has no (or: a strong / a poor) ~ / the ~ of hay (or: flowers / coffee / fried bacon) / **scentless** ['-lɪs]
	mit Duft erfüllen,	flowers ~ing the whole room
	Parfüm;	use a little ~ / a **scent-bottle** ['-ˌbɒtl] / a **scented** ['-ɪd] handkerchief
	Witterung,	dogs following (+ up) (or: losing) the ~ of a fox
	wittern	~ a fox
stink (stank, stunk) [stɪŋk, stæŋk, stʌŋk]	stinken,	sb(or: sth) ~s (+ of sth)
	Gestank	the ~ of cheap cigars

17 Taste – Geschmack

(→ 10 Parts of the face; 24 Food and drink)

taste [teɪst]	schmecken, kosten,	sth ~s nice (or: good / bad) / sth ~s of sth (or: nothing) / sth ~s like sth / ~ the pepper in the soup / ~ the soup (or: salad / wine)
	Geschmack	like (or: dislike / hate) the ~ of sth / sth has a nice ~ / sth is **tasteless** ['-lɪs] (= has no ~) / Have a ~ of the soup!
flavour ['fleɪvə*] (*BE*) = **flavor** [-r] (*AE*)	Geschmack, Geschmacksrichtung;	the ~ of strawberries (or: cheese) / sth has not much (or: plenty of) ~ / various ~s of ice-cream
	würzen	~ a sauce with onions

delicious [dɪ'lɪʃəs]	köstlich	sth tastes (or: is) ~
sweet [swi:t]	süß	sth tastes (or: is) ~ / **sweeten** ['-n] sth with sugar
acid ['æsɪd]	sauer, bitter	sth has an ~ taste
sour ['saʊə*]	sauer	sth tastes (or: is) ~ / ~ milk
bitter ['bɪtə*]	bitter	sth tastes (or: is) ~
salt [sɒ:lt]	Salz-, salzen	**salt water** ['– wɔ:tə*] / ~ the roads / The soup's too **salty** ['-ɪ].
hot [hɒt]	scharf gewürzt	a ~ curry (or: dish)
mild [maɪld]	mild	a ~ curry (or: cheese)

Touch – Tastsinn 18

(→ 178 Texture, surface)

touch [tʌtʃ]	berühren, Berührung	~ sth (or: sb) (+ lightly / firmly) sth is rough to the ~ / feel the ~ of sb's hand
feel (felt, felt) [fi:l, felt, –]	fühlen	~ sth (+ hard / soft / hot / cold) on (or: in) one's hand / ~ a pain
	tasten, abtasten	~ about (= around) (+ for sth) / ~ one's way / ~ in one's pockets for sth
	sich anfühlen	sth ~s like wool (or: glass)
feeling ['fi:lɪŋ]	Gefühl	have no ~ in one's feet
handle ['hændl]	berühren, anfassen	Please ~ with care.

Positions, movements of the body – Stellungen, Bewegungen des Körpers

Positions, changing one's position – Stellungen, Veränderungen der Stellung 19

(→ 46 Facial expression, gesture)

position [pə'zɪʃn]	Stellung, Lage	be (or: sit / lie) in a comfortable ~ / stay in the same ~ / change one's ~
still [stɪl]	regungslos	be (or: sit / stand / lie) ~
movement ['mu:vmənt]	Bewegung	make a(n) quick (or: slow / energetic) ~ / with a ~ of the hand (or: arm / foot / leg)
move [mu:v]	(sich) bewegen	~ quickly (or: slowly / energetically) / ~ one's head (or: arms / legs) / stand (or: sit / lie) without **moving** ['-ɪŋ]

graceful ['greɪsfʊl]	anmutig	be ~ / make a ~ movement / move (or: do sth) ~ly
awkward ['ɔːkwəd]	ungeschickt, linkisch	be ~ / make an ~ movement / move (or: do sth) ~ly
clumsy ['klʌmzɪ]	ungeschickt, unbeholfen	be ~ / make a ~ movement / move **clumsily** [-lɪ]
stand (stood, stood) [stænd, stʊd, –]	stehen	~ still / ~ at the window (or: by the door) / ~ about (or: around) / ~ by ([untätig] danebenstehen)
straight [streɪt]	gerade	stand (or: sit) (+ up) ~
upright ['ʌpraɪt]	aufrecht	stand (or: sit) ~
turn [tɜːn]	(sich) drehen, (sich) wenden	~ (+ round / around) to sb / ~ away (+ from sb) / ~ back (+ to sb) / ~ over onto one's back / ~ one's head (or: back) towards sb (or: sth)
lean (leant, leant, *BE* [liːn, lent, –] / leaned, leaned, *AE* [liːnd, –])	sich lehnen,	~ against a wall (or: sb's shoulder) / ~ back (+ in one's armchair) / ~ on sb's arm / ~ out (+ of the window)
	sich beugen	~ forward (or: over / down / backwards)
bend (bent, bent) [bend, bent, –]	sich bücken	~ down (or: over / forward / back) / ~ over sb / ~ down to sb
sink (sank, sunk) [sɪŋk, sæŋk, sʌŋk]	sinken	~ to the ground / ~ into sb's arms
drop [drɒp]	sich fallen lassen	~ into an armchair / ~ to the ground
crouch [kraʊtʃ]	hocken	~ (+ down) on the floor
sit (sat, sat) [sɪt, sæt, –]	sitzen,	~ on a chair (or: on a sofa / on the ground / in an armchair / at a table) / ~ up straight / ~ upright
	sich setzen	~ down / ~ back (= up) (sich aufrecht hinsetzen)
Take (took, taken) **a seat** [ˌteɪk‿ə 'siːt] = **Have** (had, had) **a seat** [ˌhæv‿ə 'siːt]	Nimm (Nehmen Sie) Platz	
kneel (knelt, knelt [niːl, nelt, –] / kneeled, kneeled [niːld, –], *AE*)	knien	~ on the floor / ~ down
lie (lay, lain) [laɪ, leɪ, leɪn]	liegen	~ in bed / ~ in the sun / ~ on one's back
stand (stood, stood) **up** [stænd, stʊd, –; – 'ʌp]	aufstehen	~ ~ when sb enters the room
get (got, got) **up** [get, gɒt, –; – 'ʌp]	aufstehen;	~ ~ from the ground
	aufstehen (sich aus dem Bett erheben)	~ ~ at seven

rise (rose, risen) [raɪz, rəʊz, 'rɪzn]	sich erheben	~ to greet sb / ~ from one's knees (or: one's seat / the ground) / ~ to one's feet
jump [dʒʌmp]	springen,	~ up (+ from one's seat) / ~ out of bed (or: one's chair) / ~ to one's feet / ~ over (or: across) / ~ forward (or: back / aside / down)
	Sprung	make a ~
spring (sprang, sprung) [sprɪŋ, spræŋ, sprʌŋ]	springen	~ to one's feet / ~ up (+ from one's seat)

Moving from place to place – sich von Ort zu Ort bewegen 20

come (came, come) [kʌm, keɪm, kʌm]	kommen	~ to a place / ~ to sb / "**Come in** !" / ~ to see ... / ~ running (or: walking)
approach [ə'prəʊtʃ]	näherkommen, sich nähern	~ the town
	Herannahen, Annäherung	an ~ to sth
arrive [ə'raɪv]	ankommen	~ at 8 o'clock / ~ home / ~ at sb's house / ~ in London / on one's **arrival** [ə'raɪvl] home
get (got, got) **to** [get, gɒt, –; '– tə]	erreichen	~ ~ London at 3 o'clock
reach [ri:tʃ]	erreichen	~ London by evening
leave (left, left) [li:v, left, –]	verlassen, wegfahren	~ at 8 o'clock / ~ a house / ~ sb
go (went, gone) [gəʊ, went, gɒn]	gehen	~ to (or: into / out of / from) ... / ~ away / ~ on foot / **get going** (sich auf den Weg machen)
walk [wɔ:k]	(zu Fuß) gehen,	~ home (or: to town / up and down)
	Spaziergang	have (or: go for) a ~ / a long (or: short / ten minutes') ~
step [step]	treten,	~ on (or: into / across / down from) sth / ~ aside (or: forward / back)
	Schritt	keep ~ with sb / take three ~s forward
pass [pɑ:s]	vorbeigehen an	~ a house
pace [peɪs]	schreiten, auf und ab gehen,	~ the room (or: platform) / ~ up and down
	Schritt, Tempo	keep ~ with ... / 10 ~s from ... / increase one's ~
march [mɑ:tʃ]	marschieren, Marsch	~ off / ~ in step / **Forward, march!** (Im Gleichschritt, marsch!) ~ up and down

stride (strode, stridden) [straɪd, strəʊd, 'strɪdn]	schreiten, (großer) Schritt	~ away (or: off) take great ~s
roam [rəʊm]	umherstreifen	~ around (or: through the streets)
wander ['wɒndə*]	schlendern	~ up and down the road
hurry ['hʌrɪ]	eilen, Eile	~ to … / ~ up (or: down) the stairs be in a ~
rush [rʌʃ]	eilen, sausen,	We needn't ~! / ~ to … / ~ off (or: away)
	Ansturm, Hektik	There has been a ~ for tickets. / the **rush hour** ['rʌʃ ˌaʊə*] (Hauptverkehrszeit)
run (ran, run) [rʌn, ræn, rʌn]	laufen, rennen	~ away (or: past / around) / ~ for sb / ~ to sb's aid / ~ after …
dash [dæʃ]	stürzen, rennen	~ (+ off) to do (or: get) sth / ~ away / ~ about all day
race [reɪs]	rennen, rasen, Wettrennen	~ down the road win (or: lose) a ~ / run a ~ against sb
climb [klaɪm]	klettern, erklimmen	~ a tree (or: mountain) / ~ onto (or: down from) … / ~ up the stairs
slide (slid, slid) [slaɪd, slɪd, –]	gleiten, rutschen	~ down the banisters (Treppengeländer)
stagger ['stægə*]	schwanken, taumeln	~ down the road
limp [lɪmp]	humpeln	~ to a chair
stumble ['stʌmbl]	stolpern, straucheln	~ down the hill / ~ over (= on) a stone
trip [trɪp]	stolpern	~ over sth and fall / ~ up the stairs
crawl [krɔːl]	kriechen, krabbeln	~ across the floor (+ on all fours) / ~ around
creep (crept, crept) [kriːp, krept, –]	kriechen, schleichen	~ towards the door / ~ along the wall (or: corridor)
hop [hɒp]	hüpfen	~ on one leg
tiptoe ['tɪptəʊ]	Zehenspitze, auf Zehenspitzen gehen	be (or: stand / walk) on ~ / ~ to the baby's bed / ~ away
slip [slɪp]	schlüpfen; rutschen	~ into (or: out of) a room / ~ away (or: out / past) / sth ~s from one's hand / My foot **slipped** [-t] and I fell. / ~ on an icy road / a **slippery** ['-ərɪ] pavement
fall (fell, fallen) [fɔːl, fel, 'fɔːlən]	fallen, stürzen,	~ over (or: from / off / into) … / ~ down (+ from) … / ~ full length (or: flat)
	Sturz	a ~ from a tree / a ~ of ten feet

Holding on to or letting go – festhalten oder loslassen 21

grope [grəʊp]	(im Dunkeln) tasten	~ about (+ for sth) / ~ one's way to (or: along / through) ...
take (took, taken) [teɪk, tʊk, 'teɪkən]	nehmen	~ sb in one's arms / ~ sb by the arm / ~ sth up with one's fingers / **take hold of** [ˌteɪk 'həʊld‿əv] sth
grasp [grɑːsp]	(er)greifen	~ sb's hand / ~ at sth
grab [græb]	gierig greifen, schnappen, (plötzlicher) Griff	~ sb / ~ sb's hand / ~ an apple make a ~ at sth
snatch [snætʃ]	erwischen, an sich reißen	~ sth (+ from sb) / ~ sth out of sb's hand
grip [grɪp]	fest greifen, packen, Griff	~ sb's hand (+ tightly) take a ~ on a rope / tighten (or: loosen) one's ~ on sth / let go one's ~ on sb (or: of sth)
seize [siːz]	ergreifen	~ sb (+ by the hand) / ~ sb's hand / ~ sth
catch (caught, caught) [kætʃ, kɔːt, –]	fangen, fassen, ergreifen	~ a thief / ~ sb by his sleeve / ~ a ball
hold (held, held) [həʊld, held, –]	(fest)halten	~ sth (+ in one's hands) / ~ sb's hand / ~ sb in one's arms / ~ one's head up (or: down)
catch hold of = **get hold of** = **take hold of** [– '– –]	ergreifen, erwischen	~ ~ ~ a robber
clasp [klɑːsp]	umklammern; falten	~ sb by the hand / ~ sth in one's hands / ~ one's hands
cling (clung, clung) [klɪŋ, klʌŋ, –]	sich anklammern, sich festhalten, sich anschmiegen	~ to sb (or: sb's arm) / ~ together
clench [klentʃ]	zusammenpressen; umklammern	~one's teeth ~ sth in one's hand
let (let, let) **go** [let, let, –; – 'gəʊ]	loslassen	~ ~ of sb (or: sth) / ~ ~ of sb's arm (or: hand) / L~ ~!
drop [drɒp]	fallen lassen	~ sth / ~ a letter in the box
lose (lost, lost) **hold** [luːz, lɒst, –; – 'həʊld]	etwas nicht mehr festhalten können	~ ~ of one's umbrella
let (let, let) **go one's hold** [– '– – ˌ–]	etwas loslassen	~ ~ ~ ~ of a rope (or: dog's lead)
leave (left, left) [liːv, left, –]	liegen lassen	~ sth in the train / ~ sth on the table

22 Touching and moving – berühren und bewegen

touch [tʌtʃ]	berühren	~ sb's arm (+ lightly) / Don't ~.
move [mu:v]	bewegen	~ one's head / ~ sth (+ away / back) / ~ sth to (or: away from) …
take (took, taken) [teɪk, tʊk, 'teɪkən]	(hin)bringen	~ letters to the post / ~ a guest home
bring (brought, brought) [brɪŋ, brɔ:t, –]	(her)bringen	~ sb a glass of water / ~ a friend home
fetch [fetʃ]	(herbei)holen, abholen	~ sb from the station
pick up [ˌpɪk 'ʌp]	aufheben	~ ~ a child / ~ sth ~ from the ground
lift [lɪft]	(auf)heben	~ sb (or: sth) (+ up) / ~ one's head (or: eyes / shoulders / arms / hands / feet when walking)
raise [reɪz]	(er)heben	~ one's head (or: eyes / arm / hand) / ~ the lid of a box
carry ['kærɪ]	tragen	~ sb (or: sth) (+ in one's arms / on one's shoulders / on one's back) / ~ sth away / sth is too heavy to ~
pull [pʊl]	ziehen	~ sb (+ by the arm / by the coat) / ~ sth (+ away / down / off / out / in) / ~ at sth (or: sb's arm / sb's coat)
draw (drew, drawn) [drɔ:, dru:, drɔ:n]	ziehen	~ sb aside / ~ back one's hand / ~ one's hat over one's eyes / ~ one's chair up to the table / ~ a card from a pack / ~ a knife (or: gun)
tear (tore, torn) [teə*, tɔ:*, tɔ:n]	zerren, reißen	~ sth off (or: out / down) / ~ sb away from sth / The shirt **tore**.
shake (shook, shaken) [ʃeɪk, ʃʊk, 'ʃeɪkən]	schütteln,	~ oneself / ~ sb by the shoulder / ~ sth (+ out) / ~ (+ up) a bottle of medicine / ~ up a cushion
	erschüttern	sth ~s the house
scratch [skrætʃ]	kratzen	~ oneself (or: one's head / ears) / ~ sth (or: the paint)
rub [rʌb]	reiben	~ one's eyes / ~ one's hands together / ~ oneself against sth
wipe [waɪp]	abputzen, wischen	~ sth clean (or: dry) / ~ one's shoes (or: feet) / ~ one's nose (+ with a hanky) / ~ one's face with … / ~ the sweat off one's brow / ~ one's tears away
bend (bent, bent) [bend, bent, –]	biegen, beugen	~ one's head (or: knees / arms) / ~ a wire

cross [krɒs]	kreuzen, verschränken	~ one's arms (or: legs) / sit with one's legs ~ed
fold [fəʊld]	falten	~ one's hands (or: arms) / ~ a letter (or: hanky) / ~ up a tablecloth / ~ sth in half
turn [tɜːn]	drehen, wenden, richten	~ one's head / ~ a key in the lock / ~ one's gun on sb
close [kləʊz]	schließen, zumachen	~ one's eyes (or: mouth) / ~ the door (or: a box / a book)
shut (shut, shut) [ʃʌt, –, –]	schließen	~ one's eyes (or: mouth) / ~ a door (or: box / cupboard)
straighten ['streɪtn]	geludemachen, durchdrücken	~ one's back (or: legs) / ~ one's hat (or: tie) / ~ a piece of wire
stretch [stretʃ]	ausstrecken	~ (+ out) one's legs
spread (spread, spread) [spred, –, –]	ausbreiten	~ (+ out) one's arms / ~ oneself (sich breitmachen) (+ out) / ~ a cloth on the table
push [pʊʃ]	schieben, stoßen, drängeln,	~ sb / ~ oneself to the front / Don't ~! / ~ sth
	Stoß, Schub	give sb (or: sth) a ~
press [pres]	drücken, pressen	~ sb's hand warmly / ~ one's nose against the window / ~ a button / ~ sth into sb's hand
tap [tæp]	klopfen, pochen, antippen	~ one's fingers on sth / ~ one's foot on the floor (+ nervously) / ~ on the door
	Klopfen	hear a ~ on the window (or: door) / a light ~
knock [nɒk]	klopfen, schlagen	~ on (or: at) the door
bind (bound, bound) [baɪnd, baʊnd, –]	binden	~ sb's hands
tie [taɪ]	verschnüren, zusammenknoten	~ one's shoelaces / ~ a knot / ~ sth into a bundle / be **tied** [taɪd] with string
fasten ['fɑːsn]	festmachen, (an-, fest-)binden	~ one's seat-belt / sth is **fastened** [-d] **to** sth
cover ['kʌvə*]	bedecken	~ one's face with one's hands
give (gave, given) [gɪv, geɪv, 'gɪvn]	geben	~ sb sth / ~ sth to sb
hand [hænd]	übergeben, reichen, aushändigen	~ sth over (+ to sb)
wrap [ræp]	einwickeln	be **wrapped** [-t] **in** paper
roll [rəʊl]	(auf-, ein-)rollen, einwickeln	~ up one's sleeves

kick [kɪk]	treten,	~ sb in (or: on) the shin / ~ a ball / ~ hard / ~ over a chair
	Tritt	give sb (or: a ball) a ~
stamp [stæmp]	trampeln, stampfen	~ the ground / ~ out a fire / ~ about in the cold / ~ one's feet
throw (threw, thrown) [θrəʊ, θrʊ:, θrəʊn]	werfen, schleudern	~ one's head back / ~ a ball / ~ sb the ball
thrust (thrust, thrust) [θrʌst, –, –]	stoßen	~ one's hands into one's pockets / ~ a knife into sb's back
put (put, put) [pʊt, –, –]	setzen, stellen, legen	~ one's head on sb's shoulder / ~ one's hand in one's pocket / ~ one's arm around sb / ~ sth in (or: out / away / down / back) / ~ sth in the cupboard / ~ sth on the table / ~ sth into one's mouth (or: a box / one's pocket)
place [pleɪs]	setzen, stellen, legen, plazieren	~ the books in the right order
lay (laid, laid) [leɪ, leɪd, –]	legen	~ (oneself) down / ~ one's hand on sb's shoulder / ~ sth down (or: aside)
lean [li:n] (leant, leant [lent, –] *BE* / leaned, leaned [li:nd, –] *AE*)	lehnen, legen	~ one's head on (or: against) sb's shoulder / ~ one's elbows on the table / ~ a bicycle against a wall
rest [rest]	liegen lassen, ruhen lassen, aufstützen	~ one's head on one's hands / ~ one's elbows on a table
open ['əʊpən]	öffnen	~ a door (or: window / box / book)
push [pʊʃ]	schieben, drücken	~ sth into the corner / ~ one's bike / ~ a button
remove [rɪ'mu:v]	beseitigen, entfernen	The police came to ~ my car because it was parked in a no parking area.
roll [rəʊl]	rollen	~ a ball / ~ down the stairs / ~ up the carpet

Eating, drinking; smoking – Essen, Trinken; Rauchen

Eat, drink, digest – essen, trinken, verdauen 23

appetite ['æpɪtaɪt]	Appetit	have a good (or: poor) ~
hunger ['hʌŋgə*]	Hunger	be dying of ~ (*inform.*) / die of ~ / be (or: feel) **hungry** ['hʌŋgrɪ]
starve [stɑːv]	hungern, vor Hunger fast umkommen (*inform.*)	be **starving** [-ɪŋ] for food / ~ to death / die of **starvation** [stɑː'veɪʃn] / Is dinner ready? **I'm starving**.
thirst [θɜːst]	Durst	satisfy (or: quench [löschen]) one's ~ / sth gives one a ~ / sth makes one **thirsty** ['-ɪ] / get (or: become / feel / be) **thirsty**
eat [iːt] (ate [et] (*BE*), [eɪt] (*AE*), eaten ['iːtn])	essen	~ sth (+ up) / ~ hungrily / ~ a lot / sth is still **eatable** ['iːtəbl] / sth is **uneatable** [ˌʌn'iːtəbl]
edible ['edɪbl]	genießbar, nicht giftig	Are these berries ~, or are they poisonous (giftig)?
feed (fed, fed) [fiːd, fed, –]	füttern, ernähren	~ a baby (+ his breakfast)
bite (bit, bitten) [baɪt, bɪt, 'bɪtn]	beißen	~ into sth / ~ off a piece of ...
chew [tʃuː]	kauen	~ sth well (or: properly) / **chewing gum** ['tʃuːɪŋ gʌm]
lick [lɪk]	lecken	~ one's lips / ~ sth off one's lips / ~ at sth
suck [sʌk]	saugen, lutschen	~ the juice from an orange / ~ a sweet / ~ sth in
drink (drank, drunk) [drɪŋk, dræŋk, drʌŋk]	trinken,	~ water (or: tea) / ~ sth down (or: up) / ~ sth from a cup / ~ (+ to) sb's health
	Schluck	give sb a ~ of water / have a ~ of water
drunk [drʌŋk] (*pred.*)	betrunken	be (or: get) ~ (+ on whisky) / be too ~ to drive a car / be a **drunkard** ['drʌŋkəd] (Trinker, Säufer)
drunken ['drʌŋkən] (*attrib.*)	betrunken	a ~ man
swallow ['swɒləʊ]	(herunter)schlucken	~ sth
choke [tʃəʊk]	sich verschlucken	~ on a fish-bone / ~ over one's food
spit (spat, spat) **out** [spɪt, spæt, –; – '–]	ausspucken	~ sth ~

digest [dɪ'dʒest], [daɪ'dʒest]	verdauen	sth is easy (or: hard) to ~ / sth ~s easily (or: hard) / sth is **digestible** [-əbl] (or: **indigestible** [ˌɪndɪ'dʒestebl])
digestion [daɪ'dʒestʃən], [dɪ'-]	Verdauung	have a good (or: normal / poor) ~ / sth is good (or: bad) for the ~
stomach ['stʌmək]	Magen; vertragen	do sth on a full (or: an empty) ~ not be able to ~ sth (*inform.*)
full (+ up) [fʊl ('– –)] (*inform.*)	satt, voll	I can't eat any more; I'm ~.
have had enough [– – '–] (*inform.*)	satt sein	Thanks, **I've had enough**.

24 Food and drink – Speisen und Getränke

(→ 17 Taste; 159 Animals on the farm; 167 Vegetables, cereals, fruit)

food	[fuːd]	Nahrungsmittel, Essen
porridge	['pɒrɪdʒ]	Haferbrei
cornflakes	['kɔːnfleɪks]	Cornflakes
milk	[mɪlk]	Milch
cream	[kriːm]	Sahne
sugar	['ʃʊgə*]	Zucker
egg	[eg]	Ei
bacon	['beɪkən]	Speck
ham	[hæm]	Schinken
flour	['flaʊə*]	Mehl
bread	[bred]	Brot
loaf	[ləʊf]	Laib
roll	[rəʊl]	Brötchen
butter	['bʌtə*]	Butter
margarine	[ˌmɑːdʒə'riːn]	Margarine
marmalade	['mɑːməleɪd]	(Zitrus-)Marmelade
jam	[dʒæm]	(Frucht-)Marmelade
honey	['hʌnɪ]	Honig
cocoa	['kəʊkəʊ]	Kakao
juice	[dʒuːs]	Saft
sandwich	['sænwɪtʃ]	Sandwich, belegtes Brot
cheese	[tʃiːz]	Käse
sausage	['sɒsɪdʒ]	Wurst
mustard	['mʌstəd]	(scharfer) Senf
soup	[suːp]	Suppe
meat	[miːt]	Fleisch
beef	[biːf]	Rindfleisch
veal	[viːl]	Kalbfleisch
pork	[pɔːk]	Schweinefleisch

mutton	['mʌtn]	Hammelfleisch
lamb	[læm]	Lammfleisch
fish and chips	[ˌfɪʃ‿ən 'tʃɪps]	Fisch mit Pommes frites
fish fingers	[ˌfɪʃ 'fɪŋgəz]	Fischstäbchen
steak	[steɪk]	Steak
chop	[tʃɒp]	Kotelett
roast beef	['rəʊst bi:f]	Roastbeef, Rinderbraten
salt	[sɔ:lt]	Salz
pepper	['pepə*]	Pfeffer
salad	['sæləd]	(Obst-, Gemüse-)Salat
ice-cream	[ˌaɪs'kri:m]	Eis
cake	[keɪk]	Kuchen, Torte
pie	[paɪ]	gefüllter Kuchen, Pastete
pastry	['peɪstrɪ]	Gebäck
biscuit (*BE*)	['bɪskɪt]	Keks
= **cookie** (*AE*)	['kʊkɪ]	
sweet (*BE*)	[swi:t]	Süßigkeit, Bonbon
= **candy** (*AE*)	['kændɪ]	
chocolate	['tʃɒkələt]	Schokolade, Praline
drink	[drɪŋk]	Getränk, alkoholisches Getränk
coffee	['kɒfɪ]	Kaffee
tea	[ti:]	Tee
squash	[skwɒʃ]	Saft (Konzentrat)
lemonade	[ˌlemə'neɪd]	Limonade
coke	['kəʊk]	Cola
beer	[bɪə*]	Bier
ale	[eɪl]	Bier (hell)
stout	[staʊt]	dunkles Starkbier
wine	[waɪn]	Wein

Meals – Mahlzeiten (→ 140 Kitchen, housework; 141 Dining-room) 25

make (made, made) **(+ oneself) sth** [meɪk, meɪd, –; ˌ– (–) '–]	(sich) etwas zubereiten	~ (+ ~) a sandwich (or: meal / cup of coffee)
recipe ['resɪpɪ]	Rezept	try (+ out) a new ~
cut (cut, cut) [kʌt, –, –]	schneiden	~ sth / ~ sb a slice of bread / ~ sth into pieces / ~ sth off (+ from sth)
slice [slaɪs]	Scheibe,	a ~ of bread (or: cheese) / a thin (or: thick) ~
	in Scheiben schneiden	~ sth (+ up) / ~ sth thin
chop [tʃɒp]	schneiden, hacken	~ meat (or: vegetables) (+ up) / ~ meat into small pieces

peel [piːl]	schälen, Schale	~ apples (or: bananas / potatoes) potato ~ / **peelings** ['-ɪŋz]
put (put, put) [pʊt, –, –]	streichen; streuen	~ some butter on one's bread ~ some salt on a tomato
spread (spread, spread) [spred, –, –]	(be)streichen	~ butter on a slice of bread
salt [sɔːlt]	salzen	~ the meat (or: fish) / **salted** ['-ɪd] butter
stir [stɜː*]	(um)rühren	~ one's tea / ~ milk into one's tea
raw [rɔː]	roh	~ eggs (or: meat)
cook [kʊk]	kochen, braten, backen	~ meat (or: vegetables) / ~ a meal / **uncooked** [ʌn'kʊkt] (= raw)
do (did, done) [duː, dɪd, dʌn]	kochen, garen	~ the beef (or: steak)
boil [bɔɪl]	(in Wasser) kochen, Kochen	The water is ~ing. / **boiled** [bɔɪld] potatoes bring sth to the ~
hard-boiled [ˌhɑːd'bɔɪld]	hartgekocht	a ~ egg
stew [stjuː]	schmoren, dünsten; Eintopf	~ed meat mutton ~ / **Irish stew** [ˌaɪərɪʃ '–]
fry [fraɪ]	(in der Pfanne) braten	sth is ~ing (or: being **fried** [-d]) / **fried** eggs (or: potatoes / fish / chicken) / **frying-pan** ['-ɪŋ pæn]
underdone [ˌʌndə'dʌn]	nicht durchgebraten	
well done [ˌwel 'dʌn]	gut durchgebraten	Pork has to be very ~ ~, or you can't eat it.
scrambled eggs [ˌskræmbld 'egz]	Rührei	make ~ ~
roast [rəʊst]	(im Backofen oder über offenem Feuer) braten, rösten, geröstet, gebraten, Braten	~ a chicken / The meat is ~ing. ~ potatoes ~ beef (or: pork / chicken) / cold ~
bake [beɪk]	backen	~ a cake / ~d beans
dish [dɪʃ]	Gericht, Essen	My favourite ~ is ...
course [kɔːs]	Gang	a meal with four ~s / the main ~
dessert [dɪ'zɜːt]	Nachtisch	have fruit (or: ice-cream) for ~
pudding ['pʊdɪŋ] (*BE*)	Nachtisch	have ice-cream for ~
offer ['ɒfə*]	anbieten	~ sb sth (= ~ sth to sb)
like [laɪk]	mögen	What would you ~? / Would you ~ some of this? / I'd ~ some rice, please. / I'd ~ some more (+ rice), please.

have (had, had) [hæv, hæd, –]	haben, nehmen	Can (or: May) I ~ some coffee, please? / H~ some tea!
take (took, taken) [teɪk, tʊk, 'teɪkən]	nehmen	~ tea / ~ sugar in one's tea
helping ['helpɪŋ]	Portion	take (or: have) a big (or: second) ~
help oneself [help wʌn'self]	sich bedienen, sich nehmen	H~ yourself. / ~ ~ to some fruit (or: another apple)
pass [pɑːs]	reichen	P~ me the sugar, please. / ~ sth (+ on) to sb
pour [pɔː*]	gießen	~ cream into (or: over) sth / ~ oneself (or: sb) a cup of tea
meal [miːl]	Mahlzeit	prepare (or: make / cook / order / serve / have / finish) a ~ / a delicious (or: hearty / rich / simple / light) ~ / The ~ is ready.
breakfast ['brekfəst]	Frühstück,	have (an early) ~ / have sth for ~ / be at ~
	frühstücken	~ with sb
snack [snæk]	Imbiß	have a ~ / a **snack-bar** ['-bɑː*]
lunch [lʌntʃ]	leichte Mahlzeit (in der Mitte des Tages) (einnehmen)	have (+ a good) ~ / have sth for ~ / be at ~ / ~ (+ with sb) at a hotel
dinner ['dɪnə*]	Hauptmahlzeit (mittags oder abends)	have (+ a delicious) ~ / have sth for ~ / be at ~ / It's time for ~ (= It's **dinner-time** ['-taɪm]). / ask sb to ~
dine [daɪn] (*form.*)	(zu Mittag oder zu Abend) essen	~ with sb / Shall we ~ together? / **dine out** [–‿'aʊt] (zum Essen ausgehen)
tea [tiː]	(als Zwischenmahlzeit)	have ~ at five o'clock / have one's five o'clock ~ / It's **tea-time** ['-taɪm].
supper ['sʌpə*]	Abendbrot	have (+ a good / a late) ~ / have sth for ~
picnic ['pɪknɪk]	Picknick	have a ~
leave (left, left) [liːv, left, –]	(vom Tisch) aufstehen	May I ~ the table?

Smoking – Rauchen 26

tobacco [tə'bækəʊ]	Tabak	smoke ~ / a mild (or: strong) ~
blend [blend]	Mischung	a ~ of the finest tobaccos of the world
cigarette [ˌsɪgə'ret]	Zigarette	take (or: smoke) a ~ / put out a ~
packet ['pækɪt] (*BE*) = **pack** [pæk] (*AE*)	Päckchen	buy (or: open) a ~ of cigarettes
brand [brænd]	Sorte, Marke	Which ~ do you prefer?

cigar [sɪ'gɑ:*]	Zigarre	
cigar box [sɪ'gɑ: ˌbɒks]	Zigarrenkiste	
pipe [paɪp]	Pfeife	fill one's ~
match [mætʃ]	Streichholz	strike (or: light / blow out) a ~ / **match-box** ['mætʃbɒks]
light (lit, lit) [laɪt, lɪt, –]	anzünden,	~ a cigarette / The cigarette was **lit** (war an). / **cigarette lighter**
	Feuer	give sb a ~ / Have you got a ~, please?
smoke [sməʊk]	rauchen,	~ a cigarette / May I ~?
	Rauch	**cigar smoke** [sɪ'gɑ: ˌ–]
have a smoke [– – '–]	rauchen	May I ~ ~ ~?
puff [pʌf]	ziehen, Zug;	~ (+ at) a cigar / take (or: have) a ~ at a cigarette
	blasen	~ cigarette smoke into (or: in) sb's face / ~ smoke into (or: in) the air
inhale [ɪn'heɪl]	inhalieren	~ deeply / ~ smoke (auf Lunge rauchen)
ash [æʃ]	Asche	the cigarette ~ falls on ... / drop cigarette ~ on the carpet / **ashtray** ['æʃtreɪ] (Aschenbecher)

Health, illness – Gesundheit, Krankheit

27 Health, illness – Gesundheit, Krankheit

health [helθ]	Gesundheit	be in good (or: poor) ~ / sth is good for one's ~ / a **healthy** ['-ɪ] climate / be (or: look) **healthy**
feel (felt, felt) [fi:l, felt, –]	sich fühlen	~ well (or: better) / I ~ ill. (*BE,* = sick, *AE*) (Mir ist übel.) / I ~ giddy. (= dizzy) (Mir ist schwindelig.)
ill [ɪl]	unwohl, krank	fall (or: become / be / look) ~ / feel ~ / have (or: suffer from) a serious **illness** ['ɪlnɪs]
disease [dɪ'zi:z]	Krankheit	catch a ~ / a skin ~ / a rare ~
sick [sɪk] (*BE: attrib.* only)	krank	a ~ child / the ~ (+ people) / a strange **sickness** ['sɪknɪs] / **mental sickness** [ˌmentl 'sɪknɪs]
sick [sɪk] (*AE: pred.* and *attrib.*)	krank	a ~ man / become (or: be) ~

sick [sɪk]	übel	feel ~ / be ~ (brechen) / A wave of **sickness** ['sɪknɪs] came over him.
disorder [dɪs'ɔːdə*]	Krankheit	physical (or: mental) ~
weak [wiːk]	schwach	be too ~ to stand up / have a ~ heart
trouble ['trʌbl]	Beschwerden	have heart (or: liver / lung) ~ / have ~ (+ in) breathing
attack [ə'tæk]	Anfall	have a **heart attack** ['hɑːt‿əˌtæk]
infect [ɪn'fekt]	anstecken	~ sb / be ~ed with cholera
contract [kən'trækt]	sich zuziehen, bekommen	~ a serious illness
contagious [kən'teɪdʒəs]	ansteckend	a ~ disease
ache [eɪk]	schmerzen, weh tun, -schmerz	My head is **aching** ['-ɪŋ]. I've got a **headache** ['hedeɪk] (or: **toothache** ['tuːθeɪk]).
hurt (hurt, hurt) [hɜːt, –, –]	schmerzen	one's legs ~
pain [peɪn]	Schmerz	be in great ~ / cry with ~ / feel a sharp ~ / feel ~s in the knee (or: back) / have stomach ~s
sore [sɔː*]	wund, schmerzhaft, entzündet	have a ~ throat (or: knee)
suffer ['sʌfə*]	leiden	~ from a disease
cold ['kəʊld]	Erkältung	catch (or: have) a ~ / a bad ~
flu [fluː] (*inform.*)	Grippe	have (+ the) ~
sneeze [sniːz]	niesen	have to ~ / ~ loudly
cough [kɒf]	husten,	be ~ing all the time
	Husten	have a bad ~
fever ['fiːvər] (*AE*) = **temperature** ['temprətʃə*] (*BE*)	Fieber	have a high (or: slight) ~ / be in bed with high ~
faint [feɪnt]	ohnmächtig werden	~ from loss of blood
unconscious [ʌn'kɒnʃəs]	ohnmächtig, bewußtlos	become (or: be) ~
be conscious [bɪ 'kɒnʃəs]	bei Bewußtsein sein	~ still ~
consciousness ['kɒnʃəsnɪs]	Bewußtsein	lose ~
heal [hiːl]	heilen	sb's wounds ~ slowly
recover [rɪ'kʌvə*]	genesen	~ from an illness / make a quick **recovery** [-rɪ]

28 Accident – Unfall

(→ 148 Services)

accident ['æksɪdənt]	Unfall	have a bad ~ / be killed in a road ~
hurt (hurt, hurt) [hɜːt, –, –]	verletzen	be (or: get) ~ / ~ one's leg / Did I ~ you?
injure ['ɪndʒə*]	verletzen	be (or: get) ~d / be badly (or: seriously / slightly) ~d / suffer serious **injuries** ['ɪndʒəriːz] (+ to the arms and legs)
ambulance ['æmbjʊləns]	Krankenwagen	
ambulance man ['æmbjʊləns ˌmæn]	Sanitäter	
first aid [ˌfɜːst 'eɪd]	erste Hilfe	give sb ~ ~
scratch [skrætʃ]	(zer)kratzen,	~ oneself (or: one's hand) on a nail / get ~ed (+ by a cat)
	Kratzer	have a ~ on one's hand / It's only a ~.
cut (cut, cut) [kʌt, –, –]	schneiden,	~ oneself (or: one's face) / ~ one's finger
	Schnittwunde	have a deep ~ on the face
wound [wuːnd]	verwunden, verletzen,	sb ~s sb / be (or: get) ~ed in the war (or: by a knife) / be badly (or: seriously / fatally [tödlich]) ~ed
	Wunde	a deep ~ / a flesh ~ / the **wounded** ['-ɪd] and the dead
bleed (bled, bled) [bliːd, bled, –]	bluten	His nose is ~ing. / One's wound is ~ing heavily. / ~ to death
bruise [bruːz]	prellen, quetschen,	fall and ~ one's leg / a ~d thumb
	Quetschung, Prellung	be covered with ~s
break (broke, broken) [breɪk, brəʊk, 'brəʊkən]	brechen	~ one's leg (or: a bone) / a **broken** leg
sprain [spreɪn]	verstauchen	a ~ed ankle
swollen ['swəʊlən]	geschwollen	have a ~ knee
poison ['pɔɪzn]	Gift, vergiften	drink a bottle of ~ by mistake / be (or: get) ~ed

29 At the doctor's – beim Arzt

patient ['peɪʃnt]	Patient	He is an old ~ of mine.
doctor ['dɒktə*]	Arzt	see a ~ (einen Arzt aufsuchen)
G. P. ['dʒiː 'piː]	Arzt für Allgemeinmedizin	

family doctor [ˌfæmɪlɪ 'dɒktə*]	Hausarzt	
surgery ['sɜːdʒərɪ]	Praxis; Sprechstunde	a doctor's ~ / the morning ~
examine [ɪg'zæmɪn]	untersuchen	~ sb carefully / have (or: undergo / carry out) a medical **examination** [-ˌ-'neɪʃn]
put (put, put) **out one's tongue** ['- - - '-]	die Zunge heraus-strecken	P~ ~ your ~, please.
temperature ['temprətʃə*]	Temperatur, Fieber	take one's ~ / Have you got a ~?
pulse [pʌlz]	Puls	take (or: feel) sb's ~
blood pressure ['blʌd ˌpreʃə*]	Blutdruck	take sb's ~ ~ / have high (or: low) ~ ~
treat [triːt]	behandeln	~ a patient (+ for his illness) / ~ an illness / need medical **treatment** ['-mənt]
prescribe [prɪ'skraɪb]	verschreiben	~ sth for sb's sore throat / take the **prescription** [ˌprɪ'skrɪpʃn] to the chemist's (*AE*: to the pharmacy)
medicine ['medsɪn]	Medizin	prescribe some ~ for sb's cough / take one's ~ / a bottle of ~
pill [pɪl]	Pille	swallow (or: take) one's ~ / be on the ~ (die „Pille" nehmen)
injection [ɪn'dʒekʃn]	Spritze	give (or: have) an ~
dress [dres]	versorgen, verbinden	~ a wound / have a wound ~ed
(+ sticking) plaster [('stɪkɪŋ) ˌplɑːstə*]	Heftpflaster	put on a (+ ~) ~
plaster(-cast) [ˌplʌstə('kɑːst)]	Gipsverband	a leg in ~
bind (bound, bound) [baɪnd, baʊnd, –]	verbinden	~ wounds
bandage ['bændɪdʒ]	verbinden, Verband	~ (+ up) sb's broken ankle / a man with a **bandaged** [-'-d] hand
scar [skɑː*]	Narbe	have a long ~ across one's cheek
x-ray [ˌeks'reɪ], ['- -]	röntgen, Röntgenaufnahme	sb's leg is ~ed / make an ~ of sb's knee

30 At the dentist's – beim Zahnarzt (→ 10 Parts of the face)

toothache ['tu:θeɪk]	Zahnschmerzen	have (or: suffer from) (+ a) ~
dentist ['dentɪst]	Zahnarzt	go to the ~'s / be at the ~'s
cavity ['kævətɪ]	Loch (im Zahn)	have a ~ in a tooth
fill [fɪl]	füllen, plombieren	~ a cavity / have a **filling** ['-ɪŋ] done
drill [drɪl]	bohren	~ sb's teeth
have (had, had) **a tooth out** [– – '– ˌ–]	einen Zahn gezogen bekommen	I'm **having a tooth out** tomorrow.
pull [pʊl]	ziehen	~ a tooth (+ out)
extract [ɪk'strækt]	ziehen	~ a tooth
(+ set of) false teeth [(– –) ˌfɔ:ls 'ti:θ]	künstliches Gebiß	
dentures ['dentʃəz]	Gebiß	wear ~

Clothing – Kleidung

31 Clothes – Kleidungsstücke

things (*inform.*)	[θɪŋgz]	Sachen
underwear	['ʌndəweə*]	Unterwäsche
= **underclothes**	['ʌndəkləʊðz]	
= **underclothing**	['ʌndəkləʊðɪŋ]	
(+ a pair of) pants	[(– '– –) 'pænts]	Unterhose (*BE*), lange Hose (*AE*)
bra	[brɑ:]	BH
slip = petticoat	[slɪp], ['petɪkəʊt]	Unterrock
(+ a pair of) stockings	[(– '– –) 'stɒkɪŋz]	Strümpfe
(+ a pair of) tights	[(– '– –) taɪts]	Strumpfhose
socks	[sɒks]	Kniestrümpfe, lange Socken
shirt	[ʃɜ:t]	Hemd
T-shirt	['ti:ʃɜ:t]	T-shirt
blouse	['blaʊz]	Bluse
sleeve	[sli:v]	Ärmel
cuff	[kʌf]	Manschette
collar	[kɒlə*]	Kragen
tie (*BE*) = **necktie** (*AE*)	[taɪ] ['nektaɪ]	Krawatte
bow-tie	[ˌbəʊ'taɪ]	Fliege
pullover	['pʊlˌəʊvə*]	Pullover
sweater	['swetə*]	dicker Pullover

jersey	['dʒɜːzɪ]	Pullover, Trikot
cardigan	['kɑːdɪgən]	Strickjacke
jacket	['dʒækɪt]	Jacke
blazer	['bleɪzə*]	Klubjacke
pocket	['pɒkɪt]	Tasche
(+ a pair of) trousers	[(– '– –) 'traʊzəz]	Hose
(+ a pair of) slacks	[(– '– –) slæks]	Hose
belt	[belt]	Gürtel
braces = suspenders (*AE*)	['breɪsɪz], [sə'spendəz]	Hosenträger
(+ a pair of) jeans	[(– '– –) dʒiːnz]	Jeans
(+ a pair of) shorts	[(– '– –) ʃɔːts]	kurze Hose
skirt	[skɜːt]	Rock
dress	[dres]	Kleid
suit	[suːt], [sjuːt]	Anzug, Kostüm
costume	['kɒstjuːm]	Kostüm (als Verkleidung; seltener: als Rock und Jacke)
(+ a pair of) shoes	[(– '– –) ʃuːz]	Schuhe
heel	[hiːl]	Absatz
boot	[buːt]	hoher Schuh, Schaftstiefel
wellington (+ boot)	['welɪŋtən (buːt)]	Gummistiefel
shoe	[ʃuː]	Schuh
coat	[kəʊt]	Mantel
cloak	[kləʊk]	Umhang, weiter Mantel
scarf (*pl.* scarves)	[skɑːf], [skɑːvz]	Halstuch, Schal
cap	[kæp]	Mütze
hat	[hæt]	Hut
(+ a pair of) gloves	[(– '– –) glʌvz]	Handschuhe
raincoat	['reɪnkəʊt]	Regenmantel
mackintosh	['mækɪntɒʃ]	Regenmantel
= mack = mac (*inform.*)	[mæk], [–]	
umbrella	[ʌm'brelə*]	Regenschirm
dinner jacket	['dɪnə ˌdʒækɪt]	Smoking
= tuxedo (*AE*)	[tʌk'siːdəʊ]	
evening dress	['iːvnɪŋ dres]	Abendkleid, Abendkleidung
evening gown	['iːvnɪŋ gaʊn]	Abendkleid
night dress	['naɪtdres]	Nachthemd
= nightie (*inform.*)	['naɪtɪ]	
(+ a pair of) pyjamas	[pə'dʒɑːməz]	Schlafanzung
= pajamas (*AE*)	[–]	
dressing gown	['dresɪŋ gaʊn]	Morgenrock, Morgenmantel
slippers	['slɪpəz]	Hausschuhe

32 Clothing accessories and jewellery – Kleidungszubehör und Schmuck

button	['bʌtn]	Knopf
buttonhole	['bʌtnhəʊl]	Knopfloch
zip fastener = zip	['zɪp ˌfɑːsnə*], [zɪp]	Reißverschluß
= **zipper** (*AE*)	['zɪpə*]	
handkerchief	['hæŋkətʃɪf]	Taschentuch
= **hanky** (*inform.*)	['hæŋkɪ]	
handbag	['hændbæg]	Handtasche (*BE*)
purse	[pɜːs]	Portemonnaie (*BE*), Handtasche (*AE*)
coin-purse (*AE*)	['kɔɪnpɜːs]	Portemonnaie
wallet	['wɒlɪt]	Brieftasche
wrist-watch	['rɪstwɒtʃ]	Armbanduhr
briefcase	['briːfkeɪs]	Aktentasche
jewellery (*BE*)	['dʒuːəlrɪ]	Schmuck, Juwelen
= **jewelry** (*AE*)	[–]	
jewel	['dʒuːəl]	Juwel, Edelstein
= **precious stone**	[ˌpreʃəs 'stəʊn]	
diamond	['daɪəmənd]	Diamant
pearl	[pɜːl]	Perle
ring	[rɪŋ]	Ring
chain	[tʃeɪn]	Kette
brooch	[brəʊtʃ]	Brosche
bracelet	['breɪslɪt]	Armband
necklace	['neklɪs]	Halskette
cuff-links	['kʌflɪŋks]	Manschettenknöpfe

33 Materials, fashion, making clothes – Stoffe, Mode, Schneidern

material [mə'tɪərɪəl]	Stoff, Material	a light (or: thin / heavy / thick / warm) ~
cloth [klɒθ]	Tuch	fine (or: coarse [rauh]) ~ / need a lot of ~
wool [wuːl]	Wolle, Woll-	This coat is (+ pure) ~. / sth is made of ~ / a ~ (= **woollen** ['-ən]) coat / a **woolly** ['-ɪ] material
cotton ['kɒtn]	Baumwolle	a ~ shirt
silk [sɪlk]	Seide, Seiden-	sth is made of ~ / ~ stockings / a **silky** ['-ɪ] material
leather ['leðə*]	Leder, Leder-	sth is made of ~ / a ~ coat

suède [sweɪd]	Wildleder, Wildleder-	a **suède jacket** ['– ˌdʒækɪt]
fur [fɜː*]	Pelz, Pelz-	a ~ coat (or: cap / collar)
linen ['lɪnɪn]	Leinen, Leinen-	a ~ sheet / bed ~
fashion ['fæʃn]	Mode	come into ~ / be in ~ / go out of ~ / sth is the latest ~ / wear **old-fashioned** [ˌəʊld'-d] clothes
fashionable ['fæʃnəbl]	modisch	~ clothes (or: colours / women) / be **fashionably** [-'-ɪ] dressed
style [staɪl]	Stil, Mode(richtung)	the ~ of the 1930's / What ~ (+ of) hats would you like to see?
elegant ['elɪgənt]	elegant	an ~ evening-dress / be ~ly dressed
smart [smɑːt]	schick, flott	a ~ jacket / be ~ly dressed
design [dɪ'zaɪn]	entwerfen,	~ a dress
	Entwurf	make a ~ for a dress
tailor ['teɪlə*]	schneidern,	~ a suit / a **well-tailored** [ˌwel'-d] suit
	Schneider	He's the Queen's ~.
size [saɪz]	Größe	take (or: have) ~ 8 (+ shoes) / It's the right (or: wrong) ~.
knit (knit, knit) [nɪt, –, –]	stricken	~ a pullover (+ out of wool) / take out one's **knitting** ['-ɪŋ]
stitch [stɪtʃ]	Stich; Masche	make long (or: short / loose) ~es drop (or: lose) a ~
needle [niːdl]	Nadel	sew (or: darn) with a ~ / **knitting needle** ['nɪtɪŋ –] / **needlework** ['niːdlwɜːk]
thread [θred]	Nähgarn,	cotton (or: nylon) ~
	einfädeln	~ a needle
sew (sewed, sown – sewed, sewed) [səʊ, səʊd, səʊn]	nähen	~ a blouse / ~ on a button / **sewing-machine** ['-ɪŋ məˌʃiːn]
pin [pɪn]	Stecknadel,	fasten sth (+ together / to sth) with a ~
	feststecken	~ sth together (or: to sth)
(+ a pair of) scissors [(– '– –) 'sɪzəz]	Schere	cut sth (+ off) with (+ ~ ~ ~) ~

Wearing clothes – Kleidung tragen 34

put (put, put) **on** [pʊt, –, –; – 'ɒn]	anziehen,	~ ~ (+ one's) trousers (or: coat / shoes)
	aufsetzen,	~ ~ a hat (or: a cap / glasses)
	anstecken,	~ ~ a ring
	umlegen	~ ~ a necklace

dress [dres]	(sich) anziehen	~ (+ oneself) quickly / It takes her hours to ~. / ~ a child / ~ (+ oneself) up as / ~ well (or: badly) / ~ in white (or: black / silk / leather) / be **well-dressed** [ˌwel'drest] / the **best-dressed** [ˌbest'drest] man / be **dressed** in white (or: in uniform) / **undress** [ˌʌn'-] quickly / be (or: get) **undressed** [ˌʌn'drest]
get (got, got) **dressed** [get, gɒt, –; – 'drest]	sich anziehen	~ ~ quickly (or: in a hurry) / It takes her hours to ~ ~.
have (had, had) **on** [hæv, hæd, –; – 'ɒn]	anhaben	~ a coat ~ / ~ black shoes ~ / ~ nothing ~
wear (wore, worn) [weə*, wɔː*, wɔːn]	tragen	~ a shirt (or: coat / hat) / Jeans are a much **worn** article of clothing.
fit [fɪt]	passen, sitzen, Sitz	sth ~s (+ well) It's a perfect ~.
tight [taɪt]	eng, stramm	~ jeans / be too ~
loose [luːs]	weit	be too ~
change [tʃeɪndʒ]	(sich) umziehen, wechseln	I must ~. / ~ the baby / ~ a dress / ~ one's wet clothes
take (took, taken) **off** [teɪk, tʊk, 'teɪkən; – 'ɒf]	ausziehen, abnehmen	~ one's coat (or: shoes) ~ ~ one's hat ~
bare [beə*]	nackt, bloß	with ~ feet (or: legs / arms) / be (or: go) **barefoot** ['beəfʊt] / **barefooted** [ˌbeə'fʊtɪd] children
naked ['neɪkɪd]	nackt	be (+ completely) ~ / be ~ to the waist
fasten ['fɑːsn]	zumachen, festmachen	~ one's jacket with a zip ~ sth to sth / **unfasten** [ˌʌn'fɑːsn] the buttons
button (+ up) ['bʌtn (ʌp)]	zuknöpfen	~ (+ ~) one's shirt (or: coat) / **unbutton** [ˌʌn'bʌtn] one's blouse
do (did, done) **up** [duː, dɪd, dʌn; '– ʌp]	zumachen	~ ~ one's shoes (or: coat)
undo (undid, undone) [ˌʌn'duː, ˌʌn'dɪd, ˌʌn'dʌn]	aufmachen	~ one's shoes (or: coat)
tie [taɪ]	zubinden, schnüren	~ one's shoes (or: scarf) / **untie** [ˌʌn'taɪ] one's shoes
knot [nɒt]	knoten, Knoten	~ one's shoelaces / ~ a tie have a ~ in one's shoelaces

lace [leɪs]	zubinden	~ one's shoes / **shoelace** ['ʃuːleɪs]
zip up [ˌzɪp 'ʌp]	(den Reißverschluß) zuziehen	~ ~ one's jacket
unzip [ˌʌn'zɪp]	(den Reißverschluß) aufmachen	~ one's jacket

Keeping clothes in order – Kleidung in Ordnung halten 35

soil [sɔɪl] = **dirty** ['dɜːtɪ]	(be)schmutzen, schmutzig werden	~ one's clothes White clothes ~ easily.
stain [steɪn]	beflecken,	be ~ed with ...
	Fleck	have (or: get) a(n) ink (or: blood) ~ on one's shirt
spot [spɒt]	Klecks	~s of ink (= **ink-spots** ['ɪŋk-s])
laundry ['lɔːndrɪ]	Wäsche,	do the ~ / The shirt is in the ~. / a ~ basket
	Wäscherei	have one's washing done in a ~
wash [wɒʃ]	waschen	~ the clothes / do the **washing** ['wɒʃɪŋ] / ~ sth in the **washing machine** ['wɒʃɪŋ məˌʃiːn]
detergent [dɪ'tɜːdʒənt]	Waschpulver	
hang (hung, hung) [hæŋ, hʌŋ, –]	(auf)hängen	~ the clothes on the line
iron ['aɪən]	bügeln	~ a shirt / do the **ironing** ['aɪənɪŋ]
press [pres]	(schnell) bügeln	~ the trousers
brush [brʌʃ]	bürsten	~ one's coat / ~ the dust off one's coat / a **clothes-brush** ['kləʊðzbrʌʃ]
polish ['pɒlɪʃ]	(blank)putzen	~ one's shoes / **shoe polish** ['ʃuː ˌpɒlɪʃ]
clean [kliːn]	putzen, saubermachen	~ one's shoes
mend [mend]	flicken, (Schuhe) reparieren	~ a hole (or: tear / sock) / have one's shoes **mended** ['-ɪd]
tear (tore, torn) [teə*, tɔː, tɔːn]	(zer)reißen, Riß	~ one's trousers / a button **tore** off have a ~ in one's trousers
darn [dɑːn]	stopfen	~ (+ the holes in) one's socks
repair [rɪ'peə*]	ausbessern	~ old shoes / ~ a shirt

Mental life – geistiges Leben

36 Mind – Geist, Verstand

mind [maɪnd]	Geist, Verstand;	have a clear (or: lively / keen / narrow / dull) ~ / be out of one's ~ / have (or: show) **presence of mind** ['prezns‿əv ˌmaɪnd]
	Sinn	sth comes (+ back) to one's ~ / change one's ~
attention [ə'tenʃn]	Aufmerksamkeit	give (= pay) ~ to ... / direct one's ~ to (= on) ... / concentrate one's ~ on ... / arrest (fesseln, erregen) sb's ~ / do sth to attract ~
attentive [ə'tentɪv]	aufmerksam	be ~ to / an ~ audience
inattentive [ˌɪnə'tentɪv]	unaufmerksam	be ~ to
concentration [ˌkɒnsən'treɪʃn]	Konzentration	have little power (or: great powers) of ~ / sth requires great ~ / try to **concentrate** ['kɒnsəntreɪt] / **concentrate** on (= upon) ...
alert [ə'lɜːt]	aufmerksam	be (or: appear to be) ~ (+ to what is going on around one)
alive [ə'laɪv]	empfänglich, achtsam	be fully ~ to ...
watchful ['wɒtʃfʊl]	wachsam, achtsam	keep a ~ eye on sb (or: sth)
mindful ['maɪndfʊl]	achtsam, bedacht	be ~ of one's duties
absent ['æbsənt]	(geistig) abwesend	look at sb in an ~ way / be very **absent-minded** [ˌæbsənt'maɪndɪd]
bore [bɔː*]	langweilen,	sb (or: sth) ~s one / ~ sb to death (or: tears) / be (or: get) **bored** [bɔːd] / a **boring** ['bɔːrɪŋ] story
	langweiliger Mensch	He's a ~.
narrow ['nærəʊ]	eng, beschränkt	have a ~ mind / be **narrow-minded** [ˌnærəʊ'maɪndɪd]
dull [dʌl]	beschränkt, dumm	have a ~ mind / be rather ~
stupid ['stjuːpɪd]	dumm	a ~ boy / a ~ thing to do
fool [fuːl]	Narr	What a ~ he is! / a **foolish** ['fuːlɪʃ] man / How **foolish**!
silly ['sɪlɪ]	albern, töricht	say ~ things / a ~ little boy / That was a ~ thing to do.
childish ['tʃaɪldɪʃ]	kindisch	Don't be ~!
smart [smɑːt]	gewitzt, pfiffig	a ~ boy (or: student) / a ~ reply

clever ['klevə*]	klug, gescheit	a ~ boy (or: remark / answer / book / piece of work) / be ~ at sth (or: doing sth) / That's very ~ of him. / admire sb's **cleverness** ['klevənɪs]
bright [braɪt]	hell, aufgeweckt	a ~ pupil
intelligence [ɪn'telɪdʒəns]	Intelligenz	have (= possess) a quick (or: sharp / lively / limited) ~ / show much (or: average / little) ~ / be **intelligent** [ɪn'telɪdʒənt] (or: **unintelligent** [ˌʌnɪn'telɪdʒənt]
wisdom ['wɪzdəm]	Weisheit, Klugheit	the ~ of our ancestors
wise [waɪz]	weise, klug	~ men [or: acts] / be ~ enough not do sth
brains [breɪnz] (*inform.*)	Grips	have a lot of ~
gift [gɪft]	Talent, Begabung	have a great ~ for sth / be very **gifted** ['gɪftɪd]
sense [sens]	Sinn (für ein bestimmtes Verhalten),	have a ~ of duty (or: justice / right and wrong / responsibility)
	Sinn (der in etwas liegt),	sth makes (+ no) ~ / make ~ of sth (sich etwas zusammenreimen) / there is no (or: little / some / not much / a lot of) ~ in doing sth (or: what one does) / I dont't know whether there is much ~ in it.
	Sinn, Urteilskraft, Verstand	have the ~ to do sth / be in possession of one's ~s / lose one's ~s
sensitive ['sensɪtɪv]	empfindlich	a ~ person
sensible ['sensəbl]	vernünftig, einsichtig	a ~ idea / What a ~ thing to do.
senseless ['senslɪs]	sinnlos, närrisch	What a ~ thing to do.
nonsense ['nɒnsəns]	Unsinn	talk (+ a lot of) ~ / That's all ~. / N~! I don't believe it.
spirit ['spɪrɪt]	Geist,	show much (or: the right) ~ / raise (or: break) sb's ~
	Schwung, Gesinnung, Stimmung	be in high (or: good / low) ~s / be out of ~s (niedergeschlagen sein)

Thinking – Denken 37

think (thought, thought) [θɪŋk, θɔːt, –]	denken,	~ hard (or: clearly / carefully / a lot) / sb is a great **thinker** ['-ə*]
	sich vorstellen, sich denken	can't ~ what (or: when / where / how / why / who) ...
think about [ˌ– ə'baʊt]	nachdenken über	~ ~ doing sth / ~ ~ a proposal / ~ ~ the past

think of ['– əv]	bedenken;	have a lot of things to ~ ~ / ~ ~ the costs (or: danger)
	sich vorstellen, sich im Traum einfallen lassen	never ~ ~ doing sth / couldn't (or: wouldn't / shouldn't) ~ ~ (+ doing) such a thing
think over [ˌ– 'əʊvə]	nachdenken über	T~ ~ what I've said. / T~ it ~ and let me know.
think to oneself ['– tə -'-]	bei sich denken	'He's not telling the truth,' I **thought to myself**.
thinking ['θɪŋkɪŋ]	Denken	do some hard ~ (on a problem) / creative (or: imaginative) ~
thought [θɔːt]	Denken, Nachdenken;	give (+ some / little / much) ~ to sth / be deep (or: lost) in ~ / act without much ~ / do sth after serious (or: long) ~
	Gedanke	sb's mind is full of ~s / a ~ enters (or: passes through) one's mind / a ~ strikes (or: occurs to / occupies) sb / the ~ of doing sth / act on second ~s (nach reiflicher Überlegung handeln)
thoughtful ['θɔːtfʊl]	nachdenklich	look (or: seem) ~ / look ~ly at sb / a ~ person (or: book)
consider [kən'sɪdə*]	bedenken, erwägen	~ (+ doing) sth / ~ what to do / ~ the possibility of doing sth / ~ing that ... (wenn man bedenkt, daß ...) / take sth into **consideration** [kənˌsɪdə'reɪʃn] / There are many **considerations** to be taken into account when buying a house.
examine [ɪg'zæmɪn]	prüfen, untersuchen	~ sth carefully (or: closely)
reflect [rɪ'flekt]	nachdenken	~ on sth / after some **reflection** [rɪ'flekʃn]
reason ['riːzn]	Vernunft, Verstand;	listen to ~ / do sth against all ~ / There is ~ in what he says. / It stands to ~ that ... (Es leuchtet ein, daß ...) / the **Age of Reason** [ˌeɪdʒ‿əv '–] (= the 18th century)
	(Vernunft-)Grund	The ~ (+ why) sb does sth is that ... / have good ~ to believe that ... / have ~ for doing sth
reasonable ['riːznəbl]	vernünftig	a ~ man / a ~ excuse / an **unreasonable** [ʌn-] fellow / Please be more ~.

idea [aɪ'dɪə*]	Idee, Vorstellung, Ahnung	get (or: form) an ~ of sth / have an (or: no / not the slightest) ~ about (= of) sth / favour (or: reject) an ~ / toy (spielen) with an ~ / sth is a good (or: not a bad / a bad) ~ / express one's ~s / an ~ enters one's mind / He's got no ~. (Er hat keine Ahnung.)
concept ['kɒnsept]	Begriff	have a (or: no) ~ of sth / Right and wrong are moral ~s. / form a **conception** [kən'sepʃn] of sth

Understanding, knowledge – Verstehen, Wissen 38

ignorant ['ɪgnərənt]	unwissend	an ~ child / be very (or: quite) ~ of sth / **Ignorance** ['ɪgnərəns] of the law is no excuse.
doubt [daʊt]	(be)zweifeln, mißtrauen,	~ sth / ~ whether (= if) ... / I don't ~ that he'll come.
	Zweifel, Mißtrauen	have one's ~s (+ about sb / about sth) / be in ~ (+ about) what to do / sth is beyond (= past) all ~
doubtful ['daʊtfʊl]	im Zweifel, zweifelhaft	be (or: feel) ~ whether ... (or: about sth) / be ~ of (= about) sb / It's ~ if ...
suppose [sə'pəʊz] (*BE*) = **guess** [ges] (*AE*)	vermuten, annehmen	~ sb will come / ~ sb is late
guess [ges]	erraten	~ how old sb is / ~ the answer
understand (understood, understood) [ˌʌndə'stænd, ˌʌndə'stʊd, –]	verstehen;	Do you ~? / ~ sb (or: each other / one another) / ~ sth (+ very well) / not fully ~ / **misunderstand** [ˌmɪsʌndə'stænd] sb (or: sth) / sth is not **understandable** [ˌʌndə'stændəbl] / give sb to ~ that ...
	(von etwas) hören;	I ~ that you are now married.
	schließen	What am I to ~ from this?
understanding [ˌʌndə'stændɪŋ]	Verständnis, Wissen;	have much ~ of sth / have a good ~ of sth / a man of great ~ / according to my ~
	Übereinkunft;	have (or: come to / reach) an ~ (+ with sb)
	Voraussetzung, Bedingung	on this ~ / on the ~ that ...

see (saw, seen) [siː, sɔː, siːn]	sehen, verstehen	Do you ~ what I mean? / ~ the joke / ~ great danger in ... / ~ no harm in ...
realize ['rɪəlaɪz]	erfassen, voll und ganz verstehen;	~ what has happened / ~ that ...
	bemerken, mitbekommen	~ an error (or: a mistake) / ~ how late it is
comprehend [ˌkɒmprɪ'hend]	verstehen, folgen können	~ sth / I'm afraid I can't ~ you. / sth is above (= beyond / past) one's **comprehension** [ˌ-'henʃn] / sth is **comprehensible** [ˌ-'hensəbl] (or: **incomprehensible** [ɪnˌ-'hensəbl])
grasp [grɑːsp]	erfassen, Fassungsvermögen, Verständnis	~ an argument / ~ the main points have a good (or: thorough) ~ of a problem / sth is within (or: beyond) one's ~
curious ['kjʊərɪəs]	neugierig;	be ~ about sth / a ~ question / ~ neighbours
	wißbegierig	be ~ to know what ... / be ~ about sth
curiosity [ˌkjʊərɪ'ɒsətɪ]	Neugier;	be dying of (or: burning with) ~ to know sth
	Wißbegier	~ about / ~ to learn about sth
find (found, found) [faɪnd, faʊnd, –]	finden	~ an answer (+ to a question) / ~ (+ **out**) when (or: where / why / how) ... / **find out** the meaning of / **find** sb **out** (ertappen)
discover [dɪ'skʌvə*]	entdecken, enthüllen	~ a secret / ~ the truth / ~ who sb is / ~ how sth has happened / sth is a great (or: an important) **discovery** [-rɪ] / make a **discovery**
explore [ɪk'splɔː]	erforschen	~ a country (or: question / problem / possibility) / be a great **explorer** [-rə*]
research [rɪ'sɜːtʃ]	forschen, Forschung	~ into a problem carry out (+ a) ~ into the causes of ...
experience [ɪk'spɪərɪəns]	Erfahrung	gain ~ / a teacher with 10 years' ~ / He has no (or: little / a lot of / much) ~ with cars (or: in repairing cars). / learn (+ sth) from (= by) ~ / know (+ sth) from (= by) ~ / an **experienced** [-t] (or: **inexperienced**) teacher

know (knew, known) [nəʊ, njuː, nəʊn]	wissen	~ the way / ~ an answer (or: all the answers) / ~ whether (or: who / what / which / how / how to do sth) / ~ nothing (or: a little / not much / a lot / everything / all) about sb (or: sth) / ~ one's mind (wissen, was man will)
	(etwas) können;	~ French / ~ how to do sth
	kennen,	~ sb (+ by sight / by name) / ~ one another
	erkennen, unterscheiden können;	He ~s a good horse when he sees one. / ~ sb from sb / ~ sth from sth
	gehört haben, kennen	~ about (or: of) sb (or: sth) / I don't ~ Mr Harris but I ~ about (= of) him.
learn (learned, learned / *AE*: learnt, learned) [lɜːn, -d, -t]	hören, Kenntnis erlangen	~ the news (or: truth) / ~ of sb's arrival
known [nəʊn]	bekannt	be ~ as ... / be **unknown** [ˌʌn'-] to sb
knowledge ['nɒlɪdʒ]	Wissen, Kenntnis	have a good ~ of sth / have no (or: little / some / much) ~ of (= about) sb (or: sth) / acquire ~ of sth / increase (or: brush up / polish up) one's ~ / lack ~ of sth / say sth to the best of one's ~
insight ['ɪnsaɪt]	Einsicht, Einblick, Verständnis	have ~ / have great ~ into sth / gain ~ into sth / sth gives a valuable ~ into sth
perceive [pə'siːv]	wahrnehmen	~ a difference between ...
aware [ə'weə*]	gewahr	be (or: become) ~ of sth (or: sb) / be fully ~ of sth / be ~ that ... / Before I was ~ ... (Ehe ich mich's versah, ...)
familiar [fe'mɪljə*]	vertraut	be ~ with sth / sth is ~ to one / a ~ face
acquainted [ə'kweɪntɪd]	vertraut, bekannt	be (+ well) ~ with sth / have an (or: some) **acquaintance** [ə'kweɪntəns] with sth
certainly ['sɜːtnlɪ]	sicher, freilich (als ausdrückliche Bestätigung, *BE*, vgl. **sure**)	'May I borrow your umbrella?' – 'C~!'

sure [ʃʊə*]	(subjektiv) sicher;	I'm ~ (= **Surely** ['-lɪ]) he didn't steal it, he's not that kind of person. / be (or: feel) (+ quite) ~ of sb (or: sth) / sb is ~ to do sth / It's ~ to rain. / I'm not ~ (= certain) where he is.
	sicher, natürlich (als ausdrückliche Bestätigung) (*inform., AE*, vgl. **certainly**, *BE*)	'May I borrow your umbrella?' – 'S~!' / 'Can you swim?' – 'I ~ can.'
To be sure [ˌ– – '–]	Sicher! Freilich!	T~ ~ ~, some people won't like this.
be conscious [biː 'kɒnʃəs]	sich bewußt sein	~ ~ of sth / ~ ~ that ...
anticipate [æn'tɪsɪpeɪt]	erwarten, rechnen mit, voraussehen; zuvorkommen	~ trouble / ~ sb's needs
make (made, made) **sure** [meɪk, meɪd, –; – 'ʃʊə*]	sich vergewissern	~ ~ of the time
certain ['sɜːtn]	(objektiv) sicher	be dead (völlig) ~ / I'm ~ he didn't lose it: I lost it myself. / He ~ly didn't lose it. / I'm not ~ (= sure) how to do it. / It's almost ~ that ...
make (made, made) **certain** [– '–] = **make sure** [– '–]	sich vergewissern	~ ~ when the train goes
no doubt [nəʊ 'daʊt]	ohne Zweifel	N~ ~ you'd like a drink.
doubtless ['daʊtlɪs]	sicher, zweifellos	'D~ you have heard of the terrible accident.'
undoubtedly [ʌn'daʊtɪdlɪ]	ohne jeden Zweifel	This is ~ true.
without doubt [wɪðˌaʊt 'daʊt]	zweifellos	

39 Traits, feelings, forms of behaviour – Eigenarten, Gefühle, Verhaltensweisen

character ['kærəktə*]	Charakter	have a good (or: bad / strong / weak) ~ / be a man of ~
trait [treɪ]	Eigenart	have specific ~s / Two ~s in his character are energy and intelligence.
temper ['tempə*]	Laune, Temperament	be in a good (or: bad) ~ be of even (or: uneven / fierce / aggressive) ~ / be **good** (or: **bad / ill**) **tempered** [ˌ– '-d] / a man with an aggressive **temperament** [-'-rəmənt]

disposition [ˌdɪspəˈzɪʃn]	Veranlagung, Neigung	a man with a cheerful ~ / have a ~ for languages
inclination [ˌɪnklɪˈneɪʃn]	Neigung, Vorliebe	have an ~ to do sth
feeling [ˈfiːlɪŋ]	Gefühl	have a strange ~ (+ about sth) / be overcome by a ~ of ... / show no (or: little / much) ~ towards sb / hurt sb's ~s
feel (felt, felt) [fiːl, felt, –]	fühlen	~ with (or: for) sb / ~ like doing sth
emotion [ɪˈməʊʃn]	Rührung, Gemütsbewegung, Gefühl	be seized (= overcome) by an ~ of ...
mood [muːd]	Stimmung, Laune	be in a peaceful (or: cheerful) ~ / be in the ~ to do sth / be in the ~ for (+ doing) sth
behaviour [bɪˈheɪvjə] (*BE*) = **behavior** [-r] (*AE*)	Verhalten, Benehmen	have (or: show) good (or: bad) ~ towards sb / criticize sb for his ~
behave [bɪˈheɪv]	sich verhalten, sich benehmen	~ well (or: badly) / a(n) **well** (or: **ill** / **badly**) **behaved** [ˌ– -ˈ-d] boy
behave oneself [-ˈ- -ˌ-]	sich anständig benehmen	**Behave yourself!**
fault [fɔːlt]	Mangel, (kleinere Schwäche)	His only ~ was that ... / **find** ~ with sb (an jmd. herummäkeln)
habit [ˈhæbɪt]	(An-)Gewohnheit	make a ~ of sth / do sth out of ~ / get into the ~ of sth
habitual [hæˈbɪtjʊəl]	gewohnheitsmäßig, Gewohnheits-	a ~ drunkard (or: liar)
manner [ˈmænə*]	Betragen, Art	I don't like his ~. / have a strange (or: an impolite) ~ / be **ill** (or: **well** / **rough**) **mannered** [ˌ– ˈ-d]
manners [ˈmænəz]	Manieren	have good (or: bad) ~ / have no ~ at all / It is bad ~ to stare at people. / forget one's ~
conduct [ˈkɒndʌkt]	Führung, Betragen	sb's ~ is good (or: bad) / show exemplary ~
tact [tækt]	Takt	have ~ / behave with ~ / **tactful** [ˈ-fʊl] / **tactless** [ˈ-lɪs]

Calm – ruhig

calm [kɑːm]	ruhig, (sich) beruhigen	a ~ man / Keep ~! ~ (+ down) / ~ sb (or: oneself)
quiet [ˈkwaɪət]	ruhig, ausgeglichen, beruhigen (*AE*)	a ~ man / have a ~ way ~ one's conscience
quieten [ˈkwaɪətən]	beruhigen (*BE*)	~ one's conscience

gentle [dʒentl]	angenehm, leise	have a ~ manner / be ~ in one's manner
ease [i:z]	Ruhe, Behaglichkeit	lead a life of ~
at ease [ət‿ˈi:z]	ungezwungen	feel ~ ~ / feel **ill at ease** [ˌɪl‿ət‿ˈi:z] (sich unbehaglich fühlen) / be ~ (+ one's) ~ / be **at ease with** sb (zwanglos mit jemandem verkehren)
patient [ˈpeɪʃnt]	geduldig	a ~ man / be ~ (+ with sb) / grow (or: become) **impatient** [ɪm-] (+ with sb) / be **impatient** to do sth
patience [ˈpeɪʃns]	Geduld	have (or: show) (+ no) ~ (+ with sb) / lose one's ~ (+ with sb) / have the ~ to do sth
serious [ˈsɪərɪəs]	ernst	try to be less ~
relaxed [rɪˈlækst]	entspannt	look very ~
comfortable [ˈkʌmfətəbl]	behaglich, bequem	be (or: feel) ~ / lead a ~ life
cool [ku:l]	kühl, gelassen	keep (or: remain) ~ / be ~ in the face of danger / have a ~ head / **play it cool** [ˌpleɪ ɪt ˈ–] (*inform.*) (es langsam gehen lassen)
nerves of iron [ˈnɜ:vz‿əv ˈaɪən]	eiserne Nerven	have ~ ~ ~

Happy – glücklich

content [kənˈtent]	zufrieden	be ~ with sth / be ~ to do sth / be (or: feel / look) **contented** [-ɪd]
please [pli:z]	gefallen	sth (or: sb) ~s one / You can't ~ everybody.
pleased [pli:zd]	erfreut, zufrieden	be greatly ~ with (= about) sth (or: sb)
pleasure [ˈpleʒə*]	Vergnügen	take (+ great) ~ in sth (or: in doing sth) / It gives one much ~ to do sth. / sth is one's chief ~ / make it a ~ to do sth
fun [fʌn]	Spaß	have (+ a lot of) ~ / say sth only in ~
funny [ˈfʌnɪ]	lustig	a ~ story
look forward to [ˌlʊk ˈfɔ:wəd tə]	sich freuen auf	We're ~ing ~ ~ the holidays.
satisfy [ˈsætɪsfaɪ]	befriedigen, zufriedenstellen	nothing ~ies one
delight [dɪˈlaɪt]	erfreuen,	sth ~s one
	Spaß haben,	~ in doing sth / be **delighted** [-ɪd] at (= with) sth / be **delighted** to do sth / be **delighted** that ...

	Spaß, Vergnügen	take ~ in doing sth / sth gives great ~ to sb / to one's great ~ / sth is one's chief ~
enjoy [ɪn'dʒɔɪ]	genießen, sich erfreuen an	~ sth / ~ good health
enjoy oneself [-'- -ˌ-]	Spaß haben	
glad [glæd]	froh	be ~ that ... / be (or: look / feel) (+ very) ~ about sth / be ~ to do sth
happy ['hæpɪ]	glücklich, zufrieden	be ~ about sth / make sb ~ / a story with a ~ ending / one's **happiness** [-nɪs] is so great that ...
joy [dʒɔɪ]	(große) Freude	wish sb ~ / in ~ and sorrow / be full of ~ / dance (or: jump) for ~ / to one's great ~ / a **joyous** ['-əs] song / **joyful** ['-fʊl] news
amuse [ə'mju:z]	(sich) belustigen	sth ~s one / ~ oneself (+ by) doing sth / keep sb **amused** [-d] with sth / be **amused** at (or: by) sth / an **amusing** story
cheerful ['tʃɪəfʊl]	heiter, munter, froh (von Personen); freundlich (von Dingen)	be (or: look) ~ / a ~ person / A sunny day makes us ~. a ~ day (or: room)
merry ['merɪ]	froh, fröhlich	have a ~ time / wish sb a M~ Christmas
cordial ['kɔ:djəl]	herzlich	a ~ welcome (or: smile / greeting)
sympathy ['sɪmpəθɪ]	Mitgefühl, Verständnis	show ~ towards (or: for) / a **sympathetic** [ˌsɪmpə'θetɪk] person
charm [tʃɑ:m]	bezaubern	~ sb / a **charming** ['-ɪŋ] young lady

Like – gern haben

like [laɪk]	mögen, gefallen, gern haben	How do you ~ it? / ~ sb (or: sth) / ~ doing sth / ~ to do sth / ~ well (or: better / best) / have a **liking** ['-ɪŋ] for sth / take a **liking** to sth (or: sb)
be fond of [bi: 'fɒnd‿əv]	gern haben	~ ~ ~ sb (or: sth) / ~ ~ ~ doing sth
kind [kaɪnd]	freundlich	be ~ to sb / it is very ~ of sb to do sth / do sth out of **kindness** ['-nɪs] / be **kind-hearted** [ˌ-'hɑ:tɪd]
nice [naɪs]	nett	a ~ man / be ~ to sb / it is very ~ of sb to do sth

polite [pə'laɪt]	höflich	a ~ boy / it is ~ to do sth / be ~ to sb / behave ~ly / be **impolite** [ˌɪmpə'laɪt] / show **politeness** [-'-nɪs] (+ towards sb)
friendly ['frendlɪ]	freundlich	be ~ with (= to) sb / be on ~ terms with sb / a ~ man / **in a friendly way**
friend [frend]	Freund	He's a ~ of mine. / my ~ Peter / make ~s (+ with sb) / make ~s again (sich wieder vertragen) / be great (or: good / close) ~s / be a good (or: dear / close / true) ~
boy-friend ['bɔɪfrend]	Freund (eines Mädchens)	Peter is Jane's ~.
girl-friend ['gɜːlfrend]	Freundin (eines Mädchens, eines Jungen)	Jane is Peter's ~.
friendship ['frendʃɪp]	Freundschaft	one's ~ with (or: for) sb / the bond of ~
familiar [fə'mɪljə*]	vertraut; (plump) vertraulich	a ~ friend / be on ~ terms with sb / be too ~ with sb / speak to sb in a very ~ way / **familiarity** [fəˌmɪlɪ'ærətɪ]
love [lʌv]	lieben,	~ sb (+ dearly / tenderly / sincerely / deeply / passionately)
	Liebe	fall (or: be) in ~ (+ with sb) / a mother's ~ for her children / ~ of adventure (or: one's country)

Help – helfen

help [help]	helfen,	~ sb (+ to do sth)
	Hilfe	need (or: get) ~ / be a great ~ (+ to sb) / be of great (or: much / little / no) ~ (+ to sb) / be **helpful** ['-fʊl] (hilfsbereit) / be **unhelpful** [ʌn'-fʊl] / be **helpless** ['-lɪs]
favour ['feɪvə*] (*BE*) = **favour** [-r] (*AE*)	Gefallen;	do sb a ~ / ask a ~ of sb
	Gunst, Wohlwollen	look with ~ on ... / win sb's ~
in favour of [– '--‿–]	zugunsten, für	
favourable ['feɪvərəbl] (*BE*) = **favorable** [–] (*AE*)	günstig	
support [sə'pɔːt]	unterstützen,	~ sb / ~ a party (or: plan)
	Unterstützung	have sb's ~ / give sb one's ~
side [saɪd]	zur Seite stehen	~ with sb

stick (stuck, stuck) **together** [stɪk, stʌk, –; – -'--] (*inform.*)	zusammenhalten	friends must ~ ~
back [bæk]	stützen, den Rücken stärken	~ sb (+ up) / have sb's **backing**
assist [ə'sɪst]	helfen, beistehen	~ sb to do sth / come to sb's **assistance** [-əns]

Trust – vertrauen

trust [trʌst]	vertrauen,	~ (+ in) sb / ~ (+ in) everything sb says
	Vertrauen;	place one's ~ in sb / have (+ no) ~ in sb
	anvertrauen,	~ sb with sth / ~ sth to sb
	sich verlassen auf	~ sb to do sth / ~ to luck (or: chance / one's memory)
trustworthy ['trʌstˌwɜːðɪ]	vertrauenswürdig	find sb to be ~
rely [rɪ'laɪ]	sich verlassen	~ on (= upon) sb (+ for help) / be **reliable** [-əbl] (or: **unreliable** [ˌʌnrɪ'laɪəbl]) / place much (or: little / no) **reliance** [-əns] on (= upon) sb
count upon [kaʊnt‿ə'pɒn]	zählen auf	~ ~ sb's help / ~ ~ sb (+ to help)
reckon on ['rekn ɒn]	rechnen auf	~ ~ sb (or: sth)
confide [kən'faɪd]	vertrauen;	~ in sb
	anvertrauen	~ a secret (or: one's troubles) to sb
confidence ['kɒnfɪdəns]	Vertrauen	have (or: lose) ~ in sb / put complete (or: much / little / no) ~ in sb / take sb into one's ~ / tell sth in strict ~
be confident of [biː 'kɒnfɪdənt‿əv]	vertrauen auf	~ ~ ~ success (or: victory / oneself)
confidential [ˌkɒnfɪ'denʃl]	vertraulich	speaking ~ly / ~ information
hope [həʊp]	hoffen,	~ to do sth / ~ that ... / ~ for the best / ~ for a change
	Hoffnung	sb's ~s are disappointed / be disappointed in one's ~s / raise sb's ~ / lose all ~ of / have some (or: no) ~ of
hopeful ['həʊpfʊl]	hoffnungsvoll	be (or: feel) ~ of (= about) sth
hopefully ['həʊpfʊlɪ]	hoffentlich	H~, he will come.
hopeless ['həʊplɪs]	hoffnungslos	a ~ case

true [truː]	wahr, echt, treu	a ~ friend / ~ friendship / be ~ to one's words (or: promise)
loyal ['lɔɪəl]	treu, ergeben	be ~ to sb (or: one's country)
adhere to [əd'hɪə tə]	stehen zu, anhängen	~ ~ one's promises (or: plans / opinion) / ~ ~ a party (Gruppe)
faith [feɪθ]	Glaube, Vertrauen	have ~ in sb (or: sth) / put (or: lose) one's ~ in sb (or: sth) / have much (or: little / no) ~ in sb / do sth in good ~
faithful ['feɪθfʊl]	treu	a ~ friend / remain ~ to sb
unfaithful [ˌʌn'feɪθfʊl]	treulos	an ~ husband

Respect – achten

respect [rɪ'spekt]	achten,	~ sb / ~ sb's wishes
	Achtung	have (or: show) great (or: no) ~ for sb / show ~ to sb / do sth out of ~ for sb
respectful [rɪ'spektfʊl]	respektvoll	be ~ (or: **disrespectful** [ˌdɪs-]) to (or: towards) sb / treat sb ~ly
respectable [rɪ'spektəbl]	anständig, ehrbar	a (+ highly) ~ person / a ~ citizen
look up to [lʊk‿ʌp tə]	aufsehen zu	The little girl ~ed ~ ~ her English teacher.
admire [əd'maɪə*]	bewundern	~ sb (+ for sth) / be a great **admirer** [-rə*] of sb (or: sth) / be full of (= filled with) **admiration** [ˌædmə'reɪʃn] for sb / sb's courage is **admirable** ['ædmərəbl]
praise [preɪz]	loben,	~ sb (+ for his work) / ~ sb's work
	Lob	deserve ~ / receive much ~ / be above (= beyond) ~
honour ['ɒnə*] (*BE*)	ehren,	~ sb
= **honor** ['ɒnər] (*AE*)	Ehre	do sth in ~ of / be a man of ~ / give one's **word of honour** [ˌwɜːd‿əv '–] / be an **honourable** [-rəbl] man
esteem [ɪ'stiːm]	hochschätzen,	~ sb / ~ sb's character (or: opinions / principles)
	Hochachtung	hold sb in great (or: high) ~
awe [ɔː]	Ehrfurcht	fill sb with ~ / have a feeling of ~
obey [ə'beɪ]	gehorchen	~ instructions (or: one's parents)

Just – gerecht

just [dʒʌst]	gerecht	be ~ to sb / a ~ decision
justice ['dʒʌstɪs]	Gerechtigkeit	treat sb with ~ / receive ~ / do sb an **injustice** [ɪn'-]

fair [feə*]	fair, gerecht	That isn't ~! / be ~ to sb / ~ play / play (or: win) **unfairly** [ˌʌn'feəlɪ]

Sincere – aufrichtig

sincere [sɪn'sɪə*]	aufrichtig	a ~ friend / be ~ about sth
honest ['ɒnɪst]	ehrlich, aufrichtig, offen	be an ~ man / be ~ about sth / be ~ with sb
frank [fræŋk]	offen, ehrlich	give a ~ answer / be quite ~ with sb / a ~ look (or: face / smile)
straight [streɪt]	gerade, ehrlich	Tell me ~! (*inform.*) / look sb ~ in the eyes / tell sb ~ out that … (*inform.*) / a **straight-forward** [ˌ-'fɔːwəd] explanation

Thankful – dankbar

thank [θæŋk]	danken	~ sb for sth / T~ you very much. / 'No, ~ you.' / 'Have a drink!' – 'T~ you. Beer, please.' / **Thanks** [-s] for the nice present.
thankful ['θæŋkfʊl]	dankbar	be ~ for sth / be ~ to sb
grateful ['greɪtfʊl]	dankbar	be ~ to sb (or: for sth) / be ~ to sb for doing sth / accept sb's help ~ly / be **ungrateful** [ʌn'-]
gratitude ['grætɪtjuːd]	Dankbarkeit	be full of ~ / show one's ~ towards sb / express one's ~ (+ to sb / for sth)

Surprise – überraschen

surprise [sə'praɪz]	überraschen, erstaunen	sth ~s one / ~ sb with a visit
	Überraschung	to my ~ / What a ~! / look up **in surprise**
amaze [ə'meɪz]	erstaunen, verblüffen	sth ~s one / be **amazed** [-d] that … / sth is **amazing** [-ɪŋ] / to my **amazement** [ə'meɪzmənt]
astonished [ə'stɒnɪʃt]	überrascht	an ~ look / be ~ to her … / to my **astonishment** [ə'stɒnɪʃmənt]

Modest – bescheiden

modest ['mɒdɪst]	bescheiden	be (or: seem / look) ~ / be ~ about one's achievements / behave ~ly
moderate (['mɒdərət], *adj.;* ['mɒdəreɪt], *v.*)	mäßig,	be ~ in one's judgements
	mäßigen, zügeln	~ one's wishes (or: demands / rage)

Care – Sorgfalt

care [keə*]	Vorsicht, Sorgfalt, Mühe,	do sth with (+ great) ~ / give much ~ to sth
	sorgen, sich kümmern,	~ for sb
	sich interessieren, sich kümmern	~ for one's own interests / I don't ~ (+ what you do). / Who ~s?
take (took, taken) **care** [teɪk, tʊk, 'teɪkən; – 'keə*]	achtgeben	~ ~ not to do sth / ~ no (or: little / much) ~ of sb (or: sth) / ~ ~ of oneself
careful ['keəfʊl]	achtsam, vorsichtig	a ~ man / be ~ about sth / be ~ (+ not) to do sth / do sth ~ly
responsible [rɪ'spɒnsəbl]	verantwortlich, verantwortungsbewußt	~ to sb / be ~ for sb (or: sth) / make sb ~ for sth / a ~ person
responsibility [rɪˌspɒnsə'bɪlətɪ]	Verantwortung	do it on one's own ~ / assume full ~ for it / have a lot of ~ties
careless ['keəlɪs]	nachlässig	be ~ (+ with one's money) / be ~ of one's clothes / do sth very ~ly
neglect [nɪ'glekt]	vernachlässigen, versäumen	~ to do (or: doing) sth ~ one's health / be **neglectful** [-fʊl] of one's appearance
negligence ['neglɪdʒəns]	Fahrlässigkeit, Nachlässigkeit	an accident due to ~
interest ['ɪntrɪst]	interessieren,	sth ~s one (+ very much) / ~ sb in sth / be **interested** [-ɪd] in sb (or: sth) / sth is very **interesting** [-ɪŋ] / an **interesting** story
	Interesse	take an (or: no / little / some / great) ~ in sth / do sth with great ~ / have (or: show) an ~ in / find no ~ in
anxious ['æŋkʃəs]	bedacht, bemüht;	be ~ for sb to do sth / be ~ to do sth / I'm ~ to see him. (*inform.*) (Ich möchte ihn unbedingt sehen.)
	ängstlich, besorgt	be (or: feel / look) ~ about sb (or: sth) / ~ feelings (or: looks / thoughts) / sth causes great **anxiety** [æŋ'zaɪətɪ]
thoughtful ['θɔːtfʊl]	rücksichtsvoll	it is ~ of sb to do sth / a ~ man
considerate [kən'sɪdərət]	rücksichtsvoll	a ~ person / be ~ towards old people / have no **consideration** [kənˌsɪdə'reɪʃn] for others / act without **consideration** for others
cautious ['kɔːʃəs]	vorsichtig, behutsam	be ~ (+ of doing sth) / a ~ man
caution ['kɔːʃn]	Vorsicht,	do sth with great ~
	warnen	~ sb to do sth

warn [wɔːn]	warnen	~ sb not to do sth / ~ sb against doing sth / ~ sb of sth / The ice cracked without **warning** ['-ɪŋ].

Courage – Mut

courage ['kʌrɪdʒ]	Mut	take (or: lose / lack) ~ / have the ~ to do sth / be a **courageous** [kə'reɪdʒəs] man / it is **courageous** of sb to do sth
brave [breɪv]	tapfer	a ~ man (or: deed) / be rewarded for one's **bravery** ['breɪvərɪ]
dare [deə*]	wagen;	sb ~ not (= ~n't) do sth / sb does not ~ (+ to) do sth / How ~ you? / I've never ~ed (+ to) do that. / a **daring** ['-rɪŋ] thing to do / a **daring** soldier
	herausfordern	~ sb to do sth
bold [bəʊld]	kühn;	a ~ plan (or: attempt / man / deed)
	dreist	be too ~
risk [rɪsk]	riskieren, wagen,	~ one's life (or: health / money)
	Risiko	do sth at one's own ~ / take (or: run) a lot of ~s / take (or: run) the ~ of doing sth

Not interested – uninteressiert

indifferent [ɪn'dɪfrənt]	gleichgültig	It's quite ~ to me. / be ~ (+ to sb / to sth) / be ~ whether ...
uninterested [ˌʌn'ɪntrɪstɪd]	uninteressiert	be completely ~ in sth
bore [bɔː*]	langweilen;	~ sb / sth ~s one / get **bored** [-d] doing sth / be **bored** stiff (or: to death / to tears) / a **boring** ['-rɪŋ] book
	langweiliger Mensch	be a ~
weary ['wɪərɪ]	überdrüssig;	be ~ of (+ doing) sth
	ermüden	~ sb with questions
tire ['taɪə*]	ermüden	~ the audience
tired ['taɪəd]	überdrüssig	be ~ of sth / be ~ of doing sth
ignore [ɪg'nɔː*]	ignorieren, nicht beachten	~ sb (or: what sb says)
cool [kuːl]	kalt, unfreundlich;	give sb a ~ greeting (or: reception)
	unverschämt (*AE*)	What ~ behaviour!
cool down [kuːl 'daʊn]	abkühlen	sb's friendship for sb ~s ~

cold [kəʊld]	kalt	be ~ towards sb / That leaves me ~. / a ~ look / a **cold-blooded** [ˌkəʊld 'blʌdɪd] (kaltblütig) murder
cold shoulder [kəʊld 'ʃəʊldə*]	kalte Schulter	give sb the ~ ~ / get the ~ ~

Sad – traurig

disappoint [ˌdɪsə'pɔɪnt]	enttäuschen	sth ~s one / ~ sb (or: sb's expectations) / be **disappointed** [-ɪd] in one's hopes / be **disappointed** to hear ... / look (+ very) **disappointed** / sth is a great **disappointment** [-mənt]
discontented [ˌdɪskən'tentɪd]	mißvergnügt, unzufrieden	be (or: seem) ~ with sth / be ~ with sb (or: sth) / have a ~ look
discontent [ˌdɪskən'tent]	Unzufriedenheit	feel (+ no) ~ with sth (or: sb)
complain [kəm'pleɪn]	(sich) beklagen	~ of (or: about) sb (or: sth) / be always ~ing / have cause for **complaint** [-t]
sad [sæd]	traurig	sth makes one ~ / be ~ that / be (or: feel / seem) ~ (+ about sth) / a ~ day / ~ news / be full of **sadness** ['-nɪs] / sth **saddens** ['sædnz] one
dissatisfied [ˌdɪs'sætɪsfaɪd]	unzufrieden	be ~ with sb (or: sth) / look ~
sorrow ['sɒrəʊ]	Leid, Trauer;	feel (+ deep) ~ at sth / have a feeling of ~ at sb's death / think **sorrowfully** [-fʊlɪ] of one's dead friend
	Bedauern	do sth without much ~ / to my great ~ / look at sb with ~
grief [gri:f]	Gram, Kummer	be mad with ~ / be driven almost insane by ~
grieve [gri:v]	sich grämen;	~ for the dead / ~ over sb's death / ~ at bad news
	Kummer bereiten	~ one's parents
cheerless ['tʃɪəlɪs]	freudlos, trostlos	be (or: look) ~ / a ~ person / a ~ day / a ~ house
miserable ['mɪzərəbl]	elend	feel (or: look) ~ / lead a ~ life / live in ~ conditions
misery ['mɪzərɪ]	Elend	live in ~
desperate ['despərət]	verzweifelt (und deshalb zu allem fähig);	a ~ criminal / a last, ~ effort / a ~ deed
	hoffnungslos	be in a ~ situation

despair [dɪ'speə*]	verzweifeln, Verzweiflung	~ of doing sth / Don't ~. sth fills one with ~
pity ['pɪtɪ]	Mitleid, bemitleiden	feel (or: have a feeling of) ~ for sb ~ sb
it's a pity [– – '–]	wie schade, leider	I~ ~ ~ it's too cold to go swimming today.
what a pity ['– – '–]	wie schade	W~ ~ ~! / W~ ~ ~ he couldn't come.
pitiless ['pɪtɪlɪs]	mitleidlos	a ~ tyrant
sorry ['sɒrɪ]	bekümmert, betrübt	be (or: feel) ~ about (or: for) sth / be ~ for sb (or: oneself) (jemanden oder sich selbst bedauern) / be ~ that ... / be ~ to hear of sth / **I'm sorry** (Leider) to say that ...

Uneasy – unruhig

uneasy [ʌn'i:zɪ]	unruhig	be (or: feel) ~ about sth / grow ~ at sth / have an ~ feeling (or: conscience)
nervous ['nɜ:vəs]	nervös	be (or: get) ~ about sth / sth makes one ~
arouse [ə'raʊz]	anregen, erregen	sth ~s one's interest (or: sympathy)
excite [ɪk'saɪt]	aufregen,	sth ~s one / ~ oneself / get (or: be) easily **excited** [-ɪd] at (= about) sth / an **exciting** [-ɪŋ] story
	erregen,	~ sb's pity / ~ admiration (or: envy / jealousy) (+ in sb)
	anstacheln	~ sb to do sth
excitement [ɪk'saɪtmənt]	Aufregung	in one's ~ / sth causes much ~ / avoid all ~ / all the ~s of a long journey
concerned [kən'sɜ:nd]	beunruhigt, besorgt	a ~ mother / **be concerned** about
tremble ['trembl]	zittern, bangen um	~ with fear (or: anger / excitement) / I ~ to think what has happened to him.
irritate ['ɪrɪteɪt]	reizen, verärgern, erbittern	sth ~s one / be **irritated** [-ɪd] at (= with / by) sb (or: sth) / be very **irritable** ['ɪrɪtəbl] (gereizt)
angry ['æŋgrɪ]	böse, zornig	be (or: get / grow) (+ very / extremely / quite) ~ (+ with sb / at sth) / an ~ man (or: look) / look at sb very ~ily / speak ~ily
mad [mæd] *(inform., AE)*	wild, verrückt, wütend	get ~ at sb for doing sth / be hopping (furchtbar) ~ / drive sb ~

rage [reɪdʒ]	Wut	be in a ~ with sb / fly into a ~ / do sth in a (+ fit of) ~
furious ['fjʊərɪəs]	wütend, rasend	be ~ (+ with sb / at sth / at what sb has done) / sth makes one ~ / speak ~ly to sb / be ~ly angry
wild [waɪld]	wild	be ~ with excitement / drive sb ~ / cry ~ly / look at sb ~ly
fierce ['fɪəs]	ungestüm, grimmig	make a ~ speech / look ~ / ~ anger

Superiority – Überlegenheit

proud [praʊd]	stolz	be ~ of sth / be too ~ to do sth
pride [praɪd]	Stolz	take (+ a) great ~ in sth / have a feeling of ~ / have far too much ~
pride oneself on ['– – –]	stolz sein auf, sich bemühen um	He ~s himself ~ having the prettiest garden in the village.
boast [bəʊst]	prahlen	be always ~ing / ~ of what one has done / be a **boastful** ['-fʊl] person / be a great **boaster** ['-ə*]
show off [ˌʃəʊ 'ɒf]	angeben	be fond of ~ing ~
haughty ['hɔːtɪ]	hochmütig, stolz	
assured [ə'ʃʊəd] = **self-assured** [ˌselfə'ʃʊəd]	selbstsicher	have a(n) ~ manner
arrogant ['ærəgənt]	arrogant	have ~ manners
look down [lʊk 'daʊn]	herabsehen	~ ~ on sb
ridicule ['rɪdɪkjuːl]	lächerlich machen, Lächerlichkeit	~ sb (or: sth) hold sb up (preisgeben) to ~ / lay oneself open to ~
mock [mɒk]	verspotten, nachäffen	~ (+ at) sb (or: sth) / hold sb up (preisgeben) to **mockery** ['-ərɪ] / sth is a **mockery** of (Travestie von)
slight [slaɪt]	kränken	~ sb / feel **slighted** ['-ɪd]
hurt (hurt, hurt) [hɜːt, –, –]	verletzen, beleidigen	~ sb's feelings / look (or: feel) ~
insult [ɪn'sʌlt]	beleidigen,	~ sb / an **insulting** [-ɪŋ] remark / **insulting** language
['ɪnsʌlt]	Beleidigung	swallow an ~
conceit [kən'siːt]	Einbildung	be full of ~ / be (or: become) **conceited** [-ɪd]
discriminate against sb [dɪ'skrɪmɪneɪt ə'genst ˌsʌmbədɪ]	jmd. benachteiligen	

embarrass [ɪm'bærəs]	in Verlegenheit bringen	
be embarrassed [bi: ɪm'bærəst]	verlegen sein	

Fear – Furcht

fear [fɪə*]	Furcht, Angst, Sorge, Befürchtung,	do sth out of ~ / ~ of death (or: one's life) / a sudden ~ comes over one / be overcome by (= with) ~ / have one's ~s
	(be)fürchten	~ death / ~ for one's life (or: safety) / ~ the worst / ~ that sth may (or: might / will / would / could) happen / be **fearful** ['-fʊl] of doing sth / be **fearless** ['-lɪs] of the consequences / a **fearless** man
afraid [ə'freɪd]	ängstlich, besorgt	be ~ of sb (or: sth) / be ~ that sth may (or: might / will / would / could) happen / be ~ to do sth / be ~ of doing sth
I'm afraid [– -'-]	Leider ...	~ ~ I can't help you.
worry ['wɒrɪ]	(sich) ängstigen, sich Sorgen machen,	~ oneself / Don't ~. / There's nothing (or: little / not much) to ~ about. / be (or: look / feel / seem) **worried** [-d] (+ over) sb (or: sth)
	Sorge	have a lot of ~ies
coward ['kaʊəd]	Feigling	sb is a ~ / a **cowardly** [-lɪ] man (or: lie) / **cowardly** behaviour
shrink (shrank, shrunk) [ʃrɪŋk, ʃræŋk, ʃrʌŋk]	zurückschrecken	~ from (+ doing) sth / ~ from responsibility (or: danger / a task)
dread [dred]	große Furcht, Grauen,	be (or: live) in ~ of sb (or: sth) / feel ~ / overcome one's ~
	sich grauen vor	~ pain (or: an examination / a visit to the dentist) / ~ that sth terrible will happen / ~ having to do sth / a **dreadful** ['-fʊl] story
fright [fraɪt]	Schrecken	get a ~ / die of ~
frighten ['fraɪtn]	erschrecken	sth ~s one / ~ sb to death / be (+ much) **frightened** [-d] by sth
scare ['skeə*]	in Schrecken versetzen	The noise ~d the baby.
scared ['skeəd]	bange	Are you ~? / What are you ~ of? / be ~ to do sth / be ~ that sth might happen

horror ['hɒrə*]	Grausen, Entsetzen;	scenes of ~ / the ~s of war / shudder (or: shiver) with ~ / turn pale with ~ / to one's ~ / The dead people were a **horrible** [-bl] sight.
	Abscheu, Widerwille	have a ~ of sth
panic ['pænɪk]	Panik,	be seized with (= by) ~
	in Panik geraten	Don't ~!
terror ['terə*]	wahnsinnige Angst,	scream with ~ / run away in ~ / have ~ of sth
	Schrecken	the ~s of war
terrible ['terəbl]	schrecklich	a ~ sight
terrify ['terɪfaɪ]	furchtbare Angst einjagen	sth ~ies one / be **terrified** [-d] by sth

Dislike – Abneigung

dislike [dɪs'laɪk]	nicht leiden mögen,	~ sb (or: sth) / ~ doing sth
	Abneigung	have a ~ of (= for) sth / take a ~ to sb
disapprove [ˌdɪsə'pruːv]	mißbilligen, tadeln	~ very strongly / ~ of sth / ~ of sb doing sth / speak with **disapproval** [-l] of sth / shake one's head **in disapproval**
displease [dɪs'pliːz]	mißfallen, zuwider sein	sth ~s one / be **displeased** [-d] at (= with) sth
object [əb'dʒekt]	einwenden, etwas dagegen haben	Do you ~ to smoking? / Do you ~ to my (= me) smoking?
mind [maɪnd]	etwas ausmachen	Do you ~ if I smoke? / Would you ~ helping me? / I don't ~.
sicken ['sɪkn]	anwidern	sth ~s one / be **sickened** [-d] by sth
disgust [dɪs'gʌst]	anekeln,	sth ~s one / be **disgusted** [-ɪd] at (= with) sb (or: sth)
	Ekel	sth fills one with ~
contempt [kən'tempt]	Verachtung	feel (or: show) ~ for sb / fall into ~ / sth brings one into ~ / look down on sb with ~
contemptible [kən'temptəbl]	verachtenswert	~ people / a ~ trick
be contemptuous of [biː kən'temptjʊəs‿əv]	keine Achtung haben vor	~ ~ ~ sb's opinion
hate [heɪt]	hassen, Haß	be filled with ~
hatred ['heɪtrɪd]	Haß, Haßgefühle	be full of ~ for sb
prejudice ['predʒʊdɪs]	Vorurteil	have (or: express) ~s / have a ~ against (= about) immigrants (or: gypsies / migrant workers) / be **prejudiced** [-t] against / racial ~

scapegoat ['skeɪpgəʊt]	Sündenbock	use others as ~s
bias ['baɪəs]	Voreingenommenheit	have a ~ towards (= against) sth

Lie – Lüge

lie [laɪ]	lügen, Lüge	~ to sb / ~ oneself out of trouble tell a ~
pretend [prɪ'tend]	so tun, als ob, vorgeben	~ to be what one is not ~ ignorance
flatter ['flætə*]	schmeicheln	~ sb (+ on sth / about sth)
slander ['slɑːndə*]	verleumden, Verleumdung	~ sb by saying that ... / ~ sb behind his back spread (or: listen to / repeat) ~ / a **slanderous** [-rəs] report
distort [dɪ'stɔːt]	verdrehen, verzerren	~ facts / ~ what sb has said / ~ the truth
mislead [ˌmɪs'liːd]	irreführen	a **misleading** [-ɪŋ] statement (or: description) / sth ~s one
put (put, put) **on** [pʊt, –, –; – 'ɒn]	heucheln, vorspiegeln	~ sth ~
put-on ['pʊtɒn]	geheuchelt	say sth with ~ sincerity
fool [fuːl]	betrügen, verleiten	~ sb (+ into believing sth)
deceive [dɪ'siːv]	täuschen, vormachen	~ sb (+ by doing sth) / ~ oneself / be **deceived** [-d] **in** sb / be **deceived into** believing sth
cheat [tʃiːt]	beschwindeln, betrügen	~ sb (+ out of his money) / ~ at cards / ~ in an examination
betray [bɪ'treɪ]	verraten	~ sb (or: oneself) / ~ one's country / **betrayal** [-əl] of one's principles
conceal [kən'siːl]	verheimlichen	~ sth from sb / ~ one's feelings / ~ the fact that ...
deceit [dɪ'siːt]	Hinterlist, Falschheit	be full of ~ / a **deceitful** [-fʊl] person
trap [træp]	Falle, eine Falle stellen	set a ~ for sb ~ sb

Aggressive – aggressiv

naughty ['nɔːtɪ]	unartig, ungezogen	a ~ child / it's ~ of sb to do sth
nasty ['nɑːstɪ]	fies, gehässig	a ~ little boy / Don't be ~. / be ~ to sb / it's ~ of sb to do sth
improper [ɪm'prɒpə*]	ungehörig	an ~ remark / ~ behaviour
rude [ruːd]	grob, unverschämt	a ~ person (or: remark / reply) / it's ~ to do sth / be ~ to sb / use ~ language

cheeky ['tʃiːkɪ]	frech	a ~ schoolboy
impudent ['ɪmpjudənt]	unverschämt	be ~ enough to do sth / it's (+ very) ~ of sb to do sth / have the **impudence** ['ɪmpjudəns] to do sth
shocking ['ʃɒkɪŋ]	schockierend	~ behaviour / How ~!
outrageous [aʊt'reɪdʒəs]	empörend	an ~ scandal / ~ behaviour / treat (or: insult) sb ~ly / behave ~ly
infamous ['ɪnfəməs]	niederträchtig; berüchtigt	~ behaviour / an ~ lie be ~ for sth
aggressive [ə'gresɪv]	aggressiv	be very ~ / behave ~ly (+ towards sb)
hostile ['hɒstaɪl] (*BE*), ['hɒstl] (*AE*)	feindlich (gesinnt)	be ~ to sb / a ~ crowd / ~ looks
fury ['fjuərɪ]	Zorn, Wut	fly into a ~ / be **furious** [-əs] with sb (or: at what sb has done)
threaten ['θretn]	(be-)drohen	~ to do sth / ~ sb (+ with sth)
threat [θret]	Drohung	utter a ~ (against sb) / carry out a ~
quarrel ['kwɒrəl]	(sich) streiten,	Children sometimes ~. / be always ~ling / ~ with sb (+ about sth) / ~ about sth
	Streit	have a ~ with sb / a ~ about sth / a ~ between / be very **quarrelsome** [-səm]
row [raʊ]	Krach, Streit	have a ~ with sb / make (or: kick up, *inform.*) a ~
fight (fought, fought) [faɪt, fɔːt, –]	kämpfen, streiten	
cruel ['krʊəl]	grausam	be (+ very) ~ to sb / a ~ man / ~ treatment / treat sb ~ly / be treated with great **cruelty** [-tɪ] / **cruelty** to animals
bully ['bʊlɪ]	einschüchtern, Raufbold (unter Schuljungen)	~ sb (+ into doing sth) be a ~
punish ['pʌnɪʃ]	bestrafen	~ sb who has done sth / ~ sb for doing sth / ~ sb severely / inflict (verhängen) (or: receive) (+ a) severe **punishment** [-mənt]
give (gave, given) **sb a lesson** [gɪv, geɪv, 'gɪvn; 'gɪv ... ə 'lesn]	jemandem eine Lektion erteilen	He gave the bully ~ ~.
spank [spæŋk]	den Hintern versohlen	get a **spanking**
beat (beat, beaten) [biːt, biːt, 'biːtn]	verprügeln (bes. mit einem Stock)	~ sb (+ up)

cane [keɪn]	Rohrstock, (mit einem Rohrstock, bes. in der Schule) züchtigen	get (or: give sb) the ~ ~ sb (+ for doing sth)
whip [wɪp]	peitschen, züchtigen	~ sb
slap [slæp]	(mit der flachen Hand) schlagen, Schlag, Ohrfeige	~ sb (+ on the face / on the cheek / on the back) give sb a ~ on the cheek
smack sb ['smæk –]	jmd. „eine knallen"	"I'll ~ you."
box on the ear ['bɒks ɒn ðɪ ˌɪə]	Ohrfeige, eine Ohrfeige geben	give sb a ~ ~ ~ ~ ~ sb ~ ~ ~
strike (struck, struck) [straɪk, strʌk, –]	einen Schlag geben	~ sb (+ a blow) on the face
knock [nɒk]	schlagen	~ sb on the head / ~ sb out / win a fight by a **knockout** ['nɒkaʊt]
hit (hit, hit) [hɪt, –, –]	schlagen, Schlag	~ sb (+ when he is down) / ~ (+ sb) below the belt make a ~ at sb's face
thrash [θræʃ]	verdreschen	~ sb (+ soundly) / get a good **thrashing** ['-ɪŋ]
offend [ə'fend]	beleidigen, (Gefühle) verletzen, gegen (Normen) verstoßen	~ sb / be **offended** [-ɪd] **at** (= **by**) sb's remarks / ~ against good manners
offence [ə'fens] (*BE*) = **offense** [–] (*AE*)	Beleidigung, Vergehen, Verstoß, Anstoß	give ~ (+ to sb) / be charged with an ~ / an ~ against good manners / take ~ (+ at sth)
revenge [rɪ'vendʒ]	(sich) rächen, Rache	~ an injustice (or: sb's death) / ~ one's dead friend / ~ oneself on sb have one's ~ (+ on sb / for sth) / take a terrible ~ on sb / do sth in ~ (+ for sth) / want ~ for sth
brutal ['bruːtl]	brutal	a ~ person (or: attack / lie) / sb is known for his **brutality** [bruː'tælətɪ]
violent ['vaɪələnt]	gewalttätig	a ~ quarrel / be in a ~ temper / use unnecessary **violence** ['vaɪələns]

Selfish – egoistisch

selfish ['selfɪʃ]	egoistisch	a very ~ person / be too ~ to do sth
put (put, put) **oneself first** [pʊt, –, –; ˌ– wʌnˌselv 'fɜːst]	sich selbst an die erste Stelle setzen	
greedy ['griːdɪ]	gierig	a ~ little boy / be ~ for sth / look at sth with ~ eyes

miserly ['maɪzəlɪ]	geizig	
hang (hung, hung) **on** [hæŋ, hʌŋ, –; ˌ– 'ɒn] (*inform.*)	zusammenhalten, hängen an	~ ~ to one's money
unthankful [ˌʌn'θæŋkfʊl]	undankbar	an ~ friend
ungrateful [ʌn'greɪtfʊl]	undankbar	be ~ (+ to sb) for sth

Blame – beschuldigen

blame [bleɪm]	die Schuld geben	Don't ~ me! / ~ sb (+ for the failure) / ~ the failure on sb / be to ~
	Schuld	lay (or: put) the ~ on sb / take (or: bear) the ~ for sth
tell (told, told) **off** [tel, təʊld, –; ˌ– 'ɒf]	tadeln	~ the children ~ for playing football
reprove [rɪ'pruːv] (*form.*)	tadeln	~ sb (+ for doing sth)
reproof [rɪ'pruːf] (*form.*)	Tadel	sth deserves ~
reproach [rɪ'prəʊtʃ]	vorwerfen,	~ sb (+ with sth / for being ...) / have nothing to ~ oneself with
	Vorwurf	give sb a look of ~ / heap ~es on sb

40 Imagination – Vorstellungskraft, Phantasie

imagination [ɪˌmædʒɪ'neɪʃn]	Vorstellungskraft, Phantasie	have great (or: much / little) ~ / sth exists only in one's ~ / sth is beyond all ~
imagine [ɪ'mædʒɪn]	sich vorstellen, sich einbilden	~ sth / ~ oneself doing sth / ~ oneself as (or: to be) ... / ~ that one is ... / Don't ~ I can give you ...
imaginable [ɪ'mædʒɪnəbl]	vorstellbar	all ~ shapes and sizes / sth is **unimaginable** [ʌn-]
imaginative [ɪ'mædʒɪnətiv]	ideenreich, phantasievoll	an ~ man / be of an ~ nature
imaginary [ɪ'mædʒɪnərɪ]	eingebildet, nur in der Phantasie vorhanden	sth is (+ purely) ~
image ['ɪmɪdʒ]	Bild, Eindruck, Image	form an ~ of sth in one's mind's eye / improve one's ~
impression [ɪm'preʃn]	Eindruck	make a good ~ on sb / sth makes a strong ~ on one / get a(n) favourable (or: unfavourable) ~ of sb / it's one's ~ that ...

invent [ɪn'vent]	erfinden, erdichten	~ a story (or: an excuse)
fancy ['fænsɪ]	Ahnung;	have a ~ that ...
	(spielerische) Phantasie	have strange ~ies about sth / sth takes (or: holds) one's ~ / **fanciful** ['fænsɪfʊl] (phantasiereich, wirklichkeitsfremd)
fantasy ['fæntəsɪ]	Einbildung, Hirngespinst	have strange ~ies / **fantastic** [fæn'tæstɪk]
illusion [ɪ'lu:ʒn]	Illusion, Täuschung	have no ~s about sth / destroy sb's ~s about sb (or: sth) / be under an ~ / an optical ~
suppose [sə'pəʊz]	angenommen	S~ a lion came out of the forest.
think (thought, thought) [θɪŋk, θɔ:t, –]	sich denken, sich vorstellen	I can't ~ why you did it.

Memory – Erinnerung, Gedächtnis 41

memory ['memərɪ]	Erinnerung, Andenken;	have pleasant ~ies of sth / awake old ~ies / sth brings back to one ~ies of sth (or: old times) / in (= to the) ~ of sb
	Gedächtnis	have a good (or: bad / poor) ~ (+ for sth) / speak from ~
remember [rɪ'membə*]	sich erinnern, daran denken	~ sb (or: sth / one's promise) / ~ that ... / ~ what (or: why / who) ... / ~ to do sth (daß man etwas tun muß) / ~ doing sth (daß man etwas getan hat) / **Not that I remember**. (Nicht, daß ich wüßte.)
remembrance [rɪ'membrəns]	Erinnerung, Andenken	have no ~ of sb (or: sth) / to the best of one's ~ / in ~ of
learn (learnt, learnt = learned, learned) **by heart** [lɜ:n, -t, -d; ˌ– baɪ 'hɑ:t]	auswendig lernen	~ sth ~ ~
think (thought, thought) **of** [θɪŋk, θɔ:t, –; '–‿əv]	sich erinnern	I can't ~ ~ his name.
bear (bore, borne) **in mind** [beɜ*, bɔ:*, bɔ:n; ˌbeər‿ɪn 'maɪnd]	bedenken	~ sth ~ ~ / ~ ~ ~ that ...
recall [rɪ'kɔ:l]	sich in die Erinnerung zurückrufen	~ sb's name (or: face) / ~ doing sth (etwas getan zu haben)

recollect [ˌrekə'lekt]	sich erinnern an	~ how to do sth (or: sth was done) / as far as one can ~
remind [rɪ'maɪnd]	(jemanden an etwas) erinnern	~ sb of (= about) sth / ~ sb to do sth
recognize ['rekəgnaɪz]	(wieder-)erkennen	~ an old acquaintance
keep (kept, kept) **in mind** ['ki:p, kept, –; ˌ– ɪn 'maɪnd]	behalten	~ sth ~ ~ / ~ ~ ~ that ...
forget (forgot, forgotten) [fə'get, fə'gɒt, fə'gɒtn]	vergessen	~ (+ about) sth / ~ to do sth / ~ what to do (or: where to go)

42 Will – Wille

(→ 58 Instruction)

will [wɪl]	Wille	have a strong (or: weak) ~ / have the ~ to do sth / get (or: have) one's ~ / be **willing** ['-ɪŋ] to do sth / be **strong-** (or: **weak-)willed** [ˌstrɒŋ(ˌwi:k)'-d]
want [wɒnt]	(etwas Erreichbares) wollen	~ sth / ~ to do sth / ~ sb to do sth / What do you ~?
wish [wɪʃ]	wünschen, wollen, (etwas Unerreichbares) wünschen,	~ to do sth / ~ sb would do sth I ~ I knew. / I ~ you would ...
	(jemandem etwas) wünschen	~ sb success (or: good luck / happiness / a happy birthday) / ~ (+ sb) good morning (or: good night / goodbye)
wish for ['wɪʃ fə]	(sich etwas sehnlich) wünschen	~ ~ an opportunity to do sth / have everything one can ~ ~
wish [wɪʃ]	Wunsch	have (or: fulfil) a ~ / get (or: have) one's ~ / grant (erfüllen) sb's ~ / express a ~
like [laɪk]	wünschen, es gern haben	~ sb to do sth / ~ to do sth / ~ doing sth
should like [ʃʊd 'laɪk] = **would like** [wʊd 'laɪk]	mögen	I ~ ~ (= I'd) ..., please. / What **would** you **like** to start with? / Where **would** you **like** to stay?
ask [ɑ:sk]	auffordern, bitten	~ sb to do sth
tell (told, told) [tel, təʊld, –]	auffordern	~ sb to do sth
desire [dɪ'zaɪə*]	verlangen, (sich sehnlich) wünschen,	~ sth / ~ to be sth / ~ sb to do sth / give sb whatever he ~s / leave much (or: nothing) to be **desired** [-d]

	Verlangen, (sehnlicher) Wunsch	have a strong ~ to do sth (or: for sth) / be filled with ~ / What is your greatest ~?
ask [ɑːsk]	auffordern, erbitten	~ sb to do sth / ~ sb's advice / ~ for sb's advice
claim [kleɪm]	beanspruchen, geltend machen	~ attention / ~ the crown [or: the throne]
keen [kiːn]	erpicht	be very ~ to do sth / be ~ on doing sth (*inform.*) / be ~ that sb should do sth / be ~ on sth
eager ['iːgə*]	bedacht	~ to do sth / be ~ for (or: about) sth
expect [ɪk'spekt]	erwarten (, daß jemand etwas tut)	~ sb to do sth / ~ obedience
require [rɪ'kwaɪə*] (*form.*)	verlangen	~ sth of sb / ~ sb to do sth / ~ that sb (+ should) do sth
demand [dɪ'mɑːnd]	fordern	~ sth / ~ to know sth / ~ that sb (+ should) do sth
direct [dɪ'rekt] (*form.*)	verfügen, anordnen	~ sb to do sth / ~ sth to be done / **as directed** [əz -ɪd] (nach Vorschrift) / give **directions** [dɪ'rekʃnz]
order ['ɔːdə*]	befehlen, anordnen,	~ sb to do sth / ~ that sb (+ should) do sth / ~ sb around (= about) (herumkommandieren)
	Befehl, Anordnung	give (or: obey) an ~ / one's ~s are to do sth
command [kə'mɑːnd]	befehlen, kommandieren,	~ sb to do sth / ~ that sb (+ should) do sth
	Befehl, Kommando	give (or: obey) a ~ / be under sb's ~
obey [ə'beɪ]	gehorchen	~ without question / ~ sb's orders / He didn't ~.
obedient [ə'biːdjənt]	gehorsam	be ~ (+ to sb) / expect **obedience** [ə'biːdjəns] from sb / **disobedient** [ˌdɪsə'biːdjənt]
decline [dɪ'klaɪn] (*form.*)	(höflich) ablehnen	~ an invitation
turn down [tɜːn 'daʊn]	zurückweisen, ablehnen	~ ~ an offer (or: a request) / ~ sb ~
reject [rɪ'dʒekt]	ablehnen	~ an offer (or: a suggestion)
refuse [rɪ'fjuːz]	verweigern, ablehnen	He ~s. / ~ to do sth / ~ sb sth / ~ an offer (or: invitation) / sb's offer meets with a cold **refusal** [-l]

Plans – Pläne (→ 186 Action) 43

plan [plæn]	planen,	~ sth / ~ to do sth
	Plan	have (or: think up / follow / make) a ~ / carry out a ~ / go according to ~

intend [ɪn'tend]	beabsichtigen	~ to do sth / ~ on doing sth / ~ that one will do sth
think of ['θɪŋk‿əv]	vorhaben	~ ~ doing sth
intention [ɪn'tenʃn]	Absicht	do sth without ~ / do sth with the ~ of doing sth / sb's ~s are good (or: bad) / have the best ~s (+ towards sb) / What are your ~s? / do sth **intentionally** [-əlɪ] (or: **unintentionally** ['ʌn-əlɪ])
deliberate [dɪ'lɪbərət]	absichtlich	a ~ lie (or: mistake) / do sth ~ly
design [dɪ'zaɪn]	planen, entwerfen	~ a house (or: dress)
scheme [ski:m]	Plan, Entwurf (*BE*); Ränke, Ränke schmieden	work to a ~ a ~ to escape taxes ~ for (or: against) sb (or: sth)
plot [plɒt]	Anschlag	lay a ~ / the **Gunpowder Plot** ['gʌnpaʊdə ˌplɒt]
idea [aɪ'dɪə]	Idee, Plan	be full of good ~s / have an ~ (+ for sth) / What a good ~!
choose (chose, chosen) [tʃu:z, tʃəʊz, 'tʃəʊzn]	wählen	~ (+ not) to do sth / ~ (+ between) doing sth and doing sth
choice [tʃɔɪs]	Wahl	make a (+ careful) ~ / take one's ~
consider [kən'sɪdə]	erwägen	~ doing sth
mean [mi:n]	vorhaben, im Sinn haben	~ to do sth
have a good mind [– – '– '–] (*inform.*)	drauf und dran sein	~ ~ ~ ~ to do sth
make (made, made) **up one's mind** ['– – – '–]	sich entschließen	~ ~ ~ ~ to do sth / ~ ~ ~ ~ to be ...
be determined [bi: dɪ'tɜ:mɪnd]	entschlossen sein	~ ~ to do sth
determination [dɪˌtɜ:mɪ'neɪʃn]	Entschlossenheit	do sth with ~ / one's ~ to do sth
decide [dɪ'saɪd]	sich entschließen, sich entscheiden	~ (+ not) to do sth / ~ that one would (+ not) do sth / ~ what to do / ~ what one should do / ~ on sth
decision [dɪ'sɪʒn]	Entschluß, Entscheidung	make (or: come to) a ~
have half a mind [– '– – ˌ–]	schwanken	~ ~ ~ ~ to do sth
postpone [ˌpəʊst'pəʊn]	aufschieben	~ a decision

Opinion – Meinung

44

opinion [ə'pɪnjən]	Meinung	have (or: form / hold) an ~ of sth / have a high ~ of sb (or: sth) / have no ~ of sb (or: sth) / be of the ~ that ... / be of one ~ / in my ~ / share the same ~ / sth is a **matter of opinion** [ˌmætər‿əv –] (Ansichtssache) / **public opinion** [ˌpʌblɪk –]
attitude ['ætɪtju:d]	Haltung, Einstellung	What's your ~ to (= towards) ...? / change (= shift) one's ~ / maintain a firm ~ / adopt a friendly ~
position [pə'zɪʃn]	Standpunkt	What's your ~ on this problem? / define one's ~ / take up a ~
stand [stænd]	Standpunkt	take the ~ that ... / take a wishy-washy ~ / **take a stand** (Farbe bekennen)
view [vju:]	Auffassung, Meinung	hold the ~ that ... / in my ~ / form a ~ of sb (or: sth) / take (or: hold) the ~ that ... / take a bright (or: rosy) ~ of sth / in ~ of (in Anbetracht) / see sth from a certain **point of view** [pɔɪnt‿əv '–] (= **viewpoint** ['-pɔɪnt]) / **view of life** [– əv 'laɪf] (Lebensanschauung)
convince [kən'vɪns]	überzeugen	~ sb (+ of sth) / ~ sb that ... / be **convinced** [-t] that ...
conviction [kən'vɪkʃn]	Überzeugung	say sth in the ~ that ... / have the courage of one's own ~s
idea [aɪ'dɪə]	Ansicht, Idee, Ahnung	have no ~ (+ of sth) / form an ~ of sb (or: sth) / have an ~ that ... (es kommt einem so vor, als ob ...)
mind [maɪnd]	Ansicht	change one's ~ (+ about sth / about sb) / to my ~
think (thought, thought) [θɪŋk, θɔ:t, –]	halten	What do you ~ (+ of it)? / ~ highly (or: well / much) of sb (or: sth) / **think the world of** [– ðe 'wɜ:ld‿əv] (wunder was halten von)
I think so. [– '– –] (*BE*) = **I guess so.** [– ˌ– '–] (*AE*)	Ich glaube, ja. Das glaube ich auch.	
outlook ['aʊtlʊk]	(Welt-)Anschauung	have a narrow (or: broad) ~ (+ on life) / sb's general ~ is liberal (or: conservative) / people of similar ~

Ourselves and the others – Wir selbst und andere

Communication – Kommunikation

45 The communication model – das Kommunikationsmodell

communicate [kə'mju:nɪkeɪt]	in Kommunikation stehen,	~ frequently / ~ by signs (or: sounds / gestures / language) / ~ with sb (or: one another)
	mitteilen	~ sth to sb / be very **communicative** [kə'mju:nɪkətɪv] (mitteilsam)
communication [kə͵mju:nɪ'keɪʃn]	Kommunikation; Mitteilung	be (+ engaged) in ~ / the ~ process a secret ~
message ['mesɪdʒ]	Nachricht, Botschaft	send (or: transmit / convey / communicate) a ~ / transmit a ~ vocally (or: graphically / verbally / non-verbally) / receive (or: get) a ~
sign [saɪn]	Zeichen	communicate by ~s / make (or: use / convey / transmit) a ~ / receive (or: understand / interpret) a ~ / respond to a ~ / a ~ refers to sth / **sign language** ['– læŋgwɪdʒ]
signal ['sɪgnl]	Signal	make a ~ / sth is a ~ for ...
code [kəʊd]	Kode, Zeichensystem	a ~ has (or: consists of) signs / use a ~ / a message is **coded** ['-ɪd] (or: **encoded** [ɪn'kəʊdɪd] / **decoded** [͵di:'kəʊdɪd]) / break a ~

46 Facial expression, gesture – Gesichtsausdruck, Gebärde

expression [ɪk'spreʃn]	Ausdruck	have an ~ of surprise on one's face
look [lʊk]	aussehen	~ angry (or: sad)
pale [peɪl]	blaß	turn ~ with fear
red [red]	rot	turn ~ with anger
blush [blʌʃ]	erröten	~ as red as a rose / ~ with (= for) shame
frown [fraʊn]	die Stirn runzeln	~ at sb (or: sth) / a ~ing look / a ~ of disapproval
raise one's eyebrows ['– – 'aɪbraʊz]	die Augenbrauen (erstaunt, zweifelnd) hochziehen	

wink [wɪŋk]	ein Auge zukneifen	~ at sb / give sb a ~
twinkle ['twɪŋkl]	zwinkern, blinzeln	~ with pleasure (or: amusement)
open one's eyes ['-- ˌ-]	die Augen aufreißen	~ ~ ~ in surprise (or: horror)
sniff [snɪf]	die Nase rümpfen; schnüffeln	
kiss [kɪs]	küssen,	~ sb
	Kuß	give sb a ~
smile [smaɪl]	lächeln,	~ at sb (or: sth)
	Lächeln	There's a ~ on sb's face.
grin [grɪn]	grinsen,	~ at sb (or: sth)
	Grinsen	have a silly ~ on one's face
make (made, made) **faces** [meɪk, meɪd, –; – 'feɪsɪz]	Grimassen schneiden	~ ~ at sb
nod [nɒd]	nicken,	He ~ded (+ his head). / ~ (+ one's) approval
	Nicken	give sb a ~
shake (shook, shaken) [ʃeɪk, ʃʊk, 'ʃeɪkn]	schütteln	~ one's head / ~ hands (+ with sb) / ~ one's finger at sb (drohen) / ~ one's fist at sb (drohend die Faust schütteln)
shrug [ʃrʌg]	mit den Schultern zucken	He ~ged (+ his shoulders).
bow [baʊ]	beugen,	~ one's head
	sich verneigen,	~ to (or: down to / before) sb
	Verbeugung	make a ~ to sb
kneel [ni:l]	knien	~ (+ down) in prayer / ~ to (or: before) sb
stretch [stretʃ]	strecken	~ one's arms (or: hands) out to (= towards) sb
hug [hʌg]	fest umarmen	~ sb (+ heartily)
grab [græb]	schnappen	~ sb by the arm (or: shoulder)
point [pɔɪnt]	zeigen	~ (+ a finger) at sth (or: sb)
stroke [strəʊk]	streicheln	~ the cat
pat [pæt]	tätscheln	~ the dog
wave [weɪv]	winken	~ goodbye to sb / ~ to sb / ~ one's hand at sb
sign [saɪn]	ein Zeichen geben,	The teacher ~ed to them to be quiet.
	Zeichen	make a ~ to sb
signal ['sɪgnl]	(herbei-)winken,	~ to the waiter
	Zeichen, Signal	give the ~ for ...
beckon ['bekn]	(herbei-)winken	I ~ed him over to me. / ~ (+ sb) to come
stamp [stæmp]	stampfen	~ one's foot in anger / ~ out of the room

47 Voice – Stimme

voice [vɔɪs]	Stimme	have a loud (or: soft / deep / low) ~ / speak in a loud ~ / raise (or: lower / drop) one's ~ / one's ~ rises (+ in anger)
aloud [ə'laʊd]	laut	read ~
call [kɔ:l]	rufen,	~ out aloud / ~ to sb / ~ for help / ~ out
	Ruf	hear a ~
cry [kraɪ]	rufen, schreien,	'Stop!' he ~ied. / ~ out with pain
	Ruf, Schrei;	give a loud ~ / a ~ of pain (or: fear / anger)
	weinen	~ bitterly / ~ with pain / ~ over sth / ~ for joy
exclaim [ɪk'skleɪm]	ausrufen	"What!" he ~ed.
shout [ʃaʊt]	schreien,	~ at sb / ~ with pain / ~ at the top of one's voice
	Schrei	hear a terrible ~
scream [skri:m]	schreien, kreischen,	~ for hours / ~ with laughter (or: pain / fright) / ~ (+ out) a warning
	Schrei	hear loud ~s
yell [jel]	(gellend) schreien	~ sth out / ~ at sb / ~ (+ out) orders at sb
shriek [ʃri:k]	(schrill) schreien	~ with laughter (or: pain / terror)
roar [rɔ:*]	brüllen;	The football crowd ~ed.
	brüllend lachen	He'll ~ (+ with laughter) when he hears ...
mutter ['mʌtə*]	murmeln, murren,	~ (+ away) to oneself / ~ threats to sb
	Gemurmel, Gemurre	hear a ~
murmur ['mɜ:mə*]	murmeln,	~ a few words
	Gemurmel	hear a ~ of voices
sigh [saɪ]	seufzen,	~ deeply
	Seufzer	give a deep ~
weep (wept, wept) [wi:p, wept, –]	weinen	~ bitterly (or: loudly)
sob [sɒb]	schluchzen,	~ bitterly / ~ oneself to sleep
	Schluchzer	be shaken by ~s of sorrow
groan [grəʊn]	stöhnen,	He ~ed (+ with pain) when he broke his arm.
	Stöhnen	hear loud ~s / give a ~
gasp [gɑ:sp]	keuchen	~ for breath / ~ with rage
hum [hʌm]	summen,	~ a song / ~ to oneself
	Summen, Gesumme	hear a ~ of voices

sing (sang, sung) [sɪŋ, sæŋ, sʌŋ]	singen	~ a song (+ to the guitar) / ~ to oneself
whistle ['wɪsl]	pfeifen	~ to oneself (or: one's dog) / ~ a tune
laugh [lɑːf]	lachen	~ a lot / ~ oneself sick
laughter ['lɑːftə*]	Gelächter	The cinema was filled with the ~ of the audience.

Say, speak – sagen, sprechen 48

say (said, said) [seɪ, sed, –]	sagen	~ sth (+ to sb) / 'Yes', he *said.* / ~ to oneself that ... / People ~ ... (Man sagt, ...)
speak (spoke, spoken) [spiːk, spəʊk, 'spəʊkn]	sprechen	learn to ~ / ~ about sth (+ to sb) / ~ of sb (or: sth) / ~ very little (or: a good deal) / ~ up (or: loudly) / ~ at a meeting / ~ (+ good) English / ~ English well / be a good (or: poor) **speaker** ['-ə*]
accent ['æksənt]	Akzent	speak with a(n) (+ foreign) ~
talk [tɔːk]	reden,	learn to ~ / ~ to sb / ~ about sb (or: sth) / ~ too much / ~ sense (or: nonsense) / ~ sth over / be a good **talker** ['-ə*]
	Gespräch	have a (+ long) ~ with sb (or: about sth / on sth) / sth is the **talk of the town** ['tɔːk‿əv ðə 'taʊn]
address [ə'dres]	anreden;	~ sb as ...
	sprechen zu	~ a meeting
converse [kən'vɜːs]	sich unterhalten	~ with sb / have a long **conversation** [ˌkɒnvə'seɪʃn] with sb
interrupt [ˌɪntə'rʌpt]	unterbrechen	~ sb
tell (told, told) [tel, təʊld, –]	sagen,	~ sb one's name (or: the time / the price / a secret) / ~ sb what one wants / ~ sb that ... / I'll ~ you what. (Ich sag' Dir was.) / Don't ~ me. (Das kann doch nicht wahr sein!)
	erzählen, mitteilen	~ sb about sth / ~ sb of sth / ~ sb the whole story / ~ (+ sb) all about it / ~ a long story / So I've been told.
mention ['menʃn]	erwähnen	~ sth (or: sb) / ~ (+ to sb) that ...
hint [hɪnt]	andeuten,	~ (+ to sb) that ...
	Andeutung	give sb a ~ (+ about how to do sth) / take a ~

suggest [sə'dʒest]	vorschlagen, nahelegen	~ (+ doing) sth / ~ that … / ~ a way to do sth / make a **suggestion** [-ʃn]
repeat [rɪ'pi:t]	wiederholen;	~ a word (or: what one has said / oneself)
	aufsagen	~ a poem beautifully
repetition [ˌrepɪ'tɪʃn]	Wiederholung	after much ~ / R~ is a good way to learn.
repeatedly [rɪ'pi:tɪdlɪ]	wiederholt	~ ask sb
deliver [dɪ'lɪvə*]	vortragen	~ a speech
inform [ɪn'fɔ:m]	informieren	~ sb of (= about) sth / ~ sb that …
let (let, let) **sb know** [let (…) 'nəʊ]	wissen lassen	L~ me ~ when you want to come.
name [neɪm]	benennen	Can you ~ all these plants?
chat [tʃæt]	plaudern,	They were ~ting (+ away).
	Plausch	have a long ~ with sb
gossip ['gɒsɪp]	tratschen,	~ over the fence
	Tratsch;	believe the ~ one hears / be fond of ~ / It's only ~.
	Schwätzchen;	have a good (or: nice) ~ with …
	Klatschbase	She's an old ~.
rumour ['ru:mə*] (*BE*) = **rumor** [-r] (*AE*)	Gerücht	R~ has it that … / There's a ~ that … / All sorts of ~ are going round. / spread ~s / there are strange ~s about (= of) sb doing sth
advise [əd'vaɪz]	raten,	~ sb to so sth / ~ sb on a question
	raten zu	~ a complete rest / ~ an early start
advice [əd'vaɪs]	Rat	Give sb a piece (or: a bit / a word) of ~ / follow (or: take) sb's ~
announce [ə'naʊns]	ankündigen, bekanntgeben	~ sb / ~ one's engagement / ~ that … / make an **announcement** [-mənt]
apologize [ə'pɒlədʒaɪz]	sich entschuldigen	~ to sb for sth
apology [ə'pɒlədʒɪ]	Entschuldigung	make an ~ (+ to sb) (+ for sth) / accept (or: refuse) an ~
criticize ['krɪtɪsaɪz]	kritisieren	~ sb's work / ~ sb for (+ not) doing sth
curse ['kɜ:s]	fluchen, Fluch;	~ sb
	verfluchen	~ sb for doing sth
emphasize ['emfəsaɪz]	betonen, Wert legen auf	~ the importance of … / put special **emphasis** ['emfəsɪs] on sth
express [ɪk'spres]	ausdrücken	~ one's thanks / ~ oneself in good clear English
protest [prə'test]	protestieren	~ about (= against) sth (+ to sb)
protest ['prəʊtest]	Protest	enter a ~ (+ against sth / do sth under (or: without) ~

promise ['prɒmɪs]	versprechen, Versprechen	"Yes, I ~." / ~ to do sth make (or: keep / break) a ~
recommend [ˌrekə'mend]	empfehlen	~ sb a book / ~ sb for a job / ~ sb to do sth / ~ doing sth

Write – schreiben 49

write (wrote, written) [raɪt, rəʊt, 'rɪtn]	schreiben	~ sb a letter / ~ to sb / ~ very badly (or: fluently)
fill in [fɪl‿'ɪn]	ausfüllen	~ ~ a form (or: cheque [tʃek])
fill out [fɪl‿'aʊt]	ausfüllen	
handwriting ['hændˌraɪtɪŋ]	Handschrift	sb's ~ is good (or: bad / rather poor)
legible ['ledʒəbl]	leserlich	
pencil ['pensl]	Bleistift	write with a ~ / sign a letter in ~ / a **pencil-sharpener** [-ˌʃɑːpnə*]
draw (drew, drawn) [drɔː, druː, drɔːn]	zeichnen	~ with a pencil / ~ a picture (or: line) / **drawing paper** ['-ɪŋ ˌpeɪpə*]
pen [pen]	Füllfederhalter, Federhalter	fill a ~ / write with a ~ dip one's ~ in the ink
ink [ɪŋk]	Tinte	write in ~ / an **inkpot** ['-pɒt]
dip [dɪp]	eintauchen	
biro ['baɪrəʊ] (*BE*) = **ball-point pen** ['bɔːlpɔɪnt ˌpen] (*AE*)	Kugelschreiber	This ~ (= ~ ~) has run out. / write with a ~ (= ~ ~)
felt-tip ['feltɪp]	Filzstift	
paper ['peɪpə*]	Papier	a piece of ~ / Give me some ~. / **writing** (or: **typewriting**) **paper** ['raɪtɪŋ / 'taɪpraɪtɪŋ ˌpeɪpə*].
sheet [ʃiːt]	Blatt	a ~ of paper / a ruled (liniert) ~
blotting-paper ['blɒtɪŋ'peɪpə*]	Löschpapier	
ruler ['ruːlə*]	Lineal	
margin ['mɑːdʒɪn]	Rand	leave a ~ / write in (= into) the ~
line [laɪn]	Zeile	write a few ~s
space [speɪs]	Zwischenraum	leave some (or: enough) ~ between the words
pad [pæd] = **writing pad** ['raɪtɪŋ ˌpæd]	Schreibblock	
shorthand ['ʃɔːthænd]	Kurzschrift	take down in ~ what is said
type [taɪp]	mit der Maschine schreiben	~ a letter / a **typewriter** ['taɪpˌraɪtə*] / **typewritten** ['taɪpˌwrɪtn]
folder ['fəʊldə*]	Aktendeckel	keep one's papers in a ~ / **loose-leaf folder** [ˌluːs'liːf ˌ–] (Ringbuch)

Punctuation marks – Satzzeichen

full stop (*BE*)	['fʊl stɒp]	Punkt
= **period** (*AE*)	['pɪərɪəd]	
comma	['kɒmə]	Beistrich, Komma
semi-colon	[ˌsemɪ'kəʊlən]	Strichpunkt, Semikolon
colon	['kəʊlən]	Doppelpunkt
question mark	['kwestʃən mɑ:k]	Fragezeichen
exclamation mark	[ˌekskləˈmeɪʃn mɑ:k]	Ausrufezeichen
quotation marks	[kwəʊ'teɪʃn ˌmɑ:ks]	Anführungszeichen
= **inverted commas**	[ɪn'vɜ:tɪd ˌkɒməz]	
hyphen	['haɪfn]	Bindestrich
dash	[dæʃ]	Gedankenstrich
three dots	[ˌθri: 'dɒts]	Auslassungspunkte
apostrophe	[ə'pɒstrəfɪ]	Auslassungszeichen, Apostroph
bracket	['brækɪt]	Klammer

50 Correspondence – Briefwechsel (→ 149 Post office)

correspond [ˌkɒrɪ'spɒnd]	sich schreiben	~ with sb / John and I have ~ed for many years. / the **correspondence** [-əns] between ... and ...
pen-friend ['penˌfrend]	Brieffreund(-in)	have many ~s
letter ['letə*]	Brief	write (or: *BE:* send, *AE:* mail) sb a ~ / get (= receive) a ~ from sb / answer a ~ / get an answer to one's ~ / **business letter** ['bɪznɪs ˌ–]
Dear ... [dɪə*]	Sehr geehrte(r) ..., Liebe(r) ...	~ Sirs, ... / ~ Mr Harris, ... / ~ John, ...
Yours, ... [jɔ:z]	Ihr ..., Dein ...	~, Peter
Yours truly [ˌjɔ:z 'tru:lɪ]	Mit freundlichen Grüßen	
With best wishes [wɪð 'best ˌwɪʃɪz]	Mit freundlichen Grüßen	
regards [rɪ'gɑ:dz]	Grüße	Give my ~ to John. / with best ~
love [lʌv]	liebe Grüße	Give my ~ to John.
envelope ['envələʊp]	Umschlag	put a letter in an ~
address [ə'dres]	Adresse, adressieren	know sb's ~ / ~ a letter
To ... [tu:, tʊ, tə]	An ...	~ Mrs Pat Harris
c/o [ˌsi: 'əʊ] (= **care of** ['keər‿əv])	bei	To Joachim Stiller, ~ Mrs Pat Harris.

Read – lesen 51

read (read, read) [riːd, red, –]	lesen	~ a book / ~ a story to sb / ~ aloud
glance [glɑːns]	überfliegen	~ at the paper / ~ through a book
reading ['riːdɪŋ]	Lesen, Lesung;	interrupt sb's ~ / listen to a ~ from Milton
	Belesenheit;	a person of wide ~
	Lektüre	a book makes good (or: easy / difficult) ~ / a book demands careful (or: close / attentive) ~
widely read ['waɪdlɪ 'red]	vielgelesen;	a ~ ~ book
	belesen	He is ~ ~.

Question, answer – Frage, Antwort 52

ask [ɑːsk]	fragen	'What time is it?' he ~ed. / ~ sb his name / ~ sb about sth / ~ after sb / ~ a question
interview ['ɪntəvjuː]	Interview	have an ~ with …
question ['kwestʃən]	Frage	have a ~ / ask (= put) a ~
demand [dɪ'mɑːnd]	wissen wollen, verlangen, bestehen auf	~ sb's name
want to know [wɒn‿tə‿'nəʊ]	wissen wollen	~ ~ ~ sb's name
inquire [ɪn'kwaɪə*]	erfragen, sich erkundigen	~ sb's name / ~ after sb's health / ~ about (= after) sb (or: sth) / make **inquiries** [-rɪz] about sb (or: sth)
who? [huː]	wer?	W~ are you?
	wen?	W~ do you mean?
who … to? ['huː (…) tuː]	wem?	W~ did you give it ~?
whose? [huːz]	wessen?	W~ book is it?
whom? [huːm]	wen?	W~ do you mean? (*form.*)
to whom? [tə 'huːm]	wem?	T~ ~ did you give it? (*form.*)
what? [wɒt]	was?	W~ did you say?
	was für?	W~ languages do you know?
	wie?	W~ do you call this in English?
which? [wɪtʃ]	welche(-r, -s)?	W~ book is yours, this one or that one?
what … like? [wɒt (…) 'laɪk]	wie?	W~ was the film ~?
what … for? [wɒt (…) 'fɔː]	warum? wozu?	W~ did you come here ~?

what sort of ['wɒt 'sɔːt‿əv] = **what kind of?** ['wɒt 'kaɪnd‿əv]	was für?	W~ ~ ~ books do you like best?
where? [weə*]	wo?	W~ are you?
	wohin?	W~ are you going? / W~ are you going in the summer holidays?
when? [wen]	wann?	W~ was that?
why? [waɪ]	warum?	W~ do you think so?
how? [haʊ]	wie?	H~ old are you?
if [ɪf]	ob	Ask him ~ he wants to come with us.
whether ['weðə*]	ob	He asked me ~ she was coming.
answer ['ɑːnsə*]	antworten,	'Yes,' he ~ed. / ~ a question / ~ a letter
	Antwort	get (or: give) an ~ / a good (or: wrong) ~
reply [rɪ'plaɪ]	erwidern,	'No,' he ~ied. / ~ to a question (or: letter)
	Erwiderung	give a ~ / make no ~ / say sth in ~ to ...
respond [rɪ'spɒnd]	(feierlich) antworten	~ to a speech
retort [rɪ'tɔːt]	(ärgerlich) antworten,	~ angrily
	(ärgerliche) Antwort	Don't give me any of your nasty ~s.

53 Affirmation, negation – Bejahung, Verneinung

yes [jes]	ja	say ~ / 'Can you swim?' – 'Y~, I can.'
of course [əv 'kɔːs]	natürlich	Yes, ~ ~.
certainly ['sɜːtnlɪ]	gewiß	Yes, ~.
all right [ɔːl 'raɪt] = **alright** [–]	schön, gut	A~ ~ (= A~), I'll do it. / That's ~ ~ (= ~) with me.
O.K. [ˌəʊ'keɪ] = **okay** [–]	in Ordnung	That's ~. / 'Let's have an ice-cream.' – 'O~.'
agree [ə'griː]	zustimmen,	~ to sb's ideas / ~ to do sth
	übereinstimmen	~ with sb / ~ on (= about) sth / There is very little **agreement** [-mənt] (+ about what to do). / be **in agreement** with sb's decision / **disagree** [ˌdɪsə'griː]
accept [ək'sept]	einverstanden sein (mit), zusagen, annehmen	~ a(n) offer (or: present / invitation / proposal) / ~ a statement (or: sb's views / an explanation)
acceptable [ək'septəbl]	annehmbar	an ~ price

consent [kən'sent]	zustimmen, Zustimmung	~ to do sth / refuse to ~ do sth with the ~ of sb / give (or: refuse) one's ~ to sth / give sb one's ~ to do sth
affirm [ə'fɜːm]	bejahen, bestätigen, bekräftigen	~ the truth of a statement / ~ that ...
confirm [kən'fɜːm]	bekräftigen, bestätigen	~ that ... / ~ a telephone message in writing / sth ~s one's opinion
assure [ə'ʃʊə*]	versichern	~ sb that ... / ~ sb of sth / ~ oneself that ... / give sb one's **assurance** [-rəns] that ...
approve [ə'pruːv]	gutheißen, anerkennen, billigen	~ a plan / ~ of sb doing sth / your plans have my **approval** [-l]
perhaps [pə'hæps]	vielleicht	P~ I'll come tomorrow. / ~ not
maybe ['meɪbiː]	möglicherweise	~ yes (or: no) / M~ I can help you.
no [nəʊ]	nein; kein	say ~ / give ~ as an answer ~ time (or: money)
not [nɒt]	nicht	I did ~ see him. / ~ good (or: bad)
not a(n) ['– –]	kein	He is ~ ~ Englishman. / N~ ~ soul was there.
not at all [nɒt‿ə't‿ɔːl]	überhaupt nicht	No, ~ ~ ~.
not ... either [nɒt (...) 'aɪðə*]	auch nicht	'I can't swim.' – 'I can't ~.'
nor [nɔː*]	auch ... nicht	Peter and Mary can't swim. N~ can their parents.
neither ['naɪðə*]	kein (von beiden); auch nicht	on ~ side / ~ of you He doesn't know and ~ do I.
none [nʌn]	kein	N~ of them is (or: are) here. / 'Have you any money left?' – 'No, ~.'
never ['nevə*]	nie	He is ~ on time. / No, ~.
nowhere ['nəʊweə*]	nirgends	~ to be found
nobody ['nəʊbədɪ] = **no one** ['nəʊ wʌn]	niemand	~ (= ~ ~) came
nothing ['nʌθɪŋ]	nichts	~ to eat

Description – Beschreibung 54

describe [dɪ'skraɪb]	beschreiben	~ sth (or: sb) / ~ sth to sb / ~ sb as ...
descriptive [dɪ'skrɪptɪv]	beschreibend	a ~ text
description [dɪ'skrɪpʃn]	Beschreibung	give an exact (or: accurate) ~ of sth / sth is beyond ~
lifelike ['laɪflaɪk]	lebensecht	a ~ description

vivid ['vɪvɪd]	lebendig	a ~ description
detailed ['di:teɪld]	in Einzelheiten gehend	a ~ description
in detail [ɪn 'di:teɪl]	genau, im Detail	describe sth ~ ~
characterize ['kærəktəraɪz]	charakterisieren	~ sb (or: sth) / ~ sb as ... / give a **characterization** [ˌkærəktəraɪ'zeɪʃn] of sb (or: sth)
characteristic [ˌkærəktə'rɪstɪk]	Merkmal	point out the ~s of sth

55 Narration – Erzählung

(→ 48 Say, speak; 63 Stories; 66 The press; 67 Radio, television)

report [rɪ'pɔ:t]	berichten, Bericht	~ an accident / ~ what one has seen give (or: write) a ~ (+ on sth)
tell (told, told) [tel, təʊld, –]	erzählen, mitteilen	~ a story
narrate [nə'reɪt]	erzählen	~ a tale from long, long ago
narrative ['nærətɪv]	erzählend	a ~ text
account [ə'kaʊnt]	Bericht	give an ~ of what happened / an **eye-witness account** ['aɪˌwɪtnɪs‿ə'kaʊnt] (Augenzeugenbericht)
contents ['kɒntents]	Inhalt	sum up the ~ / **table of contents** [ˌteɪbl‿əv '–] (Inhaltsverzeichnis)
content ['kɒntent]	Gehalt, Aussage	consider the philosophical ~ of a novel
deal (dealt, dealt) **with** [di:l, delt, –; 'di:l wið]	handeln von	
be about [bi: ə'baut]	über ... sein	

56 Exposition – Darlegung, Darstellung

explain [ɪk'spleɪn]	erklären	~ sth to sb / ~ to sb that ... / ~ to sb how (or: why) ... / ~ a problem
explanation [ˌeksplə'neɪʃn]	Erklärung	give an ~ of sth / sth needs an ~
clear [klɪə*]	klar	make sth ~ / make oneself ~ / make it ~ to sb that ...
define [dɪ'faɪn]	definieren	~ a word / sth is hard to ~ / give a precise (or: correct / wrong / false) **definition** [ˌdefɪ'nɪʃn] of sth
interpret [ɪn'tɜ:prɪt]	interpretieren	~ sb's words / ~ a poem / give (or: write) an **interpretation** [ɪnˌtəprɪ'teɪʃn] of a text

analyse ['ænəlaɪz]	analysieren	~ a sentence (or: the meaning of a text) / give (or: write) an **analysis** [ə'næləsɪs] of a text
examine [ɪg'zæmɪn]	untersuchen	~ a text (+ carefully)

Argumentation – Argumentation 57

thesis ['θiːsɪs]	These	
argue ['ɑːgjuː]	argumentieren	~ about sth / ~ with sb / ~ sb into (or: out of) sth (or: doing sth) / ~ well (or: conclusively) (schlüssig)
discuss [dɪ'skʌs]	diskutieren	~ a problem (+ with sb)
discussion [dɪ'skʌʃn]	Diskussion	a ~ arises / a ~ about sth / hold (= have) a ~
argument ['ɑːgjʊmənt]	Argument	use (or: put forward) an ~ (+ for / against) / support an ~ / a strong (or: weak) ~
prove [pruːv]	beweisen	~ an argument
disprove [ˌdɪs'pruːv]	widerlegen	~ an argument
evidence ['evɪdəns]	Beweis	... is ~ for ...
proof [pruːf]	Beweis,	have no ~ of sth / give ~ of sth
	Probe	put sth to the ~
example [ɪg'zɑːmpl]	Beispiel	find (or: give) an ~ of sth / give a concrete (or: fitting) ~
for example [fər‿ɪg'zɑːmpl] = **e.g.** ['iː 'dʒiː] = **for instance** [fə(r) 'ɪnstəns]	zum Beispiel	
quote [kwəʊt]	zitieren	~ a sentence from a book / ~ sb (or: one's favourite author)
antithesis [æn'tɪθɪsɪs]	Antithese	
object [əb'dʒekt]	einwenden	~ to an argument / have no **objection** [əb'dʒekʃn] / make an **objection to** an argument
contrast ['kɒntrɑːst]	Gegensatz,	sth is (or: forms) a ~ to sth / in ~ with (= to) ...
[kən'trɑːst]	im Gegensatz stehen;	sth ~s strongly with sth
	gegenüberstellen	~ sth with (= and) sth
distinguish [dɪ'stɪŋgwɪʃ]	unterscheiden	~ between ... and ...
distinction [dɪ'stiŋkʃn]	Unterscheidung	make (or: see) a ~ (+ between ... and ...)
consequence ['kɒnsɪkwəns]	Folge	sth has ~s / sth is of no ~ for ... / in ~ of ...

conclusion [kən'klu:ʒn]	(Schluß-)Folgerung	draw (or: come to / arrive at) the ~ that ...
conclude [kən'klu:d]	schließen	~ that ...
persuade [pə'sweɪd]	überzeugen, überreden	~ sb that ... / be ~d of sth try to ~ sb to do sth / use **persuasion** [pə'sweɪʒn] / **persuasive** [pə'sweɪsɪv] language
convince [kən'vɪns]	überzeugen	~ sb that ... / ~ sb of sth / ~ sb to do sth (*AE*) / be ~d that ... / be ~d of sth
comment ['kɒmənt]	Kommentar, kommentieren	make a ~ about sth ~ on sth
compare [kəm'peə*]	vergleichen	~ London to (= with) Paris / ~ ... and ...
comparison [kəm'pærɪsn]	Vergleich	make a ~ / in (= by) ~ with / a ~ of ... to ... (= between ... and ...)
compare with [kəm'peə wɪð]	sich vergleichen lassen	This cannot ~ ~ that.
estimate ['estɪmeɪt]	(ab-)schätzen	~ sb's age at ...
evaluate [ɪ'væljʊeɪt]	bewerten	

58 Instruction – Anweisung, Belehrung

(→ 42 Will; 73 Norm)

instruct [ɪn'strʌkt]	anweisen, belehren	~ sb in sth / ~ sb in doing sth / ~ sb how to do sth
instruction [ɪn'strʌkʃn]	Belehrung, Anweisung	give (or: receive) ~s / give sb ~s to do sth
command [kə'mɑ:nd]	befehlen, Befehl	~ sb to do sth give (or: obey) a ~
order ['ɔ:də*]	anordnen, befehlen, Anordnung, Befehl	~ sb to do sth / ~ that sb (+ should) do sth / ~ sth obey ~s / receive the ~ to do sth
direct [dɪ'rekt]	anweisen, leiten	~ sb to do sth / ~ that sb should do sth

Language – Sprache

Language – Sprache 59

language ['læŋgwɪdʒ]	Sprache (als Kommunikationssystem), (die einzelne) Sprache;	Man communicates by ~. / sign (or: computer) ~ speak a ~ (+ perfectly / fluently) / know (können) (or: master) a ~ / learn a (+ foreign) ~
	Sprache, Stil, Ausdrucksweise;	poetic ~ / use bad ~
	Fachsprache, Terminologie	legal (or: technical / scientific) ~ / the ~ of diplomacy
dialect ['daɪəlekt]	Dialekt(-)	a ~ word (or: pronunciation) / use ~ words (or: expressions / forms) / a story written in ~
slang [slæŋ]	Slang(-)	use army (or: schoolboy) ~
jargon ['dʒɑ:gən]	Jargon	speak in a meaningless ~ / the ~ of scientists
spoken ['spəʊkn]	gesprochen	the ~ language
accent ['æksənt]	Akzent	speak English with a foreign ~ / speak without an ~
written ['rɪtn]	geschrieben	the ~ language
native ['neɪtɪv]	Mutter-	English is Jack's ~ language
modern ['mɒdən]	modern, neuer	study ~ languages
speech [spi:tʃ]	(gesprochene) Sprache, Reden;	Man has the faculty (Fähigkeit) of ~. / express thoughts by ~
	Rede	give (or: make) a ~ / a(n) short (or: long / lengthy / exciting / boring) ~
simple ['sɪmpl]	einfach, klar	speak ~ English
plain [pleɪn]	einfach, schlicht	in ~ English / say sth in ~ words / speak ~ly
easy ['i:zɪ]	leicht	Do you find it ~ to speak English?
hard [hɑ:d]	schwer	~ to understand
mistake [mɪ'steɪk]	Fehler	make ~s / There's some ~ in ... / correct a ~
error ['erə*]	Fehler	make an ~ / correct an ~ / an ~ in grammar
correct [kə'rekt]	richtig;	speak ~ English
	verbessern	~ a sentence (or: mistake) / ~ an error / make **corrections** [kə'rekʃnz] in red ink

60 Word – Wort

dictionary ['dɪkʃənrɪ]	Wörterbuch	an English–German ~
look up [ˌlʊk‿'ʌp]	nachschlagen	~ ~ a word in a dictionary
mean [mi:n]	bedeuten	What does this word ~? / What's the **meaning** ['mi:nɪŋ] of this word?
sense [sens]	Sinn	In what ~ do you use this word? / in a literal (wörtlich) (or: figurative) (übertragen) ~
derived from [dɪ'raɪvd frəm]	abgeleitet von	~ ~ Latin
spell (spelt, spelt) [spel, spelt, –] (*BE*),	buchstabieren;	How do you ~ this word? / His name is spelt S-M-I-T-H.
(spelled, spelled) [speld, –] (*AE*)	(richtig) schreiben	learn to ~ / Some children can't ~ well. / correct the **spelling** ['spelɪŋ]
letter ['letə*]	Buchstabe	How many ~s are there in the word 'house'? / a small (or: capital) (Groß-) ~
alphabet ['ælfəbɪt]	Alphabet	the Roman ~ / arrange words in **alphabetical** [ˌælfə'betɪkl] order
illiterate [ɪ'lɪtərət]	Analphabet(in)	
pronounce [prə'naʊns]	aussprechen	~ badly / 'Pear' and 'pair' are ~d the same.
pronunciation [prəˌnʌnsɪ'eɪʃn]	Aussprache	have (+ a) good ~
sound [saʊnd]	Laut	The words have the same ~.
consonant ['kɒnsənənt]	Konsonant, Mitlaut	We use 'a', not 'an' before a ~.
vowel ['vaʊəl]	Vokal, Selbstlaut	We use 'an', not 'a' before a ~.
syllable ['sɪləbl]	Silbe	There are two ~s in 'letter'.
stress [stres]	betonen,	'Result' is ~ed on the second syllable.
	Betonung	In the word 'result' the ~ is on the second syllable.
intonation [ˌɪntəʊ'neɪʃn]	Tonfall, Sprachmelodie	
usage ['ju:zɪdʒ]	Sprachgebrauch	learn the finer points of ~
expression [ɪk'spreʃn]	Ausdruck	use an ~ / a polite ~
collocation [ˌkɒlə'keɪʃn]	Wortverbindung, Kollokation	
term [tɜ:m]	Ausdruck, Begriff	use a technical ~ / a specific ~
current ['kʌrənt]	gegenwärtig, aktuell	~ English / a ~ expression
common ['kɒmən]	allgemein, gängig	a word is ~ usage / a ~ expression

fit [fɪt]	passen	This word does not ~ (+ in the context). / use a **fitting** ['fɪtɪŋ] expression
idiom ['ɪdɪəm]	(einer Sprache eigentümlicher) Ausdruck	use an ~ / speak **idiomatic** [ˌɪdɪə'mætɪk] English
vocabulary [vəʊ'kæbjʊlərɪ]	Wortschatz	have a rich (or: poor) ~ / use (+ a) scientific (or: technical) ~
translate [træns'leɪt]	übersetzen	~ a book into English / read the English **translation** [træns'leɪʃn] of a book
interpret [ɪn'tɜːprɪt]	dolmetschen	~ for sb

Sentence, grammar – Satz, Grammatik 61

sentence ['sentəns]	Satz	form (or: build / construct) a ~ / write (or: read / repeat) a ~ / say a few ~s / a simple (or: compound / complex) ~
statement	['steɪtmənt]	Aussagesatz
question	['kwestʃən]	Fragesatz
command	[kə'mɑːnd]	Befehlssatz
exclamation	[ˌekskləˈmeɪʃn]	Ausrufesatz
subject	['sʌbdʒɪkt]	Subjekt
predicator	['predɪkeɪtə]	Satzkern
complement	['kɒmplɪmənt]	Ergänzung
adverbial	[əd'vɜːbjəl]	Umstandsergänzung, Adverbial
noun	[naʊn]	Substantiv, Nomen, Hauptwort
singular	['sɪŋgjʊlə*]	Singular, Einzahl
plural	['plʊərəl]	Plural, Mehrzahl
subject	['sʌbdʒɪkt]	Subjekt, Satzgegenstand
object	['ɒbdʒɪkt]	Objekt, Satzaussage
case	[keɪs]	Fall
gender	['dʒendə*]	Geschlecht
definite article	['defɪnɪt 'ɑːtɪkl]	bestimmter Artikel
indefinite article	[ɪn'defɪnɪt 'ɑːtɪkl]	unbestimmter Artikel
pronoun	['prəʊnaʊn]	Pronomen, Fürwort
personal pronoun	['pɜːsənl '–]	Personalpronomen, persönliches Fürwort
demonstrative pronoun	[dɪ'mɒnstrətɪv '–]	Demonstrativpronomen, hinweisendes Fürwort
possessive pronoun	[pə'zesɪv '–]	Possessivpronomen, besitzanzeigendes Fürwort
indefinite pronoun	[ɪn'defɪnət '–]	Indefinitpronomen, unbestimmtes Fürwort

interrogative pronoun	[ˌɪntəˈrɒgətɪv ˈ–]	Interrogativpronomen, fragendes Fürwort
relative pronoun	[ˈrelətɪv ˈ–]	Relativpronomen
reflexive pronoun	[rɪˈfleksɪv ˈ–]	Reflexivpronomen, rückbezügliches Fürwort
determiner	[dɪˈtɜːmɪnə*]	näher bestimmender Begleiter (*My* / *This* car is red.)
nominal	[ˈnɒmɪnl]	substantivischer Stellvertreter (*This* is my car.)
numeral	[ˈnjuːmərəl]	Zahlwort
cardinal number	[ˌkɑːdɪnl ˈnʌmbə*]	Kardinalzahl, Grundzahl
ordinal number	[ˌɔːdɪnl ˈnʌmbə*]	Ordinalzahl, Ordnungszahl
preposition	[ˌprepəˈzɪʃn]	Präposition, Verhältniswort
verb	[vɜːb]	Verb, Zeitwort, Tätigkeitswort
auxiliary	[ɔːgˈzɪljərɪ]	Hilfsverb, Hilfszeitwort
tense	[tens]	Tempus, Zeit
present tense	[ˈpreznt ˈtens]	Präsens, Gegenwart
past tense	[ˈpɑːst ˈtens]	Präteritum, Vergangenheit
present perfect	[ˈprezent ˈpɜːfekt]	Perfekt, vollendete Gegenwart
past perfect	[ˈpɑːst ˈpɜːfekt]	Plusquamperfekt, vollendete Vergangenheit
future	[ˈfjuːtʃə*]	Futur, Zukunft
future perfect	[ˌfjuːtʃə ˈpɜːfekt]	vollendetes Futur
simple form	[ˈsɪmpl ˈfɔːm]	einfache Form
progressive form	[prəˈgresɪv ˈfɔːm]	Verlaufsform
regular verb	[ˈregjʊlə ˈvɜːb]	regelmäßiges Verb, schwaches Zeitwort
irregular verb	[ɪˈregjʊlə ˈvɜːb]	unregelmäßiges Verb, starkes Zeitwort
infinitive	[ɪnˈfɪnətɪv]	Infinitiv, Grundform
present participle	[ˈpreznt ˈpɑːtɪsɪpl]	Partizip Präsens, Mittelwort der Gegenwart
past participle	[ˈpɑːst ˈpɑːtɪsɪpl]	Partizip Präteritum, Mittelwort der Vergangenheit
gerund	[ˈdʒerənd]	Gerundium
active voice	[ˈæktɪv ˈvɔɪs]	Aktiv, Tatform
passive voice	[ˈpæsɪv ˈvɔɪs]	Passiv, Leideform
adjective	[ˈædʒɪktɪv]	Adjektiv, Eigenschaftswort
comparison (+ of adjectives / of adverbs)	[kəmˈpærɪsn]	Steigerung
comparative	[kəmˈpærətɪv]	Komparativ, erste Steigerungsstufe
superlative	[suːˈpɜːlətɪv]	Superlativ, zweite Steigerungsstufe
adverb	[ˈædvɜːb]	Adverb, Umstandswort
adverb of manner	[ˈ–‿əv ˈmænə*]	Adverb der Art und Weise
adverb of time	[ˈ–‿əv ˈtaɪm]	Zeitadverb

adverb of place	['–‿əv 'pleɪs]	Ortsadverb
adverb of frequency	['–‿əv 'frɪ:kwensɪ]	Adverb der Häufigkeit
adverb of degree	['–‿əv dɪ'gri:]	Gradadverb
clause	[klɔ:z]	Glied, Teilsatz
main clause	['meɪn 'klɔ:z]	Hauptsatz
subclause	['sʌbˌklɔ:z],	Nebensatz
= **dependent clause**	[dɪ'pendənt ˌklɔ:z]	
conjunction	[kən'dʒʌŋkʃn]	Konjunktion, Bindewort
relative clause	['relətɪv 'klɔ:z]	Relativsatz, rückbezüglicher Nebensatz
contact clause	['kɒntækt ˌklɔ:z]	Relativsatz ohne Relativpronomen
temporal clause	['tempərəl 'klɔ:z]	Temporalsatz, Nebensatz der Zeit
causal clause	['kɔ:zl 'klɔ:z]	Kausalsatz, Nebensatz des Grundes
conditional clause	[kən'dɪʃənl 'klɔ:z]	Konditionalsatz, Bedingungssatz
direct speech	['daɪrekt 'spi:tʃ]	direkte Rede
reported speech	[rɪ'pɔ:tɪd 'spi:tʃ]	indirekte Rede

Style – Stil, Ausdruck 62

style [staɪl]	Stil, Ausdruck	use (or: employ) a ~ / write in a clear ~ / use a certain **stylistic** [staɪ'lɪstɪk] device (Mittel)

Qualities of style – stilistische Eigenschaften

plain	[pleɪn]	schlicht, klar
simple	['sɪmpl]	einfach
natural	['nætʃrəl]	natürlich
precise	[prɪ'saɪs]	genau
clear	[klɪə*]	klar
concrete	['kɒnkri:t]	anschaulich
polished	['pɒlɪʃt]	geschliffen
fluent	['flu:ənt]	flüssig
affected	[ə'fektɪd]	geziert
diffuse	[dɪ'fju:z]	unklar
confused	[kən'fju:zd]	verworren
crude	[kru:d]	primitiv

figure of speech [ˌfɪgər‿əv 'spi:tʃ]	Redefigur	use (or: employ) many ~s ~ ~
image ['ɪmɪdʒ]	Bild	use (or: employ) an ~ / use a traditional ~ / In 'Hamlet' Shakespeare uses many ~s of disease.
symbol ['sɪmbl]	Sinnbild, Symbol	sth is a ~ of (= for) ...
comparison [kəm'pærɪsn]	Vergleich	make a ~ between ... and ...

simile ['sɪmɪlɪ]	(direkter) Vergleich	use (or: employ) a ~ / a style rich in ~
repetition [ˌrepɪ'tɪʃn]	Wiederholung	use (or: employ) ~ (+ to build up tension)
exaggeration [ɪgˌzædʒə'reɪʃn]	Übertreibung	use ~ in saying sth
allusion [ə'lu:ʒn]	Anspielung	make an ~ to sth / sth is an ~ to sth
irony ['aɪərənɪ]	Ironie	speak (or: answer) with ~ / speak **ironically** [aɪ'rɒnɪkəlɪ] / an **ironic** [aɪ'rɒnɪk] remark
metaphor ['metəfə*]	Metapher	use ~ / describe sth by ~ / a word is used as a ~ for ... / a dead ~

Literature – Literatur

63 Stories – Geschichten

(→ 55 Narration)

fiction ['fɪkʃn]	Dichtung, Prosa	read (or: write) ~ / a work of ~
character ['kærəktə*]	Charakter, Figur	introduce a ~
subject ['sʌbdʒɪkt]	Gegenstand	
content ['kɒntənt]	Gehalt, Aussage	
contents ['kɒntənts]	Inhalt(sverzeichnis)	**table of contents** ['– – '–]
deal (dealt, dealt) **with** [di:l, delt, –; 'di:l wið]	handeln von	
action ['ækʃn]	Handlung (als zeitliche Abfolge)	The ~ of the novel takes place in ...
plot [plɒt]	Handlung, Fabel (als Kausalzusammenhang)	construct a ~ / **subplot** ['sʌbplɒt] (Nebenhandlung)
flashback ['flæʃbæk]	Rückblende	
setting ['setɪŋ]	Schauplatz	The ~ of ... is England. / have a fantastic (or: realistic) ~
point of view [ˌpɔɪnt‿əv 'vju:]	Standpunkt (als Beziehung des Autors oder Erzählers zum Erzählten)	write (or: speak) from the ~ ~ ~ of a factory worker
limited ['lɪmɪtɪd]	begrenzt	have a ~ point of view
omniscient [ɒm'nɪsɪənt]	allwissend	have an ~ point of view / write as the ~ narrator
author ['ɔ:θə*]	Verfasser, Autor	be the ~ of ...
writer ['raɪtə*]	Schriftsteller	
narrator [nə'reɪtə*]	Erzähler	
fable ['feɪbl]	Fabel	an animal ~

anecdote ['ænɪkdəʊt]	Anekdote	tell (or: hear) an ~ about sb
short story [ˌʃɔːt 'stɔːrɪ]	Kurzgeschichte	read a short (or: long) ~ ~
fairy tale ['feərɪ ˌteɪl]	Märchen	
detective story [ˌdɪ'tektɪv ˌstɔːrɪ]	Kriminalroman	read a ~ ~
thriller ['θrɪlə*]	spannender Krimi	
whodunit [ˌhuː'dʌnɪt] (*inform.*)	Krimi	
novel ['nɒvəl]	Roman	read (or: write) a ~

Drama – Drama (→ 129 Theatre) 64

drama ['drɑːmə]	Drama (als Gattung),	the theory of ~ / like ~ better than music
	Drama, Stück	read a ~
play [pleɪ]	Stück	a ~ by Shakespeare
tragedy ['trædʒɪdɪ]	Tragödie, Trauerspiel	
comedy ['kɒmɪdɪ]	Komödie, Lustspiel	
act [ækt]	Akt	a **one-act play** [ˌwʌn‿ækt 'pleɪ] (Einakter)
scene [siːn]	Szene	in the first ~ of Act III / a ~ plays in London / **change of scene** [ˌtʃeɪndʒ‿əv 'siːn]
monologue ['mɒnəlɒg]	Monolog	deliver a ~
soliloquy [sə'lɪləkwɪ]	Selbstgespräch	speak a ~
dialogue ['daɪəlɒg]	Dialog	enter into a ~ with others
stage directions ['steɪdʒ ˌdɪrekʃnz]	Bühnenanweisungen	
action ['ækʃn]	Handlung	
character ['kærəktə*]	handelnde Person	

Poetry – Dichtkunst 65

poem ['pəʊɪm]	Gedicht	write (or: read) a ~ / a ~ by Tennyson / recite a ~
line ['laɪn]	Zeile	a two-~ stanza / a poem has ten ~s
stanza ['stænzə]	Strophe	the first ~ of a poem / a four-line ~
verse [vɜːs]	Vers, Gedicht;	write ~ / compose ~
	Strophe, Vers, Poesie	a poem of four ~s / written in ~

rhyme ['raɪm]	Reim, (sich) reimen	a stanza has a perfect ~ the lines of a poem ~ / the first and third lines ~ with each other
lyric (+ poem) ['lɪrɪk ('–)]	(oft gefühlsbetontes) Gedicht	the ~s of Shakespeare
poet ['pəʊɪt]	Dichter	

The mass media – die Massenmedien

66 The press – die Presse

(→ 55 Narration)

newspaper ['nju:sˌpeɪpə*]	Zeitung	What ~ do you read?
paper ['peɪpə*]	Blatt, Zeitung	Have you seen today's ~? / What do the ~s say about it? / a leading ~ / the morning (or: evening) ~ / a widely read ~
daily ['deɪlɪ]	Tages-, Tageszeitung	a ~ paper the ~ies
weekly ['wi:klɪ]	Wochen-, Wochenzeitung	a ~ paper 'The Observer' is a ~.
local ['ləʊkl]	Lokal-	Most large towns have their own ~ papers.
provincial [prə'vɪnʃl]	Provinz-	a ~ paper / the ~ press
regional ['ri:dʒənl]	Regional-	a ~ paper / the ~ press
national ['næʃənl]	überregional	a ~ paper / the ~ press
serious ['sɪərɪəs]	seriös	a ~ paper / the ~ press
quality ['kwɒlətɪ]	seriös	a ~ paper / the ~ press
popular ['pɒpjʊlə*]	Massen-	read a ~ newspaper / the ~ press
the yellow press [ðə 'jeləʊ pres]	die Sensationspresse	
magazine [ˌmægə'zi:n] = **journal** ['dʒɜ:nl] = **periodical** [ˌpɪərɪ'ɒdɪkl]	Zeitschrift	a weekly (or: quarterly) ~
monthly ['mʌnθlɪ]	monatlich (erscheinend), Monatsschrift	a ~ magazine 'Reader's Digest' is a ~.
news magazine ['nju:z ˌmægə'zi:n]	Nachrichtenmagazin	
tabloid ['tæblɔɪd]	Boulevardzeitung	

edition [ɪ'dɪʃn]	Ausgabe	the morning (or: late / Sunday) ~
circulation [ˌsɜːkjʊ'leɪʃn]	Auflage	a newspaper with a ~ of a hundred thousand copies
issue ['ɪʃuː]	herausgeben, Nummer	This paper is ~d daily. This is the latest ~.
copy ['kɒpɪ]	Exemplar	This paper sells about 5,000,000 ~ies a day.
print [prɪnt]	drucken	~ a paper / This paper is ~ed in London and Manchester. / **printing office** ['prɪntɪŋ ˌɒfɪs] / **printing-press** ['prɪntɪŋ pres]
page [peɪdʒ]	Seite	the front (or: back) ~ / the middle ~s / a front-~ story
headlines ['hedlaɪnz]	Schlagzeilen	The story made the ~.
column ['kɒləm]	Spalte	the sports ~
edit ['edɪt]	herausgeben	He ~s a dozen newspapers and journals. / news (or: city / sports) **editor** ['edɪtə*] (Redakteur) / the **editorial staff** [edɪ'tɔːrɪəl stɑːf]
journalist ['dʒɜːnəlɪst]	Journalist	
reporter [rɪ'pɔːtə*]	Reporter	sports ~ / a newspaper ~
correspondent [ˌkɒrɪ'spɒndənt]	Korrespondent	our Washington ~
article ['ɑːtɪkl]	Artikel	write an ~ / a critical ~
leading article [ˌliːdɪŋ 'ɑːtɪkl] = **leader** ['liːdə*]	Leitartikel	
news story ['njuːzˌstɔːrɪ]	Nachricht (als Bericht)	
news [njuːz] (*pl.* only)	Nachricht	an interesting piece of ~ / What's the latest ~?
story ['stɔːrɪ]	Geschichte, Bericht	write a ~ on ... / a big (or: sensational) ~ / a humain interest ~
comment ['kɒmənt]	Kommentar, kommentieren	write a ~ about (= on) sth / a fair ~ ~ on sth / **commentator** ['kɒmənteɪtə*]
advertise ['ædvətaɪz]	annoncieren	~ sth / ~ in a newspaper / put an **advertisement** [əd'vɜːtɪsmənt] (= **ad** [æd]) in a newspaper
newsagent ['njuːz ˌeɪdʒənt] (*BE*) = **newsdealer** ['njuːz ˌdiːlə*] (*AE*)	Zeitungshändler	get a paper at one's local ~'s

newsboy ['nju:zbɔɪ] = **paperboy** ['peɪpəbɔɪ] (or: **papergirl** ['peɪpəgɜ:l])	Zeitungsausträger (meist ein/e Schüler/in)	
newsstand ['nju:zstænd]	Zeitungskiosk	

67 Radio, television, computer – Radio, Fernsehen, Computer

(→ 127 Music)

Radio, television – Radio, Fernsehen

aerial ['eərɪəl]	Antenne	
radio ['reɪdɪəʊ]	Radio	hear (or: listen to) sth on the ~ / What's on the ~? / buy a new ~ (= **radio set**) ['– set]
satellite TV ['sætəlaɪt ˌti:'vi:]	Satellitenfernsehen	
cable TV ['keɪbl ˌti:'vi:]	Kabelfernsehen	
goggle-box ['gɒglbɒks] (*inform.*)	„Glotze“	
television ['telɪˌvɪʒn] = **TV** [ˌti:'vi:]	Fernsehen	What's on ~? / a colour ~ / watch ~
turn on [ˌtɜ:n 'ɒn] = **switch on** [ˌswɪtʃ 'ɒn]	anschalten	~ ~ the radio (or: TV) / ~ the radio (or: TV) ~
turn up [ˌtɜ:n 'ʌp]	lauter stellen	~ the radio ~
turn down [ˌtɜ:n 'daʊn]	leiser stellen	~ the radio ~
tune in [ˌtju:n 'ɪn]	(einen Sender) einstellen	~ ~ at ten o'clock
knob [nɒb]	Knopf	turn the ~
listen ['lɪsn]	zuhören	~ (+ in) to the news / ~ (+ in) to a broadcast / ~ to an interesting programme
watch TV ['wɒtʃ ˌti:'vi:]	fernsehen	
station ['steɪʃn]	Sender	a (+ local) radio (or: TV) ~
programme ['prəʊgræm] (*BE*) = **program** [–] (*AE*)	Programm	listen to a ~ / watch a ~ on TV / a news-~ / a ~ is broadcast live / a live ~
channel ['tʃænl]	Fernsehsender, -programm	

news programme ['nju:z 'prəʊgræm]	Nachrichtensendung	"**News At Ten**"
breakfast TV ['brekfəst ˌti:'vi:]	Frühstücksfernsehen	
news report ['nju:z rɪˌpɔ:t]	Bericht (in den Nachrichten)	
commercial [kə'mɜ:ʃl]	Werbespot	a ~ for beer
broadcast ['brɔ:dkɑ:st]	Sendung	a good (or: an informative) ~ / an outside ~ (Direktübertragung)
broadcast (broadcast, broadcast) ['brɔ:dkɑ:st, –, –]	senden	~ a programme (+ of music)
announcer [ə'naʊnsə*]	Ansager	
newsreader ['nju:zˌri:də]	Nachrichtensprecher	
viewer ['vju:ə*]	(Fernseh-)Zuschauer	
listener ['lɪsnə*]	Hörer	
turn off [ˌtɜ:n‿'ɒf] = **switch off** [ˌswɪtʃ‿'ɒf]	abschalten	~ ~ the radio (or: TV)

Computer – Computer

computer [kəm'pju:tə*]	Computer, Rechner	use ~s / a **home computer** ['həʊm –]
PC ['pi: 'si:]	Personalcomputer	
hardware ['hɑ:dˌweə*]	Hardware, Gerät(e)	
keyboard ['ki:ˌbɔ:d]	Tastatur	
key [ki:]	Taste	press a ~
monitor ['mɒnɪtə*]	Monitor, Sichtgerät	
cursor ['kɜ:sə*]	Schreibmarke	move the ~ (+ to the start of the word)
chip [tʃɪp]	Chip	
disk drive ['dɪsk ˌdraɪv]	Laufwerk	
diskette [dɪs'ket]	Diskette	insert (or: remove) a ~ / save a program on ~
printer [prɪntə*]	Drucker	
software ['sɒftˌweə*]	Software, Programm(e)	
language ['læŋgwɪdʒ]	Sprache	

program ['prəʊgræm]	Programm	start (or: run) a ~ / write a ~
save [seɪv]	speichern	~ a program
delete [dɪ'li:t]	löschen	~ a program (or: file)
file [faɪl]	Datei	a program (or: text / data) ~

Computer applications – Computeranwendungen

data processing	['deɪtə prəʊˌsesiŋ]	Datenverwaltung
character	['kæræktə*]	Zeichen
string	[strɪŋ]	Zeichenfolge
field	[fi:ld]	Feld
record	['rekəd]	Datensatz
file	[faɪl]	Datei
data base	['deɪtə beɪs]	Datenbank
word processing	['wɜ:d prəʊ'sesɪŋ]	Textverarbeitung

CAD	Computer-Assisted Design	Computerunterstützte Konstruktion
CAI	Computer-Assisted Instruction	Computerunterstützter Unterricht
CAL	Computer-Assisted Learning	Computerunterstütztes Lernen
CALL	Computer-Assisted Language Learning	Computerunterstütztes Sprachenlernen

68 Film – Film

cinema ['sɪnəmə]	Kino	go to the ~
the pictures ['pɪktʃəz] (*BE*) = **the movies** ['mu:vɪz] (*AE*)	Kino, Film	go to ~ ~
box-office ['bɒksˌɒfɪs]	Kasse	buy tickets at the ~
ticket ['tɪkət]	Entrittskarte	
seat [si:t]	Platz	I'd like two ~s in the circle (= **balcony** ['bælkənɪ], *AE*).
book [bʊk]	reservieren	Can I ~ two seats for tonight?
row [rəʊ]	Reihe	Our seats are in ~ 5. / the front ~
film [fɪlm] (*BE*) = **movie** ['mu:vɪ] (*AE*)	Film	The ~ starts at 8. / a ~ star / a documentary (or: silent) ~
screenplay ['skrɪ:npleɪ]	Drehbuch	
screen [skri:n]	Leinwand	

shoot (shot, shot) [ʃu:t, ʃɒt, –]	drehen	~ a film (or: scene)
direct [dɪ'rekt]	Regie führen	~ a film / a famous **director** [-ə*]
actor ['æktə*]	Schauspieler	a famous **film** ~ ['– ˌ–] (or: **actress** ['–ˌæktrɪs])
star [stɑ:*]	Star	a great film ~ ['– –] / dream of being a film ~ one day
film studio ['fɪlm ˌstju:dɪəʊ]	Filmstudio, Atelier	

Book – Buch 69

writer ['raɪtə*]	Schriftsteller	
author ['ɔ:θə*]	Verfasser	sb is one's favourite ~
print [prɪnt]	drucken	~ a book / ~ed in Great Britain
cover ['kʌvə*]	Einband, Deckel	This book needs a new ~. / the front (or: back) ~
publish ['pʌblɪʃ]	herausgeben, veröffentlichen	first ~ed in 1976 / ~ books / **publishing company** ['pʌblɪʃɪŋ ˌkʌmpənɪ] (Verlag) / **publisher** ['pʌblɪʃə*] (Verleger)
book [bʊk]	Buch	write (or: read) a ~ / an exciting ~ / a boring ~ / a ~ is about (or: deals with) / buy a ~ at a **bookshop** ['bʊkʃɒp]
paperback ['peɪpəbæk]	Taschenbuch	
volume ['vɒlju:m]	Band	Shakespeare's works in four ~s.
sell (sold, sold) [sel, səʊld, –]	sich verkaufen	a book ~s well / a **best-seller** [ˌbest'selə*]
library ['laɪbrərɪ]	Bücherei, Bibliothek	a public (or: lending) ~ / My house has seven rooms including the ~.
borrow ['bɒrəʊ]	entleihen	~ a book from the library
chapter ['tʃæptə*]	Kapitel	
heading ['hedɪŋ]	Überschrift	
leaflet ['li:flɪt]	Flug-, Merkblatt; Heftchen, Broschüre	

Our relations with others – unsere Beziehungen zu anderen

70 Alone, with others – allein, mit anderen

leave (left, left) ['li:v, left, –]	verlassen	~ sb / ~ sb alone (in Ruhe lassen)
avoid [ə'vɔɪd]	meiden	~ sb / ~ meeting sb / ~ bad company
distance ['dɪstəns]	Abstand	keep one's ~ / keep sb at a ~
desert [dɪ'zɜ:t]	im Stich lassen	~ a friend
stay away [ˌsteɪ ə'weɪ]	wegbleiben	~ ~ from school (or: a meeting)
withdraw (withdrew, withdrawn) [wɪð'drɔ:, wɪð'dru:, wɪð'drɔ:n]	sich zurückziehen	~ from others / a **withdrawn** person / lead a **withdrawn** life
be (or: have) **done** [dʌn] **with = be** (or: have) **finished** ['fɪnɪʃt] **with**	fertig sein mit	I'm (= I've) ~ ~ you.
break (broke, broken) **up** [breɪk, brəʊk, 'brəʊkən; breɪk 'ʌp]	sich trennen	~ ~ with sb
alone [ə'ləʊn]	allein	be (or: live) (+ all) ~
by oneself [ˌbaɪ wʌn'self]	für sich	be (+ all) ~ ~
on one's own [ɒn wʌnz‿'əʊn]	auf sich selbst gestellt	be (or: live / work) ~ ~ ~
lonely ['ləʊnlɪ]	einsam, allein	be (or: feel) ~ / a ~ child / suffer from **loneliness** [-nɪs]
lonesome ['ləʊnsəm]	einsam, verlassen	get ~ / a ~ journey
together [tə'geðə*]	zusammen, gemeinsam	sit (or: live / work / go for a walk) ~ / go out ~ / call people ~
meet (met, met) [mi:t, met, –]	treffen;	~ at 2 o'clock / ~ sb in the street / ~ sb at the station (vom Bahnhof abholen)
	kennenlernen	I'd like you to ~ my wife.
meeting ['mi:tɪŋ]	Treffen, Versammlung	call (or: hold) a ~ / the ~ begins (or: ends) at ... / a sports ~ / a political ~ / a ~ between ... and ...
assemble [ə'sembl]	zusammenkommen	A great crowd ~d in the square. / a daily **assembly** [-ɪ] of pupils and staff

gather ['gæðə*]	zusammenkommen, (sich) versammeln, um sich versammeln	~ in the street (or: on the corner / round sb) / ~ together ~ a crowd round one
contact ['kɒntækt]	Verbindung, sich in Verbindung setzen	be in ~ with sb / lose ~ with sb ~ sb (+ by telephone)
join [dʒɔɪn]	sich anschließen, beitreten	~ a club / ~ sb in a walk / ~ (+ others) in a game
company ['kʌmpənɪ]	Umgang, Gesellschaft, Begleitung;	keep sb ~ / keep ~ with sb go (or: come) in ~ (+ with sb) / go with sb for ~
	Gesellschafter; Besuch, Gäste	be good (or: poor / bad) ~ have ~ (+ for dinner)
companion [kəm'pænjən]	Gefährte, Begleiter	be an excellent ~ / be not much of a ~ for sb
invite [ɪn'vaɪt]	einladen	~ sb (+ to a party / to tea)
relation [rɪ'leɪʃn]	Beziehung	business ~s / have (or: enter into / establish / end / break off) ~s with others / have personal (or: friendly / cool / hostile) ~s with others
relationship [rɪ'leɪʃnʃɪp]	Beziehung	have a (+ lasting) ~ with (= to) sb
terms [tɜːmz]	Beziehungen	be on friendly (or: good / bad) ~ with sb / come to ~ (sich einigen)
bond [bɒnd]	Band	the ~ of friendship
tie [taɪ]	Bindung	the ~s of friendship / strong family ~s / the ~s of blood
sociable ['səʊʃəbl]	gesellig	be very ~ (or: **unsociable** [ʌn-])

Competition – Konkurrenz (→ 124 Sport) 71

compete [kəm'piːt]	konkurrieren	~ with sb (+ for sth) / ~ to do sth / be in **competition** [ˌkɒmpɪ'tɪʃn] with (= against) sb (+ for sth) / be a **competitor** [kəm'petɪtə*] for sth
conflict ['kɒnflɪkt]	Konflikt	a serious ~
contest ['kɒntest]	(-)Wettbewerb	a dancing ~ / a ~ for the position of ...
ambitious [æm'bɪʃəs]	ehrgeizig	have ~ plans / an ~ man / be ~ for fame / be full of (= filled with) **ambition** [æm'bɪʃn] for sth (or: to be sth / to do sth) / realize one's **ambitions** / have great **ambitions**
challenge ['tʃælɪndʒ]	herausfordern,	~ sb (+ to do sth / to sth) / ~ sb's right to do sth
	Herausforderung	receive a ~ from sb / accept sb's ~

reckon with ['rekən wið]	rechnen mit	~ ~ sb / a man to be ~ed ~
rival ['raɪvl]	rivalisieren,	~ with sb (+ for sth)
	Rivale	be ~s for sth / have ~s / be a ~ of sb (jemandem gleichkommen) / be old ~s / be in **rivalry** [-rɪ] with sb
opponent [ə'pəʊnənt]	Gegner	
envious ['envɪəs]	neidisch	be ~ of sb
envy ['envɪ]	beneiden, Neid	~ sb sth ~ feel ~
jealous ['dʒeləs]	eifersüchtig	be ~ of sb's success / feel **jealousy** [-ɪ]
match [mætʃ]	ebenbürtiger Gegner;	find (or: meet) one's ~ / be no ~ for sb / be more than a ~ for sb
	sich messen	No one can ~ him.
success [sek'ses]	Erfolg	have great (or: much / no) ~ / wish sb ~ / be **successful** [-fʊl] (+ in life / in work) / do sth **successfully** [-fʊlɪ]
succeed [sək'si:d]	Erfolg haben	He did not ~. / ~ in life / ~ in doing sth / ~ as ...
outdo (outdid, outdone) [ˌaʊt'du:, -'dɪd, -'dʌn]	ausstechen	~ one's rivals
surpass [sə'pɑ:s]	übertreffen	~ sb in strength (or: intelligence / skill)
yield [ji:ld]	nachgeben, zurückweichen	~ to sb / ~ to anything (sich alles gefallen lassen)
give (gave, given) **in** [gɪv, geɪv, 'gɪvn; –‿'ɪn]	nachgeben, einlenken	always ~ ~ to others
fail [feɪl]	versagen;	~ utterly (or: completely / hopelessly) / ~ to do sth / ~ in an examination / be a **failure** ['-jə*]
	fehlschlagen	one's plans ~ (= end in **failure**)

72 Social position – soziale Stellung (→ 101 Class)

role [rəʊl]	Rolle	play a ~ / play one's ~ / play the ~ of ... / play a leading ~ / fill a ~
status ['steɪtəs]	soziale Stellung, Status	seek (or: lose) ~ / be of high (or: low) ~ / have great (or: little) ~ / be equal (or: unequal) in ~ to sb / sth is a **status symbol** ['– ˌsɪmbl]

prestige [pre'sti:ʒ]	Ansehen, Prestige	gain (or: lose) ~ / have high (or: little / low) ~ (+ with others) / earn (or: enjoy) much (or: little) ~
privilege ['prɪvəlɪdʒ]	Vorrecht, Privileg	have (or: hold / enjoy / inherit / be granted) a ~ / have social (or: political / economic) ~s
right [raɪt]	Recht	have the ~ to do sth / have (or: enjoy) a ~
power ['paʊə*]	Macht	have (or: use) ~ / increase (or: lose) one's ~ / have much (or: great / little / no) ~ / be a **powerful** [-fl] man / **powerless** [-lɪs]
rank [ræŋk]	Rang,	have (or: hold) a ~ / have the ~ of colonel / have a high (or: low) ~ (+ in the army)
	im Rang stehen	~ above (or: below) sb / ~ high
appoint [ə'pɔɪnt]	ernennen	~ sb / be ~ed (+ to be) headmaster / get an **appointment** [-mənt] as headmaster
promote [prə'məʊt]	befördern	~ sb (+ from clerk to manager) / be ~d (+ to) manager / get a **promotion** [prə'məʊʃn] to manager
advance [əd'vɑ:ns]	aufrücken	~ to the rank of ... / ~ rapidly in one's career
career [kə'rɪə*]	Laufbahn, Karriere	enter a ~ / have a successful ~ / make a ~ for oneself / make teaching one's ~
office ['ɒfɪs]	Amt	hold (or: occupy / fill) an ~ / be in (or: out of) ~ / resign (+ one's) ~
post [pəʊst]	Posten	have (or: get / fill / hold / find) a (+ good / responsible) ~ as ...

Norm – Norm, Regel 73

allow [ə'laʊ]	erlauben	~ sb to do sth
let (let, let) [let, –, –]	zulassen, erlauben	~ sb do sth
norm [nɔ:m]	Norm, Regel	follow (or: break) a ~
evil ['i:vl]	Übel, Böses	avoid ~ / speak no ~
conform to [kən'fɔ:m tə]	sich richten nach, sich anpassen an	~ ~ a norm / ~ fully (or: closely / slavishly) ~ norms
conformity [kən'fɔ:mətɪ]	Anpassung	be (or: act) in ~ with (= to) a standard of behaviour
deviate ['di:vɪeɪt]	abweichen	~ from a norm / express **deviant** ['di:vjənt] views / **deviant** behaviour

form [fɔːm]	Form	observe ~ / pay attention to good ~ / sth is good (or: bad) ~ / a(n) **formal** ['-l] (or: **informal** [ɪn'-l]) meeting
convention [kən'venʃn]	Übereinkunft, Konvention	follow a ~ / be a slave to ~
etiquette ['etɪket] (*sing.* only)	Umgangsformen	observe ~ / sth is against ~
custom ['kʌstəm]	Brauch, Sitte	it is the ~ to do sth / do sth according to ~ / observe a ~ / be a slave to ~ / it is **customary** [-ərɪ] to do sth
moral ['mɒrəl]	moralisch	be a ~ being (= able to understand the difference between right and wrong) / have ~ ideals
morals ['mɒrəlz]	Moral	be a man of good (or: loose / bad) ~ / criticize sb's ~
morality [mə'rælətɪ]	Sittlichkeit	have a sense of ~
conscience ['kɒnʃəns]	Gewissen	have a clear (or: good/bad) ~ / act according to (or: against) one's ~
taboo [tə'buː]	tabu, Tabu, tabuisieren	do sth that is ~ / sth is (+ under) ~ ~ sth
value ['væljuː]	Wert	sth is a ~ in society / the social (or: moral / ethical) ~s of society
tradition [trə'dɪʃn]	Tradition	follow (or: look to) ~ when doing sth / it is a ~ for sb to do sth / have **traditional** [trə'dɪʃənl] rights
rule [ruːl]	Regel	obey a ~ / make a ~ that ... / keep (or: break) a ~ / as a ~
ceremony ['serɪmənɪ]	Zeremonie	perform a ~ / stand on ~
excuse [ɪk'skuːz] [ɪk'skuːs]	entschuldigen, Entschuldigung	**Excuse me!** / make an ~
criticize ['krɪtɪsaɪz]	kritisieren	~ sb (+ for doing sth / for not doing sth)

Our family – unsere Familie

74 Courting, marriage – Werben, Heirat

single ['sɪŋgl]	ledig	a ~ girl / be (or: remain) ~
bachelor ['bætʃələ*]	Junggeselle	be a confirmed (eingefleischter) ~
spinster ['spɪnstə*] (not polite)	(alte) Jungfer	an old ~
court [kɔːt]	umwerben	John has ~ed Mary for three years.
propose [prə'pəʊz]	einen Heiratsantrag machen	~ to sb

engaged [ɪn'geɪdʒd]	verlobt	be ~ (+ to sb) / be ~ to be married / get ~ to sb
fiancé [fɪ'ɑ̃:ŋseɪ]	Verlobter	be sb's ~
fiancée [fɪ'ɑ̃:ŋseɪ]	Verlobte	be sb's ~
match [mætʃ] (*inform.*)	Partie	sb is a good ~ / make a good ~
marry ['mærɪ]	heiraten	~ sb / ~ for love / They ~ied in 1965.
married ['mærɪd]	verheiratet	be ~ (+ to sb) / get ~ (+ to sb) / a ~ man / be **unmarried** [ˌʌn-] / a ~ couple
wedding ['wedɪŋ]	Hochzeit	celebrate one's ~ / October 1st is our **wedding-day** [-deɪ]. / wear a **wedding-ring** [-rɪŋ]
marriage ['mærɪdʒ]	Hochzeit,	have a church (or: civil) ~
	Ehe	a(n) happy (or: unhappy) ~
wedding anniversary ['– ˌænɪ'vɜ:sərɪ]	Hochzeitstag	celebrate one's (+ 14th) ~ ~.
bridegroom ['braɪdgrʊm]	Bräutigam	a nervous ~
bride ['braɪd]	Braut	Here comes the ~. / a lovely ~
best man [ˌbest 'mæn]	Brautführer	
husband ['hʌsbənd]	Ehemann	a good (or: an ideal) ~
wife [waɪf] (*pl.* wives [waɪvz])	Ehefrau	Mary is Stephen's ~.
couple ['kʌpl]	Paar	a married ~ / a nice ~
honeymoon ['hʌnɪmu:n]	Flitterwochen	spend one's ~ in ...
divorce [dɪ'vɔ:s]	scheiden, sich scheiden lassen,	The court ~d them. / They ~d (+ each other). / She ~d him. / be ~d (+ from sb)
	Scheidung	obtain a ~
widow ['wɪdəʊ]	Witwe	marry a rich ~ / be **widowed** [-d]
widower ['wɪdəʊə*]	Witwer	

Family – Familie (→ 2 Sex; 3 Name; 4 Age) 75

pregnant ['pregnənt]	schwanger	be ~ / have been ~ for four months / be four months ~ / This was her second **pregnancy** ['pregnənsɪ].
baby ['beɪbɪ]	Baby	be expecting a ~ / have a ~
child [tʃaɪld] (*pl.* children ['tʃɪldrən])	Kind	have children / be married with two children
son [sʌn]	Sohn	We've got two ~s.
daughter ['dɔ:tə*]	Tochter	They've got two ~s.

brother ['brʌðə*]	Bruder	I've got two elder ~s.
sister ['sɪstə*]	Schwester	I've got two younger ~s.
twin [twɪn]	Zwilling	The ~s are always together.
parents ['peərənts]	Eltern	love one's ~
father ['fɑːðə*]	Vater	be a ~ of three children / Can you help me, F~?
dad [dæd] = **daddy** ['dædɪ]	Papa	Go and ask D~.
mother ['mʌðə*]	Mutter	This is Bill's ~. / I asked M~ for money.
mum [mʌm] = **mummy** ['mʌmɪ]	Mama	Go and ask M~.
family ['fæməlɪ]	Familie	have a large (or: small) ~ / come from a good ~

76 Relatives – Verwandte

relative ['relətɪv]	Verwandte(-r)	He is a close ~ of mine. / a distant ~ / one's nearest ~
related [rɪ'leɪtɪd]	verwandt	How are you ~ to her? / be ~ by blood
relation [rɪ'leɪʃn]	Verwandte(-r)	He is a near ~ of mine. / the poor ~s

father-in-law	['fɑːðərɪnlɔː]	Schwiegervater
mother-in-law	['mʌðərɪnlɔː]	Schwiegermutter
son-in-law	['sʌnɪnlɔː]	Schwiegersohn
daughter-in-law	['dɔːtərɪnlɔː]	Schwiegertochter
brother-in-law	['brʌðərɪnlɔː]	Schwager
sister-in-law	['sɪstərɪnlɔː]	Schwägerin
grandmother	['græn,mʌðə*]	Großmutter
grandparents	['græn,peərənts]	Großeltern
grandpa	['græn,pɑː]	Opa
grandma	['græn,mɑː]	Oma

cousin	['kʌzn]	Vetter, Kusine
nephew	['nevjuː]	Neffe
niece	[niːs]	Nichte
uncle ['ʌŋkl]	Onkel	I've got seven ~s. / U~ Bill
aunt [ɑːnt]	Tante	I've got ten ~s. / A~ Mary
descent [dɪ'sent]	Abstammung	be of British ~
descend [dɪ'send] = **be descended** [-ɪd]	abstammen	~ (= ~ ~) from an old family
ancestor ['ænsestə*]	Ahne	His ~s came from France.
generation [,dʒenə'reɪʃn]	Generation	the older (or: younger) ~

Church – Kirche

Church building – Kirchengebäude 77

church [tʃɜːtʃ]	Kirche	the ~ of St Mary / a village ~ .
cathedral [kə'θiːdrəl]	Kathedrale, Dom	**St Paul's Cathedral** [snt 'pɔːlz –]
abbey ['æbɪ]	Abtei	**Westminster Abbey** [ˌwestmɪnstər‿'æbɪ]
monastery ['mɒnəstərɪ]	Kloster	live in a ~
nunnery ['nʌnərɪ]	Nonnenkloster	live in a ~
synagogue ['sɪnəgɒg]	Synagoge	
mosque [mɒsk]	Moschee	
temple ['templ]	Tempel	
chapel ['tʃæpl]	Kapelle	
steeple ['stiːpl]	Kirchturm	climb a ~ / The ~ rises high in the air.
spire ['spaɪə*]	Turm, Helm	a tall (or: sharp / pointed) ~
bell [bel]	Glocke	the **bell tower** ['– ˌtaʊə*]
ring (rang, rung) [rɪŋ, ræŋ, rʌŋ]	läuten	~ the bells for church / The bells are ~ing.
chime ['tʃaɪm]	Geläut, läuten, schlagen	listen to the ~ of the church bells ~ the bells / The bells are ~ing. The clock ~s two.
nave [neɪv]	(Lang-, Mittel-)Schiff	the ~ of St Peter's
pillar ['pɪlə*]	Säule	a high (or: stone) ~ / The roof is supported by eight ~s.
vault [vɔːlt]	Gewölbe	a ~ed roof
pulpit ['pʊlpɪt]	Kanzel	stand in the ~
altar ['ɔːltə*]	Altar	kneel down before the ~
candle ['kændl]	Kerze	light a ~ / a **candle-stick** [-ˌstɪk]
cross [krɒs]	Kreuz	
font [fɒnt]	Taufstein	

Service – Gottesdienst 78

priest [priːst]	Priester	(esp. in the Roman Catholic Church)
minister ['mɪnɪstə*]	Geistlicher, Prediger	(in the Presbyterian and Nonconformist Churches)
parson ['pɑːsn] (*inform.*)	Pastor	(in the Church of England)
vicar ['vɪkə*]	Pastor	(in the Church of England)
Reverend ['revərənd]	Titel eines Geistlichen	(+ The) ~ John Clark

Father ['fɑːðə*]	Pater (respektvolle Anrede des katholischen Geistlichen)	~ Brown
monk [mʌŋk]	Mönch	
nun [nʌn]	Nonne	
abbot ['æbət]	Abt	
bishop ['bɪʃəp]	Bischof	
archbishop [ˌɑːtʃ'bɪʃəp]	Erzbischof	
cardinal ['kɑːdɪnl]	Kardinal	
Pope ['pəʊp]	Papst	
rabbi ['ræbaɪ]	Rabbi, jüdischer Geistlicher	
congregation [ˌkɒŋgrɪ'geɪʃn]	(die zum Gottesdienst versammelte) Gemeinde	the ~ rises (or: is kneeling)
service ['sɜːvɪs]	Gottesdienst	The evening ~ is at 6.30.
attend [ə'tend]	besuchen	~ morning service
Sunday School ['sʌndɪ skuːl]	Bibelstunde	
mass = Mass [mæs]	Messe	hear (or: say) ~ / high ~ / Sunday ~
pray [preɪ]	beten	Let us ~. / ~ to God / say **prayers** ['preɪəz] / the **Lord's Prayer** [ˌlɔːdz 'preɪə*] (das Vaterunser)
hymn [hɪm]	Kirchenlied, Choral	sing a ~ / a ~ book
psalm [sɑːm]	Psalm	
choir ['kwaɪə]	Chor	sing in the church ~ / a **choir-boy** ['-bɔɪ] (or: **choir-girl** ['-gɜːl])
organ ['ɔːgən]	Orgel	play the ~ / an **organist** ['ɔːgənɪst]
Lesson ['lesn]	Lesung	read a ~ from the New (or: Old) Testament
Gospel ['gɒspl]	Evangelium	read from the ~ according to Saint Matthew
Epistle [ɪ'pɪsl]	Epistel	read from the ~ of Saint Peter
sermon ['sɜːmən]	Predigt	give (or: hold) a ~
preach [priːtʃ]	predigen	~ a sermon (or: the gospel) / ~ on sth
collection [kə'lekʃn]	Kollekte	
Communion [kə'mjuːnjən]	Abendmahl, Kommunion	go to ~ / Holy C~
bless [bles]	segnen	~ the congregation

Faith – Glaube (→ 120 Holiday) 79

Christ [kraɪst]	Christus	Jesus ~ / believe in ~ / **Christendom** ['krɪsndəm] (Christenheit)
Christian ['krɪstjən]	Christ,	be a good ~ / **Christianity** [ˌkrɪstɪ'ænətɪ] (Christentum)
	christlich	the ~ church / a ~ country
christen ['krɪsn]	taufen	~ a baby / She was ~ed Mary. / **christening** ['krɪsnɪŋ] (Taufe)
the Bible [ðə 'baɪbl]	die Bibel	
believe [bɪ'li:v]	glauben	~ in God
belief [bɪ'li:f]	Glaube,	lose one's ~ / ~ in God
	(religiöse) Überzeugung	one's religious ~s / the ~s of the Christian church
faith [feɪθ]	Glaube	have ~ in God / put one's ~ in God / the Roman Catholic and Protestant ~s
worship ['wɜ:ʃɪp]	anbeten, verehren	~ God
God [gɒd]	Gott (der Christen)	believe in ~ / pray to ~ / the Almighty ~
god [gɒd]	Gott	Neptune was the ~ of the sea. / Venus was a Roman **goddess** ['-ɪs].
Lord [lɔ:d]	Herr, Gott, Herrgott	praise the ~ / in the year of our ~ 1990
create [krɪ'eɪt]	erschaffen	'In the beginning God ~d the heaven and the earth.' (*Genesis I, 1*)
heaven ['hevn]	Himmel	go to ~ / 'Our Father who art in H~ ...'
angel ['eɪndʒl]	Engel	
saint [seɪnt]	Heilige(-r), heilig	pray to the ~s / S~ (= St) George is the **patron saint** ['peɪtrən –] of England.
sacred ['seɪkrɪd]	heilig, geheiligt, geistlich	~ music (or: writings / animals)
holy ['həʊlɪ]	heilig	the **Holy Bible** [həʊlɪ 'baɪbl] (or: **Land** ['– lænd] / **Father** ['– 'fɑ:ðə*])
soul [səʊl]	Seele	lose one's ~ / ~s resting in heaven / the immortality (Unsterblichkeit) of the ~
commandment [kə'mɑ:ndmənt]	Gebot	the **Ten Commandments** [ten -s]
temptation [temp'teɪʃn]	Versuchung	resist a ~ / 'Lead us not into ~...'
sin [sɪn]	Sünde	commit a mortal (or: deadly) ~ / the original ~ (Erbsünde) / **sinful** ['-fʊl] / be a **sinner** ['-ə*]

guilty ['gɪltɪ]	schuldig	be ~ of many sins
the Devil [ðə 'devl]	der Teufel	
damn [dæm]	verdammen	the **damned** [-d]
hell [hel]	Hölle	go to ~
repent [rɪ'pent]	bereuen	~ one's sins / ~ having done wrong / a **repenting** [-ɪŋ] sinner
confess [kən'fes]	bekennen, beichten	~ one's sins / hear **confessions** [kən'feʃnz]
penance ['penəns]	Buße	do (+ hard) ~ (+ for one's sins)
forgive (forgave, forgiven) [fə'gɪv, fə'geɪv, fə'gɪvn]	verzeihen, begnadigen	~ one's sins
save [seɪv]	erlösen	~ a sinner / Christ the **Saviour** ['seɪvjə*]

Our school – unsere Schule

80 School building – Schulgebäude

playground = school yard = yard	['pleɪgraʊnd] ['sku:l ˌjɑ:d], [jɑ:d]	Schulhof
office	['ɒfɪs]	Sekretariat
headmaster's room = ~ office / ~ study	[hed'mɑ:stəz ˌrʊm] [– ˌɒfɪs], [– ˌstʌdɪ]	Direktorzimmer
staff room	['stɑ:f rʊm]	Lehrerzimmer
classroom	['klɑ:srʊm]	Klassenraum
language lab	['læŋgwɪdʒ ˌlæb]	Sprachlabor
biology lab	[baɪ'ɒlədʒɪ ˌlæb]	Biologiesaal
chemistry lab	['kemɪstrɪ ˌlæb]	Chemiesaal
physics lab	['fɪzɪks ˌlæb]	Physiksaal
music room	['mju:zɪk rʊm]	Musiksaal
map room	['mæp rʊm]	Kartenraum
assembly hall (*BE*) **= auditorium** (*AE*)	[ə'semblɪ hɔ:l], [ˌɔ:dɪ'tɔrɪəm]	Aula
art room	['ɑ:t rʊm]	Kunstraum
workshop	['wɜ:kʃɔp]	Werkraum
gymnasium = gym	[dʒɪm'neɪzjəm], [dʒɪm]	Turnhalle
changing room	['tʃeɪndʒɪŋ rʊm]	Umkleideraum
lavatory	['lævətərɪ]	Toilette
sports field (*BE*) **= athletics field** (*AE*)	['spɔ:ts fi:ld], [æθ'letɪks fi:ld]	Sportplatz
bicycle stands	['baɪsɪkl stændz]	Fahrradständer

Staff – Lehrkörper, die Lehrer 81

staff (*BE*)	[stɑːf],	Lehrkörper, die Lehrer und Lehrerinnen
= **faculty** (*AE*)	['fækltɪ]	
headmaster	[ˌhed'mɑːstə*]	Direktor
= **head** = **principal**	[hed], ['prɪnsəpl]	
headmistress	[ˌhed'mɪstrɪs]	Direktorin
teacher	['tiːtʃə*]	Lehrer(-in)
caretaker (*BE*)	['keəˌteɪkə*]	Hausmeister
= **janitor** (*AE*)	['dʒænɪtə*]	
form master	['fɔːm ˌmɑːstə]	Klassenlehrer
form mistress	['fɔːm ˌmɪstrɪs]	Klassenlehrerin
games teacher	['geɪmz ˌtiːtʃə*]	Sportlehrer(in)

Time-table – Stundenplan 82

schedule ['ʃedjuːl] (*AE*)	Stundenplan	
period ['pɪərɪəd]	Unterrichtsstunde (als Zeiteinheit)	have four ~s in the morning / What lesson have you got next ~?
break [breɪk] (*BE*) = **recess** [rɪ'ses] (*AE*)	Pause	have a ~ from ... to ...
lesson ['lesn]	Stunde	have an English ~
subject ['sʌbdʒɪkt]	Fach	one's favourite ~ is ... / a main ~ / take (or: drop) a ~
good at ['gʊd‿ət]	gut in	be ~ ~ English
bad at ['bæd‿ət]	schlecht, schwach in	be ~ ~ English
requirement [rɪ'kwaɪəmənt] (*AE*)	Pflichtfach	
elective [ɪ'lektɪv] (*AE*)	Wahlfach	
course [kɔːs]	Kurs	take a ~ in ...
English	['ɪŋglɪʃ]	Englisch
German	['dʒɜːmən]	Deutsch
French	[frentʃ]	Französisch
Latin	['lætɪn]	Latein
Spanish	['spænɪʃ]	Spanisch
History	['hɪstərɪ]	Geschichte
Geography	[dʒɪ'ɒgrəfɪ]	Erdkunde
Mathematics	[ˌmæθə'mætɪks],	Mathematik
= **Maths** (*inform.*)	[mæθs],	
= **Math** (*AE*)	[mæθ]	
Computer Studies	[kəm'pjuːtə 'stʌdɪz]	Informatik
Physics	['fɪzɪks]	Physik
Chemistry	['kemɪstrɪ]	Chemie

Art	[ɑːt]	Kunst
Drawing	['drɔːɪŋ]	Zeichnen
Religious Education	[rɪ'lɪdʒəs‿edjuː'keɪʃn]	Religionsunterricht
Woodwork	['wʊdwɜːk]	Werken
Music	['mjuːzɪk]	Musik
P.E. (= Physical Education)	['piː 'iː], ['fɪzɪkl ˌedjuː'keɪʃn]	Leibesübungen
Domestic Science	[də'mestɪk 'saɪəns]	Hauswirtschaft
Needlework	['niːdlwɜːk]	Handarbeit
General Studies	['dʒenərəl ˌstʌdiːz]	Gemeinschaftskunde
extra-curricular activities	[ˌekstrəkə'rɪkjələr‿æk-'tɪvətɪz]	Arbeitsgemeinschaften

83 In class – in der Klasse

classroom ['klɑːsrʊm]	Klassenraum	After break we go back to our ~.
blackboard ['blækbɔːd] = **board** [bɔːd]	Tafel	write (or: draw) sth on the ~ / clean (or: wipe) the ~
chalk [tʃɔːk]	Kreide	Isn't there a piece of ~ anywhere? / There is no ~.
duster ['dʌstə*]	Tafellappen	With a wet ~ you'll never have a clean board.
overhead projector [ˌəʊvəhed prə'dʒektə*]	Tageslichtschreiber	
map [mæp]	(Land-)Karte	fetch a ~ of Europe / hang a ~ on the **map-stand** ['-stænd]
table ['teɪbl]	Tisch	go to one's ~ / arrange the ~s in a circle (or: in groups of four)
desk [desk]	Pult	
seat [siːt]	Platz, Sitz	have a ~ in the front row
register ['redʒɪstə*]	Klassenbuch	Where is the ~? / mark the ~
be absent [biː 'æbsent]	fehlen	Who is ~ today?
note [nəʊt]	Entschuldigung (als Zettel)	You were absent yesterday. Have you got a ~?
homework ['həʊmwɜːk] = **assignments** [ə'saɪnmənts] (*AE*)	Hausaufgabe(n)	Today's h~ is to learn these new words. / Your a~ will be to read ...
get (got, got) [get, gɒt, –]	kommen (mit dem Stoff)	How far did we ~ with ...? / In the last lesson we got to page 10.

Useful classroom phrases

How do you spell ...?	Wie spricht man ... aus?
Do I need a comma?	Gehört hier ein Komma hin?
I'm not sure how to say the next word.	Ich bin mir nicht sicher, wie man das nächste Wort ausspricht.
Which tense do I need?	Welche Zeitform braucht man hier?
Could you use the ... here?	Kann man den / die / das ... hier nehmen?
What's the meaning of ...?	Was heißt / bedeutet ...?
What's the German for this word?	Was heißt das Wort auf deutsch?

Some apologies

I'm sorry I'm late; I've been to ...	Es tut mir leid, daß ich zu spät komme. Ich war (noch) bei / in ...
I'm sorry I don't know.	Das weiß ich leider nicht.
I'm afraid I've left my book at home.	Leider habe ich mein Buch zu Hause gelassen.

book [bʊk]	Buch	an English ~ / Open your ~s, page 10, line 5. / Shut your ~s.
page [peɪdʒ]	Seite	turn the ~ / turn to ~ 5
skip [skɪp]	überschlagen	~ page 5 and go on to page 6
reader ['ri:də*]	Lesebuch	
textbook ['teksbʊk]	Schulbuch	
exercise book ['eksəsaɪz bʊk]	Heft	copy sth into one's ~ ~ / hand in one's ~ ~
rough book ['rʌf bʊk]	Kladde, Konzeptheft	This exercise is to be done in your ~ ~s.
neat book ['ni:t bʊk]	Hausheft	Your homework is to be done in your ~ ~s and given in tomorrow.
prepare [prɪ'peə*]	vorbereiten	~ page 5
revise [rɪ'vaɪz]	wiederholen	~ what one has learnt up to now
written test ['rɪtn test]	Klassenarbeit	do a ~ ~
paper ['peɪpə*]	schriftliche Arbeit	a **test paper** ['test ˌ–] / return the ~s
dictation [dɪk'teɪʃn]	Diktat	write a ~
composition [ˌkɒmpə'zɪʃn]	Aufsatz	write a ~
essay ['eseɪ]	Aufsatz	plan (or: write) an ~ / write an ~ on 'The Daily Newspaper'
subject ['sʌbdʒɪkt]	Thema	The ~ of the essay is 'The Daily Newspaper'.
plan [plæn]	Gliederung	set out a ~ in detail / essay ~

introduction [ˌintrəˈdʌkʃn]	Einleitung	begin with a short ~
main body [ˈmeɪn ˈbɒdɪ]	Hauptteil	
conclusion [kənˈklu:ʒn]	Schluß	
copy [ˈkɒpɪ]	abschreiben	~ sth from the board / ~ sb's work
tally [ˈtælɪ]	übereinstimmen	Some passages ~ in every detail.
wrong [rɒŋ]	falsch	~ punctuation (or: spelling)
mark [mɑ:k] (*BE*)	korrigieren;	~ a paper
= **grade** [greɪd](*AE*)	Note	get good (or: bad) ~s
report [rɪˈpɔ:t] = **report-card** [rɪˈpɔ:tkɑ:d] (*AE*)	Zeugnis	

84 Going to school, leaving school – zur Schule gehen, die Schule verlassen

school [sku:l]	Schule	go to ~ / start (or: leave) ~ / spend 12 years at ~ / S~ begins at 8.30. / finish ~

nursery school[1]	[ˈnɜ:sərɪ sku:l]	Vorschule
infant school[2]	[ˈɪnfənt sku:l]	Grundschule (Unterstufe)
junior school[3]	[ˈdʒu:nɪə sku:l]	Grundschule (Oberstufe)
comprehensive school[4]	[ˌkɒmprɪˈhensɪv sku:l]	Gesamtschule
streaming	[ˈstri:mɪŋ]	Aufteilung der Schüler eines Jahrgangs nach ihrem Leistungsvermögen in mehrere Züge
setting	[ˈsetɪŋ]	Aufteilung der Schüler nach ihrem Leistungsvermögen innerhalb der einzelnen Fächer
mixed ability grouping	[mɪkst əˈbɪlətɪ gru:pɪŋ]	keine Aufteilung der Schüler
secondary school	[ˈsekəndrɪ sku:l]	weiterführende Schule
grammar school	[ˈgræmə sku:l]	etwa: Gymnasium
public school	[ˌpʌblɪk ˈsku:l]	etwa: Freie Schule
preparatory school = **prep school**	[prɪˈpærətrɪ sku:l] [ˈprep sku:l]	Schule, die auf den Besuch einer **public school** vorbereitet

[1] for children aged 3 to 5
[2] for children aged 5 to 7
[3] for children aged 7 to 11
[4] 90% of English school children attend a comprehensive school

pupil	['pju:pl]	Schüler(in)
schoolboy	['sku:lbɔɪ]	Schuljunge, Schüler
schoolgirl	['sku:lgɜ:l]	Schulmädchen, Schülerin
student (*AE*)	['stu:dnt]	Schüler(in)
schoolchildren	['sku:ltʃɪldrən]	Schüler(innen)
student (*BE*)	['stju:dnt]	Student(in)
C.S.E. (*BE*)[1]	[ˌsi: es 'i:]	entspricht dem Hauptschulabschluß
G.C.E. O level (*BE*)[2]	[ˌdʒi: si: 'i: 'eʊ ˌlevl]	mittlerer Bildungsabschluß (mit dem Recht, in die 'Sixth Form', etwa: Oberstufe, einzutreten)
G.C.E. A level (*BE*)[3]	[ˌdʒi: si: 'i: 'eɪ levl]	höherer Bildungsabschluß (als Voraussetzung für den Besuch einer Hochschule)
G.C.S.E. (*BE*)[4]	['dʒi: si: es 'i:]	Bildungsabschluß seit 1988, ersetzt das G.C.E. und C.S.E.
high school diploma	['haɪ sku:l dɪ'pləʊmə] (*AE*)	etwa: Mittlere Reife, Hauptschulabschluß
grade [greɪd]	Abschlußnote	receive a ~
examination [ɪgˌzæmɪ'neɪʃn]	Prüfung	take an ~ / pass (or: fail) an ~ / the G.C.E. O level ~
pass [pɑ:s]	bestehen	~ an examination / ~ a subject / ~ in five subjects
fail [feɪl]	durchfallen	~ an examination / ~ a subject
A, B, C, D, E	Sehr gut, Gut ... (im G.C.E.-Examen)	get an A in French / get two B's
1, 2, 3, 4, 5, 6	Sehr gut, Gut ... (im C.S.E.-Examen)	
college ['kɒlɪdʒ]	Schule, Kolleg (*BE*); Kolleg, Teil der Universität (*BE*), Hochschule (*BE*); Fakultät (*AE*); Kolleg, Studienschule (die auf die Universität vorbereitet) (*AE*)	**Eton College** [ˌi:tn 'kɒlɪdʒ] **King's College**, [ˌkɪŋz 'kɒlɪdʒ], Cambridge a technical ~ / a teacher-training ~ the ~ of medicine (or: law) Peter will go to ~ next year when he finishes school.

[1] Certificate of Secondary Education [sə'tɪfɪkeɪt‿əv 'sekəndərɪ ˌedju:'keɪʃn]
[2] General Certificate of Education Ordinary level [ˌdʒenərəl sə'tɪfɪkeɪt‿əv ˌedju:'keɪʃn 'ɔ:dnrɪ 'levl]
[3] General Certificate of Education Advanced level [– əd'vɑ:nst 'levl]
[4] General Certificate of Secondary Education [– 'sekəndərɪ –]

Our country – unser Land

85 Constitution – Verfassung

constitution [ˌkɒnstɪ'tju:ʃn]	Verfassung	the ~ of the U.S.A. / draw up (or: change / abolish) a ~ / a(n) written (or: unwritten) ~
freedom ['fri:dəm]	Freiheit	have ~s / the basic (or: fundamental / human) ~s / ~ of speech (or: religious worship / the press) / ~ from want (or: fear / arbitrary arrest – willkürliche Verhaftung)
democracy [dɪ'mɒkrəsɪ]	Demokratie	
democratic [ˌdemə'krætɪk]	demokratisch	
liberty ['lɪbətɪ]	(die bürgerliche) Freiheit	~ of conscience / religious ~ / struggle for (+ civil) ~ies
equality [i:'kwɒlətɪ]	Gleichheit	"**Liberty**, **equality**, **fraternity**" (Brüderlichkeit)
rights [raɪts]	Rechte	stand up for one's ~ / have ~s / protect (or: defend) the **rights of man** / fight for one's ~
article ['ɑ:tɪkl]	Artikel	the seven ~s of the US Constitution
amend [ə'mend]	(eine Verfassung) ergänzen	~ a constitution / the **Ten Original Amendments** [-mənts] to the American Constitution
citizen ['sɪtɪzn]	Bürger	be a ~ of the United Kingdom
subject ['sʌbdʒɪkt]	Untertan	the King's ~s
national ['næʃənl]	Staatsangehöriger	foreign ~s / German ~s in the U.K. / have (or: possess) British **nationality** [ˌnæʃə'nælətɪ]
government ['gʌvnmənt]	Herrschaft, Regierung	"G~ of the people, by the people, for the people." / central (or: local / military) ~
head of state ['hed‿əv 'steɪt]	Staatsoberhaupt	Elizabeth II is the ~ ~ ~ of the United Kingdom.
crown [kraʊn]	Krone (als Amt), Krone (als Herrschaftszeichen), krönen	succeed to the C~ / wear a ~ / ~ sb king
coronation [ˌkɒrə'neɪʃn]	Krönung	the ~ of Queen Elizabeth II

king [kɪŋ]	König	be (or: become) ~ / be crowned ~ / K~ Henry VIII
queen [kwi:n]	Königin	be (or: become) ~ / Q~ Elizabeth II
rule [ru:l]	herrschen, regieren,	~ a country
	Herrschaft, Regierung	under the ~ of ... / the ~ of the Tudors / be the **ruler** ['-ə*] of ...
reign [reɪn]	regieren,	~ from ... to ... / The Queen of England ~s but doesn't rule.
	Herrschaft, Regierungszeit	during Henry VIII's ~
royal ['rɔɪəl]	königlich	the **Royal Family** [ˌ– 'fæməlɪ]
throne [θrəʊn]	Thron	sit on the ~ / come to the ~ / lose one's ~
ascend [ə'send]	besteigen	~ the throne
abdicate ['æbdɪkeɪt]	abdanken	~ (+ from the throne)
president ['prezɪdənt]	Präsident	elect a ~ / be elected ~ / the P~ of the United States / Mr P~ / a **presidential** [ˌprezɪ'denʃl] election
prime minister [ˌpraɪm 'mɪnɪstə*]	Premierminister	
chancellor ['tʃɑ:nsələ*]	Kanzler	
power ['paʊə*]	Macht, Gewalt	have (= possess) ~ / use (= exercise) ~ / have much (or: great / little) ~ / come to ~

Party – Partei 86

party ['pɑ:tɪ]	Partei	found (or: form / organize) a ~ / belong to a ~ / an area is a traditional stronghold (Hochburg) of a ~
leader ['li:də*]	Vorsitzender, Führer	be a party ~ / follow a ~
following ['fɒləʊɪŋ]	Gefolge	a political leader with a large ~
headquarters [ˌhed'kwɔ:təz]	Zentrale	party ~
member ['membə*]	Mitglied	be a party ~
programme ['prəʊgræm] (*BE*) = **program** [–] (*AE*)	(politisches) Programm	a party ~ / adopt (verabschieden) a ~
platform ['plætfɔ:m]	(Wahl-)Programm	adopt a ~
policy ['pɒləsɪ]	Politik, politische Linie, politische Absicht	follow a ~ / carry out one's ~ / foreign (or: incomes) ~
ideology [ˌaɪdɪ'ɒlədʒɪ]	Ideologie, Weltanschauung (gleich welcher Richtung)	support an ~ / adhere to an ~

87 Election – Wahl

candidate ['kændɪdət]	Kandidat	be a ~ for mayor / stand as a ~ for Parliament
stand (stood, stood) **for** [stænd, stʊd, –; '– fə*] (*BE*) = **run** (ran, run) **for** [rʌn, ræn, rʌn; '– fər](*AE*)	kandidieren für	~ ~ Parliament / ~ ~ the Presidency / ~ ~ an office
seat [siːt]	Sitz	win (or: lose) a ~ / a safe (or: marginal) ~ / gain 25 ~s
constituency [kən'stɪtjʊənsɪ] (*BE*)	Wahlkreis	a small (or: large) ~
congressional district [kəŋ'greʃnl 'dɪstrɪkt] (*AE*)	Wahlkreis	the 18th ~ ~ of New York
campaign [kæm'peɪn]	Wahlkampf	fight a ~
vote [vəʊt]	Stimme,	give one's ~ to sb (or: for sth) / receive a lot of ~s
	stimmen, wählen;	~ for sb (or: sth) / ~ yes (or: no) / have the right to ~
	Vertrauensvotum, Abstimmung, Wahl;	a ~ of confidence
	Stimmrecht	have the ~
voter ['vəʊtə*]	Wähler	win over ~s
poll [pəʊl]	Wahl, Abstimmung;	go to the ~s / the ~ begins at ...
	Wahlbeteiligung,	a heavy (or: light / low / poor) ~
	(Stimmen) auf sich vereinigen	~ one-third of the votes cast
elect [ɪ'lekt]	wählen	~ a president / ~ sb as one's M. P. / ~ sb (+ to be) president / be ~ed president
election [ɪ'lekʃn]	Wahl	hold (or: fight / win / lose) an ~ / put sb up for an ~ / **General Election** [ˌdʒenrəl –] (Unterhauswahl) / **by-election** ['baɪ-] (Nachwahl)
polling booth ['pəʊlɪŋ buːð]	Wahlkabine	
polling station ['pəʊlɪŋ ˌsteɪʃn]	Wahllokal	
polling day ['pəʊlɪŋ deɪ]	Wahltag	

ballot ['bælət]	Wahlgang, (geheime) Abstimmung	a secret ~ vote by ~
turnout ['tɜ:naʊt]	Wahlbeteiligung	a high (or: low) ~
return [rɪ'tɜ:n]	(in das Parlament) wählen	~ sb to Parliament
ballot paper ['bælət ˌpeɪpə*]	Stimmzettel	

Parliament, Congress – Parlament 88

Parliament ['pɑ:ləmənt]	(das englische) Parlament, Unterhaus	enter (or: go into / get into) ~ / stand for ~ / speak in ~ / the **Houses of Parliament** [ˌhaʊzɪs əv '–]
sit (sat, sat) [sɪt, sæt, –]	tagen	Parliament ~s at Westminster. / The House is ~ting.
rise (rose, risen) [raɪz, rəʊz, 'rɪzn]	die Sitzung beenden	Parliament ~s.
summon ['sʌmən]	einberufen	Parliament is ~ed to meet.
dissolve [dɪ'zɒlv]	auflösen	~ Parliament
House of Commons [ˌhaʊs‿əv 'kɒmənz] (*BE*)	Unterhaus	be a member of the ~ ~ ~ / the rights (or: liberties) of the ~ ~ ~
M.P. [ˌem'pi:]= **MP** = **Member of Parliament** ['membər‿əv '–] (*BE*)	Mitglied des Parlaments	Sir Harold Wilson, former ~
front bench [ˌfrʌnt 'bentʃ]	eine der beiden vorderen Bänke (auf denen die führenden Abgeordneten ihren Platz haben)	sit on the ~ ~es / a ~-~ ['--] MP / the Government (or: opposition) ~ ~ / be a **front-bencher** [ˌfrʌnt'bentʃə*]
back bench [ˌbæk 'bentʃ]	eine der hinteren Bänke (auf denen die übrigen Abgeordneten ihren Platz haben)	sit on the ~ ~es / a ~-~ ['- -] MP / be a **back-bencher** [ˌbæk 'bentʃə*]
opposition [ˌɒpə'zɪʃn]	Opposition	be in ~ / go into ~ / Her Majesty's loyal O~
Shadow Cabinet [ˌʃædəʊ 'kæbɪnɪt]	Schattenkabinett	be a member of the ~ ~
the Speaker [ðe 'spi:kə*]	der Sprecher[1]	

[1] Vorsitzender des Unterhauses (*BE*); Präsident des Repräsentantenhauses (*AE*)

House of Lords [ˌhaʊs‿əv 'lɔ:dz] (*BE*)	Oberhaus	have a seat in the ~ ~ ~
peer [pɪə*] (*BE*)	Peer, Adliger (mit Sitz im Oberhaus)	a hereditary (or: life) ~ / raise sb to the **peerage** ['-rɪdʒ] (Peerswürde)
congress ['kɒŋgres] (*AE*)	Kongress	be a member of ~ / **congressman** [-mən] / **congresswoman** [-wʊmən]
House of Representatives ['– – ˌreprɪ'zentətɪvz] (*AE*)	Repräsentantenhaus	
Senate ['senɪt] (*AE*)	Senat	
senator ['senətər] (*AE*)	Senator	an influential ~

89 Sitting – Sitzung

sitting ['sɪtɪŋ]	Sitzung	attend a ~ / an all-night ~
meet (met, met) [mi:t, met, –]	zusammentreten	The House will ~ at 2.30 p.m.
proceedings [prə'sidɪŋz]	Verhandlungen, Beratungen	bring the ~ to a conclusion
order ['ɔ:də*]	Geschäftsordnung	call to ~ / O~! O~!
order of the day ['ɔ:dər‿əv ðə 'deɪ]	Tagesordnung	pass to the ~ ~ ~ ~
question time ['kwestʃən taɪm]	Fragestunde	hold ~ ~
bill [bɪl]	Gesetzesvorlage	introduce (or: bring in / debate) a ~
read (read, read) [ri:d, red, –]	lesen, beraten	~ a bill / the **First** (or: **Second** / **Third**) **Reading** [ˌfɜ:st / ˌsekənd / ˌθɜ:d 'ri:dɪŋ]
committee [kə'mɪtɪ]	Ausschuß	examine a bill in ~ / sit on a ~
chairman ['tʃeəmən]	Vorsitzender	
report [rɪ'pɔ:t]	Bericht (an das Plenum)	debate on a ~
debate [dɪ'beɪt]	Debatte,	open a ~ / speak in a ~ / hold a ~ on sth
	debattieren	~ a question
speech [spi:tʃ]	Rede	make (= deliver) a ~ / the freedom (= liberty) of ~
motion ['məʊʃn]	Antrag	make (or: put / bring forward) a ~ / a ~ is carried (or: lost)
move [mu:v]	beantragen	~ an amendment (Abänderung)

vote [vəʊt]	abstimmen, Abstimmung; Stimme	~ 'No' / ~ 'Aye' [aɪ] take a ~ give one's ~ for ...
carry ['kærɪ]	durchbringen	~ a bill (or: motion)
pass [pɑːs]	verabschieden, verabschiedet werden	~ a bill a bill ~es
act [ækt]	Gesetz	pass an ~ / an **Act of Parliament** [ˌ–‿əv 'pɑːləmənt] (or: **Congress** [ˌ–‿əv 'kɒŋgres])

Government – Regierung 90

govern ['gʌvn]	regieren	~ a country / Do you know how Britain is ~ed? / a Labour (or: Conservative) **Government** [-mənt]
policy ['pɒləsɪ]	Politik, politische Linie	
politics ['pɒlɪtɪks]	Politik, Staatskunst	
overthrow (overthrew, overthrown) [ˌəʊvə'θrəʊ, -'θruː, -'θrəʊn]	stürzen	~ the Government
resign [rɪ'zaɪn]	zurücktreten	The Government has ~ed.
administration [ədˌmɪnɪ'streɪʃn]	Regierung (*AE*); Verwaltung, Durchführung	the Busch A~ / the national ~ the ~ of law
Prime Minister [ˌpraɪm 'mɪnɪstə*] (*BE*)	Premierminister	
President ['prezɪdənt] (*AE*)	Präsident	be elected (+ to the office of) ~
term [tɜːm]	Amtszeit	be elected for a four-year ~ / serve two ~s
cabinet ['kæbɪnɪt]	Kabinett	a ~ meeting
department [dɪ'pɑːtmənt]	Ministerium	run a ~ / the government ~s

Public finance – öffentliche Finanzen 91

budget ['bʌdʒɪt]	Etat, Haushaltsplan	introduce the ~ (+ in the House of Commons / in Congress)
expenditure [ɪk'spendɪtʃə*]	Ausgabe	control (or: increase / limit) public ~

revenue ['revənju:]	Einnahme	public (or: Government) ~ / **Inland Revenue** [ˌɪnlənd '–] (Finanzverwaltung) (*BE*) / the raising of ~
tax [tæks]	Steuer,	pay ~es / increase ~es (+ by 2.5%) / pay **income tax** ['ɪŋkəm ˌ–]
	besteuern	~ sth (+ heavily) / grumble (= complain) about high **taxation** [tæk'seɪʃn] / **sales tax** ['seɪlz –] (Warenumsatzsteuer)
VAT [ˌvi: eɪ 'ti:] = **Value Added Tax** [ˌvælju: 'ædɪd 'tæks]	Mehrwertsteuer	charge 14% ~
rate [reɪt]	Gemeindesteuer	pay ~s / the water ~ / **rate-payer** ['– ˌpeɪə*]
customs ['kʌstəmz]	Zoll	pass (= get) through the ~ / **customs officer** ['– ˌɒfɪsə]
declare [dɪ'kleə*]	deklarieren, (beim Zoll) angeben	have nothing to ~
duty ['dju:tɪ]	Abgabe, Zoll	pay ~ on sth / pay ~ at the customs / a **duty-free** [ˌ– 'fri:] shop

92 Foreign policy – Außenpolitik

international [ˌɪntə'næʃnl]	international	~ relations (or: politics) / **international law** (Völkerrecht)
foreign ['fɒrən]	auswärtig	~ relations / the ~ service / the **Foreign Office** [ˌ– 'ɒfɪs] (*BE*)
diplomat ['dɪpləmæt]	Diplomat	join (or: be in) the **diplomatic service** [ˌdɪplə'mætɪk '–]
ambassador [æm'bæsədə*]	Botschafter	the French ~ in London / send (or: receive) an ~ / the French ~ to the USA
embassy ['embəsɪ]	Botschaft	the German ~ in Washington
power ['paʊə*]	Macht	the **Great Powers** [greɪt '-z] / a sea ~
tension ['tenʃn]	Spannung	reduce international ~
conference ['kɒnfərəns]	Konferenz	hold a ~ / a ~ of West European states
summit meeting ['sʌmɪt ˌmi:tɪŋ]	Gipfeltreffen	
negotiate [nɪ'gəʊʃɪeɪt]	verhandeln	~ with sb on sth / ~ for a peaceful settlement / start (or: enter into / carry on) **negotiations** [nɪˌgəʊʃɪ'eɪʃnz]

agreement [ə'gri:mənt]	Übereinkunft	come to (or: arrive at / make / reach / sign / break) an ~ / a **trade agreement** ['treɪd –]
treaty ['tri:tɪ]	Vertrag	conclude (or: sign / break) a ~ / a **peace treaty** ['pi:s ˌtri:tɪ] / the **North Atlantic Treaty Organization (NATO)** ['neɪtəʊ]
pact [pækt]	Pakt	make (or: conclude / sign / break / ignore) a ~ / a ~ between two nations
ally ['ælaɪ]	sich verbünden	be **allied**[1] [ə'laɪd] with a country / the **allied**[1] ['ælaɪd] forces / enter into an **alliance** [ə'laɪəns] with another country / make (= form) an **alliance** / an **alliance** between two countries / the **allied** status of Berlin
allies ['ælaɪz]	Alliierte, Verbündete	
neutral ['nju:trəl]	neutral	a ~ country / be (or: remain) ~ / **neutrality** [nju:'trælətɪ]
peace [pi:s]	Friede	make ~ (+ with sb) / be at ~ with a country / sign a **peace treaty** ['– ˌtri:tɪ]

The armed forces – die Streitkräfte 93

service ['sɜ:vɪs]	Wehrdienst	see active ~ in a war / be on active ~ / military ~ / **serviceman** [-mən] (*BE*)
services ['sɜ:vɪsɪz] = **forces** ['fɔ:sɪz]	Streitkräfte	be in (or: join) the (+ armed) ~
army ['ɑ:mɪ]	Heer, Armee	join the ~ / be in the ~ / an ~ officer the 8th A~
navy ['neɪvɪ]	Marine	join the ~ / be in the ~ / have a small ~ of 25 ships
fleet [fli:t]	Flotte	
air force ['eəfɔ:s]	Luftwaffe	join the ~ ~ / be in the ~ ~
RAF [ˌɑ:r‿eɪ 'ef], [ræf] (*inform.*)	die königliche Luftwaffe	join the ~
call up [kɔ:l 'ʌp] (*BE*)	einberufen	He was ~ed ~ in 1942. / be ~ed ~ for military service
draft [drɑ:ft], [dræ:ft] (*AE*)	einberufen	be ~ed into the army / a **draftee** ['-i:] (Wehrpflichtiger)
serve [sɜ:v]	dienen	~ in the army

[1] allied is generally pronounced ['ælaɪd] when attributive

conscientious objector [kɒnʃɪˌenʃəs əb'dʒektə*]	Kriegsdienstverweigerer	
desert [dɪ'zɜːt]	desertieren	~ one's post / ~ the colours
drill [drɪl]	Exerzieren, drillen	perform (or: carry out) ~ ~ soldiers / soldiers are ~ed in sth
order ['ɔːdə*]	Befehl	give an ~ / shout (or: bark) an ~ / obey an ~
soldier ['səʊldʒə*]	Soldat	a brave (or: fine) ~
uniform ['juːnɪfɔːm]	Uniform	wear (+ a) ~
the ranks [ðə 'ræŋks] (*BE*) = **enlisted men** [ɪn'lɪstɪd men] (*AE*)	die Mannschaften	belong to ~ ~ (= the ~ ~)
N.C.O. [ˌen siː 'əʊ]	Unteroffizier	~'s
officer ['ɒfɪsə*]	Offizier	be an army ~

94 War – Krieg

war [wɔː*]	Krieg	declare ~ (+ on ...) / be at ~ (+ with ...) / go to ~ (+ against ...) / put an end to ~ / **the Great War** [ðə ˌgreɪt '–] (der Erste Weltkrieg) / **the Second World War** [ðə 'sekənd ˌwɜːld '–] / **prisoner of war** [ˌprɪznər‿əv '–] (= *P.O.W.*)
warfare ['wɔːfeə*]	Kriegführung	chemical (or: total / nuclear) ~
attack [ə'tæk]	angreifen,	~ the enemy (or: a town / a fleet) / ~ bravely
	Angriff	make (or: begin) an ~ (+ on the enemy) / come under ~ / repel (abschlagen) an ~
raid [reɪd]	(überraschender) Angriff	make a ~ on a town (or: the coast) / be killed in an **air-raid** ['eə-]
advance [əd'vɑːns]	vormarschieren, Vormarsch	~ in the direction of ... the German ~ through Belgium
storm [stɔːm]	Sturmangriff, stürmen	take by ~ ~ a position
surround [sə'raʊnd]	umzingeln	~ the enemy
take (took, taken) [teɪk, tʊk, 'teɪkən] = **seize** [siːz]	einnehmen	~ a town
occupy ['ɒkjʊpaɪ]	besetzen	~ a country (or: town)

besiege [bɪ'siːdʒ]	belagern	~ a town
action ['ækʃn]	Kampfhandlung, Einsatz	ready for ~ / killed in ~
fight [faɪt]	Kampf, Gefecht, kämpfen	a bloody (or: fierce) ~ ~ against (= with) a country
battle [bætl]	Schlacht	win (or: lose) a ~ / die in ~ / a great (or: bloody / murderous) ~
defence [dɪ'fens] (*BE*) = **defense** [–] (*AE*)	Verteidigung	organize the ~
defend [dɪ'fend]	verteidigen	~ a position
cover ['kʌvə*]	Deckung	take ~ (+ from enemy fire)
retreat [rɪ'triːt]	Rückzug, sich zurückziehen	make a ~ / be in full ~ force the enemy to ~ / ~ from ... to ...
flight [flaɪt]	Flucht	take ~ / put the enemy to ~
flee (fled, fled) [fliː, fled, –]	fliehen	~ (+ from) a battlefield (or: the enemy)
withdraw (withdrew, withdrawn) [wɪð'drɔː, -'druː, -'drɔːn]	sich zurückziehen, zurückziehen	The army had to ~ ~ the army
defeat [dɪ'fiːt]	besiegen, Niederlage	~ an army (+ totally) suffer (+ total) ~
surrender [sə'rendə*]	kapitulieren, sich ergeben, Kapitulation	~ (+ oneself) to the enemy demand ~ / unconditional ~
enemy ['enəmɪ]	Feind	fear the ~ / defend the country against its ~ies

Weapons – Waffen

weapon ['wepən]	Waffe	modern ~s / atomic (or: biological / chemical) ~s / a deadly ~
ammunition [ˌæmju'nɪʃn]	Munition	run short of ~ / live (scharfe) ~
bullet ['bʊlɪt]	Kugel	be hit by a ~ / a 9 mm ~
powder ['paʊdə*]	Pulver	**gunpowder** ['gʌnˌ-] (Schießpulver)
pistol ['pɪstl]	Pistole	fire a ~ / carry a ~
rifle ['raɪfl]	Gewehr	load (or: fire) a ~ / hear a **rifleshot** [-ʃɒt]
tank [tænk]	Panzer	
invade [ɪn'veɪd]	einmarschieren (in)	~ a country / **invasion** [ɪn'veɪʒn]
aim [eɪm]	zielen, Ziel	~ at sb (or: sth) take ~ at sb (or: sth)

shoot (shot, shot) [ʃu:t, ʃɒt, –]	schießen, anschießen, erschießen	~ at sb (or: sth) ~ sb (+ dead) / be shot in the arm
shot [ʃɒt]	Schuß	fire a ~ / be wounded by a ~
hit (hit, hit) [hɪt, –, –]	treffen	~ a target (Ziel)
miss [mɪs]	vorbeischießen	~ sb (or: sth)
gun [gʌn]	Feuerwaffe; Geschütz	carry (or: load / fire) a ~ a 16-inch ~
shell [ʃel]	Granate, mit Granatfeuer belegen	~s bursting all around ~ the enemy lines
grenade [grɪ'neɪd]	Handgranate	throw a ~
bomb [bɒm]	Bombe	drop a ~ / A-~ / H-~ / **neutronic bomb** [ˌnju:'trɒnɪk –] / plant a ~ in a building
missile ['mɪsaɪl] (*BE*), ['mɪsl] (*AE*)	Geschoß, Rakete	guided (or: intercontinental / ballistic) ~
rocket ['rɒkɪt]	Rakete	fire (or: launch) a ~
explode [ɪk'spləʊd]	explodieren	shells (or: bombs / mines) ~ / a terrible **explosion** [ɪk'spləʊʒn]
blow (blew, blown) **up** [bləʊ, blu:, bləʊn; ˌ– 'ʌp]	sprengen; explodieren	~ ~ a bridge a bomb ~s ~
destroy [dɪ'strɔɪ]	zerstören	~ a bridge (or: town)
destruction [dɪ'strʌkʃn]	Zerstörung	leave a town in complete ~
damage ['dæmɪdʒ]	beschädigen, Schaden, Beschädigung	be badly **damaged** [-d] / do great ~ to

95 Crime – Verbrechen

crime [kraɪm]	Verbrechen	commit a ~ / accuse sb of a ~ / a frightful (or: horrible) ~ / **organized crime** ['ɔ:gənaɪzd ˌ–] (Bandenverbrechen) / **criminal** ['krɪmɪnl] (Verbrecher)
murder ['mɜ:də*]	Mord, ermorden	commit (+ a) ~ / the ~ of sb by sb / a **murderer** [-ə*] ~ sb / a **murderous** [-rəs] plan
rape [reɪp]	Vergewaltigung, vergewaltigen	be sent to prison for ~ ~ a woman / a **rapist** [-ɪst]
kidnap ['kɪdnæp]	entführen	~ a child / **kidnapper** [-ə*]
theft [θeft]	Diebstahl	be accused of ~
thief [θi:f] (*pl.* thieves [θi:vz])	Dieb	catch (or: stop / arrest) a ~ / Stop, ~!

steal (stole, stolen) [sti:l, stəʊl, 'stəʊlən]	stehlen	~ sb's purse (or: money)
shoplift ['ʃɒpˌlɪft]	Ladendiebstahl begehen	~ sth / a **shoplifter** [-ə*] / be guilty of **shoplifting** [-ɪŋ]
mug [mʌg]	überfallen und ausrauben	~ sb / be (or: get) ~ged / a **mugger** ['-ə]
burglar ['bɜ:glə*]	Einbrecher (nur nachts)	arrest (or: catch / seize) a ~ / There have been a lot of **burglaries** [-rɪz].
crook [krʊk]	Gauner	
housebreaker ['haʊsˌbreɪkə*]	Einbrecher (tagsüber)	
arson ['ɑ:sn]	Brandstiftung	commit ~
set (set, set) **fire to** [set, –, –; – 'faɪə tə]	in Brand stecken	~ ~ ~ a house
fraud [frɔ:d]	Betrug	get (= obtain) sth by ~
deceive [dɪ'si:v]	betrügen	~ sb
counterfeit ['kaʊntəfɪt]	(Geld) fälschen, gefälscht	~ money / a ~ coin
rob [rɒb]	(be-)rauben	~ a bank / ~ sb of sth / I've been **robbed**! [-d] / a **robber** ['-ə*] / commit **robbery** ['-ərɪ]
bribe ['braɪb]	bestechen,	~ sb with sth / ~ sb to do sth / guilty of **bribery** [-ərɪ]
	Bestechungsgeld	give (or: take) a ~
blackmail ['blækmeɪl]	erpressen	~ sb (+ into doing sth)
treason ['tri:zn]	Landesverrat	commit ~
spy [spaɪ]	Spion	cover up a ~
high treason ['haɪ 'tri:zn]	Hochverrat	commit ~ ~

Police – Polizei 96

police [pə'li:s]	Polizei, Polizei-	call the ~ / a **policeman** [-mən] / **police constable** [ˌ– 'kʌnstəbl] (= **P. C.**) (Wachtmeister) / take sb to the **police station** ['– steɪʃn]
patrolman [pə'trəʊlmən] (*AE*)	Streifenpolizist	
officer ['ɒfɪsə*]	Beamter;	a **police officer** [pə'li:s –]
	Anrede für einen Polizeibeamten	'Please, O~, could you tell me ...?'
beat [bi:t]	Streife	be on one's ~

squad car ['skwɒd ˌkɑːr] (*AE*) = **patrol car** [pə'trəʊl ˌkɑː*] (*BE*)	Streifenwagen	
mystery ['mɪstərɪ]	Geheimnis, Rätsel	solve the ~ of a robbery / unravel (enthüllen) a ~
investigate [ɪn'vestɪgeɪt]	untersuchen	~ a crime (or: murder) / carry out **investigations** [ɪnˌvestɪ'geɪʃnz] / sth is under **investigation**
inquire [ɪn'kwaɪə*]	ermitteln	~ into a robbery / make careful **inquiries** [-rɪz] about
clue [kluː]	Anhaltspunkt	find (or: get) a ~ to a mystery / sth gives the police a ~ / have no ~s
fingerprint ['fɪŋgəprɪnt]	Fingerabdruck	leave (+ one's) ~s on the door
footprint ['fʊtprɪnt] = **footmark** ['fʊtmɑːk]	Fußabdruck	leave (+ one's) ~s in the mud
suspect [sə'spekt] (*v.*), ['sʌspekt] (*n.*)	verdächtigen, Verdächtiger	~ sb of sth (or: doing sth) question a ~
suspicion [sə'spɪʃn]	Verdacht	have a ~ that … / have ~s about sth / sb's behaviour is very **suspicious** [sə'spɪʃəs] / be **suspicious** about (= of) sb (or: sth)
search [sɜːtʃ]	fahnden; durchsuchen	~ for a wanted man ~ a thief thoroughly
warrant ['wɒrənt]	Haftbefehl	there is a ~ out for sb's arrest / a ~ to arrest sb
wanted ['wɒntɪd]	gesucht	~ for murder / ~ by the police
detect [dɪ'tekt]	aufdecken, entlarven	~ a crime (or: murderer) / escape **detection** [dɪ'tekʃn]
detective [dɪ'tektɪv]	Detektiv, Kriminalbeamter	**detective sergeant** [– 'sɑːdʒənt] / **private detective** [ˌpraɪvɪt –]
arrest [ə'rest]	verhaften, Verhaftung	~ a thief have a warrant for sb's ~
handcuff ['hændkʌf]	Handschelle, Handschellen anlegen	put ~s on sb ~ sb
question ['kwestʃən]	verhören	~ sb closely / be ~ed by the police / The police gave him a thorough **questioning** [-ɪŋ].

Court – Gericht

law [lɔː]	Gesetz, Recht	break the ~ study ~ / English ~
legal ['liːgl]	Rechts-, legal	~ affairs / take ~ action (+ against sb) / a ~ offence
court [kɔːt]	Gericht; Gerichtssaal	go to ~ / appear in ~ / take sb to ~ have the ~ cleared / in the **court-room** ['-rʊm]
case [keɪs]	Fall;	a civil (or: criminal) ~ / a ~ of murder / take a ~ to court
	Prozeß, Rechtsstreit	win (or: lose) one's ~
trial ['traɪəl]	Gericht (als Verfahren),	go on ~ (vor Gericht kommen) / bring sb to ~ / put sb on ~ for sth / be (= stand) on ~ for sth
	Verfahren	be given a fair ~ / **trial by jury** [– baɪ ˌdʒʊərɪ] (Schwurgerichtsverfahren)
try [traɪ]	verhandeln	~ a case / be ~ied for stealing
prosecute ['prɒsɪkjuːt]	anklagen	~ sb for murder (or: stealing) / **prosecuting counsel** ['-ɪŋ 'kaʊnsl] (Ankläger) / start a **prosecution** [ˌprɒsɪ'kjuːʃn] against sb / the **prosecution** (Staatsanwaltschaft) / **public prosecutor** [ˌpʌblɪk -ər] (Staatsanwalt)
charge [tʃɑːdʒ]	Anklage, anklagen	bring a ~ of murder against sb ~ sb with murder
action ['ækʃn]	Klage	bring an ~ against sb / ~ for damages (auf Schadenersatz)
sue [sjuː]	verklagen	**suit** [suːt] (Klage, Prozeß)
accuse [ə'kjuːz]	beschuldigen	~ sb of murder / **the accused** [ðiː -d] / bring an **accusation** [ˌækjʊː'zeɪʃn] against sb / a false **accusation**
dock [dɒk]	Anklagebank	be in the ~
plead [pliːd]	sich bekennen	~ (+ not) guilty (+ to murder)
defend [dɪ'fend]	verteidigen	~ oneself (or: sb) / **defending counsel** [dɪˌfendɪŋ 'kaunsl] (Verteidiger) / the **defendant** [-ənt] (Angeklagter) / conduct one's own **defence** [dɪ'fens] (*BE*) = **defense** [–] (*AE*)
object [əb'dʒekt]	Einspruch erheben	'I ~.'
deny [dɪ'naɪ]	abstreiten	'I ~ it all.' / ~ that one has done sth / ~ a charge

evidence ['evɪdəns]	Beweis;	a piece of ~ / enough ~ to prove sb guilty / **circumstantial evidence** [ˌsɜːkəm'stænʃl –] (Indizienbeweis) / on grounds of insufficient ~ (aus Mangel an Beweisen)
	Zeugenaussage	give ~ / call sb in ~ (als Zeugen aufrufen)
witness ['wɪtnɪs]	Zeuge,	call (or: hear) a ~ / an **eyewitness** [ˌaɪ'wɪtnɪs]
	(als Zeuge) aussagen,	~ to the truth of sth / ~ against the accused / ~ to seeing the accused do sth
	Zeugenaussage	give ~ on behalf of the accused
cross-examine [ˌkrɒsɪg'zæmɪn]	ins Kreuzverhör nehmen	~ a witness
statement ['steɪtmənt]	Aussage	make a ~ / prove one's ~
swear (swore, sworn) [sweə*, swɔː*, swɔːn]	schwören	~ by God / ~ by (= on) the Bible / ~ to the truth of a statement
oath [əʊθ]	Eid	take an ~ / be under (= on) ~ / swear an ~ / a false ~
perjury ['pɜːdʒərɪ]	Meineid	commit ~
admit [əd'mɪt]	zugeben	~ that one has done sth / ~ a crime (or: one's guilt)
confess [kən'fes]	gestehen	~ a crime / make a **confession** [kən'feʃn]
truth [truːθ]	Wahrheit	tell (= speak) the ~ / the whole ~ and nothing but the ~
convict [kən'vɪkt]	überführen	~ sb of murder
guilt [gɪlt]	Schuld	prove sb's ~ / be **guilty** ['-ɪ] of murder / prove sb **guilty**
innocent ['ɪnəsnt]	unschuldig	be ~ of sth / prove one's (or: sb's) **innocence** ['ɪnəsəns]
jury[1] ['dʒʊərɪ]	die Geschworenen	The ~ found him guilty.
verdict ['vɜːdɪkt]	Spruch der Geschworenen	hear the ~ / return a ~ of (+ not) guilty
lawyer ['lɔːjə*] (*BE*) = **attorney** [ə'tɜrnɪ] (*AE*)	Rechtsanwalt	
judge [dʒʌdʒ]	Richter	a J~ of the High Court
judgment ['dʒʌdʒmənt] (*BE*) = **judgement** [–] (*AE*)	Verurteilung; Strafe	give ~ / pass a ~ on sb; a ~ of £250 against Mr Miller

[1] The jury decides whether the accused is guilty or not; it does not decide what the punishment should be.

punish ['pʌnɪʃ]	bestrafen	~ sb severely / ~ sb with (= by) a fine / **capital punishment** [ˌkæpɪtl -mənt] (Todesstrafe)
sentence ['sentəns]	Urteil,	pass a ~ of imprisonment (or: life imprisonment) on (= upon) sb / pass the **death sentence** ['deθ ˌ–] on sb
	verurteilen	~ sb to two years in prison / ~ sb to pay a fine / ~ sb to death
life [laɪf]	lebenslänglich	get ~ / sentence sb to ~ (+ imprisonment)
fine [faɪn]	Geldstrafe,	sentence sb to pay a ~ / pay a ~
	zu einer Geldstrafe verurteilen	~ sb £200 / ~ sb for an offence
appeal [ə'pi:l]	Berufung	the right to ~ / make an ~ to a higher court
acquit [ə'kwɪt]	freisprechen	~ sb of robbery (or: a crime)

Prison – Gefängnis 98

prison [prɪzn]	Gefängnis	spend two years in ~ / go to ~ (+ for two years) / be in ~
imprison [ɪm'prɪzn]	ins Gefängnis stecken	be ~ed for two years / ~ sb / sentence sb to ten months' **imprisonment** [-mənt]
custody ['kʌstədɪ]	Haft	take into ~ / remand (verwahren) in ~
gaol [dʒeɪl] = **jail** [dʒeɪl]	Gefängnis	be sent to ~ / three years in ~
cell [sel]	Zelle	lock sb up in a ~
escape [ɪ'skeɪp]	Flucht,	make an ~
	fliehen	~ from prison
release [rɪ'li:s]	entlassen,	be ~d from prison
	Entlassung	be due (anstehen) for ~
pardon ['pɑ:dn]	begnadigen,	~ a prisoner
	Begnadigung	ask for ~ / a general ~
bail [beɪl]	Bürgschaft, Kaution	be (+ let) out on ~ / refuse ~

Country – Land 99

country ['kʌntrɪ]	Land,	the European ~ies / "**God's own country**" (*AE inform.*) / a beautiful (or: nice) ~
	(Heimat-, Vater-)Land	serve one's ~ / fight (or: die) for one's ~ / one's **mother country** ['mʌðə ˌkʌntrɪ]

countryman ['kʌntrɪmən]	Landsmann	
native ['neɪtɪv]	Heimat-, Mutter-	one's ~ country (or: language)
foreign ['fɒrən]	Aus-, Fremd-	a ~ country (or: language)
abroad [ə'brɔːd]	im (ins) Ausland	live (or: go) ~
frontier ['frʌnˌtɪə*]	Grenze	cross the ~ (+ at ...) / a country has ~s with ... / the French-Spanish ~ / a ~ runs along a river / defend one's ~
boundary ['baʊndərɪ]	Grenze, Grenzlinie	fix the ~ies of a country
border ['bɔːdə*]	Grenze, Grenzgebiet,	guard the ~ / escape over the ~ / cross the ~ / within our ~s / a **border town** [– taʊn] / **the Border** (zwischen England und Schottland)
	grenzen	France and Germany ~ on each other. / Germany ~s on Denmark in the north.
passport ['pɑːspɔːt]	Paß	show one's ~ / have a German ~
land [lænd]	Land	the **Holy Land** ['həʊlɪ –]
empire ['empaɪə*]	(Kaiser-, Welt-)Reich	the **British Empire** [ˌbrɪtɪʃ –] / **emperor** ['empərə*] (Kaiser) / **empress** ['emprɪs] (Kaiserin)
imperial [ɪm'pɪərɪəl]	kaiserlich, Reichs-	**His** (or: **Her**) **Imperial Highness** [– – ˌhaɪnɪs] / ~ policy
Commonwealth ['kɒmənwelθ]	die britische Völkergemeinschaft	The British ~ / The Queen is the Head of the ~
state [steɪt]	Staat;	rule (or: govern) a ~ / a **state visit** to a country / the relationship between Church and S~ / a **statesman** ['-smən]
	Bundesstaat	the 50 ~s of the US / the ~s of Australia
independence [ˌɪndɪ'pendəns]	Unabhängigkeit	gain ~ (+ from another country) / fight for ~ / a country declares its ~ / an **independent** [ɪndɪ'pendənt] state
sovereign ['sɒvrɪn]	souverän, unabhängig	a ~ state / defend the **sovereignty** ['sɒvrəntɪ] of one's country
colony ['kɒlənɪ]	Kolonie	have many ~ies / live in the ~ies / the American **colonists** [-sts] / a **colonial** [kə'ləʊnjəl] (jemand, der lange Zeit in einer Kolonie gelebt hat) / fight against **colonialism** [kə'ləʊnɪelɪzm] / **colonize** ['kɒlənaɪz] a country

territory ['terɪtərɪ]	Staatsgebiet,	British ~ / British **territorial** [ˌterɪ'tɔːrɪəl] waters
	Gebiet	travel through unknown ~
federation [ˌfedə'reɪʃn]	Bundesstaat	the hope of founding a European ~
federal ['fedərəl]	Bundes-	a ~ republic / the **Federal Republic** ['– rɪ'pʌblɪk] (= W. Germany) / the ~ government in Washington
confederacy [kən'fedərəsɪ]	Staatenbund	**the German Confederacy** (der Deutsche Bund, 1815–1866)
confederate [kən'fedəret]	konföderiert	the **Confederate States of America** [– ˌsteɪts‿əv‿ə'merɪkə] (= the 11 Southern states which left the Union in 1861 and 1862)
kingdom ['kɪŋdəm]	Königreich	the **United Kingdom** [juːˌnaɪtɪd –] (= **U. K.** [ˌjuː 'keɪ])
republic [rɪ'pʌblɪk]	Republik	
dictator [dɪk'teɪtə*]	Diktator	a cruel ~ (or: **dictatorship** [-ʃɪp])
nation ['neɪʃn]	Nation	a rich (or: poor / powerful / peaceful) ~ / have **national** ['næʃənl] pride / a **national** holiday / be a fanatical **nationalist** ['næʃnəlɪst]
patriot ['pætrɪət]	Patriot	be a loyal (or: good) ~
traitor ['treɪtə*]	Verräter	
national anthem [ˌnæʃnəl 'ænθəm]	Nationalhymne	sing the ~ ~
flag [flæg]	Fahne, Flagge,	hoist a ~ / the national ~
	beflaggen	~ the streets in honour of sb
capital ['kæpɪtl]	Hauptstadt	Washington, D.C. is the ~.
province ['prɒvɪns]	Provinz	people from the ~s / Ontario is a Canadian ~. / a **provincial** [prə'vɪnʃl] paper
county ['kaʊntɪ]	Grafschaft (*BE*),	the ~ of Essex
	etwa: Kreis (*AE*)	Mifflin ~

Society – Gesellschaft

100 The social system – das soziale System

(→ 45–58 Communication; 70–73 Our relations with others)

interaction [ˌɪntər'ækʃn]	zwischenmenschliches Handeln	be engaged in ~ with others / social ~
organization [ˌɔːgənaɪ'zeɪʃn]	Organisation (als Ordnung), Organisation (als Gruppe)	sth works well (or: badly) by reason of its efficient (or: inefficient) ~ belong to a large (or: small) ~
system ['sɪstəm]	System	the social (or: political / cultural) ~ / introduce a new ~ of doing sth
structure ['strʌktʃə*]	Struktur, Ordnung	have a complex (or: simple) social ~
order ['ɔːdə*]	Ordnung	establish (or: change / overthrow) a social ~ / a democratic (or: undemocratic) social ~
society [sə'saɪətɪ]	Gesellschaft (als Wort dafür, daß Menschen in Gruppen leben), Gesellschaft (als Gesamtheit miteinander verbundener Gruppen)	live in ~ / modern (or: present-day) ~ a ~ rises (or: grows/develops)/live in a(n) underdeveloped (or: backward / primitive / developed / advanced / industrial / post-industrial) ~

101 Class – Klasse

(→ 72 Social position)

class [klɑːs]	Klasse	belong to the upper (or: middle / lower / working) ~
estate [ɪ'steɪt] (*hist.*)	Stand	the three ~s of the realm / the **First** (or: **Second** / **Third**) **Estate**
clergy ['klɜːdʒɪ]	Geistlichkeit	
nobility [nəʊ'bɪlətɪ]	Adel	belong to the ~ / be a member of the ~ / be born (or: marry) into the ~
aristocracy [ˌærɪ'stɒkrəsɪ]	Aristokratie	belong to the ~ / be a member of the ~ / be an **aristocrat** ['ærɪstəkræt]
noble [nəʊbl]	adlig	be of ~ rank (or: birth) / a **nobleman** ['-mən] / a **noblewoman** ['-wʊmən] / **the nobles** [ðə '-z]
bourgeoisie [ˌbʊəʒwɑː'ziː]	Bürgertum, Bourgeoisie	
proletariat [ˌprəʊlɪ'teərɪət]	Proletariat	

elite [eɪ'li:t]	Elite	belong to the ~ in society / the social (or: military / political / governing) ~
the Establishment [ði: ɪ'stæblɪʃmənt]	das Establishment	belong to ~ ~ / attack ~ ~

Ranks in the nobility – Adelstitel

duke [dju:k]	Herzog	**duchess** ['dʌtʃɪs]	Herzogin
marquess = marquis ['mɑ:kwɪs]	Markgraf	**marchioness** ['mɑ:ʃənɪs]	Markgräfin
earl [ɜ:l]	Graf		
count [kaʊnt]	(nichtenglischer) Graf	**countess** ['kaʊntɪs]	Gräfin
viscount ['vaɪkaʊnt]	Vicomte	**viscountess** ['vaɪkaʊntɪs]	Vicomtess
baron ['bærən]	Baron, Freiherr	**baroness** ['bærənɪs]	Baronin, Freifrau

gentry ['dʒentrɪ]	niederer Adel	
baronet ['bærənɪt]	Baronet	
knight [naɪt]	Ritter	
My Lord! [maɪ 'lɔ:d]	Gnädiger Herr (Anrede für ein Mitglied des höheren Adels)	
My Lady! [maɪ 'leɪdɪ]	Gnädige Herrin	
Sir [sɜ:*], **Lady** ['leɪdɪ]	Anrede	~ Winston Churchill / ~ Jane Grey / **Sir** Winston [sə 'wɪnstən] (Vorname) and **Lady** Churchill (Nachname)

Social group – soziale Gruppe (→ 70 Alone, with others) 102

group [gru:p]	Gruppe	found (or: join / belong to / leave) a ~ / a(n) formal (or: informal / stable / unstable) ~ / analyze ~ life
leader ['li:də*]	Führer	have a powerful (or: influential) ~ / be the ~ of a group / be under sb's **leadership** [-ʃɪp]
follower ['fɒləʊə*]	Gefolgsmann	be sb's ~ / have many ~s / have a large (or: small) **following** ['fɒləʊɪŋ]
star [stɑ:*]	Star	be a ~
pair [peə*]	Paar	
outsider [ˌaut'saɪdə*]	Außenseiter	be an ~
club [klʌb]	Club, Verein	meet sb in one's ~ / belong to a sports ~

member ['membə*]	Mitglied	be (or: become) a ~ of a club / **membership** [-ʃɪp]
association [əˌsəʊsɪ'eɪʃn]	Verband; Verbindung	form an ~ to help old people work in ~ with sb
society [sə'saɪətɪ]	Gesellschaft, Verein, Verband	a film ~
gang [gæŋ]	Gruppe; Rotte, Bande, sich zusammenrotten	a ~ of criminals (or: youths) belong to a ~ / be a **gangster** ['-stə*] ~ up on (= against) sb
crowd [kraʊd]	Menge, Masse, sich drängen	~s of people / a ~ waiting at the bus stop ~ round sb (or: sth) / ~ into a room
community [kə'mju:nətɪ]	Gemeinde, Gemeinschaft	be born into a ~ / grow up in a ~ / belong to a ~ / live in a ~ / a farming (or: rural / village) ~ / an urban ~ / the Catholic (or: Jewish / Negro) ~ of New York

103 Population – Bevölkerung

population [ˌpɒpju'leɪʃn]	Bevölkerung	a country has a ~ of ... / the ~ of London is about 8½ million / a large (or: small) ~ / a ~ rises (= increases) (+ at a rate of 2% per year) / the **population explosion** [– ɪk'spləʊʒn] / **population growth** [– 'grəʊθ]
populate ['pɒpjʊleɪt]	bevölkern	an area is ~d by ... / a **thickly-populated** ['θɪklɪ-ɪd] area
census ['sensəs]	Volkszählung	conduct a ~
migration [maɪ'greɪʃn]	Wanderung	the great ~ of the Germanic peoples / overseas ~
immigrate ['ɪmɪgreɪt]	einwandern	~ into a country / Millions of **immigrants** ['ɪmɪgrənts] came from Asia to America.
immigration [ˌɪmɪ'greɪʃn]	Einwanderung	
emigrate ['emɪgreɪt]	auswandern	~ from a country / a ship full of **emigrants** ['emɪgrənts] going to America
refugee [ˌrefjʊ'dʒi:] (*BE*) ['refjʊdʒi:] (*AE*)	Flüchtling(s-)	a **refugee camp** [– kæmp]

minority [maɪ'nɒrətɪ]	Minderheit	belong to a ~ / a country has a large (or: strong) black ~ / a country has a ~ problem / an ethnic (or: racial) ~
persecute ['pɜːsɪkjuːt]	verfolgen	~ a minority
ethnic ['eθnɪk]	Volks-	the ~ groups in the US / an ~ minority
assimilate [ə'sɪmɪleɪt]	(kulturell) eingliedern, assimilieren	be (or: become) ~d into a society
integration [ˌɪntɪ'greɪʃn]	Integration	racial ~
segregation [ˌsegrɪ'geɪʃn]	Rassentrennung	
colour bar ['kʌlə bɑː*] (*BE*) = **color bar** ['kʌlər bɑr] (*AE*)	Rassenschranke	
emancipation [ɪˌmænsɪ'peɪʃn]	Befreiung, Gleichberechtigung	fight for the ~ of a minority / the ~ of the slaves

Reform, revolution – Reform, Revolution 104

change [tʃeɪndʒ]	Wandel	social (or: political / economic / cultural) ~ (= ~s) / a sudden (or: radical / violent / rapid / gradual / revolutionary) ~
progress ['prəʊgres] (*BE*), ['prɒgres] (*AE*)	Fortschritt	make no (or: little / rapid) ~ / support ~ / moral (or: social / intellectual) ~ / be **progressive** [prəʊ'gresɪv]
reform [rɪ'fɔːm]	Reform,	propose (or: demand) ~s / call for ~s / bring about ~s / carry out ~s / a great (or: radical / complete / general) ~ of sth / oppose a ~
	reformieren	~ sth slowly (or: radically / cautiously)
demonstration [ˌdemən'streɪʃn]	Demonstration	take part in a ~ / **demo** ['deməʊ] / **demonstrate** ['demənstreɪt] for (or: against) sth
unrest [ˌʌn'rest]	Unruhe	social (or: political) ~
riot ['raɪət]	Krawall, Aufstand,	put down a ~ / a **riotous** [-əs] crowd
	sich zusammenrotten	~ for sth / ~ against the Government
uproar ['ʌprɔː*]	Aufruhr, Tumult	
rebel ['rebl] (*n.*)	Rebell	imprison a ~
[rɪ'bel] (*v.*)	rebellieren	~ against the Government

rebellion [rɪ'beljən]	Rebellion	be in ~ against the Government / a ~ breaks out / put down a ~
revolt [rɪ'vəʊlt]	Revolte, Aufstand,	a ~ breaks out (or: flames up / spreads) / incite (or: provoke / stir up / fan) a ~ / drive the population to ~ / repress (or: put down) a ~ / be in ~
	revoltieren	~ against the Government
terrorist ['terərɪst]	Terrorist	
rise (rose, risen) [raɪz, rəʊz, 'rɪzn]	sich erheben	~ (+ up) against the Government
plot [plɒt]	Verschwörung, Anschlag,	form (or: draw up / conceive) a ~ / discover (= detect) a ~ / get involved in a ~
	sich verschwören, (verschwörerisch) planen	~ against sb / ~ to kill sb ~ sb's murder
conspire [kən'spaɪə]	sich verschwören, konspirieren	~ against the Government / form a **conspiracy** [kən'spɪrəsɪ] against ... / be involved in a **conspiracy**
revolution [ˌrevə'luːʃn]	Revolution	begin (or: prepare / end) a ~ / a ~ erupts (or: breaks out) / a ~ aims at (or: is directed against) sth / a ~ takes place (or: rages / collapses) / a **revolutionary** [-ərɪ] party / **the Industrial Revolution** [ðiː ɪn'dʌstrɪəl –]

Our working life – Unser Arbeitsleben

Work – Arbeit

Employment – Beschäftigung 105

firm [fɜːm] = **company** ['kʌmpənɪ]	Firma	
apply [ə'plaɪ]	sich bewerben	~ for a job / write an **application** [ˌæplɪ'keɪʃn]
applicant ['æplɪkənt]	Bewerber	There were ten ~s for the job.
interview ['ɪntəvjuː]	Vorstellung	go for an ~
employ [ɪm'plɔɪ]	beschäftigen	~ fifty men / be ~ed in a bank / be in (or: out of) **employment** [-mənt] / **employee** [ˌemplɔɪ'iː] (Beschäftigte(r)) / **employer** [-ə*] (Arbeitgeber)
work [wɜːk]	Arbeit,	find ~ / be out of ~ / do one's ~
	arbeiten	~ hard / ~ in an office (or: at a farm) / Where do you ~?
labour ['leɪbə*] (*BE*) = **labor** [-r] (*AE*)	(mehr Kraft als Geschicklichkeit erfordernde) Arbeit;	earn one's living by manual ~ / a **labourer** [-rə]
	Arbeiterschaft, Arbeitskräfte	skilled and unskilled ~ / have not enough skilled ~ / the **Labour Party** ['leɪbə ˌpɑːtɪ]
job [dʒɒb]	Stelle	find a (+ good) ~ / be without a ~ / a **part-time job** ['pɑːtˌtaɪm –]
position [pə'zɪʃn]	Stellung	have a good ~ / apply for the ~ of assistant manager
duty ['djuːtɪ] (*BE*), ['duːtɪ] (*AE*)	Pflicht, Dienst	do one's ~ / have a sense of ~ / be **on duty** / be **off duty**
5-day week [faɪv deɪ 'wiːk]	Fünftagewoche	work a ~ ~
overtime ['əʊvətaɪm]	Überstunden	work ~ / be on ~
worker ['wɜːkə*]	Arbeiter	a skilled (Fach-) ~
workman (*pl.* workmen) ['wɜːkmən]	(Hand-)Arbeiter, Handwerker	a good (or: bad) ~
craftsman (*pl.* craftsmen) ['krɑːftsmən]	Handwerker	a fine ~ / a master ~

master ['mɑːstə*]	Meister	a ~ carpenter
foreman ['fɔːmən]	Vorarbeiter	
apprentice [ə'prentɪs]	Lehrling	an ~ carpenter / be ~d to a carpenter
trainee [treɪniː]	Praktikant	a ~ reporter
manpower ['mæn,paʊə*]	Arbeitskräfte	be short of ~
personnel [,pɜːsə'nel]	Personal	the ~ manager
colleague ['kɒliːg]	Kollege	
staff [stɑːf]	Belegschaft, Personal	a ~ of 20
notice ['nəʊtɪs]	Kündigung	give ~ to sb / give sb his ~ / give sb a week's ~
dismiss [dɪs'mɪs]	entlassen	~ sb (+ from his job)
fire ['faɪə*] = **sack** [sæk] (*inform.*)	feuern	~ sb / "You are fired (or: sacked)!"
unemployed [,ʌnɪm'plɔɪd]	arbeitslos	be ~ / draw **unemployment benefit** [,ʌnɪm'plɔɪmənt 'benɪfɪt] (Arbeitslosenunterstützung)
employment office [ɪm'plɔɪmənt ,ɒfɪs]	Arbeitsamt	
be on the dole [– – – 'dəʊl] (*inform.*)	stempeln gehen	
retire [rɪ'taɪə*]	in den Ruhestand treten oder versetzen	He ~d at the age of 60.
jobcentre ['dʒɒb,sentə*]	Arbeitsvermittlung	

106 Occupations – Berufe[1]

farmer	['fɑːmə*]	Bauer, Landwirt
forester	['fɒrɪstə*]	Förster; Waldarbeiter
gardener	['gɑːdenə*]	Gärtner
florist	['flɒrɪst]	Blumenhändler
miller	['mɪlə*]	Müller
baker	['beɪkə*]	Bäcker
butcher	['bʊtʃə*]	Metzger, Schlachter
cook	[kʊk]	Koch
weaver	['wiːvə*]	Weber
tailor	['teɪlə*]	Herrenschneider
dressmaker	['dres,meɪkə*]	Damenschneider(in)
shoemaker	['ʃuː,meɪkə*]	Schuhmacher

[1] Die Bezeichnungen gelten in den meisten Fällen für männliche wie für weibliche Berufstätige.

cobbler	['kɒblə*]	Flickschuster
barber	['bɑːbə*]	Herrenfriseur
hairdresser	['heəˌdresə*]	Damenfriseur
sailor	['seɪlə*]	Seemann
fisherman	['fɪʃəmən]	Fischer
docker (*BE*) = **longshoreman** (*AE*)	['dɒkə*], ['lɒŋʃɔːmən]	Hafenarbeiter
pilot	['paɪlət]	Pilot; Lotse
captain	['kæptɪn]	Kapitän
engine driver (*BE*) = **engineer** (*AE*)	['endʒɪn ˌdraɪvə*], [ˌendʒɪ'nɪər]	Lokomotivführer
busdriver (*BE*)	['bʌsdraɪvə*]	Busfahrer
lorry driver (*BE*) = **truck driver** (*AE*)	['lɒrɪ ˌdraɪvə*], ['trʌk draɪvər]	Lastwagenfahrer
soldier	['səʊldʒə*]	Soldat
policeman	[pə'liːsmən]	Polizist
customs officer	['kʌstəmz 'ɒfɪsə*]	Zollbeamter
postman (*BE*) = **mailman** (*AE*)	['pəʊstmən], ['meɪlmən]	Briefträger
miner	['maɪnə*]	Bergmann
mechanic	[mɪ'kænɪk]	(Kfz-)Mechaniker
engineer	[ˌendʒɪ'nɪə*]	Ingenieur, Techniker; Maschinist (*BE*); Lokomotivführer (*AE*)
fitter	['fɪtə*]	Monteur
locksmith	['lɒksmɪθ]	Schlosser
blacksmith	['blæksmɪθ]	Schmied
clockmaker = **watchmaker**	['klɒkˌmeɪkə*], ['wɒtʃˌmeɪkə*]	Uhrmacher
carpenter	['kɑːpəntə*]	Zimmermann
plumber	['plʌmə*]	Installateur
electrician	[ˌɪlek'trɪʃn]	Elektriker
bricklayer	['brɪkˌleɪə*]	Maurer
tiler	['taɪlə*]	Dachdecker; Fliesenleger
painter	['peɪntə*]	Anstreicher
decorator	['dekəreɪtə*]	Maler, Anstreicher
paperhanger	['peɪpəˌhæŋə*]	Tapezierer
chimney-sweep	['tʃɪmnɪswiːp]	Schornsteinfeger
architect	['ɑːkɪtəkt]	Architekt
artist	['ɑːtɪst]	Künstler(in)
sculptor	['skʌlptə*]	Bildhauer(in)
painter	['peɪntə*]	Maler(in)
singer	['sɪŋə*]	Sänger(in)
actor	['æktə*]	Schauspieler
actress	['æktrɪs]	Schauspielerin
journalist	['dʒɜːnəlɪst]	Journalist

reporter	[rɪ'pɔːtə*]	Reporter
printer	['prɪntə*]	Drucker
bookbinder	['bʊkˌbaɪndə*]	Buchbinder
bookseller	['bʊkˌselə*]	Buchhändler
doctor	['dɒktə*]	Arzt
dentist	['dentɪst]	Zahnarzt
nurse	['nɜːs]	Krankenschwester
male nurse	['meɪl 'nɜːs]	Pfleger
chemist (*BE*) =	['kemɪst],	Apotheker, Drogist
pharmacist (*AE*) =	['fɑrməsɪst],	Apotheker
druggist (*AE*)	['drʌgɪst]	
optician	[ɒp'tɪʃn]	Optiker
banker	['bæŋkə*]	Bankier
bank-clerk	['bæŋkklɑːk]	Bankangestellter
book-keeper =	['bʊkˌkiːpə*],	Buchhalter
accountant	[ə'kaʊntənt]	
salesman	['seɪlzmən]	Verkäufer; Vertreter
saleswoman	['seɪlzˌwʊmən]	Verkäuferin; Vertreterin
shop assistant (*BE*)	['ʃɒpəˌsɪstənt],	Verkäufer(in)
= **sales clerk** (*AE*)	['seɪlz klɜrk]	
clerk	[klɑːk]	kaufmännischer Angestellter
manager	['mænɪdʒə*]	Geschäftsführer
civil servant	[ˌsɪvl 'sɜːvənt]	Beamter
shop keeper (*BE*) =	['ʃɒp ˌkɪːpə*],	Händler, Kaufmann
store-keeper (*AE*)	['stɒrˌkiːpər]	
lawyer (*BE*) =	['lɔːjə*],	Rechtsanwalt, -anwältin
attorney (*AE*)	[ə'tɜrnɪ]	
solicitor	[sə'lɪsɪtə*]	Rechtsanwalt, Rechtsberater(in)
barrister	['bærɪstə*]	Rechtsanwalt, bei höheren Gerichten zugelassen
secretary	['sekrətrɪ]	Sekretär(in)
fireman	['faɪəmən]	Feuerwehrmann

107 Income – Einkommen

pay [peɪ]	Bezahlung, Lohn	get one's ~ every Friday / bring home good ~
wage [weɪdʒ]	Lohn	get a ~ of £70 a week / earn a good ~ / pay high (or: low) ~s
salary ['sælerɪ]	Gehalt	earn a ~ of £4,500 a year / pay a good ~
income ['ɪŋkʌm]	Einkommen	have a large (or: high / good / small / low / poor) ~
earn [ɜːn]	verdienen	~ a lot of money / ~ £80 a week

live on ['lɪv ɒn]	leben von	~ ~ a small income
living ['lɪvɪŋ]	Lebensunterhalt	earn one's ~ / work for one's ~ / make a ~ in industry
livelihood ['laɪvlɪhʊd]	Auskommen, Lebensunterhalt	make a ~ doing sth / make (or: earn) one's ~ by doing sth / Teaching is my ~.
pension ['penʃn]	Rente, Pension, pensionieren	get a ~ / retire on a ~ / an old-age ~ ~ sb off / be of **pensionable** [-əbl] age / a **pensionable** job
rich [rɪtʃ]	reich	a ~ man / be (or: become / grow) ~ / **the rich** / amass great **riches** ['-ɪz]
well-to-do [ˌweltə'duː]	wohlhabend	come from a ~ ['---] family
well off [ˌwel‿'ɒf]	wohlhabend	be very ~ ~
wealth [welθ]	Reichtum	have a lot of ~ / a **wealthy** ['-ɪ] man
fortune ['fɔːtʃuːn]	Vermögen	make a ~ / sth is worth a ~
luxury ['lʌkʃərɪ]	Luxus	live in ~ / a ~ hotel / live in **luxurious** [lʌg'zjʊərɪəs] surroundings
poor [pʊə*]	arm	be very ~ / a ~ man / **the poor**
poverty ['pɒvətɪ]	Armut	fall into ~ / live in ~
badly off [ˌbædlɪ 'ɒf]	arm (dran sein)	be ~ ~

Trade union, strike – Gewerkschaft, Streik 108

trade union = trades union [ˌtreɪd(z) 'juːnɪən] (*BE*) **= labor union** ['leɪbər ˌjuːnɪən] (*AE*)	Gewerkschaft	form(or: organize) ~ ~s / join (or: belong to / be a member of) a ~ ~ / a ~ ~ leader / a **trade unionist** [ˌ– '-ɪst]
T.U.C. [ˌtiː juː 'siː] (*BE*)[1]	etwa: Gewerkschaftsbund	
AFL-CIO ['eɪ əf 'el ˌsiː aɪ 'əʊ] (*AE*)[2]	etwa: Gewerkschaftsbund	
shop steward [ˌʃɒp 'stjʊəd]	Vertrauensmann	
working conditions ['wɜːkɪŋ kən'dɪʃnz]	Arbeitsbedingungen	fight for better ~ ~
strike [straɪk]	Streik	start (or: call) a ~ / be on ~ for (or: against) sth
strike (struck, struck) [straɪk, strʌk, –]	streiken	~ as a protest against sth / ~ for better wages (or: higher pay / shorter hours / improved conditions)

1 T.U.C. = Trades Union Congress
2 AFL-CIO = American Federation of Labor and Congress of Industrial Organizations

general strike [ˌdʒenrəl 'straɪk]	Generalstreik	
wildcat strike ['waɪldkæt –]	wilder Streik	
picket ['pɪkɪt]	Streikposten; Streikwache stehen	place ~s at the factory gates ~ in front of the factory
blackleg ['blækleg] (*BE*)	Streikbrecher	
lockout ['lɒkaʊt]	Aussperrung	
lock out [lɒk 'aʊt]	aussperren	

Production – Produktion

109 Power, energy – Kraft, Energie

power ['paʊə*]	Kraft	electric (or: water / steam) ~
energy ['enədʒɪ]	Energie	the sources of ~ / use atomic (or: hydroelectric) ~ / save (or: waste) ~
coal [kəʊl]	Kohle	burn ~
mine [maɪn]	Zeche, Bergwerk,	work in a ~ / a gold (or: tin / coal) ~ / a coal **miner** ['-ə*]
	fördern, abbauen	~ coal
electricity [ɪˌlek'trɪsətɪ]	Elektrizität, Strom	convey ~ from ... to ...
electric [ɪ'lektrɪk]	elektrisch, Elektro-	an ~ battery / ~ lights / an **electrical engineer** [-l ˌendʒɪ'nɪə*] / generate ~ power
current ['kʌrənt]	Strom	use alternating ~ (= A. C.) (Wechselstrom) / use direct ~ (= D. C.) (Gleichstrom)
voltage ['vəʊltɪdʒ]	Volt	produce high ~s
power station ['paʊə steɪʃn] (*BE*) = **power-plant** ['paʊərplænt] (*AE*)	Kraftwerk	a nuclear ~
reservoir ['rezəvwɑː*]	Stausee	store water in a ~
dam [dæm]	Damm	build a ~ / the **Hoover Dam** (on the Colorado River, USA)
oil [ɔɪl]	Öl	the **oil-producing** ['-prə'djuːsɪŋ] countries / strike ~ (auf Öl stoßen)
crude oil ['kruːd 'ɔɪl]	Rohöl	

oil-well ['ɔɪlwel]	Ölquelle	
oil-field ['ɔɪlfi:ld]	Ölfeld	
derrick ['derɪk]	Bohrturm	
refinery [rɪ'faɪnərɪ]	Raffinerie	
pipeline ['paɪplaɪn]	Pipeline	
fuel ['fjʊəl]	Brennstoff, Kraftstoff	burn (or: save) ~

Manufacturing, tools – Herstellen, Werkzeuge 110

raw material [ˌrɔ: mə'tɪərɪəl]	Rohstoff	turn ~ ~s into another product
produce [prə'dju:s]	herstellen, produzieren	~ food (or: cars / goods)
production [prə'dʌkʃn]	Produktion	increase the ~ of sth / **mass production** [ˌmæs –]
manufacture [ˌmænju'fæktʃə*]	(in großen Mengen und mit Maschinen) herstellen,	~ goods (or: cars / shoes) / **manufactured goods** [-d gʊdz] (Fertigwaren) / **car manufacturer** ['kɑ: -rə*]
	Herstellung	the ~ of shoes
factory ['fæktərɪ]	Fabrik	work in a ~ / a shoe-~
mill [mɪl]	Fabrik, Werk	a spinning- (or: cotton- / paper- / steel- / weaving-) ~
works [wɜ:ks]	Fabrik, Werk, Betrieb	an iron ~ / a glass (or: gas) ~ / the ~ canteen
plant [plɑ:nt]	Werk, Anlage;	a chemical ~ / an industrial ~
	Maschinerie, Anlage	a power-~ for electricity
workshop ['wɜ:kʃɒp]	Werkstatt	send a broken machine to the ~
industry ['ɪndəstrɪ]	Industrie(-zweig)	~ and commerce (Handel) / the clothing (or: iron and steel / shipping / car / textile / electrical) ~ / a town with many ~ies / an **industrial nation** [ɪn'dʌstrɪəl ˌneɪʃn]
machine [mə'ʃi:n]	Maschine	a **sewing machine** ['səʊɪŋ məˌʃi:n] / use ~s / work with ~s / the **machine age**
engine ['endʒɪn]	Motor, (Antriebs-) Maschine	a **steam engine** ['sti:m ˌ–]
motor ['məʊtə*]	Motor	an electric ~
tool [tu:l]	Werkzeug	use a ~ / a **tool bag** ['– bæg] (= **toolkit** ['-kɪt])

Some tools and what we do with them – Werkzeug und was wir damit tun

axe [æks] (*BE*) = **ax** [–] (*AE*)	Axt	cut sth off (or: down) with an ~ / split logs with an ~
spade [speɪd]	Spaten	dig the garden with a ~
shovel ['ʃʌvl]	Schaufel	move the snow (or: sand) with a ~
hammer ['hæmə*]	Hammer	drive a nail into the wood with a ~ / break the window with a ~
pincers ['pɪnsəz]	Kneifzange	pull nails from wood with a pair of ~
pliers ['plaɪəz]	Kombizange	bend and cut wire (or: hold small things) with a pair of ~
spanner ['spænə*] (*BE*) = **wrench** [rentʃ] (*AE*)	Schraubenschlüssel	tighten or loosen nuts with a ~
screwdriver ['skru: ˌdraɪvə*]	Schraubenzieher	tighten or loosen screws with a ~
bolt [bəʊlt]	Schraube	fasten the iron bar to the wood with a ~
nut [nʌt]	Mutter	tighten (or: loosen) a ~
plug [plʌg]	Dübel	fit a ~ into a **plughole** ['-həʊl]
screw [skru:]	(Holz-)Schraube	fix the shelf (Brett) to the wall with some ~s
nail [neɪl]	Nagel	knock (or: hammer) a ~ into the wall
drill [drɪl]	Bohrer	
file [faɪl]	Feile	smooth metal (or: wood) with a ~
chisel ['tʃɪzl]	Stecheisen, Meißel	shape wood (or: stone) with a ~
saw [sɔ:]	Säge	cut up wood (for a fire) with a ~

111 Factory – Fabrik

management ['mænɪdʒmənt]	Management	
shop [ʃɒp]	Abteilung	the machine ~
shop floor [ˌʃɒp 'flɔ:*]	Betrieb, Belegschaft	the men on the ~ ~
workbench ['wɜ:k bentʃ]	Werkbank	work at a ~
conveyor belt [kən'veɪə belt]	Fließband	stand (+ all day) at a ~ ~
assemble [ə'sembl]	montieren	~ cars / **assembly line** [ə'semblɪ laɪn] (Fließband)
piecework ['pi:swɜ:k]	Akkordarbeit	do ~ / be on ~
overtime ['əʊvətaɪm]	Überstunden	work ~ / be on ~

shift [ʃɪft]	Schicht	the early (or: late) ~ / work on the day (or: night) ~
clock in [klɒk 'ɪn]	(den Arbeitsbeginn an der Kontrolluhr) stechen	~ ~ at 7 o'clock
clock out [klɒk 'aʊt]	(das Arbeitsende an der Kontrolluhr) stechen	~ ~ at 3 o'clock
factory whistle ['fæktərɪ ˌwɪsl]	Fabriksirene	The ~ ~ blows at 6 and 2.

Farm – Bauernhof 112

(→ 159 Animals on the farm; 163 Man and animal; 165 The animal; 167 Vegetables, cereals, fruit; 168 Man and plant; 169 The plant)

farm [fɑːm]	Bauernhof	live (or: work) on a ~ / a cattle (or: chicken / poultry / pig / fruit) ~ / **farmhouse** ['fɑːmhaʊs] / in the **farmyard** ['fɑːmjɑːd]
farmer ['fɑːmə*]	Bauer, Landwirt	
farm hand ['fɑːm hænd]	Knecht, Landarbeiter	
farming ['fɑːmɪŋ]	Landwirtschaft, besonders Ackerbau und Viehzucht	
agriculture ['ægrɪkʌltʃə*]	Landwirtschaft, besonders Ackerbau	**agricultural** [ˌ--'--rəl] products
dairy products ['deərɪ ˌprəʊdʌkts]	Milchprodukte	
ranch [ræntʃ] (*AE*)	Viehfarm	a cattle- (or: horse- / sheep-) ~ / **rancher** ['-ə*]
shed [ʃed]	Schuppen, (Kuh-)Stall	keep the farm equipment in the ~ **cowshed** ['kaʊ-] / a **cattle shed** ['kætl –]
pigsty ['pɪgstaɪ]	Schweinestall	
stable [steɪbl]	Pferdestall	
barn [bɑːn]	Scheune	
hen house ['hen haʊs]	Hühnerstall	

Trade – Handel

113 Buying, selling – Kaufen, Verkaufen

trade [treɪd]	handeln, Handel;	~ in coffee do a lot of ~ with sb / a **trade agreement** [ˌ– əˈgriːmənt] between England and Germany
	eintauschen	~ sth for sth
commerce [ˈkɒmɜːs]	Handel	~ between England and the United States / **Chamber of Commerce** [ˌtʃeɪmbər‿əv ˈkɒmɜːs] (Handelskammer)
business [ˈbɪznɪs]	Geschäft, Geschäftsleben	do (+ some / a lot of) ~ together (or: with sb) / How's ~? / go into ~ / be in the wool ~
market [ˈmɑːkɪt]	Markt	We buy our vegetables at the ~. / on ~ day / a cattle ~ / find a ~ for a product / there is a great ~ for a product
fair [feə*]	Messe	a book ~ / the **Hanover Fair** [ˈhænəʊvə ˈ–]
import [ɪmˈpɔːt]	importieren	~ sth from a country
export [ekˈspɔːt]	exportieren	~ sth to a country
offer [ˈɒfə*]	anbieten,	~ sb sth (+ for $10,000) / ~ sb £2,000 for sth
	Angebot	make sb an ~ / make an ~ of $50 for sth
advertise [ˈædvətaɪz]	annoncieren	~ sth / ~ in a newspaper / put an **advertisement** [ədˈvɜːtɪsmənt] in the newspaper
deal (dealt, dealt) [diːl, delt, –]	handeln, Handel treiben,	~ in tobacco / a **car dealer** [ˈkɑː -ə*]
	(regelmäßig) kaufen,	~ at a store
	in geschäftlicher Verbindung stehen	~ with a store / ~ with sb
sell (sold, sold) [sel, səʊld, –]	verkaufen,	~ sb sth (+ for $50) / ~ sth off at reduced prices
	sich verkaufen	sth ~s well (or: badly)
sold out [seʊld ˈaʊt]	ausverkauft	We're (+ all) ~ ~.
sale [seɪl]	Verkauf	sth is for ~ / make a ~ / **'For Sale'** / get sth at a ~ (als Sonderangebot) / a **wholesale** [ˈhəʊl-] (Großhandels-)

		business (or: dealer / price) / **wholesaler** ['həʊl-ə*] / regular price £5, **wholesale price** £3.50
order ['ɔːdə*]	bestellen, Bestellung	~ sth / ~ oneself a new suit execute an ~ / send in an ~
customer ['kʌstəmə*]	Kunde	be a ~ at a shop / be a good ~
shopping ['ʃɒpɪŋ]	Einkauf(en)	go ~ / do one's ~ / go ~ for some new clothes
shopping centre ['– ˌsentə*]	Einkaufszentrum	the ~ ~ of a town
shopping street ['– ˌstriːt]	Einkaufsstraße	
shopping precinct ['– ˌpriːsɪŋkt]	Einkaufszone	
shopping mall ['– ˌmɔl], ['– ˌmæl] (*AE*)	Einkaufszone	
buy (bought, bought) [baɪ, bɔːt, –]	kaufen,	~ sth (+ for 50p) / ~ sth new (or: cheap) / ~ sth from sb
	guter Kauf	It's a real ~ at such a low price.
bargain ['bɑːgɪn]	handeln,	~ with sb about (= over) a price
	gutes Geschäft,	make a ~ / sth is a real ~
	gute Gelegenheit	pick sth up as a ~ / hunt for ~s
window shopping ['wɪndəʊ ˌʃɒpɪŋ]	Schaufensterbummel	go ~ ~
get (got, got) [get, gɒt, –]	bekommen	Where can I ~ a nice picture-postcard of London?
I'd like [aɪd 'laɪk]	Ich hätte gern	~ ~ a picture-postcard of New York.
exchange [ɪks'tʃeɪndʒ]	umtauschen	I want to ~ this shirt; it's not the right size.

Shop – Laden, Geschäft 114

shop [ʃɒp] (*BE*)	Laden, Geschäft	keep (or: run) a ~ / go to a ~ / a big (or: large / small / little) ~ / the local village ~ / ~s open (or: close) at ...
store [stɔːr] (*AE*)	(großes) Geschäft, Laden, Geschäft	a furniture (or: hardware) ~ the local village ~ / a general ~
department store [dɪ'pɑːtmənt stɔː*]	Kaufhaus	A ~ ~ sells a variety of goods.
department [dɪ'pɑːtmənt]	Abteilung	the shoe ~

supermarket ['suːpəˌmɑːkɪt]	Supermarkt	buy sth in a ~
shop window ['ʃɒp wɪndəʊ]	Schaufenster	I want the coat in the ~ ~.
window display ['wɪndəʊ dɪ'spleɪ]	Auslage	see sth in the ~ ~ / sth is in the ~ ~
counter ['kaʊntə*]	Theke	stand behind the ~ / put the articles on the ~
cash-register ['kæʃ ˌredʒɪstə*]	Ladenkasse	put money in the ~
shopping ['ʃɒpɪŋ]	Einkaufs-	~-trolley (*BE*) (= -cart (*AE*)) / ~-basket (or: bag)
cash desk ['kæʃ desk]	Kasse (in einem Supermarkt oder Warenhaus)	
shopkeeper ['ʃɒpˌkiːpə*] (*BE*) = **store-keeper** ['stɔːrˌkiːpər] (*AE*)	Ladenbesitzer	
shop assistant ['ʃɒp əˌsɪstənt] (*BE*) = **sales clerk** ['seɪlz klɜrk] (*AE*)	Verkäufer(-in)	

Shops, shopkeepers, and what they sell – Geschäfte, Händler und was sie verkaufen

grocer ['grəʊsə*]	Lebensmittelhändler	(→ 24 Food and drink)
grocery ['grəʊsərɪ]	Lebensmittelgeschäft	
greengrocer ['griːnˌgrəʊsə*]	Obst- und Gemüsehändler	(→ 167 Vegetables, cereals, fruit)
greengrocery ['griːnˌgrəʊsərɪ]	Obst- und Gemüseladen	
butcher ['bʊtʃə*]	Metzger, Fleischer	(→ 24 Food and drink)
butcher's ['bʊtʃəz]	Metzgerei, Fleischerei	
baker ['beɪkə*]	Bäcker	(→ 24 Food and drink)
baker's ['beɪkəz]	Bäckerei	
pharmacist ['fɑːməsɪst]	Apotheker	(→ 29 At the doctor's)
pharmacy ['fɑːməsɪ]	Apotheke	
chemist ['kemɪst] (*BE*)	Apotheker, Drogist	(→ 29 At the doctor's; 139 Bathroom, hygiene)
chemist's ['kemɪsts] (*BE*)	Apotheke, Drogerie	
druggist ['drʌgɪst] (*AE*)	Drogist	

drugstore ['drʌgstɔːr] (*AE*)	Drogerie (manchmal mit Apotheke)	
ironmonger ['aɪən,mʌŋgə*]	Eisenwarenhändler	(→ 140 Kitchen, housework; 110 Manufacturing; 168 Man and plant)
hardware ['hɑːdweə*]	Eisenwaren	
tobacconist [tə'bækənɪst]	Tabakhändler	(→ 26 Smoking)
tobacconist's [tə'bækənɪsts]	Tabakladen	
confectioner [kən'fekʃnə*]	Konditor, Zuckerbäcker	(→ 24 Food and drink)
confectioner's [kən'fekʃnəz] = **sweet shop** ['swiːt ʃɒp] (*BE*) = **candy store** ['kændɪ stɔːr] (*AE*)	Süßwarenladen	
confectionery [,kən'fekʃnərɪ]	Süßwaren	
newsagent ['njuːz,eɪdʒənt] (*BE*) = **newsdealer** ['nuːz,diːlər] (*AE*)	Zeitungshändler	(→ 66 The press)
newsagent's ['njuːz,eɪdʒənts]	Zeitungsladen	
newsstand ['njuːzstænd]	Zeitungskiosk	
bookseller ['bʊkselə*]	Buchhändler	(→ 69 Book)
bookshop ['bʊkʃɒp] = **bookstore** ['bʊkstɔːr] (*AE*)	Buchhandlung	
stationer ['steɪʃnə*]	Schreibwarenhändler	(→ 49 Write; 50 Correspondence)
stationer's ['steɪʃnəz]	Schreibwarengeschäft	
stationery ['steɪʃnərɪ]	Schreibwaren	
record shop ['rekɔːd ʃɒp]	Schallplattengeschäft	
souvenir shop [,suːvə'nɪə ʃɒp]	Andenkenladen	
antique dealer [æn'tiːk 'diːlə]	Antiquitätenhändler	
antique-shop [æn'tiːkʃɒp]	Antiquitätenladen	

115 Goods – Güter, Waren

goods [gʊds]	Güter, Waren	There is a large variety of ~ in the shops. / sell many kinds of ~
product ['prɒdʌkt]	Erzeugnis	sell one's ~s
produce ['prɒdju:s]	landwirtschaftliche Erzeugnisse	The farmer takes his ~ to the market.
article ['ɑ:tɪkl]	Artikel	~s of clothing / An ~ sells well.
store [stɔ:*]	Vorrat, Lager	keep sth in ~
storehouse ['stɔ:haʊs]	Lagerhaus; Fundgrube	
store-room ['stɔ:rʊm]	Lagerraum, Vorratskammer	
stock [stɒk]	Vorrat, Warenbestand, Lager;	sth is in (or: out of) ~ take ~ (Inventur machen)
	Standard-	sell all ~ sizes
warehouse ['weəhaʊs]	Lagerhaus	the ~s by the river
deliver [dɪ'lɪvə*]	liefern	~ goods to the door / guarantee prompt **delivery** [-vərɪ]
forward ['fɔ:wəd]	zusenden	~ goods to sb
return [rɪ'tɜ:n]	zurückgeben	~ empty bottles to the shop
selection [sɪ'lekʃn]	Auswahl	a shop has a good (or: large / fine) ~ (+ of sth)
range [reɪndʒ]	Auswahl	a shop has a large ~ of sth
contain [kən'teɪn]	enthalten	a bottle ~s wine (or: a pint of beer) / boxes, bottles, cans are **containers** [-əz]
hold (held, held) [həʊld, held, –]	fassen, enthalten	a bottle ~ing 1 litre
pack [pæk]	verpacken	~ goods / ~ up a parcel
wrap [ræp]	einwickeln	~ sth in brown paper (Packpapier)
carry ['kærɪ]	tragen	~ sth in a **paperbag** ['peɪpəbæg]
tie [taɪ]	(ver-)schnüren	~ a parcel up / ~ a knot (+ in a piece of string)
knot [nɒt]	knoten,	~ a rope tightly
	Knoten	tie sth with a ~
string [strɪŋ]	Bindfaden	a ball of ~ / a piece of ~
glue [glu:]	Klebstoff,	
	kleben	~ sth to sth

How things are sold – Wie etwas verkauft wird

by **weight** [weɪt]	nach Gewicht	two pounds of tea (or: cheese / potatoes / pork)
by **quantity** ['kwɒntətɪ]	nach Quantität	six (or: a dozen) eggs / twenty cigars
in **slices** ['slaɪsɪz]	(in Scheiben) geschnitten	six ~ of ham (or: cheese)
in **packets** ['pækɪts] (*BE*)	in Tüten, Päckchen, Packungen	two ~ of cigarettes (or: biscuits / butter)
in **packs** [pæks] (*AE*)	in Päckchen	two ~ of cigarettes
in **tubes** [tju:bz]	in Tuben	two ~ of toothpaste
in **bottles** ['bɒtlz]	in Flaschen	two ~ of wine (or: sauce / juice)
in **tins** [tɪnz] (*BE*)	in Dosen, Konserven, Büchsen	two ~ of beans (or: fish / fruit / milk)
in **cans** [kænz] (*AE*)	in Dosen	two ~ of beer (or: beans / fish / milk)
in **bars** [bɑ:z]	Tafel, Riegel	two ~ of milk chocolate (or: soap)
in **jars** [dʒɑ:z]	in Gläsern	two ~ of jam (or: honey / marmalade / mixed pickles)
in **boxes** ['bɒksɪz]	in Schachteln	two ~ of matches (or: cigars / chocolate)
in **sacks** [sæks]	in Säcken	two ~ of potatoes (or: rice)
in **barrels** ['bærəlz]	in Fässern	two ~ of beer
in **cartons** ['kɑ:tənz]	in Kartons, in Stangen	two ~ of eggs (or: milk) a **carton** ['kɑrtn] of 200 cigarettes (*AE*)
in **crates** [kreɪts] (*BE*)	in Kästen	two ~ of beer
in **cases** ['keɪsɪz] (*AE*)	in Kästen	two ~ of soda (Sprudel)
in **bunches** ['bʌntʃɪz]	in Stauden, als Strauß	two ~ of grapes (or: bananas) two ~ of flowers
in **bags** [bægz]	in Beuteln, in Tüten	two five-pound ~ of potatoes
in bundles ['bʌndlz]	in Bündeln, in Ballen	

Price – Preis 116

price [praɪs]	Preis	What's the ~ of ...? / The ~ will be something like £10. / pay a high ~ for sth / ~s are high (or: low) / ~s rise (or: drop / fall) / raise (or: reduce / lower) ~s / at a reasonable ~

How much is this?	Was kostet das?	
How much are these?	Was kosten diese?	
It's 50p.	Das kostet 50p.	
They're 50p.	Die kosten 50p.	

cost (cost, cost) [kɒst, kɒst, –]	kosten	sth ~s a lot of money (or: too much / 50p / very little) / What (or: How much) does it ~?
	Kosten	What is the ~ of ...? / **cost of living** [ˌ–‿əv 'lɪvɪŋ]
charge [tʃɑːdʒ]	berechnen	~ sb $50 (+ for sth)
expensive [ɪk'spensɪv]	teuer	a very ~ car (or: restaurant) / at one's own **expense** [ɪk'spens] / pay sb's **expenses** [-ɪz]
cheap [tʃiːp]	billig	sth is fairly ~ / sth is dirt ~ (*inform.*) (spottbillig) / buy sth ~ly / sth is ~ at the price
cost-effective [ˌkɒstɪ'fektiv]	kostengünstig	
costly ['kɔstlɪ] (*AE*)	kostspielig	a ~ sport
dear [dɪə*] (*BE*)	teuer, kostspielig	It's too ~, I can't afford it.
discount ['dɪskaʊnt]	Rabatt	allow 3% ~ for cash (+ payment)
hire-purchase [ˌhaɪə'pɜːtʃəs] (*BE*)	Ratenkauf	buy a TV (or: car) on ~
credit ['kredɪt]	Raten	buy sth on ~
invoice ['ɪnvɔɪs]	Lieferschein	
reminder [rɪ'maɪndə*]	Mahnung	
receipt [rɪ'siːt]	Quittung	
fee [fiː]	Honorar, Gebühr	a doctor's ~ / school ~s
bill [bɪl] (*BE*) = **check** [tʃek] (*AE*)	Rechnung	pay the ~ after a meal
pay [peɪ]	(be)zahlen	~ the bill / ~ for sth (or: sb)

Money – Geld

117 Currency – Währung

currency ['kʌrənsɪ]	Währung, Devisen	The German ~ is strong. Foreign ~ies (+ not) accepted.
coin [kɔɪn]	Münze	insert (einwerfen) the ~s before speaking

note [nəʊt] (*BE*) = **bill** [bɪl] (*AE*)	Schein	change a £5 ~ / pay with a $5 ~
penny ['penɪ]	Penny	You can't buy anything for a ~
pence [pens]	(Mehrzahl, als Wert)	It costs ten ~
pennies ['penɪz]	(Mehrzahl, als Münzen)	Give me five ~ for this five-pence piece, please.
pound [paʊnd]	Pfund	It costs five ~s. / a **five-pound note** / a hundred pence to the ~
cent [sent]	Cent	Five ~s are called a **nickel** ['nɪkəl]. / Ten ~s are called a **dime** [daɪm]. / Twenty-five cents are called a **quarter** ['kwɔːrtər].
dollar ['dɒlər] (*AE*)	Dollar	It costs five ~s.
change [tʃeɪndʒ] = **exchange** [ɪks'tʃeɪndʒ]	Wechselgeld; umtauschen	Have you got ~ for £5? ~ pounds for dollars.

We write:	*We say:*	*We write:*	*We say:*
5p	['faɪv 'piː]	**5c**	['faɪv 'sents]
£3	['θriː 'paʊndz]	**$1.50**	[ə 'dɒlər 'fɪftɪ]
£8.20	['eɪt paʊndz 'twentɪ]	**$3.08**	['θriː 'dɒləz eɪt 'sents]

Banking, insurance, stock exchange – Bankwesen, Versicherung, Börse 118

bank [bæŋk]	Bank	the **Bank of England** [ˌ–‿əv 'ɪŋglənd] / have money in the ~
savings bank ['seɪvɪŋz ˌbæŋk]	Sparkasse	
branch [brɑːntʃ]	Zweigstelle, Filiale	a bank with ~es all over the country
account [ə'kaʊnt]	Konto	have (or: open) an ~ (+ at a bank) / have money in one's ~ / an empty ~
current account ['kʌrənt‿əˌkaʊnt]	laufendes Konto	
savings account ['seɪvɪŋz əˌkaʊnt]	Sparkonto	
pay (paid, paid) **in** [peɪ, peɪd, –; ˌ– 'ɪn]	einzahlen	~ ~ £100 / ~ £100 ~ to one's account
draw (drew, drawn) [drɔː, druː, drɔːn] = **withdraw** [wɪð'-]	abheben	~ money (+ from one's account)

overdraw [ˌəʊvəˈdrɔː], [-druː], [-drɔːn]	überziehen	~ one's account
balance [ˈbæləns]	ausgleichen, saldieren	~ an account
bank statement [ˈbæŋk ˌsteɪtmənt]	Kontoauszug	
finance [faɪˈnæns]	finanzieren	~ a project / have **financial** [faɪˈnænʃl] problems
transfer [trænsˈfɜː*]	überweisen	~ £50 (+ to sb / to sb's account)
standing order [ˈstændɪŋ ˈɔːdə*]	Dauerauftrag	pay rates (or: insurances) by ~ ~
cheque [tʃek] (*BE*) = **check** [–] (*AE*)	Scheck	pay by ~ / cash a ~ / draw (ausstellen) a ~ (+ on one's bank) / a ~ for 50 dollars
cheque card [ˈtʃek kɑːd] (*BE*) = **check card** [ˈ– kɑrd] (*AE*)	Scheckkarte	apply for a ~ ~
chequebook [ˈtʃekbʊk] (*BE*) = **checkbook** [–] (*AE*)	Scheckheft	
crossed check [ˈkrɒst tʃek]	Verrechnungsscheck	
bill [bɪl]	Wechsel	draw (ausstellen) (or: accept) a ~
loan [ləʊn]	Darlehen	get a ~ (+ from one's bank) / grant a ~ / a 5,000 dollar ~
interest [ˈɪntrɪst]	Zinsen	pay 5% ~ (+ on a loan)
interest rate [ˈɪntrɪst ˌreɪt]	Zinsfuß	Lend money at 8% ~ ~
invest [ɪnˈvest]	anlegen	~ money (+ in a business)
counter [ˈkaʊntə*]	Schalter	wait at the ~
cashier [kæˈʃɪə*] (*BE*) = **teller** [ˈtelər] (*AE*)	Kassierer	
safe	Safe	deposit documents in a ~ / **safe-breaker** [ˈ-ˌbreɪkə*] (= **safe-cracker** [ˈ-ˌkrækər], AE)
insure [ɪnˈʃʊə*]	versichern	~ oneself (or: one's life / one's car / one's house) / be **insured** [-d] against fire
insurance [ɪnˈʃʊərəns]	Versicherung	have a life (or: fire) ~ / an ~ policy / pay monthly premiums on one's ~
stock exchange [ˈstɒk‿ɪksˌtʃeɪndʒ]	Börse	the New York ~ ~

share [ʃeə*]	Aktie	hold (= own) (+ 100) ~s in a company
quotation [kwəʊ'teɪʃn]	Notierung	The ~ for GM was 49¾–50¼.
dividend ['dɪvɪdend]	Dividende	pay a ~
speculate ['spekjʊleɪt]	spekulieren	~ in gold mines / a **speculative** ['spekʊlətɪv] sale / **speculator** [-ə*]
broker ['brəʊkə*]	Börsenagent	give an order to the ~

Spend money, owe money – Geld ausgeben, Geld schulden 119

money ['mʌnɪ]	Geld	have (or: earn) (+ a lot of) ~ / get **pocket money** ['pɒkɪt ˌ–] (+ every Sunday)
sum [sʌm]	Summe	spend large ~s of money
amount [ə'maʊnt]	Betrag,	owe (or: pay) an ~
	sich belaufen auf,	The bill ~s to £40.
	Summe, Menge	spend large ~s of money
cash [kæʃ]	Bargeld	I have no ~ on me. / pay ~
pay (paid, paid) [peɪ, peɪd, –]	bezahlen	~ for sth / ~ 50 dollars (+ for sth) / ~ a bill / ~ sb
spend (spent, spent) [spend, spent, –]	ausgeben	~ £5,000 for (= on) a new car / ~ a lot of money on sth / ~ 20 dollars a week
afford [ə'fɔːd]	sich leisten,	be able to ~ a new car every two years / Can you ~ to lend me some money?
	aufbringen	be able to ~ £20,000 for a new house
mean [miːn]	geizig, knauserig	be ~ about money
waste [weɪst]	verschwenden	~ money
short of ['ʃɔːt‿əv]	knapp an	be ~ ~ money
borrow ['bɒrəʊ]	leihen	~ money (+ from a bank)
lend (lent, lent) [lend, lent, –]	(aus-)leihen	~ sb money
credit ['kredɪt]	Kreditwürdigkeit,	sb's ~ is good for £10,000
	gutschreiben	~ 100 dollars to a customer / ~ an amount to one's bank account
debt [det]	Schuld	pay one's ~s / be in (or: out of) ~ / run into ~ / a ~ of 50 dollars
owe [əʊ]	schulden	~ sb money
save [seɪv]	sparen, ersparen	This will ~ you a lot of money. / be **saving** ['-ɪŋ] money (+ for sth)
thrifty ['θrɪftɪ]	sparsam	a ~ housewife

Our leisure time – Unsere Freizeit

Holidays – Ferien

120 Holiday – Feiertag, Ferien, Urlaub

holiday ['hɒlɪdeɪ]	Feiertag,	Christmas is a ~ in most countries. / a public ~
	Ferien, Urlaub (*BE*),	go (or: be) on ~ / Where are you going for your ~s? / spend one's ~s at the seaside / take a month's ~ in summer / the school ~s
	Urlaub machen	~ in France / **holiday-maker** [– ˌmeɪkə*]
vacation [və'keɪʃn] (*BE*), [veɪ'-] (*AE*)	Ferien, Urlaub (*AE*);	be on ~ / Where are you going for your ~?
	Semesterferien (*BE*)	The college is closed during (+ the) ~.
leave [li:v]	Urlaub (des Soldaten oder Beamten)	be on ~ / absent without ~ / home ~ every 18 months
feast [fi:st]	(kirchlicher) Feiertag	celebrate a ~ / a movable ~
Good Friday [ˌgʊd 'fraɪdɪ]	Karfreitag	
Easter ['i:stə*]	Ostern	
Whitsun ['wɪtsn]	Pfingsten	
Christmas ['krɪsməs] **(+ Day)** [ˌ– 'deɪ]	Weihnachten	
Christmas Eve [ˌkrɪsməs 'i:v]	Heiligabend	
Boxing Day ['bɒksɪŋ deɪ] (*BE*)	Zweiter Weihnachtstag	
Thanksgiving ['θæŋksˌgɪvɪŋ] **(+ Day)** (*AE*) **= Harvest Festival** [ˌhɑ:vɪst 'festəvl] (*BE*)	Erntedankfest	
bank holiday [ˌbæŋk 'hɒlədɪ] (*BE*)	Bankfeiertag	
New Year's Day [ˌnju: jɪəz 'deɪ]	Neujahr	
New Year's Eve [ˌnju: jɪəz 'i:v]	Silvester	

Hallowe'en [ˌhæləʊ'iːn]	wird am 31. Oktober gefeiert	
Remembrance Sunday [rɪ'membrəns ˌsʌndɪ]	etwa: Volkstrauertag	
Poppy Day ['pɒpɪ deɪ]	volkstüml. Name für 'Remembrance Day'	
Guy Fawkes' Night ['gaɪ fɔːks naɪt]	wird am 5. November gefeiert	
May Day ['meɪ deɪ]	1. Mai	
leisure ['leʒə] (*BE*), ['liːʒər] (*AE*)	Muße, Freizeit	spend one's ~ doing sth / have little ~ time / do sth at ~
weekend [ˌwiːk'end]	Wochenende	spend the ~ at the seaside

Travelling – Reisen (→ 91 Public finance; 99 Country; 151–157 Transport) 121

travel agency ['trævl ˌeɪdʒənsɪ]	Reisebüro	go to a ~ ~
book [bʊk]	buchen	~ a flight / Could you ~ me a double room, please?
ticket ['tɪkɪt]	Fahrkarte, Flugschein	buy a ~
package tour ['pækɪdʒ tʊə*]	Pauschalreise	book a ~ ~
luggage ['lʌgɪdʒ] (*BE*) = **baggage** ['bægɪdʒ] (*AE*)	Gepäck	have a lot of ~ with one / pack one's ~ / Where's your **hand luggage**?
suitcase ['suːtkeɪs]	Koffer	carry a light (or: heavy) ~
bag [bæg]	Tasche	
holdall ['həʊldɔːl]	Reisetasche	
trunk [trʌŋk] (*BE*)	Seemannskoffer	
pack [pæk]	packen	~ a suitcase (or: one's luggage) / **unpack** [ˌʌn'pæk] a suitcase
start [stɑːt]	aufbrechen	~ for London / ~ early
set (set, set) **off** [ˌset 'ɒf]	aufbrechen	~ ~ on a journey (or: a trip)
leave (left, left) [liːv, left, –]	abreisen von	~ London / ~ for (aufbrechen nach) India
travel ['trævl]	reisen,	~ by air (or: train / car / bus) / ~ through France (or: to Spain / round the world) / ~ 100 miles a day / **traveller** [-ə*] / **traveller's cheque** [ˌ-əz 'tʃek]
	Reise	I saw these things on (= during) my ~s.

journey ['dʒɜːnɪ]	Reise	make a ~ by car / a long ~ / go on a ~ / It's a two-day (= days') ~ from here to ...
trip [trɪp]	Vergnügungsreise, Ausflug	go on (= for) a ~ to Brighton for the day / make a ~ (+ on the Thames)
tour [tʊə*]	Rundreise, eine Rundreise machen, bereisen;	a ~ round Europe / ~ England / a **touring** ['-rɪŋ] holiday
	Rundgang	a ~ of London (or: a castle) / go on a guided ~ round the castle
voyage ['vɔɪɪdʒ]	Seereise	go on a long ~ / a ~ round the world / make a ~ / the ~ from England to Spain
tourist ['tʊərɪst]	Tourist,	a town full of ~s in summer
	Touristen-	~ class / ~ information
the sights [ðə 'saɪts]	die Sehenswürdigkeiten	see ~ ~ of London
sightseeing ['saɪtˌsiːɪŋ]	Besichtigung;	go ~ / sth attracts many **sightseers** ['saɪtsiːəz]
	Besichtigungs-	go on a ~ **tour**
guide [gaɪd]	Fremdenführer;	The ~ showed us some of the sights of London.
	Reiseführer (als Buch)	a ~ for visitors to Britain / a ~ to London

122 Hotel – Hotel

hotel [həʊ'tel]	Hotel	stay at a ~ (+ for two nights) / a small (or: large / big / good / comfortable) ~ / an expensive ~
guest house ['gest haʊs]	Pension	
reception [rɪ'sepʃn]	Empfang	leave the key at the ~ / ~ desk
lobby ['lɒbɪ] (*AE*)	Empfangshalle	meet sb in the (+ hotel) ~
reserve [rɪ'zɜːv]	reservieren	~ a room in a hotel / Have you got a **reservation** [ˌrezə'veɪʃn], Sir?
book [bʊk]	buchen, reservieren lassen	I've ~ed two rooms for tonight. / Could you ~ me a double room, please?
room [ruːm]	Zimmer	book a ~ with (or: without) a bath (or: shower) / a double (or: single) ~
register ['redʒɪstə*]	sich anmelden, die Anmeldeformulare ausfüllen	Please, ~ before going up to your room. / ~ at a hotel
porter ['pɔːtə*] (*BE*)	Portier	The ~ will call a taxi for you.

lift [lɪft] (*BE*) = **elevator** ['elɪveɪtər] (*AE*)	Fahrstuhl	Please take the ~.
key [kiː]	Schlüssel	Leave your ~ at the desk.
call [kɔːl]	wecken	Please ~ me at seven tomorrow.
hall [hɔːl]	Hotelhalle	wait for sb in the ~
lounge [laʊndʒ]	Gesellschaftsraum	watch TV in the ~

Camping – Camping 123

camp [kæmp]	zelten, campen;	~ for the night by a little brook / go **camping** ['-ɪŋ]
	Ferienlager	stay in a ~
camping site ['kæmpɪŋ ˌsaɪt] = **camp site** ['kæmp saɪt]	Zeltplatz	
caravan site ['kærəvæn ˌsaɪt]	Campingplatz (für Wohnwagen)	
caravan park ['kærəvæn ˌpɑːk]	Campingplatz (mit Mietwohnwagen)	
tent [tent]	Zelt	put (= set) up a ~ / sleep in ~s
pitch [pɪtʃ]	aufschlagen	~ a tent
strike (struck, struck) [straɪk, strʌk, –]	abbrechen	~ a tent
peg [peg]	Pflock, Hering	hammer the ~s into the ground
canvas ['kænvəs]	Segeltuch	
sleeping bag ['sliːpɪŋ ˌbæg]	Schlafsack	
rucksack ['rʌksæk]	Rucksack	carry a ~
caravan ['kærəvæn]	Wohnwagen	
motor caravan ['məʊtə ˌkærəvæn]	Wohnmobil	
motorhome ['məʊtərˌhəʊm] (*AE*)	Wohnmobil	
trailer ['treɪlər] (*AE*)	Wohnwagen, Anhänger	

Sports and games – Sport und Spiel

124 Sport – Sport

(→ 71 competition)

sport [spɔːt]	Sport, Sportart	go in for ~ / be fond of ~ Football, hockey and baseball are ~s.
sports [spɔːts]	(Leichtathletik-) Wettkampf, Sportfest	Our **School Sports Day** [skuːl '– ˌdeɪ] will be on Thursday.
match [mætʃ]	Wettkampf, -spiel, Partie, Kampf	win (or: lose) a ~ a football (or: tennis / boxing / cricket) ~
game [geɪm]	Spiel	Let's have a ~ of billiards. / the **Olympic Games** [ə'lɪmpɪk 'geɪmz]
compete [kəm'piːt]	(an einem Wettkampf) teilnehmen	~ in a championship (or: tournament / race) / a(n) national (or: international) **competition** [ˌkɒmpɪ'tɪʃn] (Wettkampf)
sportsman (*pl.* sportsmen ['spɔːtsmən])	Sportler; (der faire) Sportsmann	be a good ~
sportswoman ['spɔːtswʊmən] (*pl.* sportswomen [-wɪmɪn])	Sportlerin	
sportsmanship ['spɔːtsmənʃɪp]	sportliches Verhalten	
athlete ['æθliːt]	(Leicht-)Athlet	
amateur ['æmətə*]	Amateur	
professional [prə'feʃənl]	Berufssportler	turn ~ (= become a ~ player)
team [tiːm]	Mannschaft	Our ~ has won.
captain ['kæptɪn]	Mannschaftsführer	
train [treɪn]	trainieren	~ a team / ~ for the next match
shape [ʃeɪp] = **form** [fɔːm]	Form	get (or: stay) in ~ / be out of ~ / be in (+ good / bad) ~
coach [kəʊtʃ]	Trainer	an athletics (or: football) ~
play [pleɪ]	spielen	~ (+ a game of) football / a football (or: cricket) **player** [-ə*]
win (won, won) [wɪn, wʌn, –]	gewinnen	~ a game (or: match / race)
beat (beat, beaten) [biːt, –, 'biːtn]	schlagen	~ sb (+ at tennis)

cup [kʌp]	Pokal	win the ~ / ~ final / a **challenge cup** ['tʃælɪndʒ –] (Wanderpokal)
score [skɔː]	erzielen, Ergebnis	~ points (or: a goal) What's the ~?
medal ['medl]	Medaille	win the gold ~
record ['rekɔːd]	Rekord	hold (or: set up / break) a ~ / improve a ~ / **world record** ['wɜːld '–]
champion ['tʃæmpjən]	Meister	be the **world champion** ['wɜːld –]
championship ['tʃæmpjənshɪp]	Meisterschaft; Meistertitel	the heavyweight ~ of the world / the U.S. open golf ~
draw [drɔː]	Unentschieden	The game was (or: ended in) a ~.
lose (lost, lost) [luːz, lɒst, –]	verlieren	~ a game / ~ by 1 goal (or: set) to 2 / ~ badly
referee [ˌrefə'riː]	Schiedsrichter (Fußball, Rugby, Basketball, Hockey, Ringen)	
umpire ['ʌmpaɪə*]	Schiedsrichter (Baseball, Cricket, Tennis, Tischtennis, Volleyball)	
rule [ruːl]	Regel	the ~s of tennis / sth is against the ~s
fair [feə*]	fair, sportlich	~ play / **unfair** [ˌʌn'-] play / play ~
foul [faʊl]	unfair, regelwidrig	~ shot (or: hit) / There was a great deal of ~ play in the football match.

Games, sports – Spiele, Sportarten 125

gymnastics	[dʒɪm'næstɪks]	Turnen
athletics	[æθ'letɪks]	Leichtathletik
running	['rʌnɪŋ]	Laufen
jogging	['dʒɒgɪŋ]	Joggen
long jump	['lɒŋ dʒʌmp]	Weitsprung
high jump	['haɪ dʒʌmp]	Hochsprung
pole vault	['pəʊl vɔːlt]	Stabhochsprung
shot-put	['ʃɒtpʊt]	Kugelstoßen
the diskus throw	[ðə 'dɪskəs θrəʊ]	Diskuswerfen
the javelin throw	[ðə 'dʒævlɪn θrəʊ]	Speerwerfen
football	['fʊtbɔːl]	Fußball
= soccer	['sɒkə*]	
football = American football	[əˌmerɪkən '–] (*AE*)	amerikanischer Fußball
rugby	['rʌgbɪ]	Rugby

volleyball	['vɒlɪbɔ:l]	Volleyball
baseball	['beɪsbɔ:l]	Baseball
basket-ball	['bɑ:skɪtbɔ:l]	Basketball
tennis	['tenɪs]	Tennis
table tennis	['teɪbl ˌtenɪs]	Tischtennis
golf	[gɒlf]	Golf
cricket	['krɪkɪt]	Cricket
handball	['hændbɔ:l]	Handball
rowing	['rəʊɪŋ]	Rudern
canoeing	[kə'nu:ɪŋ]	Kanusport
swimming	['swɪmɪŋ]	Schwimmen
surfing	['sɜ:fɪŋ]	Surfen
skiing	['ski:ɪŋ]	Schifahren
yachting	['jɒtɪŋ]	Segeln
= **sailing**	['seɪlɪŋ]	
skating	['skeɪtɪŋ]	Eislaufen
roller-skating	['rəʊlə ˌskeɪtɪŋ]	Rollschuhlaufen
boxing	['bɒksɪŋ]	Boxen
aerobics	[e'rəʊbɪks]	Aerobic
body-building	['bɒdɪ'bɪldɪŋ]	Bodybuilding
bowling	['bəʊlɪŋ]	Kegeln, Bowling
wrestling	['reslɪŋ]	Ringen
weight lifting	['weɪt ˌlɪftɪŋ]	Gewichtheben
cycling	['saɪklɪŋ]	Radfahren

race [reɪs]	Rennen, Wettlauf	a 100 meter (or: one mile) ~ / a relay ~ (Staffel) / go to the (+ horse / greyhound) ~s

126 Football, soccer – Fußball

football ['fʊtbɔ:l] = **soccer** ['sɒkə*]	Fußball	play ~ / the ~ field (= the pitch) / a ~ match / a ~ fan / the ~ season
stadium ['steɪdjəm] (*pl.* **stadia** [steɪdjə])	Stadion	The ~ is full.
halfway line ['hɑ:fweɪ ˌlaɪn]	Mittellinie	
touch line ['tʌtʃ ˌlaɪn]	Seitenlinie	
penalty ['penltɪ]	Elfmeter(-)	a ~ goal / kick off from the ~ spot
penalty area ['penltɪ ˌeərɪə]	Strafraum	
penalty spot ['penltɪ ˌspɒt]	Elfmeterpunkt	

goal [gəʊl]	Tor	score a ~ / win (+ by) two ~s to nil (= 2–0)
net [net]	Netz	The ball is in the ~.
goalkeeper ['gəʊl͵ki:pə*]	Torwart	
the defence [ðe dɪ'fens]	die Verteidigung	
defenders [dɪ'fendəz]	Verteidiger	
midfield players ['mɪdfi:ld ͵pleɪəz]	Mittelfeldspieler	
strikers ['straɪkəz]	Stürmer	
kick-off [͵kɪk'ɒf]	Anstoß	The ~ is at 2.30.
pass [pɑ:s]	Paß,	make a long ~
	passen	~ the ball to sb
kick [kɪk]	schießen	~ the ball
shoot (shot, shot) [ʃu:t, ʃɒt, –]	schießen	be in a good position to ~
throw-in ['θrəʊɪn]	Einwurf	take a ~
corner ['kɔ:nə*]	Eckball	take a ~
foul [faʊl]	Foul	be sent off the field for a ~
free kick [͵fri: 'kɪk]	Freistoß	It's a ~ ~ to the 'Whites'. / take a ~ ~
shirt [ʃɜ:t]	Trikot	
stand [stænd]	Tribüne	hit a ball into the ~
spectator [spek'teɪtə*]	Zuschauer	
scoreboard ['skɔ:bɔ:d]	Anzeigetafel	
terraces ['terəsɪz]	Stehtribüne	
hooligan ['hu:lɪgən]	Rowdy	
champion ['tʃæmpjən]	Meister	**championship** [-ʃɪp]
cup [kʌp]	Pokal(wettbewerb)	**cup winner** ['– ͵–] (Pokalsieger) / **cup final** [͵– 'faɪnl] / **world cup** ['wɜ:ld '–]
cup-tie ['kʌptaɪ]	Pokalspiel	
division [dɪ'vɪʒən]	Liga	be top of the **First Division** [͵fɜ:st –]
be promoted [bi: prə'məʊtɪd]	aufsteigen	~ ~ to the next division
be relegated [bi: 'relɪgeɪtɪd]	absteigen	~ ~ to the second division

Art and entertainment – Kunst und Unterhaltung

127 Music – Musik

instrument ['ɪnstrʊmənt]	Instrument	play an ~ / tune (stimmen) an ~
play [pleɪ]	spielen	~ the piano (or: trumpet) / ~ by ear
flute [flu:t]	Flöte	
clarinet [ˌklærɪ'nət]	Klarinette	
saxophone ['sæksəfəʊn]	Saxophon	
trombone [trɒm'bəʊn]	Posaune	
trumpet ['trʌmpɪt]	Trompete	blow the ~
violin ['vaɪəlɪn]	Geige	
piano [pɪ'ænəʊ]	Klavier	
drum [drʌm]	Trommel	beat the ~s (Schlagzeug)
guitar [gɪ'tɑ:*]	Gitarre	
note [nəʊt]	Note	
bar [bɑ:*]	Takt	the 50th ~
time [taɪm]	Takt	beat the ~ / be in (or: out of) ~ / get out of ~ / keep good (or: exact) ~
key [ki:]	Tonart	in major (or: minor) ~
major ['meɪdʒə*]	Dur	in C ~
minor ['maɪnə*]	Moll	in F ~
melody ['melədɪ]	Melodie, Lied	sing (or: whistle) a ~ / a simple ~
tune [tju:n]	Melodie	a gay (or: lively) ~ / play (or: sing) sth to the ~ of ... / know the ~ to a song
music ['mju:zɪk]	Musik;	write (or: compose / study / play) ~ / pop (or: chamber) ~ / a **musical** [-l] child
	Noten	play sth without ~
orchestra ['ɔ:kɪstrə]	Orchester	play the violin in the school ~ / conduct (dirigieren) an ~
conduct [kən'dʌkt]	dirigieren	**conductor** [-ə*] (Dirigent)
concert ['kɒnsət]	Konzert	go to a ~
band [bænd]	Kapelle, Band	a dance (or: military) ~ / **band leader** ['– ˌli:də*] / **band master** ['– ˌmɑ:stə*] (*mil.*)
busker ['bʌskə*]	Straßenmusikant	
sing (sang, sung) [sɪŋ, sæŋ, sʌŋ]	singen	~ a song (+ to the guitar)
voice [vɔɪs]	Stimme	have a good ~ / a song arranged for 3 ~s

song [sɒŋ]	Lied	sing a ~ / a popular ~ / a **love-song** ['lʌvsɒŋ] / a **folk-song** ['fəʊksɒŋ]
hit [hɪt]	Schlager	a top ~ / **hit parade** ['– pəˌreɪd]
evergreen ['evəgri:n]	Evergreen	
number ['nʌmbə*]	Nummer	a popular ~
words ['wɜ:dz] = **lyrics** ['lɪrɪks]	Text, Worte	
choir ['kwaɪə*]	(Kirchen-, Schul-)Chor	sing in the church (or: school) ~ / ~ boy / ~ master / **Vienna Boys' Choir** [vɪˌenə 'bɔɪz –]
chorus ['kɔ:rəs]	Chor, Gesangsgruppe;	The ~ was very good. / a men's (or: women's) ~
	Chorlied;	a ~ for men's voices / sing a ~
	Refrain	The girls sang the verses of the song and the boys sang the ~.
quartet [kwɔr'tet]	Quartett	**barber-shop** ~ ['bɑ:bəʃɔp –] (trad. amerik. Gesangsformation)
record ['rekɔ:d]	Schallplatte	play a ~ (+ by the Beatles) / listen to a ~ / put on a ~ / a **record player** [– ˌpleɪə*]
stereo ['sterɪəʊ]	Stereo	I bought myself some new ~ **equipment**. (Stereoanlage)
tape recorder ['teɪp rɪˌkɔ:də*]	Tonbandgerät	
tape [teɪp]	Tonband	
reel [ri:l]	Spule	
control [kən'trəʊl]	Regler	the forward (or: rewind / stop / pause / playback) ~
microphone ['maɪkrəfəʊn]	Mikrophon	
cassette recorder [kə'set rɪˌkɔ:də*]	Kassettenrecorder	
Walkman ['wɔ:kmən]	*Walkman*	carry a ~
CD ['si: 'di:] = **compact disc** ['kɒmpækt ˌdɪsk]	CD, Schallplatte mit digitalisierter Aufnahme	**CD-player** [-pleiə*]

128 Dancing – Tanzen

disco ['dɪskəʊ]	Diskothek	go to a ~
ball [bɔːl]	Ball	go to a ~ / a fancy dress ~ (Maskenball) / a **ballroom** ['bɔːlrʊm]
danceband ['dɑːns,bænd]	Tanzkapelle	
dance [dɑːns] (*BE*), [dæːns] (*AE*)	Tanz,	The waltz is a beautiful ~. / a traditional (or: country) ~ / **square dance** ['skweər dæns] (trad. amerik. Gruppentanz)
	tanzen,	~ a waltz / be a good **dancer** [-ə*] / go to a **dancing school** ['-ɪŋ skuːl]
	Tanz(-veranstaltung)	go to a ~
ballroom dancing ['bɔːlrʊm ,dɑːnsɪng]	Gesellschaftstanz	
waltz [wɔːls]	Walzer	
tango ['tæŋgəʊ]	Tango	
ballet ['bæleɪ] (*BE*), [bæ'leɪ] (*AE*)	Ballett	learn (= study) ~

129 Theatre – Theater

(→ 64 Drama)

theatre ['θɪətə*] (*BE*) = **theater** [-r] (*AE*)	Theater	go to the ~ / a provincial ~
produce [prə'djuːs]	inszenieren	~ a play / a(n) interesting (or: shocking / successful) **production** [prə'dʌkʃn] / a new **production** of 'Macbeth'
direct [dɪ'rekt]	Regie führen	~ a play / a play is under sb's **direction** [dɪ'rekʃn]
rehearse [rɪ'hɜːs]	proben	~ a play / a play is in **rehearsal** [-l] / **dress rehearsal** [,dres -l] (Generalprobe)
cast [kɑːst]	Besetzung	the ~ of a play
part [pɑːt]	Rolle	play (or: take / learn) a ~ / speak one's ~ / The ~s of Macbeth and Lady Macbeth are played by ...
chorus ['kɔːrəs]	Tanz- oder Gesangsgruppe	a girl in the ~ line
act [ækt]	darstellen	~ Hamlet / be an **actor** ['-ə*] (or: **actress** ['-rɪs])
perform [pə'fɔːm]	aufführen	~ a play / ~ 'Macbeth' / a successful **performance** [-əns]

stage [steɪdʒ]	Bühne	be on ~ / enter (or: leave) the ~ / **stage direction** ['– dɪˌrekʃn] (Bühnenanweisung)
curtain ['kɜːtn]	Vorhang	The ~ rises (or: falls).
scenery ['siːnərɪ]	Bühnenbild	The ~ is realistic.
act [ækt]	Akt	a one-~ play
scene [siːn]	Szene	a ~ plays in ... / change of ~ / a key ~
entrance ['entrəns]	Auftritt	make one's ~ from the left (or: right)
enter ['entə*] ...	... tritt auf	~ Hamlet.
exit ['eksɪt]	Abgang;	make one's ~ to the left (or: right)
	... geht ab	~ Polonius
audience ['ɔːdjens]	Zuschauer	There was a large (or: small) ~ in the theatre.
applaud [ə'plɔːd]	applaudieren	~ for five minutes / ~ an actor / win the **applause** [ə'plɔːz] of the audience
cheer [tʃɪə*]	(zu-)jubeln	The audience ~ed. / The actor was ~ed loudly.
stamp [stæmp]	stampfen	The audience ~ed (+ their feet) enthusiastically.
boo [buː]	(aus-)buhen	~ (+ the players / the performance)
hoot [huːt]	johlen	~ (+ the actor off the stage)

Painting, drawing, sculpture – Malen, Zeichnen, Bildhauerei 130

(→ 14 Sight)

museum [mjuː'zɪəm]	Museum	go to a ~ / the **British Museum** [ˌbrɪtɪʃ –]
gallery ['gælərɪ]	Galerie	an art ~ / the **National Gallery** [ˌnæʃnəl '–]
exhibition ['eksɪ'bɪʃn]	Ausstellung	an ~ of modern art
art [ɑːt]	Kunst	a work of ~ / an ~ gallery / the **fine arts** [ˌfaɪn‿ɑːts] / modern (or: abstract) ~ / be a great **artist** ['-ɪst]
craft [krɑːft]	Kunstfertigkeit, Handwerk	the potter's ~ / learn the ~ of a wood-carver
paint [peɪnt]	malen,	~ flowers (or: a landscape) / ~ (+ a picture of) sb / ~ sth blue / a famous **painter** [-ə*] / a nice **painting** ['-ɪŋ] (+ of sb)
	Farbe	mix ~s
canvas ['kænvəs]	Leinwand	paint on ~
draw (drew, drawn) [drɔː, druː, drɔːn]	zeichnen	~ a line (or: circle) / ~ a picture (+ of sb / of sth) / a nice **drawing** ['-ɪŋ]

cartoon [kɑː'tuːn]	Witzzeichnung	draw a ~
caricature ['kærɪkə,tjʊə*]	Karikatur	draw a ~
sketch [sketʃ]	Skizze, skizzieren	make a ~ of sb (or: sth) ~ sb (or: sth)
picture [pɪktʃə*]	Bild	see (or: describe / draw / paint / hang) a ~ / A ~ hangs on the wall.
portray [pɔː'treɪ]	porträtieren	~ sb (+ as ...) / a picture ~ing sth
portrait ['pɔːtrɪt]	Porträt	have one's ~ painted / sit for a ~ / a flattering (or: faithful / lifelike) ~
water-colours ['wɔːtə,kʌləz]	Wasserfarben	paint in ~
oils [ɔɪlz]	Ölfarben, Öl	paint in ~
foreground ['fɔːgraʊnd]	Vordergrund	What can you see in the ~?
middle distance ['mɪdl ,dɪstəns]	Mittelgrund	
background ['bækgraʊnd]	Hintergrund	
frame [freɪm]	Rahmen, rahmen	a wooden ~ ~ a picture / a **framed** [-d] picture
sculpture ['skʌlptʃə*]	Bildhauerei;	study painting and ~ / a **sculptor** ['skʌlptə*]
	Skulptur, Plastik	Michelangelo made some famous ~s.
statue ['stætjuː]	Statue	a ~ of Abraham Lincoln / make a ~ (+ of stone / marble / clay / metal / wood)
carve [kɑːv]	schnitzen, meißeln	~ a statue (+ out of wood) / ~ a statue from marble
shape [ʃeɪp]	formen, modellieren	~ a pot / ~ clay into a pot / ~ a figure out of clay

131 Photography – Fotografieren

camera ['kæmərə]	Kamera, Fotoapparat	load a ~ / a pocket ~
film [fɪlm]	Film	develop a ~ / a **colour film** ['kʌlə –]
photograph ['fəʊtəgrɑːf]	Fotografie,	take a ~ (= **photo** ['fəʊtəʊ]) of sb (or: sth) / take a flash ~ / a **photographer** [fə'tɒgrəfə*]
	fotografieren	~ sb (or: sth)
picture ['pɪktʃə*]	Bild, Foto	take a ~
snap [snæp]	Schnappschuß	take a ~ (= **snapshot** ['-ʃɒt]) of sb (or: sth)
wind (wound, wound) **on** [waɪnd, waʊnd, –; –'ɒn]	weiterdrehen	~ ~ to the next frame

print [prɪnt]	Abzug	make five ~s from the negative
enlargement [ɪn'lɑːdʒmənt]	Vergrößerung	make ~s
flash [flæʃ]	Blitzlicht	use (+ a) ~ (= **flashlight** ['-laɪt]) / take a ~ photo
album ['ælbəm]	Album	stick pictures in an ~
slide [slaɪd]	Dia	take colour ~s / show ~s of one's holidays

Circus, fun fair, variety show – Zirkus, Jahrmarkt, Varieté 132

circus ['sɜːkəs]	Zirkus	go to the ~
ring [rɪŋ]	Manege	enter the ~ / the **ringmaster** ['-mɑːstə*]
artiste [ɑː'tiːst]	Artist	a trapeze [trə'piːz] ~
acrobat ['ækrəbæt]	Akrobat	
handstand ['hændstænd]	Handstand	do a ~
somersault ['sʌməsɔːlt]	Salto	turn a ~
stunt [stʌnt]	Kunststück	do ~s on the trapeze
tightrope ['taɪtrəʊp]	Seil	walk a ~ / a ~ walker
juggle ['dʒʌgl]	jonglieren	~ balls / a **juggler** [-ə*]
clown [klaʊn]	Clown	
antics ['æntɪks]	Clownerien	laugh at sb's ~ / do one's ~
lion tamer ['laɪən ˌteɪmə*]	Löwenbändiger	
magic ['mædʒɪk]	Zauberkunst, Magie	
magician [mə'dʒɪʃn]	Zauberer	
trick [trɪk]	Trick, Zauberkunststück	
fun fair ['fʌn feə*]	Jahrmarkt	
shooting gallery ['ʃuːtɪŋ ˌgælərɪ]	Schießbude	
merry-go-round ['merɪgəʊˌraʊnd] (*BE*) = **carousel** [ˌkærə'sel] (*AE*)	Karussel	ride on a ~

The world around us – Die Welt um uns

Our home – unser Haus

133 Building a house – ein Haus bauen

build (built, built) [bıld, bılt, –]	bauen	~ a house / a house **built of** brick
site [saıt]	Bauplatz	Our house will be built on this ~.
architect ['ɑ:kıtekt]	Architekt	a good ~ / modern **architecture** ['ɑ:kıˌtektʃə*]
design [dı'zaın]	entwerfen,	~ a new house / Our new house has been ~ed by Francis Moore.
	Entwurf	make a ~
plan [plæn]	Plan, Grundriß,	draw (+ up) a ~ (+ for a new house)
	planen, zeichnen	~ a new house
construction [kən'strʌkʃn]	Bau, Bau-	be under ~ / ~ firm / ~ site
foundation(s) [faʊn'deıʃn(z)]	Fundament	lay the ~ (+ of a new house)
brick [brık]	Ziegel(-stein), Backstein,	a house made of ~ (= **bricks**) / stack (aufstapeln) ~s / a **bricklayer** ['-leıə*] (Maurer) / lay ~s (mauern)
	aus Ziegel	The house is ~, not wood. / a ~ wall
mortar ['mɔ:tə*]	Mörtel	bricks and ~
cement [sı'ment]	Zement	a bag of ~ / mix ~ with water / **cement-mixer** [-ˌmıksə*]
concrete ['kɒnkrı:t]	Beton	make (or: mix) ~ / **reinforced concrete** [ˌri:ın'fɔ:st –] (Stahlbeton)
beam [bi:m]	Balken, Träger	
rafter ['rɑ:ftə*]	Sparren	**rafters** [-z] (Dachstuhl)
tile [taıl]	Dachpfanne,	fit the ~s / a **tiled** [-d] roof
	(ein Dach) decken,	~ a roof / bathroom ~s
	Fliese	
put (put, put) **in** [pʊt, –, –; – 'ın]	einsetzen,	~ ~ window panes (or: frames)
	installieren	~ ~ pipes
lay (laid, laid) **on** [leı, leıd, –; – 'ɒn]	anlegen, installieren	~ ~ water (or: gas / electricity)
put (put, put) **on** [pʊt, –, –; – 'ɒn]	anschlagen, einsetzen	~ ~ a door

install [ɪn'stɔːl]	installieren	~ electric light (or: a fireplace / the bathroom / the heating)
paper ['peɪpə*]	tapezieren	~ the walls (+ with **wallpaper** ['wɔːlˌ-])
paint [peɪnt]	anstreichen	~ the walls (or: ceiling / window frames / doors)
repair [rɪ'peə*]	reparieren,	The window needs ~ing. / ~ the door
	Reparatur	make ~s to the house. / in good ~ (baulicher Zustand) / out of ~ (baufällig)
renovate ['renəʊveɪt]	renovieren	~ a house (or: room)
pull down [ˌpʊl 'daʊn]	abreißen	~ ~ a house
demolish [dɪ'mɒlɪʃ]	abbrechen	~ a house

Owner, tenant – Hausbesitzer, Mieter 134

landlord ['lænlɔːd]	Hauswirt	
landlady ['lænˌleɪdɪ]	Hauswirtin	
owner ['əʊnə*]	Hausbesitzer	be the ~ of a house
property ['prɒpətɪ]	Haus- und Grundbesitz	own two ~ies
real estate ['rɪəl ɪˌsteɪt]	Immobilien	~ ~ in Florida
mortgage ['mɔːgɪdʒ]	Hypothek	raise a ~ (+ on one's house) / take out a ~ (+ on one's house)
rate [reɪt]	(Kommunal-)Abgabe	House owners pay ~s to the local government. / pay ~s for water supply (or: the upkeep of roads)
let (let, let) [let, –, –]	vermieten	~ a house at a rent of £ … a week / **room** (or: **house**) **to let**
tenant ['tenənt]	Mieter	be a ~ / one's rights as a ~
rent [rent]	Miete;	pay ~ for a flat / pay (+ a) high (or: low) ~
	(ver-)mieten	~ a house from sb / ~ a house to sb
notice ['nəʊtɪs]	Kündigung	give ~ to quit (aus der Sicht des Vermieters) / give ~ that one is leaving (aus der Sicht des Mieters)
move [muːv]	umziehen	We're going to ~. / ~ to London / ~ in (or: out) / ~ to a new house / **removal** [rɪ'muːvl] (Umzug) / **removal van** [rɪ'muːvl væn] (Möbelwagen)

135 Live – wohnen

live [lɪv]	wohnen	Where do you ~? / ~ at 22, High Street / ~ next door to sb / ~ in a flat / ~ together (or: alone)
stay [steɪ]	sich aufhalten, bleiben	~ with friends / ~ at a hotel / Where are you ~ing?
lodge [lɒdʒ]	(zeitweilig, meist gegen Entgelt) wohnen	~ at Mrs Miller's / ~ with friends / be sb's **lodger** ['-ə*] / take in a **lodger**
lodgings ['lɒdʒɪŋz]	Unterkunft	find ~ for the night / My ~ are only two rooms.
board [bɔːd]	Verpflegung, Kost,	get ~ and lodging for £30 a week / pay £30 for ~ and lodging / have full ~
	Unterkunft und Kost erhalten oder gewähren	~ with a friend / ~ at a friend's house / ~ some students from the university / take in **boarders** ['-əz] / live in a **boarding house** ['-ɪŋ haʊs] / a **boarding school** ['-ɪŋ skuːl] (Internat)
bed and breakfast [ˌbed‿ən 'brekfəst]	Zimmer mit Frühstück (in einem Privathaus)	have ~ ~ ~
room [ruːm]	Zimmer	rent a ~ / **room to let** [ˌruːm tə 'let]
furnished ['fɜːnɪʃt]	möbliert	rent a ~ room (or: house) / an **unfurnished** [ˌʌn-] room
flat [flæt] (*BE*)	(Miet-, Etagen-) Wohnung	live in a ~
block of flats [ˌblɒk‿əv 'flæts] (*BE*)	Mietshaus	live in a ~ ~ ~
apartment [ə'pɑːtmənt]	großer, oft luxuriöser Raum mit Küche und Bad, Appartement (*BE*);	an ~ in an expensive part of town
	Wohnung (*AE*) (vgl. **flat**);	an ~ in New York
	luxuriöse Wohnung (*BE*)	an ~ in the best part of town
apartments [ə'pɑːtmənts]	möblierte Mietwohnung, besonders Ferienwohnung; Mietshaus (*AE*) (vgl. **block of flats**)	From these ~ you can see the sea.
apartment house [ə'pɑrtmənt haʊs] (*AE*)	Mietshaus	

house [haʊs]	Haus	live in a ~ / a large (or: big / small) ~ / build (or: rent / let) a ~ / move into a new ~
home [həʊm]	Haus, Heim, Wohnung	be at ~ / go ~ / stay at ~
cottage ['kɒtɪdʒ]	kleines Haus auf dem Lande	have a ~ in Suffolk
hut [hʌt]	Hütte	live in a small ~
bungalow ['bʌŋgələʊ]	Bungalow	
terraced house [ˌterəst 'haʊs] (*BE*)	Reihenhaus	
semi-detached house [ˌsemɪdɪˌtætʃt 'haʊs] (BE) = **semi** ['semɪ]	Haus (als Hälfte eines Doppelhauses)	
detached house [dɪˌtætʃt 'haʊs] (*BE*)	freistehendes Haus	
duplex (+ **apartment**) ['du:pleks] (*AE*)	Haus mit zwei Wohnebenen	
high-rise ['haɪraɪz]	Hochhaus	
mansion ['mænʃn]	stattliches Wohnhaus	a ~ ten miles from London / a country ~
mansions ['mænʃnz] (*BE*)	Häuserblock mit komfortablen Wohnungen	

House – Haus

(→ 168 Man and plant)

136

fence [fens]	Zaun	a ~ round the house / a wire (or: wooden) ~ / look over the ~
wall [wɔ:l]	Mauer	a ~ round the house / jump (or: climb) onto a ~ / sit on a ~ / a garden ~
gate [geɪt]	Pforte, Tor	go through a ~ / open (or: close / shut) a ~ / drive through the **gateway** ['-weɪ]
drive [draɪv]	Auffahrt	walk (or: drive) up the ~ to a house / a house is approached by a ~
garden ['gɑ:dn]	Garten	have a big (or: large / small) ~ around the house / lay out a ~ / a well-kept ~ / We haven't much of a ~.
grounds [graʊndz]	Anlagen (z. B. eines Landhauses, eines Schlosses)	the ~ of Windsor Castle

yard [jɑːd]	Hof, Garten	play in the ~
dustbin ['dʌstbɪn] (*BE*) = **garbage can** ['gɑrbɪdʒ kæn] (*AE*)	Mülleimer	empty the ~ (= ~ ~)
garage ['gærɑːʒ] (*BE*), [gə'rɑːʒ] (*AE*)	Garage	keep one's car in the ~
terrace ['terəs]	Terrasse	sit on the ~
enter ['entə*]	eintreten in	~ a house / wait at the **entrance** ['entrəns]
indoor ['ɪndɔː*]	im Haus	an ~ game
indoors [ˌɪn'dɔːz] (*attrib.*)	ins Haus, im Haus	go (or: stay) ~
step [step]	Stufe	Mind the ~!
threshold ['θreʃhəʊld]	Schwelle	cross the ~ / carry one's bride over the ~
front door [ˌfrʌnt 'dɔː*]	Haustür	go in the ~ ~ / enter by the ~ ~
letter box ['letə bɒks] (*BE*) = **mail-box** ['meɪlbɒks] (*AE*)	Briefkasten	
bell [bel] = **doorbell** ['dɔːbəl]	Klingel	ring the ~
handle ['hændl]	Türgriff	turn (or: press down) the ~
key [kiː]	Schlüssel	turn the ~
lock [lɒk]	Schloß; schließen	put the key in the ~ ~ the door
hall [hɔːl] (*BE*) = **lobby** ['lɒbɪ] (*AE*)	Diele	enter (= go in) the ~ / walk through the ~
stairs ['steəz]	Treppe	climb the ~ / go up (or: down) the ~ / pass sb on the ~ / **staircase** ['steəkeɪs] (Treppenhaus)
upstairs [ˌʌp'steəz]	treppauf, oben (im Haus); oben gelegen	go (or: be) ~ an ~ room
downstairs [ˌdaʊn'steəz]	trepp ab, unten (im Haus); unten gelegen	go (or: be) ~ a ~ room
storey (*BE*) = **story** (*AE*) ['stɔːrɪ]	Stockwerk	there are five ~s (= **stories**, *AE*) including the ground floor / a 3–~ed (= **storied**, *AE*) house
floor [flɔː*]	Stock, Etage, Geschoß	live on the 4th ~ / Our office is on the 10th ~. / the **ground floor** [ˌgraʊnd '–] (Erdgeschoß)
cellar ['selə*]	Keller	
basement ['beɪsmənt]	Kellergeschoß	in the ~
lift [lɪft] (*BE*) = **elevator** ['elɪveɪtər] (*AE*)	Fahrstuhl	take the ~ (+ to the 10th floor / to the 10th storey) / use the ~

corridor ['kɒrɪdɔː*] (*BE*) = **passage** ['pæsɪdʒ] (*AE*)	Flur, Korridor, Gang	go along the ~ / a dark ~
balcony ['bælkənɪ]	Balkon	sit on the ~
attic ['ætɪk]	Dachboden	keep old things in the ~
gable ['geɪbl]	Giebel	a house has two ~s / a **gabled** ['-d] house
roof [ruːf]	Dach	fall from the ~ / a **span** ~ (Satteldach) / a **flat** ~ (Flachdach)
chimney ['tʃɪmnɪ]	Schornstein	sweep the ~ / Smoke goes up the ~.
lightning conductor ['laɪtnɪŋ kən͵dʌktə*]	Blitzableiter	A ~ ~ conducts lightning into the ground.
televison aerial ['telə͵vɪʒən 'eərɪel]	Fernsehantenne	put up a ~ ~ on the roof
housing estate ['haʊzɪŋ ɪs'teɪt]	Siedlung	

Room – Raum, Zimmer 137

room [ruːm]	Raum, Zimmer	go into a ~ / enter a ~ / a bright (or: dark) ~
door [dɔː*]	Tür	open (or: shut) the ~
wall [wɔːl]	Wand	hang a picture on the ~ / paper (or: paint) the ~s green (= in green)
window ['wɪndəʊ]	Fenster	open (or: shut) the ~ / The ~ is open (or: shut). / look through (or: out of) a ~ / lean out of a ~ / a vase of flowers on the **window-sill** [-sɪl]
pane [peɪn]	Scheibe	knock at the (+ **window**-)~ / a broken (or: cracked) ~
curtain ['kɜːtn] (*BE*) = **drape** [dreɪp] (*AE*)	Vorhang	draw the ~s / The ~s hang well. / hang ~s in front of the window
blinds [blaɪndz] (*BE*) = **window shade** ['wɪndəʊ ͵ʃeɪd] (*AE*)	Jalousie	pull down the ~
floor [flɔː*]	Fußboden	sit on the ~ / drop sth on the ~
carpet ['kɑːpɪt]	Teppich	have thick ~s on the floor / a large (or: small / Persian) ~
wall-to-wall carpeting [͵wɔːl tə 'wɔːl 'kɑːpɪtɪŋ]	Teppichboden	have ~ ~
rug [rʌg]	(kleiner) Teppich, (Bett-)Vorleger	a room covered with ~s
hearth-rug ['hɑːθrʌg]	Kaminvorleger	

ceiling ['si:lɪŋ]	Decke	a room with a high (or: low) ~
lamp [læmp]	Lampe	a ~ hanging from the ceiling
standard lamp ['stændəd læmp]	Stehlampe	
lamp-shade ['læmp ʃeɪd]	Lampenschirm	
spotlight ['spɒtlaɪt]	Strahler	direct a ~ on to sb (or: sth)
switch on [swɪtʃ 'ɒn] = **turn on** [tɜ:n 'ɒn]	einschalten	~ ~ a lamp
switch off [– 'ɒf] = **turn off** [– 'ɒf]	ausschalten	~ ~ a lamp
light [laɪt]	Licht	electric ~ / read by **lamplight** ['læmp-]
bulb [bʌlb]	Birne	put a new ~ in the lamp / change the ~
socket ['sɒkɪt]	Fassung; Steckdose	fix a bulb tightly into the ~ put the plug into the ~
plug [plʌg]	Stecker	put the ~ into the socket
flex [fleks] (*BE*) = **cord** [kɔ:rd] (*AE*)	Schnur, Kabel	a long telephone ~
fuse [fju:z]	Sicherung	The ~ melts (or: blows).
heat [hi:t]	heizen	~ a room / ~ electrically (or: by gas) / have **central heating** [ˌsentrəl '-ɪŋ]
stove [stəʊv]	Ofen	heat a room with a(n) coal (or: gas / electric / oil) ~
radiator ['reɪdɪeɪtə*]	Heizkörper	turn the ~ on (or: off)
fireplace ['faɪəpleɪs]	Kamin	sit by (or: round) the ~
furniture ['fɜ:nɪtʃə*]	Möbel	a piece of ~ / period ~ (Stilmöbel) / **furniture-polish** ['-pɒlɪʃ]
furnish ['fɜ:nɪʃ]	einrichten, möblieren	~ a room with new furniture / rent a(n) **furnished** [-t] (or: **unfurnished** [ˌʌn-]) room (or: house)
furnishings ['fɜ:nɪʃɪŋz]	Einrichtung	buy new ~

138 Bedroom, rest – Schlafzimmer, ruhen

bed [bed]	Bett	go to ~ / be (or: lie / stay) in ~ / get to ~ (+ late) / get into (or: out of) ~ / It's time for ~. / It's **bedtime** ['-taɪm]. / put a child to ~ / make the ~ / **bed-linen** ['-ˌlɪnɪn] (= **bedclothes** ['-kləʊðz]) / a **bedside-table** ['-saɪd ˌteɪbl] / a **bedside lamp** ['-saɪd ˌlæmp]

sheet [ʃi:t]	Bettuch	change the ~s every week / put clean ~s on the bed
mattress ['mætrɪs]	Matratze	
bedstead ['bedsted]	Bettgestell	
cot [kɒt] (*BE*) = **crib** [krɪb] (*AE*)	Babybett	
cradle ['kreɪdl]	Wiege	
pillow ['pɪləʊ]	Kopfkissen	rest one's head on a ~ / a **pillow-case** [-keɪs] (= **pillow-slip** [-slɪp])
blanket ['blæŋkɪt]	Bettdecke	fold a ~ / put a (+ woollen) ~ on one's bed / get under the ~ / cover oneself with a ~
quilt [kwɪlt]	Steppdecke	a continental ~ (Federbett)
alarm clock [ə'lɑ:m klɒk]	Wecker	set the ~ ~ (+ for 7 o'clock) / The ~ ~ is ringing.
wardrobe ['wɔ:drəʊb]	Kleiderschrank	hang up clothes in the ~
dressing-table ['dresɪŋˌteɪbl]	Frisierkommode	
chest of drawers [ˌtʃest əv 'drɔ:əz]	Kommode	
tire ['taɪə*]	ermüden	sth ~s one (or: sb) (+ out) / sth is **tiring** [-rɪŋ] (= **tiresome** [-səm])
tired ['taɪəd]	müde	be (or: get / become / feel / look) ~ / be very (or: dreadfully / awfully / terribly / dead) ~ / sth makes one (or: sb) ~ / be **overtired** [ˌəʊvə-] / be ~ out (erschöpft)
worn out [ˌwɔ:n‿aʊt]	abgekämpft, erschöpft	be ~ ~ after two sleepless nights
weary ['wɪərɪ]	erschöpft	be ~ after one's day's work
exhausted [ɪg'zɔ:stɪd]	erschöpft	be completely ~
sleepy ['sli:pɪ]	schläfrig	be (or: feel) ~ / a ~ face
yawn [jɔ:n]	gähnen,	~ sleepily
	Gähnen	give a loud (or: hearty) ~ / hide (or: suppress) a ~
stretch [stretʃ]	sich strecken,	He ~ed (+ himself). / ~ one's limbs
	Strecken	have a good ~ / get up with a ~ and a yawn
rest [rest]	ruhen, sich ausruhen,	He ~ed (+ for a while). / have to ~
	Ruhepause	have (or: take / need) a ~ (+ from sth / from doing sth) / get some ~
relax [rɪ'læks]	sich entspannen	He ~ed (+ for a while). / sth ~es one

sleep (slept, slept) [sli:p, slept, –]	schlafen,	~ long (or: for an hour) / ~ well (or: through)
	Schlaf	go to ~ / get eight hours' ~ / have (or: get) (+ not) enough ~ / not get much ~ / I can't get to ~ (einschlafen).
asleep [ə'sli:p]	im Schlaf, in Schlaf	be ~ / be fast (tief) ~ / fall (= drop) ~
dream (dreamt, dreamt [dri:m, dremt, –] (*BE*) = dreamed, dreamed [-d, –] (*BE, AE*))	träumen	~ of (= about) sth / ~ that ...
dream [dri:m]	Traum	have a (+ bad) ~ / have a ~ about sb (or: sth) / awake from a ~ / a **dreamless** ['-lɪs] sleep
snore [snɔ:*]	schnarchen	Don't ~ so loudly.
wake (woke, woken) [weɪk, wəʊk, 'wəʊkən] (= waked, waked [weɪkt, –])	aufwachen, wecken	~ early / ~ up / W~ up! ~ sb up / sth ~s one up / Please ~ me at seven.
waken ['weɪkən]	wecken, aufwachen	The alarm-clock ~s me at seven.
awake (awoke, awoken [ə'weɪk, ə'wəʊk, ə'wəʊkən] = awaked [ə'weɪkt])	wach werden	~ early in the morning
awake [ə'wəɪk] (*pred.*)	wach	be ~ / be wide ~ (hellwach)
get (got, got) **up** [get, gɒt, –; – 'ʌp]	aufstehen	~ ~ early / ~ ~ at seven
rise (rose, risen) [raɪz, rəʊz, 'rɪzn]	sich erheben	~ very early / a(n) early (or: late) **riser** ['-ə*]

139 Bathroom, hygiene – Badezimmer, Körperpflege

bath [bɑ:θ] (*BE*), [bæ:θ] (*AE*)	Badezimmer;	two rooms, kitchen, and ~
	Badewanne;	a brown (or: metal) ~ (= **bathtub** ['-tʌb])
	Bad;	have (*BE*) (or: take) (*AE*) a ~ / have a hot (or: warm / cold) ~ / give sb a ~
	baden	She ~s [bɑ:θs = bæθs] every morning. / She has just ~ed the baby.
bathe [beɪð]	(im Freien) baden, Bad (im Freien)	~ in the sea / have a ~ in the sea

shower ['ʃaʊə*]	Brause, duschen	have (*BE*) (= take) (*AE*) a ~ / step under the ~
washbasin ['wɒʃˌbeɪsn] = **sink** [sɪŋk]	Waschbecken	wash one's hands in the ~
tap [tæp] = **faucet** ['fɔːsɪt] (*AE*)	Wasserhahn	turn the ~ on (or: off) / The ~ is dripping (or: running). / repair the ~
plug [plʌg]	Stopfen	**plughole** ['plʌghəʊl] (Abflußöffnung]
bathroom cabinet ['bɑːθrʊm ˌkæbɪnət]	Toilettenschränkchen	
wash [wɒʃ]	(sich) waschen	~ in cold water / ~ oneself (+ one's hands) / ~ the dirt off (+ one's hands)
wet [wet]	naß; naßmachen	My hair is still ~. ~ one's hands (or: hair)
soap [səʊp]	Seife; (ein)seifen	a bar of ~ ~ (+ up) one's hands
towel ['taʊəl]	Handtuch	hang the ~ on **towel rail** [– reɪl] / dry one's hands on a ~ / rub oneself down with a ~
dry [draɪ]	trocken, trocknen	be (or: get) ~ ~ one's hands on a towel / ~ oneself down with a towel
brush [brʌʃ]	bürsten, Bürste	~ one's nails (or: hair / teeth) clean one's hands with a ~ / a **nail-brush** ['neɪl-] / a **hairbrush** ['heə-]
comb [kəʊm]	kämmen, Kamm	~ one's hair
mirror ['mɪrə*]	Spiegel	look into a ~ / see oneself in a ~
toothpaste ['tuːθpeɪst]	Zahnpaste	put (or: squeeze) some ~ onto one's **toothbrush** ['tuːθbrʌʃ]
cream [kriːm]	Creme	put some ~ on one's face (or: hands)
spray [spreɪ]	Spray, sprühen	use a hair (or: deodorant) ~ ~ oneself with a perfume / ~ a deodorant under one's arms
make (made, made) **up** [meɪk, meɪd, –; – 'ʌp]	schminken	~ ~ one's face
make-up ['meɪkʌp]	Schminke	use ~
lipstick ['lɪpstɪk]	Lippenstift	use ~
perfume [pə'fjuːm] = **scent** [sent]	Parfüm	put some ~ on one's face
shave [ʃeɪv]	(sich) rasieren,	~ off one's beard / ~ twice a day / a **clean-shaven** [ˌkliːn'ʃeɪvn] face / use a **shaver** ['-ə*] (Trockenrasierer)
	Rasur	need (or: have) a ~

razor ['reɪzə*]	Rasierapparat	shave off one's beard with an **electric razor** [ɪˌlektrɪk –] / **safety razor** ['seɪftɪ ˌ–] / **razor blade** [– ˌbleɪd] (Rasierklinge)
toilet ['tɔɪlɪt] (*BE*) = **bathroom** ['bæθrʊm] (*AE*)	Toilette	go to the ~ / be in the ~
W.C. [ˌdʌbəlju: 'si:] (*BE*)	W.C.	go to the ~
loo [lu:] (*BE inform.*) = **john** [dʒɒn] (*AE inform.*)	Klo	go to the ~
toilet roll ['tɔɪlɪt rəʊl]	Toilettenpapierrolle	
cistern ['sɪstən]	Spülkasten	
flush [flʌʃ]	spülen	~ the toilet

140 Kitchen, housework – Küche, Hausarbeit

(→ 25 Meals; 141 Dining-room)

cooker ['kʊkə*] (*BE*)	Herd	put sth on the ~ / switch (= turn) on (or: off) the ~
stove [stəʊv] (*AE*)	Herd	put sth on the ~
oven ['ʌvn]	Backofen	bake a cake in the ~
microwave oven ['maɪkrəweɪv ˌʌvn]	Mikrowellenherd	
pan [pæn]	Pfanne, Topf, Kochtopf	heat sth slowly in a ~ / fry eggs in a **frying pan** ['fraɪɪŋ ˌ–]
saucepan ['sɔ:spən]	Schmortopf, Kochtopf	stew meat in a ~
pot [pɒt]	Kochtopf	boil potatoes in a ~
kettle [ketl]	Kessel	put the ~ on the stove
sink [sɪŋk]	Spüle	wash the dishes in the ~
wash up [ˌwɒʃ‿ʌp]	aufwaschen	~ ~ the dishes
dry up [ˌdraɪ 'ʌp]	abtrocknen	
food mixer ['fu:d ˌmɪksə*]	Mixer	
dishwasher ['dɪʃwɒʃə*]	Geschirrspülmaschine	put the dishes in the ~
refrigerator [rɪ'frɪdʒəreɪtə*] = **fridge** [frɪdʒ] (*inform.*) = **icebox** ['aɪsbɒks] (*inform.*)	Kühlschrank	put (or: keep) sth in the ~
deep-freeze [ˌdi:p'fri:z], ['- -] (*AE*)	Kühltruhe	

freezer ['fri:zə*]	Kühltruhe	
freezing compartement ['fri:zɪŋ kəm,pɑ:tmənt]	Tiefkühlfach	
cupboard ['kʌbəd]	Schrank	put the dishes into the ~
clean [kli:n]	sauber, saubermachen	keep the house ~ ~ the floor (or: bath / window)
broom [bru:m]	Besen	
sweep (swept, swept) [swi:p, swept, –]	fegen	~ the floor (or: room / house / garden / garden path)
dust [dʌst]	abstauben, Staub	~ the furniture There is thick (or: a lot of / a thick layer of) ~ on the shelves. / a **dusty** ['-ɪ] room / a **duster** ['-ə*] (Staublappen)
wipe [waɪp]	(ab)wischen; abtrocknen	~ the floor (or: table) ~ the dishes
vacuum-cleaner ['vækjʊəmkli:nə*] = **hoover** ['hu:və*] (*BE*)	Staubsauger	use (or: take) the ~ / clean the floor (or: carpet / furniture) with the ~
tidy ['taɪdɪ]	aufräumen, aufgeräumt	~ (+ up) one's room a ~ room

Dining-room – Eßzimmer (→ 25 Meals; 140 Kitchen, housework) 141

table ['teɪbl]	Tisch	sit at the ~ / lay the ~ / clear the ~
tablecloth ['teɪblklɒθ]	Tischtuch	spread a ~ on the table
napkin ['næpkɪn]	Serviette	fold a ~
nappy ['næpɪ]	Lätzchen	
tray [treɪ]	Tablett	carry a ~ (+ with dishes) / put sth on a ~
cutlery ['kʌtlərɪ]	Besteck	
spoon [spu:n]	Löffel	take two ~s of sugar on one's tea
teaspoon ['ti:spu:n]	Teelöffel	add one ~ of sugar / two teaspoonfuls ['-ˌfʊlz] of sugar
tablespoon ['teɪblspu:n]	Eßlöffel	
fork [fɔ:k]	Gabel	
knife [naɪf] (*pl.* knives [-vz])	Messer	cut sth with a ~
plate [pleɪt]	Teller	

saucer ['sɔːsə*]	Untertasse	
cup [kʌp]	Tasse	a ~ of tea (or: coffee)
bowl [bəʊl]	Schüssel, Schale	a salad ~
dish [dɪʃ]	Schüssel, Platte	a meat (or: vegetable) ~
glass [glɑːs]	Glas	a ~ of wine / a **wine glass** ['waɪn –]
mug [mʌg]	Krug, Becher	
pot [pɒt]	Kanne	a **teapot** ['tiː-] / a **coffeepot** ['kɒfɪ-]
jug [dʒʌg]	Krug / Kanne	a **milk jug** ['mɪlk –]
pitcher ['pɪtʃər] (*AE*)	Krug, Kanne	
sugar bowl ['ʃʊgə bəʊl]	Zuckerdose	Pass me the ~, please.
eggcup ['egkʌp]	Eierbecher	

142 Study – Arbeitszimmer

den [den] (*AE*)	Arbeitszimmer	
bookcase ['bʊkkeɪs]	Bücherschrank	keep one's books on three large ~s
shelf [ʃelf] (*pl.* shelves [ʃelvz])	Regal(boden)	put books on the top (or: middle / bottom / second) ~ / take a book from the ~ / My **shelves** are full of books.
filing cabinet ['faɪlɪŋ ˌkæbɪnɪt]	Aktenschrank	
desk [desk] = **writing table** ['raɪtɪŋ ˌteɪbl] = **writing desk** ['– desk]	Schreibtisch	sit (or: work) at one's ~ (= ~ ~)
drawer ['drɔːə*]	Schublade	a desk with three ~s / open (or: pull out / push in / shut / close) a ~
swivel-chair ['swɪvltʃeə*]	Drehstuhl	
table lamp ['teɪbl læmp]	Schreibtischlampe	an adjustable (verstellbar) ~ ~
reading lamp ['riːdɪŋ læmp]	Leselampe	turn on the ~ ~
file ['faɪl]	Ordner, Hefter; abheften	~ away letters
card-index ['kɑːdˌɪndeks]	Kartei	
record card ['rekəd kɑːd]	Karteikarte	
waste-paper basket [ˌweɪst'peɪpə ˌbɑːskɪt]	Papierkorb	throw (or: drop) sth in the ~ ~

Sitting-room – Wohnzimmer 143

sofa ['səʊfə] = **settee** [se'tiː]	Sofa	sit on a ~
couch [kaʊtʃ] = **davenport** ['dævnpɔːt] (*AE*)	Liegesofa	lie on a ~
armchair [ˌɑːm'tʃeə*]	Sessel	sit in an ~ / drop into an ~ / a comfortable ~
cushion ['kʊʃn]	Sofakissen	push a ~ behind one's back (or: neck)
cabinet ['kæbɪnɪt]	Vitrine, Schrank	keep one's good china in the ~
candle ['kændl]	Kerze	light (or: put out) a ~ / a ~ is burning / soft **candle-light** [-laɪt] / a **candlestick** [-stɪk]
vase [vɑːz] (*BE*), [veɪz] (*AE*)	Vase	put the flowers in a ~
chair [tʃeə*]	Stuhl	sit on a ~

Nursery – Kinderzimmer 144

cradle ['kreɪdl]	Wiege	lie (or: sleep) in a ~ / rock the ~
pram [præm] (*BE*) = **baby carriage** ['beɪbɪ ˌkærɪdʒ] (*AE*)	Kinderwagen	push a ~ (= ~ ~) / take a baby for a walk in the ~ (= ~ ~)
bottle ['bɒtl]	Flasche	give a baby the ~
toy [tɔɪ]	Spielzeug	play with one's ~s / a ~ car (or: train)
ball [bɔːl]	Ball	play ~ (+ with sb) / throw (or: catch) a ~
doll [dɒl]	Puppe	play (+ with) ~s / a **doll's house** ['dɒlz 'haʊs]
picture book ['pɪktʃə bʊk]	Bilderbuch	look at a ~ ~
colour ['kʌlə*] (*BE*) = **color** [-r] (*AE*)	buntmalen, mit Buntstiften malen	~ a picture / ~ the car red / a **coloured** [-d] pencil
model [mɒdl]	Modell-	build a ~ ship / a ~ plane / play with a ~ train
jigsaw puzzle ['dʒɪgsɔː ˌpʌzl]	Puzzle	fit together the pieces of a ~ ~
game [geɪm]	Spiel	have (or: play) a ~ of chess (or: poker / cards)
chess [tʃes]	Schach	play ~

draughts [drɑ:fts] (*BE*) = **checkers** ['tʃekərz] (*AE*)	Dame	play ~
card [kɑ:d]	Spielkarte, Karte	play ~s / **playing-cards** ['pleɪɪŋ -z] / a **pack of cards** [ˌpæk‿əv 'kɑ:dz] (ein Blatt Karten) / shuffle ~s (mischen)

Our town, our village – unsere Stadt, unser Dorf

145 Town, village – Stadt, Dorf

(→ 146 Buildings and places; 147 Street; 136 House)

town [taʊn]	Stadt;	live in a ~, not in the country / a large (or: small / old / dirty) ~ / go (+ up / down) to ~[1] / be in ~[1]
	Geschäfts-, Einkaufszentrum einer Stadt;	go to ~ to do some shopping
	alle Bewohner einer Stadt	the whole ~ / sth is the talk of the ~
the town [ðə 'taʊn]	die Stadt (im Gegensatz zum Land)	like ~ ~ better than the country / leave the country for ~ ~
city ['sɪtɪ]	Stadt, Großstadt	the ~ of London (or: New York) / the **city centre** [ˌ– 'sentə*] / the **city arms** [ˌ– 'ɑ:mz] (Stadtwappen)
the City [ðə 'sɪtɪ]	die City, das Londoner Banken- und Börsenviertel	work in ~ ~
centre ['sentə*] (*BE*) = **center** [-r] (*AE*)	Zentrum, Stadtmitte	the business (or: shopping) ~
market square ['mɑ:kɪt skweə*]	Marktplatz	
circus ['sɜ:kəs] (*BE*)	(runder) Platz	Piccadilly C~
square ['skweə*]	Platz (wo mehrere Straßen zusammenlaufen)	live in Portman S~ / Trafalgar S~ / Times S~
street [stri:t]	Straße	the city ~s were full of people
road [rəʊd]	Straße	the ~ to London
communications [kəˌmju:nɪ'keɪʃnz]	(Verkehrs-) Verbindungen)	have excellent ~ with / have poor road ~ with
building ['bɪldɪŋ]	Gebäude	
house [haʊs]	Haus	

[1] "Town" in this phrase is often used in England when speaking of London.

suburb ['sʌbɜːb]	Vorort	live in a ~ / live in the ~s / **suburban** [sə'bɜːbən] streets with rows of identical houses
outskirts ['aʊtskɜːts]	Stadtrand	on the ~ of Manchester
environs [ɪn'vaɪərənz]	Umgebung	in the ~ of Liverpool
village ['vɪlɪdʒ]	Dorf	live in a ~ / a small ~
inhabitant [ɪn'hæbɪtənt]	Einwohner	the ~s of a town / ... has 25,000 ~s
live [lɪv]	wohnen	~ in London / ~ at 49, Greencroft Road, London SE1 8BA
neighbour ['neɪbə*] (*BE*) = **neighbor** [-r] (*AE*)	Nachbar	be a good ~ / be good ~s / one's next-door ~ / live in a quiet **neighbourhood** [-hʊd]
next door [ˌnekst 'dɔː*]	nebenan	The Hunters live ~ ~ (+ to us).

Buildings and places – Gebäude und Örtlichkeiten 146

town hall [ˌtaʊn 'hɔːl]	Rathaus	
church [tʃɜːtʃ]	Kirche	(→ 77–79 Church)
school [skuːl]	Schule	(→ 80–84 Our school)
library ['laɪbrərɪ]	Bibliothek, Bücherei	(→ 69 Book)
museum [mjuː'zɪəm]	Museum	(→ 130 Painting, drawing, sculpture)
theatre ['θɪətə*] (*BE*) = **theater** [-r] (*AE*)	Theater	(→ 64 Drama; 129 Theatre)
cinema ['sɪnəmə] (*BE*) = **movie theatre** ['muːvɪ ˌθɪətər] (*AE*)	Kino	(→ 68 Film)
railway station ['reɪlweɪ ˌsteɪʃn] (*BE*) = **railroad station** ['reɪlrəʊd ˌ–] (*AE*)	Bahnhof	(→ 155 By train)
underground station ['ʌndəgraʊnd ˌ–] (*BE*) = **subway station** ['sʌbweɪ ˌ–] (*AE*)	U-Bahnhof	(→ 154 By bus, by underground)
bus stop ['bʌs stɒp]	Bushaltestelle	(→ 154 By bus, by underground)
airport ['eəpɔːt]	Flughafen	(→ 156 By plane)
harbour ['hɑːbə*] (*BE*) = **harbor** ['hɑːrbər] (*AE*)	Hafen	(→ 157 By ship)
hotel [həʊ'tel]	Hotel	(→ 122 Hotel)

restaurant ['restərɔ̃:ŋ]	Restaurant	(→ 150 Restaurant)
snack bar ['snæk bɑ:*]	Imbiß	(→ 150 Restaurant)
pub [pʌb] (*BE, inform.*) = **public house** [ˌpʌblɪk 'haʊs] (*BE, form.*)	Kneipe	(→ 150 Restaurant)
ice-cream parlor ['aɪskri:m ˌpɑ:lə*]	Eisdiele	
police station ['pəli:s steɪʃn]	Polizeistation	(→ 96 Police)
fire station ['faɪə steɪʃn]	Feuerwache	(→ 148 Services)
hospital ['hɒspɪtl]	Krankenhaus	(→ 27–30 Health, illness)
court [kɔ:t]	Gericht	(→ 97 Court)
castle ['kɑ:sl]	Schloß, Burg	
power station ['paʊə steɪʃn]	Kraftwerk	(→ 109 Power, energy)
water works ['wɔ:tə wɜ:ks]	Wasserwerk	
sewage works ['sju:ɪdʒ wɜ:ks]	Kläranlage	
gasworks ['gæswɜ:ks]	Gasanstalt	
stadium ['steɪdɪəm]	Stadion	(→ 124–126 Sports and games)
sports ground ['spɔ:ts graʊnd]	Sportplatz	(→ 124–126 Sports and games)
(+ swimming) pool [('swɪmɪŋ) pu:l]	Bad	(→ 124–126 Sports and games)
playground ['pleɪgraʊnd]	Spielplatz	
park [pɑ:k]	Park	
bench [bentʃ]	Parkbank	
zoo [zu:]	Zoo	(→ 162 Animals in the zoo)
cemetery ['semɪtrɪ]	Friedhof	(→ 6 Death)
car park ['kɑ: pɑ:k]	Parkplatz; Parkhaus	
multi-storey (car park) [ˌmʌltɪ'stɔ:rɪ ('––)]	Parkhaus	
parking lot ['pɑ:kɪŋ lɔt] (*AE*)	Parkplatz	
parking space ['pɑ:kɪŋ speɪs]	Einstellplatz, Parkbox	

Street – Straße (→ 153 Road) 147

street [stri:t]	Straße	a long (or: broad / wide / narrow / busy / noisy / crowded) ~ / go down (or: along / across) a ~ / walk across (or: in / up / down) the ~ / meet sb in (= on) the ~ / Which ~ do you live in? / cross a ~
Street = St	Straße (in Straßennamen)	27, Carter Street, London E 13 / 42nd Street
Road [rəʊd] = **Rd**	Straße (in Straßennamen)	42, Camp Road, London NW4 8QZ
corner ['kɔ:nə*]	Ecke	on (= at) the ~ (+ of Clapham Pk Rd and Bedford Rd)
turning ['tɜ:nɪŋ] (*BE*) = **turn** [tɜrn] (*AE*)	Abzweigung	take the second ~ on the left
crossroads ['krɒsrəʊdz] (*BE*) = **intersection** [ˌɪntər'sekʃn] (*AE*)	Kreuzung	
roadway ['rəʊdweɪ]	Fahrbahn	Don't stand in (= on) the ~
pavement ['peɪvment]	Bürgersteig (*BE*); Straßenpflaster, Belag, Platten (*AE*)	Please walk on the ~.
sidewalk ['saɪdwɔ:k] (*AE*)	Bürgersteig	Please keep to the ~.
gutter ['gʌtə*]	Gosse	a dirty ~
alley ['ælɪ]	enge Gasse	a dark ~
kerb [kɜ:b] (*BE*) = **curb** [kɜrb] (*AE*)	Bordsteinkante	**kerbstone** ['-stəʊn] (= **curbstone** [-stəʊn]) (Bordstein)
crossing ['krɒsɪŋ]	Überweg	a **zebra** ~ [ˌzi:brə '–] / a **pedestrian** ~ [pɪˌdestrɪən –] / a **level** [ˌlevl] (*AE*: **grade** [ˌgreɪd]) ~ (Bahnübergang)
lamppost ['læmppəʊst] (*BE*) = **street lantern** ['stri:t ˌlæntərn] (*AE*)	Laternenpfahl	
signpost ['saɪnpəʊst]	Wegweiser	Follow the ~s for Oxford.
parking meter ['pɑ:kɪŋ ˌmi:tə*]	Parkuhr	Park at a ~ ~.
pedestrian [pɪ'destrɪən]	Fußgänger	P~s must use the pavement (or: sidewalk). / a ~ **precinct** [– ˌpri:sɪŋkt] (*BE*) (Fußgängerzone)
motorist ['məʊtərɪst]	Autofahrer	

traffic ['træfɪk]	Verkehr	there is a lot of ~ on the roads / heavy ~ / **traffic lights** [– ˌlaɪts] (Ampel)
rush hour ['rʌʃ ˌaʊə*]	Hauptverkehrszeit	in (or: during) the ~ ~
traffic jam ['træfɪk dʒæm]	Verkehrsstau	The accident caused a ~ ~.
holdup ['həʊldʌp] (*BE*) = **tail-back** ['teɪlbæk] (*AE*)	Stau	a two-mile ~ (= ~)

148 Services – Dienste

police [pə'li:s]	Polizei	(→ 96 Police)
fire brigade ['faɪə brɪˌgeɪd] (*BE*) = **fire department** ['faɪər dɪˌpɑrtmənt] (*AE*)	Feuerwehr	
ambulance ['æmbjuləns]	Krankenwagen	(→ 28 Accident)
doctor ['dɒktə*]	Arzt	(→ 29 At the doctor's)
dentist ['dentɪst]	Zahnarzt	(→ 30 At the dentist's)
hospital ['hɒspɪtl]	Krankenhaus	go to ~ / be in ~ (→ 27 Health, illness)
petrol station ['petrəl ˌsteɪʃn] (*BE*) = **gas station** ['gæs ˌsteɪʃn] (*AE*)	Tankstelle	(→ 152 By car)
garage ['gærɑ:ʒ]	Tankstelle (und/oder Werkstatt)	(→ 152 By car)
taxi ['tæksɪ] (*BE*) = **cab** [kæb] (*AE*)	Taxi	
bus [bʌs]	Bus	(→ 154 By bus, by underground)
underground ['ʌndəgraʊnd] (*BE*) = **subway** ['sʌbweɪ] (*AE*)	U-Bahn	(→ 154 By bus, by underground)
railway ['reɪlweɪ]	Eisenbahn	(→ 155 By train)
airport ['eəpɔ:t]	Flughafen	(→ 156 By plane)
travel agency ['trævl ˌeɪdʒənsɪ]	Reisebüro	(→ 121 Travelling)
bank [bæŋk]	Bank	(→ 118 Banking, insurance, stock exchange)
post office ['pəʊst ˌɒfɪs]	Post	(→ 149 Post office)

embassy ['embəsɪ]	Botschaft	(→ 92 Foreign policy)
consulate ['kɒnsjʊlət]	Konsulat	(→ 92 Foreign policy)

49 Post office – Postamt

(→ 50 Correspondence)

post office ['pəʊst ˌɒfɪs]	Postamt	Where is the nearest ~ ~?
mail [meɪl]	Post (die man erhält oder versendet);	Is there any ~ this morning? / The ~ has not arrived yet. / have a lot of ~ / open the ~ / send a letter by **air mail** ['eə –]
	einwerfen, aufgeben (*AE*)	~ a letter
post [pəʊst]	Post (die man erhält oder versendet);	Has the ~ been yet? / Has any ~ come for me?
	Post (als Einrichtung);	send sth by ~
	einwerfen, aufgeben (*BE*)	~ a letter
counter ['kaʊntə*]	Schalter	There was a long queue at the ~.
postman ['pəʊstmən] (*BE*) = **mailman** ['meɪlmən] (*AE*)	Postbote	Has the ~ been here yet?
PO Box [ˌpiː 'əʊ bɒks]	Postfach	
telegram ['telɪgræm]	Telegramm	send sb a ~ / get a ~ from sb
telephone ['telɪfəʊn] = **phone** [fəʊn] (*inform.*)	Telefon;	be on the ~ / talk to sb on the ~ / **phone number** ['– ˌnʌmbə*]
	anrufen	~ sb
British Telecom ['brɪtɪʃ 'telɪkɒm]	staatl. Gesellschaft für Telekommunikation (Telefon und Datenübertragung)	
call [kɔːl]	Anruf,	make a ~ / give sb a ~
	anrufen	~ sb / make a(n) local (or: national / international) ~
ring (rang, rung) [rɪŋ, ræŋ, rʌŋ]	läuten;	The telephone is ~ing.
	anrufen	~ sb up (or: back) (*BE*)
dial ['daɪəl]	wählen	~ 999 / ~ the police
directory [dɪ'rektərɪ]	Telefonbuch	look up a number in the ~
phone book ['fəʊn bʊk] (= **PB**)	Telefonbuch	
Yellow Pages ['jeləʊ 'peɪdʒɪz] (= **YP**)	Branchenverzeichnis	

enquiries [ɪn'kwaɪərɪz]	Auskunft	dial 191 for ~
phone box ['fəʊn bɒks]	Telefonzelle	There's a ~ ~ over there.
phone booth ['fəʊn bu:θ]	Telefonzelle	
stamp [stæmp]	Briefmarke	a 5p ~ / stick a ~ on an envelope / collect ~s / have a **stamp collection** ['– kəˌlekʃn]
postage ['pəʊstɪdʒ]	Porto	The ~ for this parcel will be 70p.
parcel ['pɑ:sl] (*BE*) = **package** ['pækɪdʒ] (*AE*)	Paket	send (or: open) a ~ / We got a ~ in the post today.
small packet [ˌsmɔ:l 'pækɪt]	Päckchen	

150 Restaurant – Restaurant

(→ 23 – 26 Eating, drinking, smoking)

restaurant ['restərɔ̃:ŋ]	Restaurant	go to have a meal at an Italian ~ / a cheap (or: an expensive) ~
snack bar ['snæk bɑ:*]	Imbiß	go to the ~ ~ round the corner
café ['kæfeɪ] (*BE*), [kæ'feɪ] (*AE*)	Café	
pub [pʌb] (*BE, inform.*) = **public house** [ˌpʌblɪk 'haʊs] (*BE, form.*)	Kneipe	go to a ~ (= ~ ~)
bar [bɑ:*]	Theke, Bar	go to the ~ for a drink
self-service [ˌself'sɜ:vɪs]	Selbstbedienungs-	a ~ restaurant (= **cafeteria**) [kæfɪ'tɪərɪə]
service ['sɜ:vɪs]	Bedienung, Service	No ~ in the garden. / Prices include a **service charge** [– tʃɑ:dʒ] (Trinkgeld).
table ['teɪbl]	Tisch	A ~ for two, please.
waiter ['weɪtə*]	Ober, Kellner	The ~ will give us the menu.
waitress ['weɪtrɪs]	Kellnerin	The ~es had a lot do do.
serve [sɜ:v]	bedienen, servieren	We don't ~ dinner after 10 p.m.
order ['ɔ:də*]	bestellen	~ a bottle of wine
menu ['menju:]	Speisekarte	Can I have the ~, please? / choose sth from the ~
choose (chose, chosen) [tʃu:z, tʃəʊz, 'tʃəʊzn]	wählen	Have you chosen something from the menu?
start [stɑ:t]	beginnen	What would you like to ~ with?

I'd like [ˌaɪd 'laɪk]	Ich hätte gern	~ ~ roast chicken, please.
bill [bɪl] (*BE*) = **check** [tʃek] (*AE*)	Rechnung	Can I have my ~, please?
tip [tɪp]	Trinkgeld, ein Trinkgeld geben	expect a ~ ~ the waiter
eat (ate, eaten) **out** [iːt, et, 'iːtn, ˌ– 'aʊt]	essen gehen	
takeaway ['teɪkəweɪ]	Restaurant für Außer-Haus-Verkauf	
tea-shop ['tiːʃɒp]	etwa: Café	
wine bar ['waɪn bɑː*]	Weinstube	

Transport – Transport, Verkehrswesen

By bicycle, by motor-cycle – mit dem Fahrrad, mit dem Motorrad 151

bicycle ['baɪsɪkl] = **bike** [baɪk] (*inform.*)	Fahrrad, Rad	go by ~
ride (rode, ridden) [raɪd, rəʊd, 'rɪdn]	(mit dem Fahrrad oder Motorrad) fahren	~ one's bike (or: motor-cycle)
saddle [sædl]	Sattel	The ~ is too high.
brake [breɪk]	Bremse	The ~s are O.K.
handlebars ['hændlbɑːz]	Lenker	The ~ are too low.
wheel [wiːl]	Rad	The front ~ is not O.K.
cycle ['saɪkl]	mit dem Rad fahren	
moped ['məʊpəd] (*BE*)	Moped	
motor scooter ['məʊtə ˌskuːtə*]	Motorroller	
motorcycle ['məʊtəˌsaɪkl] = **motorbike** ['məʊtəbaɪk] (*inform.*)	Motorrad	a powerful ~ / **motorcyclist** [-ɪst]
crash-helmet ['kræʃˌhelmɪt]	Sturzhelm	wear a ~

152 By car – mit dem Auto

car [kɑː*]	Auto	go (or: travel) by ~ / a second-hand ~ (Gebrauchtwagen)
automobile ['ɔːtəməʊbiːl] (*AE*) = **motor car** ['məʊtə kɑː*] (*BE*)	Auto	
model ['mɒdl]	Modell	a new (or: an old) ~ / a 1980 ~
van [væn] (*BE*)	Lieferwagen	a baker's ~
coach [kəʊtʃ] (*BE*) = **bus** [bʌs] (*AE*)	Reisebus	a ~ (+ going) to London (or: from New York to Chicago)
lorry ['lɒrɪ] (*BE*) = **truck** [trʌk] (*AE*)	Lastwagen	a ~ full of . . .
learner driver [ˌlɜːnə 'draɪvə*]	Fahrschüler	
driving licence ['draɪvɪŋ ˌlaɪsəns] (*BE*) = **driver's licence** ['draɪvərz ˌlaɪsəns] (*AE*)	Führerschein	have a ~ ~ / renew one's ~ ~
numberplate ['nʌmbəpleɪt] (*BE*) = **licence plate** ['laɪsəns pleɪt] (*AE*)	Nummernschild, Kennzeichen	
key [kiː]	Schlüssel	look for one's car ~ / put the ~ in the ignition / **ignition key** [ɪg'nɪʃn kiː] (Zündschlüssel)
body ['bɒdɪ]	Karosserie	
engine ['endʒɪn]	Motor	start the ~
bonnet ['bɒnɪt] (*BE*) = **hood** [hʊd] (*AE*)	Haube	open the ~
boot [buːt] (*BE*) = **trunk** [trʌŋk] (*AE*)	Kofferraum	put everything in the ~
gear ['gɪə*]	Gang	change into second ~ (or: reverse ~ [Rückwärtsgang])
gear-lever ['gɪəˌlevə*] (*BE*) = **gear-shift** ['gɪəʃɪft] (*AE*)	Schaltknüppel	
steering wheel ['stiːrɪŋ wiːl]	Lenkrad	hold the ~ ~
clutch [klʌtʃ]	Kupplung	press the ~
tyre ['taɪə*] (*BE*) = **tire** [-r] (*AE*)	Reifen	have a flat ~ (Platten)

go (went, gone) [gəʊ, went, gɒn]	fahren	~ by car / ~ fast
drive (drove, driven) [draɪv, drəʊv, 'drɪvn]	(ein Auto) fahren	~ a car / ~ well / be a good **driver** ['-ə*]
ride (rode, ridden) [raɪd, rəʊd, 'rɪdn]	(in einem Auto) fahren, (Auto-)Fahrt	~ in a car go for a ~ in a car
speed (sped, sped) [spi:d, sped, –]	(zu) schnell fahren;	~ along (or: down) the motorway / be fined (Geldstrafe bekommen) for ~ing
	Geschwindigkeit	travel along at a slow (or: steady) ~ / exceed (überschreiten) (or: keep within) the **speed limit** ['– ˌlɪmɪt] / gain ~
fast [fɑ:st]	schnell	drive ~
overtake (overtook, overtaken) [ˌəʊvə'teɪk, -'tʊk, -'teɪkn]	überholen	~ a lorry / '**No overtaking**'
brake [breɪk]	bremsen	~ suddenly (or: hard)
park [pɑ:k]	parken	~ a car / leave the car in a **car park** ['kɑ: pɑ:k]
petrol ['petrəl] (*BE*) = **gas** [gæs] (*AE*)	Benzin	fill (+ the car / her) up with ~ / be short of ~ / be low on gas
filling station ['fɪlɪŋ ˌsteɪʃn] (*BE*) = **service station** ['sɜ:vɪs ˌ–] (*BE*) = **petrol station** ['petrəl ˌ–] (*BE*) = **gas station** ['gæs ˌ–] (*AE*)	Tankstelle	drive to the next ~ ~
tank [tæŋk]	Tank	have only a little petrol in the ~
fill up [ˌfɪl 'ʌp]	volltanken	F~ her ~, please.
oil [ɔɪl]	Öl	check the ~
breakdown ['breɪkdaʊn]	Panne	have a ~ with one's car
repair [rɪ'peə*]	reparieren	have one's car ~ed
spare part ['speə pɑ:t]	Ersatzteil	

153 Road – (Land-)Straße (→ 147 Street)

road [rəʊd]	(Land-)Straße	go (or: travel) by ~ / drive along a ~ / It takes two hours by ~. / Is this the ~ to Walton? / I was on the ~ for 2 hours.
roadway ['rəʊdweɪ]	Fahrbahn	Don't stop on the ~; draw up on the side.
roadside ['rəʊdsaɪd]	Straßenrand	sit by the ~
lane [leɪn]	Fahrspur;	the right (or: left / inside / outside) ~ / keep to the inside ~ / get into ~ (sich einordnen)
	(ein von Hecken, Mauern usw. eingefaßter) Weg; Gasse (in der Stadt)	a narrow (or: shady) ~
bend [bend]	Kurve	go slowly around a ~ / Do not overtake when approaching a ~.
curve [kɜːv]	Kurve	take a ~ (+ at high speed) / cut a ~
crossroads ['krɒsrəʊdz] (*BE*) = **intersection** ['ɪntərsekʃn] (*AE*)	Kreuzung	come to a(n) ~
traffic lights ['træfɪk ˌlaɪts]	Ampel	wait at the ~ ~
signpost ['saɪnpəʊst]	Wegweiser	
roundabout ['raʊndəbaʊt] (*BE*) = **rotary** ['rəʊtərɪ] (*AE*)	Kreisverkehr	double ~ ahead / enter a ~
detour ['dɪːˌtʊə*]	Umweg	make a ~ because the main road is closed
diversion [daɪ'vɜːʃn]	Umleitung	There is a ~ because of road repairs.
highway ['haɪweɪ]	Überlandstraße	
trunk road ['trʌŋk rəʊd] (*BE*)	Fernverkehrsstraße	
motorway ['məʊtəweɪ] (*BE*) = **freeway** ['friːweɪ] (*AE*)	Autobahn	
bypass ['baɪpɑːs] (*BE*) = **expressway** [ɪk'spresweɪ] (*AE*)	Umgehungsstraße	
road sign ['rəʊd saɪn]	Verkehrsschild	

Some common texts on road signs – Texte auf Verkehrsschildern

Keep in lane	in der Spur bleiben	**Give way** (*BE*) = **Yield** (*AE*)	Vorfahrt achten
No parking	Parken verboten	**No entry**	Einfahrt verboten
Turn left	Links abbiegen	**No overtaking**	Überholen verboten
Turn right	Rechts abbiegen	**Winding road**	kurvenreiche Strecke
Slow	Langsam fahren	**Level crossing** (*BE*) = **Grade crossing** (*AE*)	Eisenbahn kreuzt
Slow down	Abbremsen (oft vor Kurven)		

By bus, by underground – mit dem Bus, mit der U-Bahn 154

bus stop ['bʌs stɒp]	Bushaltestelle	wait at the ~
number ['nʌmbə*]	Linie	take the ~ 12 (+ bus)
queue [kjuː] (*BE*)	Schlange,	stand in a long ~ / jump the ~ (sich vordrängen)
	Schlange stehen	~ (+ up) for the bus
line [laɪn] (*AE*)	Schlange	stand in ~ / cut into the ~ (sich vordrängen)
bus [bʌs]	Bus	go by ~ / take the ~
passenger ['pæsɪndʒə*]	Fahrgast	All the ~s got off.
conductor [kən'dʌktə*] (*BE*)	Schaffner	The bus ~ had no change.
get (got, got) **in** [get, gɒt, –; – 'ɪn] = **get on** [– 'ɒn]	einsteigen	The bus was so full that nobody else could ~ ~.
get (got, got) **off** [get, gɒt, –; – 'ɒf] = **get out of** [get 'aut əv]	aussteigen	Do not ~ ~ (= ~ ~ ~) the bus before it comes to a complete halt.
'Fares, please' ['feəz ˌpliːz] = **'All fares'** ['ɔːl feəz]	„Noch jemand ohne Fahrschein?“	
fare ['feə*]	Fahrgeld	pay one's ~
ticket ['tɪkɪt]	Fahrschein	a bus ~
underground ['ʌndəgraʊnd]	U-Bahn	go by (= on the) ~
tube ['tjuːb] (*BE inform.*)	U-Bahn (in London)	travel by ~ / a ~ train
subway ['sʌbweɪ] (*AE*)	U-Bahn	the New York ~

line [laɪn]	Linie	take the Victoria ~
station ['steɪʃn]	U-Bahnhof	A train sped into the ~.
escalator ['eskəleɪtə*]	Rolltreppe	go down to the platform by ~
ticket machine ['tɪkɪt məˌʃiːn]	Fahrkartenautomat	get a 20p ticket from the ~ ~

155 By train – mit der Eisenbahn

railway ['reɪlweɪ] (*BE*) = **railroad** ['reɪlrəʊd] (*AE*)	Eisenbahn	a ~ station / a ~ line / a ~ crossing
rail [reɪl]	Schiene	go off the ~s
signal ['sɪgnəl]	Signal	change a ~
station ['steɪʃn]	Bahnhof	meet sb at the ~ / see sb off at the ~
passenger ['pæsɪndʒə*]	Fahrgast	
commuter [kə'mjuːtə*]	Pendler(in)	
ticket ['tɪkɪt]	Fahrkarte	buy a ~ / a single (*BE*) (= one-way, *AE*) ~ / a return (*BE*) (= round-trip, *AE*) ~
single ['sɪŋgl]	einfache Fahrt	The price is £2.50 ~.
return [rɪ'tɜːn]	hin und zurück	The price is £4.80 ~.
timetable ['taɪmteɪbl] = **schedule** ['ʃedjuːl] (*BE*), ['skedʒʊl] (*AE*)	Fahrplan	look at the ~
waiting room ['weɪtɪŋ rʊm]	Warteraum	sit in the ~ ~
platform ['plætfɔːm] (*BE*)	Bahnsteig, Gleis	wait on the ~ / The train arrives at ~ 3.
track [træk] (*AE*)	Gleis	The train leaves from ~ 23.
train [treɪn]	Zug	go (or: travel) by ~ / Is this the right ~ for London? / take the 10.30 ~ (+ to London)
engine ['endʒɪn] (*BE*) = **locomotive** ['ləʊkəˌməʊtɪv] (*AE*)	Lokomotive	a(n) steam (or: diesel / electric) ~ / an **engine driver** ['– draɪvə*] (*BE*) (= **engineer** [ˌendʒɪ'nɪər], AE)
express train [ɪk'spres treɪn]	Schnellzug	
inter-city train [ˌɪntəˌsɪtɪ 'treɪn]	Intercity	
carriage ['kærɪdʒ] (*BE*) = **car** [kɑr] (*AE*)	Personenwaggon	the second ~

compartment [kəm'pɑːtmənt]	Abteil	the ~ is a (+ non-) smoker
conductor [kən'dʌktə*] (*BE*) = **guard** [gɑrd] (*AE*)	Schaffner	
first class [ˌfɜːst 'klɑːs]	erste Klasse	travel ~ ~
rack [ræk]	Gepäckablage	put one's suitcases on the ~
communication cord (*BE*) [kəˌmjunɪ'keɪʃn kɔːd] = **emergency brake** [ɪ'mɜːdʒənsɪ breɪk] (*BE / AE*)	Notbremse	pull the ~ ~
catch (caught, caught) **the train** [kætʃ, kɔːt, –; '– ðə ˌtreɪn]	den Zug bekommen	be just in time to ~ ~ ~
leave (left, left) [liːv, left, –]	abfahren	The train ~s at 10.30.
miss the train ['mis ðe ˌtreɪn]	den Zug verpassen	~ ~ ~ by a few minutes
change [tʃeɪndʒ]	umsteigen;	~ at Colchester for Cambridge / ~ trains
	aussteigen	'All ~!'
connect with [kə'nekt wɪð]	Anschluß haben (von einem Zug gesagt)	~ ~ the 9.30 train at Colchester
connection [kə'nekʃn]	Anschluß	catch (or: miss) one's ~
delay [dɪ'leɪ]	Verspätung	There'll be a ~ of 10 minutes. / The train was ~ed (hatte Verspätung) (+ for) 10 minutes.
arrive [ə'raɪv]	ankommen	The train ~s at 12.30.
terminus ['tɜːmɪnəs]	Endstation	King's Cross is the ~.

By plane – mit dem Flugzeug 156

airline ['eəlaɪn]	Fluggesellschaft	
airport ['eəpɔːt]	Flughafen	Gatwick A~, London / an international ~
airfield ['eəfiːld] (*mil.*)	Fliegerhorst	
airstrip ['eəstrɪp]	Landeplatz	
flight [flaɪt]	Flug	book a ~ / F~ KLM 173 has just arrived.

check in [ˌtʃek 'ɪn]	durch die Abfertigung gehen	~ ~ at the airport an hour before the plane leaves
gate [geɪt]	Ausgang (zur Rollbahn)	Flight LH 735 to Hamburg is boarding now through G~ 12.
airliner ['eəlaɪnə*]	(Verkehrs-)Flugzeug	too small for ~s
cabin ['kæbɪn]	Kabine	
passenger ['pæsɪndʒə*]	Passagier	'P~s for London please go to Gate 12.'
seat [siːt]	Sitz	fasten the ~ belts
runway ['rʌnweɪ]	Rollbahn	taxi (rollen) to the ~ / a 7,000-ft. ~
control tower [kən'trəʊl ˌtaʊə*]	Kontrollturm	
take (took, taken) **off** [teɪk, tʊk, 'teɪkn; – 'ɒf]	starten	The plane ~s ~ at 10.30.
climb [klaɪm]	steigen	~ higher and higher
fly (flew, flown) [flaɪ, fluː, fləʊn]	fliegen,	~ a plane / ~ to New York / I don't like ~ing.
	mit ... fliegen,	~ Lufthansa
	überfliegen	~ the Atlantic in six hours
stewardess ['stjuːədɪs]	Stewardess	Two ~es brought coffee.
land [lænd]	landen	~ safely
touch down [ˌtʌtʃ 'daʊn]	aufsetzen	no smoking during ~ ~
crash [kræʃ]	abstürzen,	~ into a mountain
	Absturz	be killed in a ~
cancel ['kænsl]	absagen	be ~led
aircraft ['eəkrɑːft]	Luftfahrzeug(-e)	
aeroplane ['eərəpleɪn] (*BE*) = **airplane** ['eərpleɪn] (*AE*)	Flugzeug	
helicopter ['helɪkɒptə*]	Hubschrauber	
hover ['hɒvə*]	schweben	
balloon [bə'luːn]	Ballon	
glider ['glaɪdə*]	Segelflugzeug	
airship ['eəʃɪp]	Luftschiff, Zeppelin	

By ship – mit dem Schiff

ship [ʃɪp]	Schiff	travel (+ to New York) by ~ / go aboard a ~
passenger ['pæsɪndʒə*]	Passagier	first-class ~ / deck ~s
aboard [ə'bɔːd]	an Bord	go ~ a ship / 'Welcome ~.'
embark [ɪm'bɑːk]	sich einschiffen	The passengers ~ed on the QE2.
board [bɔːd]	Bord,	go (or: be) on ~ (+ a ship)
	an Bord gehen	~ a ship
cabin ['kæbɪn]	Kabine	book a ~
bunk [bʌŋk] = **berth** [bɜːθ]	Koje	sleep in a ~
put (put, put) (+ **out**) **to sea** [pʊt, –, –; – (ˌaʊt) tə 'siː]	auslaufen, in See stechen	The liner first ~ (+ ~) ~ ~ in 1952.
sail [seɪl]	(mit dem Schiff) fahren,	~ for London
	Segel,	hoist (heißen) the ~s
	segeln	a **sailing boat** ['-ɪŋ bəʊt]
course [kɔːs]	Kurs	steer a ~ of 160° / be on (or: off) ~ / keep on ~ / set ~ for
head [hed]	steuern	~ south (or: for the mainland)
bearing ['beərɪŋ]	Peilung	take a compass ~ on a landmark / get (= take) one's ~s (peilen)
navigate ['nævɪgeɪt]	navigieren	~ by the stars
steer ['stɪə*]	steuern	~ a course of 270° / ~ a boat / ~ northward (or: for the coast / for the harbour)
sailor ['seɪlə*] = **seaman** (*pl.* seamen) ['siːmən]	Seemann, Matrose	become a ~
go (went, gone) **to sea** [gəʊ, went, gɒn; ˌ– tə 'siː]	zur See fahren	~ ~ ~ at the age of 14
captain ['kæptɪn]	Kapitän	be the ~ of a ship
crew [kruː]	Besatzung	The ~ has gone ashore.
deck [dek]	Deck	go on ~ / on (or: below) ~
bridge [brɪdʒ]	Brücke	stand on the ~
lifeboat ['laɪfbəʊt]	Rettungsboot	
lifebelt ['laɪfbelt]	Rettungsring	
life-jacket ['laɪfˌdʒækɪt]	Schwimmweste	inflate (aufblasen) a ~
lighthouse ['laɪthaʊs]	Leuchtturm	pass a ~

put (put, put) **in** [pʊt, –, –; – 'ɪn]	einlaufen	The 'King George' ~s ~ at Harwich ['hærɪdʒ] at 6.30 a.m.
anchor ['æŋkə*]	Anker,	drop (+ the) ~ / lie at ~
	ankern	~ a boat
pilot ['paɪlət]	Lotse, lotsen	~ ships into (or: out of) the harbour / **pilot boat** [– bəʊt]
disembark [ˌdɪsɪm'bɑːk]	von Bord gehen	The passengers ~ed at 2 a.m.
harbour ['hɑːbə*] (*BE*) = **harbor** ['hɑːrbər] (*AE*)	Hafen	reach (or: lie in / leave) the ~ / enter a ~ / Plymouth ~ / a natural (or: manmade / fishery) ~
port [pɔːt]	Hafen(-stadt)	the ~ of Rotterdam / reach (or: leave) ~ / put into a ~ / call at (anlaufen) several ~s / **Port Said** [ˌpɔːt 'saɪd]
marina [mə'riːnə]	Yachthafen, Sporthafen	
quay [kiː]	Kai	A lot of ships were tied up alongside the ~.
pier [pɪə*]	Pier, Landungssteg	She sails from ~ 29.
moor [mʊə*]	vertäuen, festmachen	~ a ship in a harbour
load [ləʊd]	Ladung,	The ship was carrying a ~ of bananas.
	laden	~ a ship with sth
cargo ['kɑːgəʊ]	Ladung	a ~ of coal
hatch [hætʃ]	Luke	open a ~
crane [kreɪn]	Kran	load a cargo with ~s

Ships and boats – Schiffe und Boote

sailing boat	['seɪlɪŋ bəʊt]	Segelboot
rowing boat (*BE*)	['rəʊɪŋ bəʊt]	Ruderboot
= **rowboat** (*AE*)	['rəʊbəʊt]	
canoe	[kə'nuː]	Kanu, Kanadier
kayak	['kaɪæk]	Kajak, Paddelboot
dinghy	['dɪŋgɪ]	Jolle
yacht	[jɒt]	Jacht
motor boat	['məʊtə bəʊt]	Motorboot
freighter	['freɪtə*]	Frachter
ferry	['ferɪ]	Fährschiff
steamer	['stiːmə*]	Dampfer
= **steam ship**	['stiːm ʃɪp]	
liner	['laɪner]	Passagierschiff

Animals around us – Tiere um uns

Animals in the house – Tiere im Haus 158

dog [dɒg]	Hund	call (or: feed) one's ~ / take one's ~ for a walk (= walk the ~)
puppy ['pʌpɪ]	Welpe	have six ~ies
bark [bɑ:k]	bellen	~ at the moon
sniff [snɪf]	schnüffeln	~ (+ at) sb's shoes
kennel ['kenl]	Hundehütte	sleep in a ~
breed [bri:d]	Rasse,	What ~ is it?
	züchten	She ~s terriers.
cat [kæt]	Katze	a black (or: white / grey / ginger) ~ / a Siamese ~
kitten ['kɪtn]	Kätzchen	a playful ~
mew [mju:] = **miao** [mi:'aʊ]	miauen	~ pitifully (kläglich)
scratch [skrætʃ]	kratzen	~ sb
budgie ['bʌdʒɪ] (*inform.*)	Wellensittich	a yellow ~
canary [kə'neərɪ]	Kanarienvogel	a blue ~
cage [keɪdʒ]	Käfig	a small ~
pigeon ['pɪdʒɪn]	Taube	a grey ~
dove [dʌv]	Taube	**dovecot** ['-kɒt] (Taubenschlag)
fish [fɪʃ]	Fisch	keep a **goldfish** ['gəʊldfɪʃ] in a tank
tank [tæŋk]	Aquarium	There are 20 fish in the ~.
hamster ['hæmstə*]	Hamster	a hungry ~
guinea pig ['gɪnɪ pɪg]	Meerschweinchen	a dirty ~ ~
pet [pet]	zahmes Tier, Haustier, Lieblingstier	keep a ~ / be one's ~

Animals on the farm – Tiere auf dem Bauernhof 159

pig	[pɪg]	Schwein
goat	[gəʊt]	Ziege
sheep (*pl.* sheep)	[ʃi:p]	Schaf
lamb	[læm]	Lamm
horse	[hɔ:s]	Pferd
donkey (*BE*)	['dʌŋkɪ],	Esel
= **ass** (*AE*)	[æs]	
mule	[mju:l]	Maultier, Maulesel
pony	['pəʊnɪ]	Pony
cattle	[kætl]	(Rind-)Vieh

cow	[kaʊ]	Kuh
calf (*pl.* calves)	[kɑːf], ['kɑːvz]	Kalb
ox (*pl.* oxen)	[ɒks], ['ɒksən]	Ochse
bull	[bʊl]	Bulle
fowl	[faʊl]	Huhn (als Art)
chicken	['tʃɪkɪn]	Huhn (als Art)
fowls = poultry	[faʊlz], ['pəʊltrɪ]	Geflügel
chick	[tʃɪk]	Küken
cock (*BE*)	[kɒk],	Hahn
= **rooster** (*AE*)	['ruːstər]	
hen	[hen]	Henne
duck	[dʌck]	Ente (als Art oder als weibliches Tier)
drake	[dreɪk]	Erpel
goose (*pl.* geese)	[guːs], [giːs]	Gans (als Art oder als weibliches Tier)
gander	['gændə*]	Ganter, Gänserich
turkey	['tɜːkɪ]	Truthahn, Truthenne, Pute, Puter

160 Animals in the fields and forests – Tiere des Feldes und Waldes

deer (*pl.* deer)	[dɪə*]	Hirsch, Reh; Rotwild
roe = roe-deer	[rəʊ], ['rəʊˌdɪə*]	Reh, Hirschkuh; Rehwild
roebuck	['rəʊbʌk]	Rehbock
wild boar	['waɪld bɔː*]	Wildschwein
fox	[fɒks]	Fuchs
vixen	['vɪksn]	Füchsin
squirrel	['skwɪrəl]	Eichhörnchen
hare	[heə*]	Hase
rabbit	['ræbɪt]	Kaninchen
rat	[ræt]	Ratte
mouse (*pl.* mice)	[maʊs], [maɪs]	Maus
beaver	['biːvə*]	Biber
racoon	[rə'kuːn]	Waschbär
skunk	[skʌŋk]	Stinktier
hedgehog	['hedʒhɒg]	Igel
mole	[məʊl]	Maulwurf
bat	[bæt]	Fledermaus
bird	[bɜːd]	Vogel
sparrow	['spærəʊ]	Spatz
finch	[fɪntʃ]	Fink
bullfinch	['bʊlfɪntʃ]	Dompfaff
tit	[tɪt]	Meise
wren	[ren]	Zaunkönig

nightingale	['naɪtɪŋgeɪl]	Nachtigall
robin	['rɒbɪn]	Rotkehlchen
blackbird	['blækbɜːd]	Schwarzdrossel, Amsel
starling	['stɑːlɪŋ]	Star
crow	[krəʊ]	Krähe
raven	['reɪvn]	Rabe
magpie	['mægpaɪ]	Elster
lark	[lɑːk]	Lerche
swallow	['swɒləʊ]	Schwalbe
cuckoo	['kʊkuː]	Kuckuck
woodpecker	['wʊd,pekə*]	Specht
pheasant	['feznt]	Fasan
partridge	['pɑːtrɪdʒ]	Rebhuhn
stork	[stɔːk]	Storch
crane	[kreɪn]	Kranich
falcon	['fɔːlkən]	Falke
eagle	['iːgl]	Adler
buzzard	['bʌzəd]	Bussard
hawk	[hɔːk]	Habicht
vulture	['vʌltʃə*]	Geier
owl	[aʊl]	Eule
reptile	['reptaɪl]	Kriechtier
lizard	['lɪzəd]	Eidechse
snake	[sneɪk]	Schlange
poisonous snake	['pɔɪznəs –]	Giftschlange
adder	['ædə*]	Kreuzotter
butterfly	['bʌtəflaɪ]	Schmetterling
moth	[mɒθ]	Motte
caterpillar	['kætəpɪlə*]	Raupe
bee	[biː]	Biene
bumble-bee	['bʌmblbiː]	Hummel
wasp	[wesp]	Wespe
hornet	['hɔːnɪt]	Hornisse
fly	[flaɪ]	Fliege
maggot	['mægət]	Made
mosquito	[mə'skiːtəʊ],	Stechmücke
= **gnat** (*BE*)	[næt]	
flea	[fliː]	Floh
louse (*pl.* lice)	[laʊs], [laɪs]	Laus
ant	[ænt]	Ameise
beetle	['biːtl]	Käfer
bug	[bʌg]	Wanze; (selten) Käfer, Insekt (*AE*)
locust	['ləʊkəst]	Heuschrecke
grasshopper	['grɑːshɒpə*]	Grashüpfer
cricket	['krɪkɪt]	Grille, Heimchen
spider	['spaɪdə*]	Spinne

worm	[wɜːm]	Wurm
earthworm	['ɜːθwɜːm]	Regenwurm
snail	[sneɪl]	Schnecke
slug	[slʌg]	Nacktschnecke

161 Animals in or near the water – Tiere im oder am Wasser

swan	[swɔːn]	Schwan
frog	[frɒg]	Frosch
tadpole	['tædpəʊl]	Kaulquappe
toad	[təʊd]	Kröte
herring	['herɪŋ]	Hering
plaice	[pleɪs]	Scholle
haddock	['hædək]	Schellfish
sole	[səʊl]	Seezunge
carp	[kɑːp]	Karpfen
bass	[bæs]	Barsch
trout	[traʊt]	Forelle
pike	[paɪk]	Hecht
cod	[kɒd]	Kabeljau
eel	[iːl]	Aal
salmon	['sæmən]	Lachs
shark	[ʃɑːk]	Hai, Haifisch
shellfish	['ʃelfɪʃ]	Schalentier
clam	[klæm]	Muschel
oyster	[ɔɪstə*]	Auster
crab	[kræb]	Krabbe
crayfish	['kreɪfɪʃ]	Flußkrebs
lobster	['lɒbstə*]	Hummer
shrimp	[ʃrɪmp]	Garnele
star fish = sea star	['stɑː fɪʃ], ['siː stɑː*]	Seestern
sea urchin = sea hedgehog	['siː ˌɜːtʃɪn], ['siː ˌhedʒhɒg]	Seeigel
octopus	['ɒktəpəs]	Krake
cuttlefish	['kʌtlfɪʃ]	Tintenfisch
coral	['kɒrəl]	Koralle

162 Animals in the zoo – Tiere im Zoo

wolf (*pl.* wolves)	[wʊlf], [wʊlvz]	Wolf
jackal	['dʒækɔːl]	Schakal
hyena	[haɪ'iːnə]	Hyäne
dingo	['dɪŋgəʊ]	Dingo
kangaroo	[ˌkæŋgə'ruː]	Känguruh

lion	['laɪən]	Löwe
tiger	['taɪgə*]	Tiger
leopard	['lepəd]	Leopard
panther	['pænθə*]	Panther
puma	['pju:mə]	Puma
jaguar	['dʒægjʊə]	Jaguar
lynx	[lɪŋks]	Luchs
wild cat	['waɪld kæt]	Wildkatze
bear	[beə*]	Bär
polar bear	[ˌpəʊlə 'beə*]	Eisbär
elephant	['elɪfənt]	Elefant
hippo	['hɪpəʊ],	Flußpferd
= **hippopotamus**	[ˌhɪpə'pɒtəməs]	
rhinoceros	[raɪ'nɒsərəs]	Nashorn
bison	['baɪsn]	Bison
buffalo	['bʌfələʊ]	Büffel
camel	['kæməl]	Kamel
giraffe	[dʒɪ'rɑ:f]	Giraffe
zebra	['zi:brə]	Zebra
antelope	['æntɪləʊp]	Antilope
elk	[elk]	Elch
reindeer	['reɪnˌdɪə*]	Rentier
monkey	['mʌŋkɪ]	Affe
ape	[eɪp]	(Menschen-)Affe
gorilla	[gə'rɪlə]	Gorilla
chimp(anzee)	[(ˌ)tʃɪmp(ən'zi:)]	Schimpanse
orang outang	[ɔ:ˌræŋ u:'tæŋ]	Orang-Utan
= **orang utang**		
seal	[si:l]	Seehund
whale	[weɪl]	Wal
dolphin	['dɒlfɪn]	Delphin
crocodile	['krɒkədaɪl]	Krokodil
lizard	['lɪzəd]	Eidechse
penguin	['peŋgwɪn]	Pinguin
ostrich	['ɒstrɪtʃ]	Strauß
peacock	['pi:kɒk]	Pfau

Man and animal – Mensch und Tier 163

wild [waɪld]	wild, ungezähmt;	~ animals / a ~ horse / the ~ beasts (die großen Raubtiere)
	wild, gefährlich	a ~ dog
fierce ['fɪəs]	wild, gefährlich	a ~ tiger (or: dog)
tame [teɪm]	zähmen, bändigen,	~ a wild horse / a lion **tamer** ['-ə*]
	zahm, gezähmt	a ~ fox (or: wolf) / This dog is quite ~.

train [treɪn]	dressieren, abrichten	~ an animal (+ to do sth) / a ~ed animal
raise [reɪz]	züchten, halten	~ pigs (or: chickens)
keep (kept, kept) [ki:p, kept, –]	halten	~ bees (+ for honey) / ~ sheep (+ for wool)
pet [pet]	(zahmes) Haustier, Lieblingstier	have a lot of ~s / keep a mouse as a ~
domestic animal [dəʊˌmestɪk 'ænɪməl] = **farm animal** ['fɑ:m ˌ–]	Haus- und Nutztier	Cows (or: Pigs) are ~ ~s.
feed (fed, fed) [fi:d, fed, –]	füttern	~ cows on hay in winter
milk [mɪlk]	melken,	~ a cow (+ by hand)
	Milch	A cow gives ~. / breed cows for ~
fatten ['fætn]	mästen	~ (+ up) pigs
slaughter ['slɔ:tə*]	schlachten	~ pigs (or: oxen) / **slaughter-house** [-haʊs]
shoot (shot, shot) [ʃu:t, ʃɒt, –]	schießen	~ a wild duck
go (went, gone) **shooting** [gəʊ, went, gɒn; – 'ʃu:tɪŋ]	(zu Fuß) auf Jagd gehen	~ ~ in the woods
hunt [hʌnt]	(mit Pferden und Hunden, *BE*; zu Fuß oder mit Pferden und Hunden, *AE*) jagen,	~ deer (or: foxes) / go **hunting** ['–ɪŋ]
	Jagd	a long ~
game [geɪm]	(jagdbares) Wild,	hunt ~
	(Jagd-)Beute;	carry home one's ~
	jagdbar	a ~ bird
trap [træp]	eine Falle stellen	~ beavers / a **trapper** ['-ə*]
fish [fɪʃ]	fischen, angeln	~ for herrings / be out ~ing / a **fishing net** ['fɪʃɪŋ net] / a **fisherman** ['fɪʃəmən]
catch (caught, caught) [kætʃ, kɔ:t, –]	fangen	~ fish
angle ['æŋgl]	angeln	go **angling** [-ɪŋ]
bait [beɪt]	Köder	use worms or small fish as (+ a) ~

The sounds of animals – Tierstimmen 164

bark (dogs)	[bɑːk]	bellen
growl (dogs)	[graʊl]	knurren
mew (cats)	[mjuː]	miauen
purr (cats)	[pɜː*]	schnurren
squeak (mice)	[skwiːk]	quietschen
grunt (pigs)	[grʌnt]	grunzen
squeal (pigs)	[skwiːl]	quieken
bleat (goats)	[bliːt]	meckern
bleat (sheep)	[bliːt]	blöken
neigh (horses)	[neɪ]	wiehern
moo (cows)	[muː]	muhen
crow (cocks, *BE* = roosters, *AE*)	[krəʊ]	krähen
cackle (hens)	['kækl]	gackern
sing (birds)	[sɪŋ]	singen
hiss (snakes)	[hɪs]	zischen
hum = buzz (bees)	[hʌm], [bʌz]	summen
croak (frogs)	[krəʊk]	quaken
roar (lions)	[rɔː*]	brüllen
trumpet (elephants)	['trʌmpɪt]	trompeten
growl (bears)	[graʊl]	brummen
bray (donkeys)	[breɪ]	schreien

The animal – das Tier 165

animal ['ænɪml]	Tier(-);	~s and plants / the ~ kingdom / study ~ behaviour
	Vierbeiner	~s, birds, or fish
wildlife ['waɪldlaɪf]	die Tierwelt	
male [meɪl]	männlich,	a ~ bird
	Männchen	With most birds the ~ is bigger.
female ['fiːmeɪl]	weiblich,	a ~ bird
	Weibchen	The ~ is wilder.
mate [meɪt]	Partner,	find a ~
	sich paaren	Birds ~ in the spring.
breed (bred, bred) [briːd, bred, –]	sich fortpflanzen	Some animals won't ~ in the zoo. / These cows are good **breeders** ['-əz].
litter ['lɪtə*]	Wurf	have two ~s a year
egg [eg]	Ei	lay ~s
nest [nest]	Nest, nisten	a bird's ~ / build a ~ in trees
brood [bruːd]	brüten,	That hen is ~ing.
	Brut	a ~ of chicken (or: insects / fish)

hatch [hætʃ]	ausbrüten; schlüpfen	~ eggs (or: chickens) Three eggs (or: chickens) have ~ed already.
young [jʌŋ]	Junge	feed (or: care for) the ~ / a fox and its ~
pack [pæk]	Rudel	a ~ of wolves / hunt in ~s / the leader of the ~
herd [hɜːd]	Herde	a ~ of cows (or: elephants) / live in ~s
flock [flɒk]	Herde, Schwarm	a ~ of sheep a ~ of birds
shoal [ʃəʊl] = **school** [skuːl]	Fischschwarm	a ~ of herrings
eat (ate, eaten) [iːt, et, 'iːtn]	fressen	Cows ~ grass.
feed (fed, fed) [fiːd, fed, –]	sich ernähren, grasen	~ on grass (or: fish) ~ in the fields (or: meadows)
graze [greɪz]	grasen, äsen	cows (or: deer / sheep) ~ / ~ in the fields
hunt [hʌnt]	jagen	Wolves ~ in packs.
prey [preɪ]	Beute, (Beute) jagen; Raub-	The lion ate its ~. / be (or: become / fall) ~ to a lion ~ at night a **beast of prey** [ˌbiːst‿əv '–] / a **bird of prey** [ˌbɜːd‿əv '–]
catch (caught, caught) [kætʃ, kɔːt, –]	fangen	~ mice
mammals ['mæmlz]	Säugetiere	A mouse and an elephant are ~.
birds ['bɜːdz]	Vögel	keep ~ in cages
reptiles ['reptaɪlz]	Reptilien, Kriechtiere	R~ have existed for millions of years.
amphibians [æm'fɪbɪənz]	Amphibien, Lurche	A~ are faster in water.
fish [fɪʃ]	Fische	
fur [fɜː]	Pelz, Fell	have thick (or: long / short) ~
mane [meɪn]	Mähne	a lion's (or: horse's) ~
horn [hɔːn]	Horn	a cow's (or: goat's / antelope's) ~
feather ['feðə*]	Feder	have soft (or: long / brightly coloured) ~s
shell [ʃel]	Schale, Gehäuse; Panzer	Snails have ~s. Tortoises (Schildkröten) have ~s.
skin [skɪn]	Haut	a smooth (or: slimy / dry) ~
feeler ['fiːlə*]	Fühler	an insect's ~
mouth [maʊθ]	Maul	The dog holds (or: catches) sth in its ~.

beak [bi:k]	(meist gebogener) Schnabel	the parrot's (or: buzzard's) ~
bill [bɪl]	Schnabel	the canary's ~
claw [klɔ:]	Kralle	The cat (or: tiger) showed its ~s. / It dug its ~s into the flesh.
paw [pɔ:]	Pfote	a cat's ~
hoof [hu:f] (*pl.* hooves [hu:vz], hoofs [-fs])	Huf	a horse's ~s (= ~ves)
fin [fɪn]	Flosse	a fish's ~s
flipper ['flɪpə*]	Flosse (von Säugern)	a dolphin's (or: whale's / seal's) ~
wing [wɪŋ]	Flügel	the ~s of a bird (or: insect)

Plants around us – Pflanzen um uns

Flowers, bushes, trees – Blumen, Sträucher, Bäume 166

(→ 169 The plant)

tulip	['tju:lɪp]	Tulpe
daffodil	['dæfədɪl]	Osterglocke, gelbe Narzisse
rose	[rəʊz]	Rose
dahlia	['deɪljə]	Dahlie
geranium	[dʒɪ'reɪnjəm]	Geranie
forget-me-not	[fə'getmɪnɒt]	Vergißmeinnicht
bluebell	['blu:bel]	Glockenblume
sunflower	['sʌnflaʊə*]	Sonnenblume
daisy	['deɪzɪ]	Gänseblümchen
poppy	['pɒpɪ]	Mohn
carnation = pink	[kɑ:'neɪʃn], [pɪŋk]	Nelke
thistle	['θɪsl]	Distel
heather	['heðə*]	Heidekraut
mistletoe	['mɪsltəʊ]	Mistel
ivy	['aɪvɪ]	Efeu
oak	[əʊk]	Eiche
beech	[bi:tʃ]	Buche
poplar	['pɒplə*]	Pappel
birch	[bɜ:tʃ]	Birke
ash	[æʃ]	Esche
willow	['wɪləʊ]	Weide
elm	[elm]	Ulme
fir	[fɜ:*]	Tanne; Fichte, Föhre
spruce	[spru:s]	Fichte
pine	[paɪn]	Kiefer, Föhre; Pinie

palm	[pɑ:m]	Palme
larch	[lɑ:tʃ]	Lärche
yew	[ju:]	Eibe
plane (+ **-tree**)	[pleɪn ('-tri:)]	Platane
apple tree	['æpl tri:]	Apfelbaum

167 Vegetables, cereals, fruit – Gemüse, Getreide, Früchte

potato (*pl.* potatoes)	[pə'teɪtəʊ], [-z]	Kartoffel
onion	['ʌnjən]	Zwiebel
carrot	['kærət]	Möhre
spinach	['spɪnɪdʒ]	Spinat
lettuce	['letɪs]	Salat
cabbage	['kæbɪdʒ]	Kohl
cauliflower	['kɒlɪˌflaʊə*]	Blumenkohl
turnip	['tɜ:nɪp]	Rübe
sprouts	[spraʊts]	Rosenkohl
tomato (*pl.* tomatoes)	[tə'mɑ:təʊ], [-z]	Tomate
bean	[bi:n]	Bohne
pea	[pi:]	Erbse
cucumber	['kju:kʌmbə*]	Gurke
cereal	['sɪərɪəl]	Getreide
corn	[kɔ:n]	Getreide, bes. Weizen (*BE*); Mais (*AE*)
wheat	[wi:t]	Weizen
rye	[raɪ]	Roggen
barley	['bɑ:lɪ]	Gerste
oat = oats	[əʊt], [əʊts]	Hafer
rice	[raɪs]	Reis
maize (*BE*) = **corn** (*AE*)	[meɪz], [kɔrn]	Mais
fruit	[fru:t]	Obst, Frucht, Früchte
fruits	[fru:ts]	Obst- oder Fruchtsorten
apple	['æpl]	Apfel
pear	[peə*]	Birne
plum	[plʌm]	Pflaume
peach	[pi:tʃ]	Pfirsich
cherry	['tʃerɪ]	Kirsche
berry	['berɪ]	Beere
strawberry	['strɔ:bərɪ]	Erdbeere
gooseberry	['gʊzbərɪ]	Stachelbeere
blackberry	['blækbərɪ]	Brombeere
raspberry	['rɑ:zbərɪ]	Himbeere
grape	[greɪp]	Weintraube

lemon	['lemən]	Zitrone
orange	['ɒrɪndʒ]	Apfelsine
grapefruit	['greɪpfruːt]	Pampelmuse
banana	[bə'nɑːnə]	Banane
pineapple	['paɪnˌæpl]	Ananas
coconut	['kəʊkənʌt]	Kokosnuß
walnut	['wɔːlnʌt]	Walnuß
chestnut	['tʃesnʌt]	Kastanie
peanut	['piːnʌt]	Erdnuß

Man and plant – Mensch und Pflanze 168

Garden – Garten

garden ['gɑːdn]	Garten	lay out a ~ / a well-kept ~ / a vegetable (or: kitchen) ~
greenhouse ['griːnhaus]	Gewächshaus	
park [pɑːk]	Park	go for a walk in the ~ / have a rest on the **park-bench** ['-bentʃ]
gardening ['gɑːdnɪŋ]	Gartenarbeit	G~ is my hobby. / know sth about ~ / do some ~
lawn [lɔːn]	Rasen	mow (or: cut) the ~ / play on the ~
mow [məʊ]	mähen	~ the lawn with a **lawnmower** ['lɔːn-ə*]
flower ['flaʊə*]	Blume	grow (or: pick) ~s
vegetables ['vedʒtəblz]	Gemüse	grow (or: plant) ~
fruit [fruːt]	Obst	grow (or: pick) ~s
grow (grew, grown) [grəʊ, gruː, grəʊn]	anbauen	~ flowers (or: vegetables)
bed [bed]	Beet	prepare a **flower-bed** ['flaʊə-]
dig (dug, dug) [dɪg, dʌg, –]	(um-)graben	~ the ground (or: garden) with a spade / ~ a hole
sow (sowed, sown = sowed, sowed) [seʊ, səʊd, səʊn]	säen	~ carrots / ~ a bed with carrot-seeds
plant [plɑːnt]	(be-)pflanzen	~ flowers / ~ a garden / ~ a bed with tulips
water ['wɔːtə*]	gießen	~ the garden (or: flowers)
weed [wiːd]	Unkraut, Unkraut jäten	a flower-bed full of ~ ~ the garden
orchard ['ɔːtʃəd]	Obstgarten	an **apple**-(or: **cherry-)orchard**

pick [pɪk]	pflücken	~ (+ sb) a rose / ~ a bunch (Strauß) of flowers / ~ apples (or: fruit)
gather ['gæðə*]	sammeln, pflücken	(+ go to) ~ flowers (or: berries)

Farm – Bauernhof (→ 112 Farm; 170 Land)

field [fi:ld]	Feld, Acker;	a ~ of corn
	Wiese, Weide	a ~ full of sheep / The sheep are in the ~.
fence [fens]	Zaun,	a field with a ~ around it
	einzäunen	The field is ~d (+ in) to keep the cows in.
meadow ['medəʊ]	Wiese	a rich ~
pasture ['pɑ:stʃə*]	Weide	drive cattle to a ~ / graze in a ~ / a rich ~ / The cows are in the ~.
grow (grew, grown) [grəʊ, gru:, grəʊn] = **raise** [reɪz]	anbauen	~ corn in a field
cultivate ['kʌltɪveɪt]	anbauen;	~ spinach (or: tomatoes)
	bebauen, bestellen	~ the ground (or: field)
crop [krɒp]	Nutzpflanze;	Wheat (or: salad) is a widely grown ~.
	Ernte, Ertrag	have a big wheat ~ / the potato ~ of 1980
plough [plaʊ] (*BE*) = **plow** [–] (*AE*)	Pflug,	a horse- (or: tractor-) drawn ~ / A ~ breaks up the ground.
	pflügen	~ a field
ripe [raɪp]	reif	The corn is ~.
ripen ['raɪpn]	reifen,	The corn ~s in the sun.
	reifen lassen	The sun ~s the corn.
cut (cut, cut) [kʌt, –, –]	schneiden	~ the corn (or: grass)
reap [ri:p]	mähen, ernten	~ the corn
harvest ['hɑ:vɪst]	Ernte (als Arbeit),	help with the ~
	Ernte (als Ertrag),	gather in the ~ / a rich (or: good / large / poor) ~ / the **wheat-harvest** [wi:t'-]
	Erntezeit,	at ~
	ernten	~ the crops
mill [mɪl]	Mühle	a **miller** ['-ə*] / a **windmill** ['wɪn-]
grind (ground, ground) [graɪnd, graʊnd, –]	mahlen	~ the corn to flour
straw [strɔ:]	Stroh	~ for the animals
hay [heɪ]	Heu	make ~

vine [vaɪn]	Wein, Weinrebe	grow (= cultivate) ~ / grow ~s in a **vineyard** ['vɪnjəd]
grape [greɪp]	Weintraube, Weinbeere	pick (= gather) ~s / press ~s
wine [waɪn]	Wein (als Getränk)	a noble (or: new / heavy / mild / light) ~ / a **wine cellar** ['– ˌselə*]
plantation [plæn'teɪʃn]	Plantage	work on a tea (or: tobacco / cotton) ~

Field, forest – Feld, Wald

hedge [hedʒ]	Hecke	a field surrounded by a ~
bush [bʊʃ]	Busch	hide in the ~es
undergrowth ['ʌndəgrəʊθ]	Unterholz	stumble through the ~
wood [wʊd]	Wald, Gehölz	go for a walk in the ~s / a dense (or: cool / shadowy) ~
forest ['fɒrɪst]	Wald, Forst	a thick (or: dark) ~
fell [fel]	fällen	~ a tree
cut (cut, cut) [kʌt, –, –]	schlagen	~ firewood / ~ (+ down) a tree
log [lɒg]	Baumstamm	transport ~s down the river
sawmill ['sɔːmɪl]	Sägewerk	the noise of a ~

The plant – die Pflanze (→ 166 Flowers, bushes, trees) 169

plant [plɑːnt]	Pflanze	a tall (or: small / beautiful / lovely / common / strange / rare / wild) ~ / an uncommon (or: exotic) ~
flower ['flaʊə*]	Blume	rare (or: common / beautiful / wild) ~s / water the ~s
shrub [ʃrʌb]	Staude, Strauch, Busch	a large (or: small) ~ / **shrubby** ['-ɪ] hills / a terrace sheltered (geschützt) by thick **shrubbery** ['-ərɪ] (Buschwerk)
bush [bʊʃ]	Busch, Strauch, Gebüsch	plant (or: grow / cultivate) ~es / cut (or: trim) a ~
tree [triː]	Baum	plant (or: chop / cut down / fell) a ~ / climb a ~
grass [grɑːs]	Gras	rich (or: high / thick / short / meagre) ~ / water (or: cut / mow) ~
fern [fɜːn]	Farn	
mushroom ['mʌʃrʊm]	Pilz	go to gather (or: pick) ~s
toadstool ['təʊdstuːl]	(meist giftiger) Pilz	
moss [mɒs]	Moos	soft ~ / covered with ~ / the **mossy** ['-ɪ] ground under the trees

Parts of the plant – Pflanzenteile

root [ru:t]	Wurzel;	the ~s of a flower (or: tree) / take ~ / pull a plant up by the ~s
	anpflanzen;	~ a plant in the garden
	Wurzeln schlagen	Roses ~ easily.
stalk [stɔ:k]	Stengel	the ~ of a lily
stem [stem]	Stiel, Stengel	the ~ of a leaf (or: plant) / a thin (or: thick / long / short) ~ / A ~ bears leaves and blossoms. / a ~ bending (or: waving) in the wind
trunk [trʌŋk]	Stamm (eines Baumes)	a thick (or: thin / straight / crooked / bent) ~ / a **tree-trunk** ['tri:-]
bark [bɑ:k]	Rinde, Borke	a tree has (+ a) thin (or: thick) ~
branch [brɑ:ntʃ]	Ast	The ~es swayed in the wind.
twig [twɪg]	Zweig	a bird sitting on a ~
leaf [li:f] (*pl.* leaves [li:vz])	Blatt	Many trees shed (abwerfen) their ~ves in autumn. / a green (or: new / dry / dead / large / thick / thin / small) ~ / an **oak-leaf** ['əʊk-]
withered ['wɪðəd]	verwelkt, welk	~ leaves
rustle ['rʌsl]	rascheln (lassen)	hear the leaves ~ / The wind ~d the dead leaves.
needle ['ni:dl]	Nadel	fir-~s / pine-~s
pine-cone ['paɪnkəʊn]	Tannenzapfen	pick up ~s
acorn ['eɪkɔ:n]	Eichel	collect ~s
thorn [θɔ:n]	Dorn	be pricked by a ~
bud [bʌd]	Knospe,	**rose-buds** ['rəʊz-z] / Trees are in ~.
	knospen, treiben	Trees are ~ding.
blossom ['blɒsəm]	Blüte (eines Baumes oder Strauches),	**apple-blossoms** ['æpl-z] / a tree covered with ~s / be in (+ full) ~
	blühen	The apple trees are ~ing.
flower ['flaʊə*]	Blüte (als Teil der Pflanze),	the beautiful ~s of a rose / The roses are in ~ just now.
	blühen	Most plants ~ in spring. / **flowering plant** [-rɪŋ plɑ:nt] (Blütenpflanze)
bloom [blu:m]	(auf-)blühen,	The roses are ~ing now.
	Blüte	in full ~
fruit [fru:t]	Frucht	The ~ ripens.
stone [stəʊn]	Stein	the ~ of a peach (or: cherry)
core [kɔ:*]	Gehäuse	the ~ of an apple
kernel ['kɜ:nl]	Kern	the ~ of a nut

skin [skɪn]	Schale	the ~ of an orange (or: apple) / a banana ~
peel [piːl]	Schale, schälen	apple (or: orange) ~ ~ a(n) apple (or: pear / orange / banana)
shell [ʃel]	Schale	the ~ of a coconut
seed [siːd]	Samen	the ~ of a plant (or: berry) / raise from ~

Earth – die Erde

Land – Land 170

globe [gləʊb]	Globus, Erdball	
land [lænd]	Land (im Gegensatz zum Meer)	be on ~, not at sea / reach ~ / travel by ~ / sight (or: come in sight of) ~ / go on ~
continent ['kɒntɪnənt]	Erdteil, Kontinent	the seven ~s / a **continental** [ˌkɒntɪ'nentl] climate

Europe	['jʊərəp]	Europa
Asia	['eɪʃə]	Asien
Africa	['æfrɪkə]	Afrika
Australia	[ɒ'streɪljə]	Australien
North America	[ˌnɔːθ ə'merɪkə]	Nordamerika
South America	[ˌsaʊθ ə'merɪkə]	Südamerika
Antarctica	[ænt'ɑːktɪkə]	Antarktis

the Continent [ðə 'kɒntɪnənt]	Europa (aus der Sicht des Engländers, d. h. ohne die Britischen Inseln)	go for a holiday on ~ ~
mainland ['meɪnlənd]	Festland	the ~ of Scotland / The ship left the island and headed for the ~.
island ['aɪlənd]	Insel	live on an ~ / a South Sea **islander** [-ə*]
area ['eərɪə]	Gebiet	There aren't many towns in this ~. / a(n) desert (or: urban / rural / corn-growing) ~
region ['riːdʒən]	Gebiet, Gegend	the cold ~s of the world / the Arctic ~ / a forest ~

country ['kʌntrɪ]	Land (im Gegensatz zur Stadt)	stay (or: live) in the ~ / spend a day in the ~ / go to the ~ (+ for a summer holiday)
countryside ['kʌntrɪsaɪd]	Landschaft, Gegend	go for a walk in the ~ / a lovely (or: beautiful) ~
landscape ['lænskeɪp]	Landschaft (wie sie sich dem Auge darbietet)	We stood on a high hill and admired the beautiful ~ below. / The trees and the hills make a beautiful ~. / a mountain ~
picturesque [ˌpɪktʃə'resk]	malerisch	a ~ landscape (or: countryside / village)

Land form – Topographie

hill [hɪl]	Anhöhe, Hügel, Berg	go up (or: down) the ~ / a high ~ / go **uphill** [ˌʌp'-] / go **downhill** [ˌdaʊn'-] / a **hilly** ['-ɪ] country (or: road)
hillside ['hɪlsaɪd]	Hang	sit on a grassy ~ / slide down the ~
mountain ['maʊntɪn]	Berg	This ~ is 6,000 ft. high. / climb a ~ / a range (Zug) of ~s
mountains ['maʊntɪnz]	Gebirge	spend one's holidays in the ~ / the **Rocky Mountains** [ˌrɒkɪ –] / a **mountainous** ['maʊntɪnəs] country
Mount [maʊnt] = **Mt**	Berg (vor Eigennamen)	~ **Everest** is the highest mountain in the world.
volcano [vɒl'keɪnəʊ] (*pl.* volcanoes [-z])	Vulkan	A ~ erupted.
top [tɒp]	Gipfel, Spitze	reach the ~ / walk up to the ~ / the ~ of a mountain (or: hill)
summit ['sʌmɪt]	Gipfel	reach the ~ (+ of a mountain / of a hill) / The ~ was covered with mist (Nebel).
peak [pi:k]	Spitze	The (+ mountain) ~s are covered with snow.
ridge [rɪdʒ]	Grat, Kamm	walk along the mountain ~ / The sun is setting behind the ~.
slope [sləʊp]	Abhang,	climb a ~ (+ to the top of a hill) / walk up a ~ / roll (or: slide) down a ~
	abfallen	The hill ~s downward to a river.
steep [sti:p]	steil	a ~ hill (or: mountain / slope)
valley ['vælɪ]	Tal	look down on a deep (or: wide / narrow) ~ / walk down into a ~ / pass through a ~

highland ['haɪlənd]	Bergland, Hochland	These flowers are only found in the ~(s). / the mid-German ~(s) / the H~(s) of Scotland
upland ['ʌplənd]	Hochland, hoch gelegen	The climate is rougher in the ~. an ~ region
plateau ['plætəʊ], [-ˈ-]	Hochebene	the **Plateau of Tibet** [– əv tɪ'bet]
plain [pleɪn]	Ebene	fly over the (+ vast) ~s of Australia / the rolling ~s of Canada
flat [flæt]	flach, eben	~ land (or: country)
lowland ['ləʊlənd]	Tiefland	When we came down from the hills we reached the flat ~(s)

Ground – Boden (→ 168 Man and plant)

land [lænd]	Erde, Boden, Ackerland	good (or: rich / poor / rough) ~ / **wasteland** ['weɪst-] (Ödland) / buy a piece of ~ / a plot of ~ / a **landslide** ['-slaɪd] (Erdrutsch)
earth [ɜːθ]	Erde, Boden	Plants grow in the ~.
ground [graʊnd]	Oberfläche, Grund, Boden, -platz	sit (or: lie) on the ~ / fall to the ~ / sandy (or: stony / level / flat) ~ / plant seeds in the ~
soil [sɔɪl]	Boden, Ackerland	good (or: rich / poor / heavy / muddy / sandy / dry) ~ / an area of rich ~
fertile ['fɜːtaɪl]	fruchtbar	~ (or: **infertile** [ɪn-]) land (or: soil)
rock [rɒk]	Fels,	a house built on ~ / solid (or: strong) ~ / a **rocky** ['-ɪ] hill / the **Rocky Mountains** [ˌ-ɪ 'maʊntɪnz]
	Felsbrocken	~s rolling down the side of a mountain
stone [stəʊn]	Stein (als Material), (der einzelne) Stein	a house built of ~. a house built of large ~s / a road covered with ~s / a **stony** ['-ɪ] path / the **Stone Age** ['– eɪdʒ]
marble ['mɑːbl]	Marmor, Marmor-, marmorn	a statue made of ~ a ~ pillar (or: statue)
granite ['grænɪt]	Granit	
chalk [tʃɔːk]	Kreide	
sandstone ['sændstəʊn]	Sandstein	
clay [kleɪ]	Ton	
sand [sænd]	Sand	play in the ~ / a **grain of sand** [greɪn əv '–] (Sandkorn)
desert ['dezət]	Wüste	the **Sahara Desert** [sə'hɑːrə ˌ–]

swamp [swɔːmp]	Sumpf	This land is mainly ~. / The land around the lake is very **swampy** ['-ɪ].
bog [bɒg]	Moor	
marsh [mɑːʃ]	Marsch	
moor [mʊə] = **moors** [-z]	Hochmoor	
common ['kɒmən] (*BE*)	offenes Grasland (das jeder betreten kann)	
fen [fen]	Marschland, Niederung	
heath [hiːθ]	Heide	
prairie ['preərɪ]	Prärie	
steppe [step] = **steppes** [-s]	Steppe	

171 Water – Wasser

River, canal, lake – Fluß, Kanal, See

source [sɔːs]	Quelle	the ~s of the Nile / Where does the Nile have its ~?
rise (rose, risen) [raɪz, rəʊz, 'rɪzn]	entspringen	Where does the Nile ~?
brook [brʊk]	Bach	a small (or: clear) ~
stream [striːm]	(kleiner) Fluß;	a deep (or: small / wide / broad / swift / slow / shallow) ~
	Strömung, Strom	swim with (or: against) the ~ / go **upstream** [ˌʌp'-] / go **downstream** [ˌdaʊn'-]
river ['rɪvə*]	Fluß	the **River Thames** [ˌrɪvə 'temz] / a great (or: long / deep / large / small / narrow / wide) ~ / have a swim in the ~ / jump into the ~ / sail up (or: down) a ~
canyon ['kænjən]	Cañon, Felsschlucht	
shallow ['ʃæləʊ]	flach, seicht	~ water / a ~ river
course [kɔːs]	Lauf	follow the ~ of a river
flow [fləʊ]	fließen, strömen	~ to (or: towards / into) the sea / ~ fast (or: smoothly)
float [fləʊt]	(auf dem Wasser) schwimmen, (im Wasser) treiben	
run (ran, run) [rʌn, ræn, rʌn]	fließen	~ into the sea
current ['kʌrənt]	Strömung	a strong (or: feeble) ~
overflow [ˌəʊvə'fləʊ]	überschwemmen	The river is ~ing.

flood [flʌd]	überfluten,	The river ~ed the fields. / The river is ~ed with heavy rain.
	Überschwemmung	a terrible ~ / the **Great Flood** [greɪt '–] (Sintflut)
join [dʒɔɪn]	zusammenfließen; in ... fließen	Which two rivers ~ at Koblenz? Where does this stream ~ the Rhine?
confluence ['kɒnflʊəns]	Zusammenfluß	at the ~ of the Rhine and the Mosel
bank [bæŋk]	Ufer	on the ~s of the Thames / on the left (or: right) ~ .
bridge [brɪdʒ]	Brücke	cross a river on (or: by) a ~ / a ~ across a river / walk across a ~
flow into ['fləʊ ˌɪntʊ]	münden	The Nile ~s ~ the Mediterranean.
mouth [maʊθ]	Mündung	Cairo is at the ~ of the Nile.
canal [kə'næl]	Kanal	build (or: construct) a ~ / The **Suez Canal** ['sʊɪz –] joins the Red Sea and the Mediterranean.
lock [lɒk]	Schleuse	pass (or: go through) a ~
pond [pɒnd]	Teich	sail a model ship on a ~
lake [leɪk]	(der) See	a great (or: large / small / peaceful) ~ / This ~ is 200 feet deep. / walk along the banks of a ~ / **Lake Michigan** [– 'mɪʃɪgən] / the **Great Lakes** [greɪt '-s]

Sea – Meer, (die) See

sea [siː]	Meer, (die) See,	swim in the ~ / live by the ~ / Brighton is on (or: by) the ~. / go to ~ (zur See gehen) / by land and ~
	See (in Eigennamen);	the **North Sea** ['nɔːθ –] / the **Irish Sea** ['aɪərɪʃ –]
	Seegang, See	a calm (or: smooth / rough / heavy) ~ / a choppy (bewegt) ~
sea level ['siː 'levl]	Meeresspiegel	above (or: below) ~ ~
overseas [ˌəʊvə'siːz]	(in, nach) Übersee,	go (or: live) ~
	Übersee-	~ trade
ocean ['əʊʃn]	Ozean	cross the ~ / the wide ~ / the **Atlantic Ocean** [ət'læntɪk '–]
transatlantic [ˌtrænzət'læntɪk]	transatlantisch	a ~ flight (or: voyage)
bay [beɪ]	Bucht	a small ~ / **Hudson Bay** ['hʌdzən '–]
gulf [gʌlf]	Golf	the **Gulf Stream** ['– striːm] / the **Gulf of California** [– əv ˌkælɪ'fɔːnjə]
strait [streɪt]	Meerenge, Straße	the **Straits of Dover** [-s əv 'dəʊvə*]
channel ['tʃænl]	Meerenge, Kanal	the **English Channel** [ˌɪŋglɪʃ '–] / the **Bristol Channel** [ˌbrɪstl '–]

wave [weɪv]	Welle	a big (or: large / high / heavy / long / short) ~ / plough through the ~s / ~s washing against a rock / ~s rolling over the deck of a ship
foam [fəʊm]	Schaum, schäumen	waves crowned with ~ waves ~ing along the beach
surf [sɜːf]	Brandung	a heavy ~ / ride the ~ / a **surfboard** ['-bɔːd] / go **surfing** ['-ɪŋ]
break (broke, broken) [breɪk, brəʊk, 'brəʊkən]	branden, sich brechen	waves ~ing over (or: on / against) the rocks / the sea ~ing on the beach / a **breaker** ['-ə*] / the **breakers** ['-əz] (Brandung)
tide [taɪd]	die Gezeiten, Flut, Wasser	The ~ is coming in (or: going out). / at high (= flood) ~ / at low (= ebb) ~
coast [kəʊst]	Küste	Cromer is (= lies) on the east ~. / sail along the ~ / **coastal** ['-əl] shipping (or: waters)
seaside ['siːsaɪd]	Meeresküste	go to the ~ / spend one's holidays at the ~
off [ɒf]	vor (der Küste von)	lie at anchor 5 miles ~ Harwich
shore [ʃɔː*]	Strand	go (or: be) on ~ / on the ~ of a lake / walk along the ~ / the **seashore** ['siː-]
ashore [ə'ʃɔː*]	an Land, auf Land	go (or: stay) ~ / The ship ran ~. / The ship was driven ~.
beach [biːtʃ]	Strand	play on the ~ / a sandy ~ / a pebbly (mit Kieseln bedeckt) ~
cliff [klɪf]	Klippe	a steep ~ / climb the ~s / the White C~s of Dover
cape [keɪp]	Kap	
promontory ['prɒməntrɪ]	Vorgebirge	

172 Sky, weather, climate – Himmel, Wetter, Klima

(→ 179 Temperature)

weather ['weðə*]	Wetter	have good (or: bad) ~ / What's the ~ like? / The ~ is fine. (Look at 'rain', 'wind', 'snow', etc. below for more words describing the weather.)
weather report ['weðə rɪˌpɔːt]	Wetterbericht	
weather map ['weðə mæp]	Wetterkarte	
weatherman ['weðəmæn]	Meteorologe (im Fernsehen oder Radio)	

forecast ['fɔːkɑːst]	Vorhersage,	make a weather ~ / hear the weather ~ on the radio
	vorhersagen	~ rain (or: sunny conditions)
spell [spel]	Periode	have a long ~ of good weather / have a cold ~ in January
climate ['klaɪmɪt]	Klima	a country has a mild (or: pleasant / rough) ~ / The ~ here is mild.

Rain, fog – Regen, Nebel

overcast ['əʊvəkɑːst]	bewölkt, bedeckt	an ~ sky
cloud [klaʊd]	Wolke	There are heavy (or: thick / grey / black / white) ~s in the sky. / a **cloudy** ['-ɪ] (or: **cloudless** ['-lɪs]) sky
dull [dʌl]	trüb	a ~ day (or: sky) / ~ weather
rain [reɪn]	Regen,	~ falls (or: sets in / comes down) / be caught in the ~
	regnen	It's going to ~. / It starts (or: stops) ~ing. / ~ hard (or: heavily) / **rain-drops** ['-drɒps]
rainy ['reɪnɪ]	regnerisch	a ~ day / ~ weather
patter ['pætə*]	trommeln	hear the rain ~ on the roof
pour [pɔː*]	gießen	It's ~ing (+ with rain). / Rain is ~ing down. / stand in the ~ing rain
puddle ['pʌdl]	Pfütze	step (or: fall) into a ~
mud [mʌd]	Schlamm	get stuck in the ~ / a **muddy** ['-ɪ] road
soaked [səʊkt]	durchnäßt	get ~ (+ through) / be ~ to the skin
wet [wet]	naß	get ~ (+ with rain) / be ~ (+ through) / a ~ day / ~ weather
umbrella [ʌm'brelə]	Regenschirm	open (or: shut) an ~
fog [fɒg]	Nebel	~ rises (or: comes down) / have (or: get) much ~ / thick ~ / It's **foggy** ['-ɪ]. / a **foggy** day / **foggy** weather
visibility [ˌvɪzɪ'bɪlətɪ]	Sichtweite	drive slowly in poor (or: low) ~ / fog with a ~ under (or: of less than) 50 metres
mist [mɪst]	Dunst, Nebel	~ falls (or: rises / clears) / thick (or: fine) ~ / be hidden (or: covered) by ~ / a **misty** ['-ɪ] day / **misty** weather
haze [heɪz]	leichter Nebel, Dunst	The sun breaks (or: shines) through the morning ~. / a **hazy** ['-ɪ] day

Wind – Wind

breeze [bri:z]	Lüftchen, Brise	a light (or: slight) ~ / **breezy** ['-ɪ] weather / a **breezy** day
wind [wɪnd]	Wind	there is no (or: little / quite a) ~ / the ~ rises (or: drops) / a strong (or: light) ~ / a northerly ~ / a **windy** ['-ɪ] (or: **windless** ['-lɪs]) day
blow (blew, blown) [bləʊ, blu:, bləʊn]	blasen, wehen	The wind is ~ing hard. / It's ~ing hard. / ~ sth off / sth ~s (or: is blown) off
storm [stɔ:m]	Sturm	a ~ rises (or: blows / rages) / a heavy (or: wild / violent) ~ / a **stormy** ['-ɪ] day / **stormy** weather
gale [geɪl]	steife Brise, Sturm	It's blowing a ~. / a stiff (or: violent / terrific) ~ / a **gale warning** ['-ˌwɔ:nɪŋ]
calm [kɑ:m]	ruhig, windstill	a ~ day
hurricane ['hʌrɪkən]	Orkan	a ~ blows up

Cold weather – kaltes Wetter

cool [ku:l]	kühl,	The weather is rather ~ today. / It's ~. / a ~ evening
	Kühle	the ~ of the evening
cold [kəʊld]	kalt,	a ~ day (or: night) / ~ weather / a ~ wind
	Kälte	a biting ~ / tremble with ~
chilly ['tʃɪlɪ]	frostig, kühl	~ weather
freeze (froze, frozen) [fri:z, frəʊz, 'frəʊzn]	gefrieren	It's **freezing** ['fri:zɪŋ]. / **freezing point** ['-ɪŋ pɔɪnt] / The lake **froze over**.
frozen ['frəʊzn]	gefroren	a ~ road (or: lake) / be ~ in
frost [frɒst]	Frost(-periode)	a hard (or: sharp) ~ / have ten degrees of ~ / We've had several ~s this winter.
ice [aɪs]	Eis	slide (or: slip) on ~ / slippery with ~ / be covered with thick (or: thin) ~ / an **icy** ['-ɪ] road / **icy** cold / The roads **iced** [-t] **over**.
sleet [sli:t]	Graupel	~ turning to rain
hail [heɪl]	Hagel	a ~ storm
snow [snəʊ]	Schnee,	fresh (or: deep / thick / crisp) ~ / ~ falls (or: lies) / deep in ~ / a **snow-covered** ['-ˌkʌvəd] (= **snowy** ['-ɪ]) roof / **snowy** weather
	schneien	It's ~ing (+ heavily).

flake [fleɪk] = **snowflake** ['snəʊ-]	Schneeflocke	thick ~s
snowball ['snəʊbɔːl]	Schneeball	throw ~s
snowman ['snəʊmæn]	Schneemann	build a ~
melt [melt]	schmelzen	ice (or: snow) ~s / The sun ~s the snow.
thaw [θɔː]	Tauwetter, tauen	A ~ sets in. / wait for the ~ It's ~ing. / ice ~s

Warm weather – warmes Wetter

sun [sʌn]	Sonne	the ~ shines (or: beats down) / sit (or: lie) in the (+ hot / burning) ~
sunshine ['sʌnʃaɪn]	Sonnenschein	have much (or: little) ~ / come out into the ~
sunny ['sʌnɪ]	sonnig	a ~ day / ~ weather (or: spells)
shine (shone, shone) [ʃaɪn, ʃɒn, –]	scheinen	The sun is **shining** ['-ɪŋ]. / ~ brightly (or: clearly)
heat [hiːt]	Hitze	the ~ of the sun / suffer from the ~ / What a dreadful ~! / a **heat wave** ['–weɪv]
hot [hɒt]	heiß	It's ~. / a ~ day / ~ weather / a ~ spell (Hitzeperiode)
sultry ['sʌltrɪ]	schwül	~ weather / It's ~.
oppressive [ə'presɪv]	drückend	~ weather / It's ~.
thunder ['θʌndə*]	Donner	hear a loud crash (or: a long roll / a rumble, a peal) of ~ / ~ and lightning
lightning ['laɪtnɪŋ]	Blitz	be struck (or: killed) by ~ / thunder and ~
thunderstorm ['θʌndəstɔːm]	Gewitter	

Fine weather, bad weather – schönes Wetter, schlechtes Wetter

fine [faɪn]	schön, sonnig	~ weather / a ~ day / It's ~. / F~ day today, isn't it?
bright [braɪt]	hell, strahlend	a ~ day / ~ weather / ~ sunshine
settled ['setld]	beständig	a period of ~ weather
changeable ['tʃeɪndʒəbl]	veränderlich	The weather is ~.
nasty ['nɑːstɪ]	unangenehm	~ weather / a ~ day
chilly ['tʃɪlɪ]	unangenehm kalt	a ~ day / ~ winds

Environmental problems – Umweltprobleme

pollution [pə'lu:ʃən]	Verschmutzung	air ~ / ~ of the atmosphere
pollute [pə'lu:t]	verschmutzen	~ the atmosphere / become ~d with nitrates
waste [weɪst]	Abfall(-)	poisonous (or: radioactive) ~ / a river thick with industrial ~ / **waste paper** [ˌ– 'peɪpə*]
refuse ['refju:s]	Müll, Abfall	collect ~ / **domestic refuse** [də'mestɪk –] (Hausmüll)
refuse dump ['refju:s dʌmp]	Müllkippe	
garbage ['gɑ:bɪdʒ]	(Küchen-)Abfall	throw sth into the **garbage can** ['– ˌ–]
rubbish ['rʌbɪʃ]	Abfall, Müll, Schutt	a local **rubbish dump** ['– dʌmp]
trash (*AE*) [træʃ]	Abfall, Müll	a yard filled with ~
rubble ['rʌbl]	Schutt	a building reduced to ~
scrap (+ metal) ['skræp (ˌmetl)]	Schrott	sell sth for ~
sewage ['sju:ɪdʒ]	Abwasser	urban ~ / **sewage works** [– ˌwɜ:ks] (Kläranlage)
sewer ['sju:ə*]	Abwasserleitung	
sewerage ['sju:ərɪdʒ]	Kanalisation	
emission [ɪ'mɪʃn]	Emission	~ of gas (or: radiation) / reduce CO_2 ~
acid rain ['æsɪd reɪn]	saurer Regen	
deforestation [di:ˌfɒrɪ'steɪʃən]	Abholzung	the ~ of the Amazon Basin
extinction [ɪk'stɪŋkʃən]	Aussterben	be in danger of ~ / be threatened with ~
overpopulation [ˌəʊvəˌpɒpjʊ'leɪʃən]	Überbevölkerung	

Preservation of the environment – Umweltschutz

preserve [prɪ'zɜ:v]	bewahren	~ the environment
protect [prə'tekt]	schützen	~ the environment
conservation [ˌkɒnsə'veɪʃn]	(Umwelt-)Schutz	the ~ of forests
ecology [i:'kɒlədʒɪ]	Ökologie	
environmentalist [ɪnˌvaɪrən'mentəlɪst]	Umweltschützer, Grüner	
reclaim [rɪ'kleɪm]	wiederverwerten	~ raw materials
recycle [ri:'saɪkl]	zurückgewinnen	~ waste paper / ~d paper
reprocess [rɪ'prəʊses]	wiederaufbereiten	~ raw materials

reprocessing plant [rɪ'prəʊsesɪŋ plɑ:nt]	Wiederaufbereitungsanlage	
refuse-sorting plant ['refju:sˌsɔ:tɪŋ plɑ:nt]	Müllsortieranlage	
lead-free ['led'fri:]	bleifrei	~ petrol / a ~ petrol station

Universe – das Universum

Space – der Weltraum 173

sky [skaɪ]	Himmel	a blue (or: bright / clear / dark) ~ / an overclouded ~ / see clouds (or: stars) in the ~ / under the open ~
sun [sʌn]	Sonne	The ~ rises in the east and sets in the west.
moon [mu:n]	Mond	The ~ shines in the sky at night. / There is a (or: no) ~. / a **moonlit** ['-lɪt] (or: **moonless** ['-lɪs]) night / **moonlight** ['-laɪt] shines
lunar ['lu:nə*]	Mond	the ~ surface
wax [wæks]	zunehmen	the ~ing moon
wane [weɪn]	abnehmen	the moon waxes and ~s
full moon [ˌfʊl 'mu:n]	Vollmond	It is ~ ~.
half moon [ˌhɑ:f 'mu:n]	Halbmond	
new moon [ˌnju: 'mu:n]	Neumond	
planet ['plænɪt]	Planet	a distant ~ / observe the ~s / the **planetary system** ['-ərɪ ˌsɪstəm]
orbit ['ɔ:bɪt]	Umlaufbahn	calculate the ~
star [stɑ:*]	Stern	a **fixed star** [ˌfɪkst '–] / a **shooting star** [ˌʃu:tɪŋ '–] / see many ~s in the sky / the **Polar Star** [ˌpəʊlə '–]
zodiac ['zəʊdɪæk]	Sternkreis	the signs of the ~
constellation [ˌkɒnstə'leɪʃn]	Sternbild	recognize ~s
meteor ['mi:tjə]	Meteor	see a ~ flash across the sky
comet ['kɒmɪt]	Komet	

galaxy ['gæleksɪ]	Galaxie	The universe is made up of many ~ies.
Milky Way [ˌmɪlkɪ 'weɪ]	Milchstraße	fly through the ~ ~
space [speɪs]	Weltraum, Raum	outer ~ / travel through ~ / the ~ age / ~ research
universe ['ju:nɪvɜ:s]	Universum, Weltall	the vastness (or: immensity) of the ~
world [wɜ:ld]	Erde, Welt; Universum, Welt	all over the ~ "He's got the whole ~ in his hands."
astronomy [ə'strɒnəmɪ]	Astronomie	A~ is not a new science.
telescope ['telɪskəʊp]	Fernrohr	look through a ~
observatory [əb'zɜ:vətrɪ]	Sternwarte	watch the stars from an ~

174 Space flight – Raumflug

probe [prəʊb]	Raumsonde	send a ~ into outer space
satellite ['sætəlaɪt]	(künstlicher) Satellit	launch a ~ / hear the bleeps (Piepen) of a ~
rocket ['rɒkɪt]	Rakete	launch a ~
stage [steɪdʒ]	Stufe	a three-~ rocket / the first ~
engine ['endʒɪn]	Antrieb, Motor	start (or: fire) an ~ / an ~ shuts off
thrust [θrʌst]	Schub	provide a maximum ~ of 230,000 pounds
spacecraft ['speɪskrɑ:ft]	Raumschiff	go to the moon in a ~
astronaut ['æstrənɔ:t]	Astronaut	The ~s were in space for 10 days.
cosmonaut ['kɒzmənɔ:t]	Kosmonaut	
spacesuit ['speɪssu:t]	Raumanzug	put on a ~
countdown ['kaʊntdaʊn]	Countdown	stop the ~
launch [lɔ:ntʃ]	starten	~ a rocket (or: satellite)
ignite [ɪg'naɪt]	zünden	~ the first stage / The first stage ~s.
gravitational pull [ˌgrævɪ'teɪʃnəl 'pʊl]	Erdanziehung	overcome the ~ ~
orbit ['ɔ:bɪt]	Umlaufbahn	be in ~ / enter into an ~ / leave an ~
coast [kəʊst]	(ohne Antrieb durch den Raum) gleiten	~ through space
course correction ['kɔ:s kəˌrekʃn]	Kurskorrektur	carry out a ~ ~

dock [dɒk]	ankoppeln	begin (or: complete) a **docking manoeuvre** [ˌ– mə'nuːvə] (*BE*) (= maneuver, *AE*)
land [lænd]	landen	~ on the moon
re-entry [riː'entrɪ]	Wiedereintritt (in die Erdatmosphäre)	~ into the Earth's atmosphere
splashdown ['splæʃdaʊn]	Niedergehen (im Ozean)	a ~ in the Atlantic
land [lænd]	landen	~ back on earth
space lab ['speɪs læb]	Raumlabor	sent up a ~ ~
space shuttle ['speɪs ˌʃʌtl]	Raumfähre	launch a ~ ~

Matter – Materie

Matter – Materie 175

atom ['ætəm]	Atom	the structure of the ~ / **atomic energy** [əˌtɒmɪk 'enədʒɪ] (or: bomb)
nucleus ['njuːklɪəs] (*pl.* nuclei ['njuːklɪaɪ])	Kern	the ~ of a hydrogen atom
nuclear ['njuːklɪə*]	Kern-	~ energy / ~ fission (Kernspaltung)
radiation [ˌreɪdɪ'eɪʃn]	Strahlung	emit (aussenden) ~ / radioactive ~
element ['elɪmənt]	Element	be an ~
chemical sign ['kemɪkl saɪn]	chemisches Zeichen	O is a ~ ~

carbon (C)	['kɑːbən]	Kohlenstoff
hydrogen (H)	['haɪdrədʒən]	Wasserstoff
oxygen (O)	['ɒksɪdʒən]	Sauerstoff
nitrogen (N)	['naɪtrədʒən]	Stickstoff
sulphur (S)	['sʌlfə*]	Schwefel
copper (Cu)	['kɒpə*]	Kupfer
iron (Fe)	['aɪən]	Eisen
zinc (Zn)	[zɪŋk]	Zink
lead (Pb)	[led]	Blei
tin (Sn)	[tɪn]	Zinn
uranium (U)	[jʊ'reɪnjəm]	Uran
silver (Ag)	['sɪlvə*]	Silber
gold (Au)	[gəʊld]	Gold

join [dʒɔɪn]	eine Verbindung eingehen	Atoms have the power to ~ with other atoms.
compound ['kɒmpaʊnd]	Verbindung	
composed of [kəm'pəʊzd əv]	zusammengesetzt aus	
react [rɪ'ækt]	reagieren	When acids ~ with bases salts are formed.
molecule ['mɒlɪkju:l]	Molekül	Elements combine to form ~s.
matter ['mætə*]	Materie	mind and ~ / the ~ of the universe
base [beɪs]	Base, Lauge	
acid ['æsɪd]	Säure	
salt [sɔ:lt]	Salz	
metal ['metl]	Metall	
rust [rʌst]	Rost,	(+ be) covered with ~
	rosten (lassen)	~ away / Rain will ~ the iron roof. / sth is very **rusty** ['-ɪ]
ore [ɔ:*]	Erz	obtain metals from ~ / ~ deposits (Lagerstätten)
made of ['meɪd əv]	aus	~ ~ iron
brass [brɑ:s]	Messing	a vase made of ~
bronze [brɒnz]	Bronze	a statue (or: bell) made of ~
substance ['sʌbstəns]	Substanz, Stoff	a hard (or: soft) ~
material [me'tɪərɪəl]	Material, Stoff	a good (or: solid / worthless) ~

176 Weight, mass – Gewicht, Masse

Metric weights – metrische Gewichte

gram = gramme = g	[græm], [–]	Gramm, g
kilogram = kilogramme = kg	['kɪləʊgræm], [–]	Kilogramm, Kilo, kg
tonne = (+ metric) ton	[('metrɪk) tʌn]	Tonne

Avoirdupois [ˌævədəˈpɔɪz] (the system of weight used formerly in Britain; still in use in the United States) – *früheres angelsächsisches Gewichtssystem*

ounce [aʊns] = **oz**	28,3g	**16 ounces** ['-ɪz] = **ozs**	= 1 pound
pound [paʊnd] = **lb**	ca. 450 g	**14 pounds** [-z] = **lbs**	= 1 stone
stone [stəʊn]	ca. 6,35 kg	**2 stone**	= 1 quarter
quarter ['kwɔːtə*]	ca. 12,7 kg	**4 quarters** [-z]	= 1 hundredweight
hundredweight ['hʌndrədweɪt] **= cwt**	ca. 50,8 kg	**20 hundredweight = cwt**	= 1 ton
ton [tʌn]	ca. 1016 kg		

weigh [weɪ]	wiegen	~ five kilos / ~ sth (or: sb / oneself) / ~ sth in one's hand
weight [weɪt]	Gewicht	have much (or: little) ~ / sb's ~ is 83 kilos
scales ['skeɪlz]	Waage	stand on the ~
heavy ['hevɪ]	schwer	a ~ weight / too ~
light [laɪt]	leicht	a ~ weight / too ~
load [ləʊd]	Last,	carry a ~ / a heavy ~
	laden	~ sth into (or: onto) sth
burden ['bɜːdn] (*form.*)	Last, Bürde	put on (or: off) a ~ / a heavy (or: light) ~
pressure ['preʃə*]	Druck	the ~ of air (or: water) / a ~ of 4 lbs to the square inch
bear [beə*]	tragen, aushalten	sth ~s one's weight
support [sə'pɔːt]	(ab-, unter-) stützen;	be ~ed by two vertical pillars
	Stütze	a building with steel ~s

State – Zustand 177

solid ['sɒlɪd]	fest, massiv,	become ~ / a ~ piece of sth / sth is (+ of) ~ silver / a ~ building / ~ furniture / on ~ ground
	fester Stoff	~s and liquids
hard [hɑːd]	hart	as ~ as rock / on ~ ground / a ~ kind of wood / **harden** ['-n] steel
strong [strɒŋ]	stark	a very ~ material / a ~ rope (or: stick)
firm [fɜːm]	fest, stark, hart	sth stands ~ / a ~ support / put sth into the refrigerator to make it ~
grind (ground, ground) [graɪnd, graʊnd, –]	mahlen	~ sth to pieces / ~ corn into flour / ~ coffee

powder ['paʊdə*]	Pulver	**soap powder** ['səʊp ˌ–] / **baking powder** ['beɪkɪŋ ˌ–]
dust [dʌst]	Staub	~ blowing in the streets / a thick layer of ~ / a **dusty** ['-ɪ] road
weak [wi:k]	schwach	a very ~ material
delicate ['delɪkət]	zart, zerbrechlich	~ china (Porzellan)
crumb [krʌm]	Krume	bread ~s
crumble ['krʌmbl]	(zer-)krümeln, (zer-) bröckeln	~ bread / a **crumbling** [-ɪŋ] wall
crack [kræk]	zersplittern, springen,	~ sth / sth ~s
	Sprung, Riß	~s in the ice / a ~ in a cup
break (broke, broken)	(zer-)brechen	~ a window / ~ off a piece of sth / sth ~s easily
[breɪk, brəʊk, 'brəʊkən]	Bruch	repair a ~ / sth is **breakable** ['breɪkəbl]
bend (bent, bent) [bend, bent, –]	biegen, sich biegen lassen	~ a wire / ~ the end of a wire (+ up / down / back) / sth ~s easily
melt [melt]	schmelzen	The snow is ~ing. / ~ two metals together / ~ sth down (einschmelzen) / a **melting pot** ['-ɪŋ pɒt] (Schmelztiegel) / **melted** ['-ɪd] chocolate (or: ice-cream)
molten ['məʊltən]	geschmolzen, flüssig	~ metal (or: rock)
liquid ['lɪkwɪd]	flüssig,	~ food (or: air)
	Flüssigkeit	Don't add too much ~ to the mixture. / solids and ~s
drop [drɒp]	Tropfen	a ~ of water (or: blood) / fall in ~s / a **raindrop** ['reɪn-]
flow [fləʊ]	fließen,	~ through (or: into / out of) ... / ~ easily (or: smoothly)
	(Durch-)Fluß	a ~ of water
pour [pɔ:*]	gießen, schütten;	~ sth into a bottle / ~ out a cup of tea / ~ sth out of sth
	strömen	water (or: rain) ~s down / tears ~ down
spill (spilt, spilt) [spɪl, spɪlt, –]	verschütten	~ milk (or: sugar)
boil [bɔɪl]	sieden	Water ~s at 100° C. / **boiling point** ['-ɪŋ pɔɪnt]
bubble ['bʌbl]	sprudeln	The water is **bubbling** [-ɪŋ]. / blow **soap bubbles** ['səʊp ˌ-z] (Seifenblasen)
steam [sti:m]	(Wasser-)Dampf,	clouds of ~ / a jet (Strahl) of ~ rises / produce (or: get up / let off) ~
	dampfen	The ground is ~ing after the rain.

gas [gæs] (*pl.* gases, *BE;* gases, gasses, *AE*)	Gas	There are several kinds of ~(s)es in the air. / put the kettle on the ~ / be in the **gaseous** ['gæsjəs] state
air [eə*]	Luft	have some fresh ~ / get some fresh ~
fire ['faɪə*]	Feuer	a bright (or: hot / glowing / warming / crackling) ~ / a burnt-out (= dead) ~ / catch ~ / make (or: light) a ~ / be on ~ / put a ~ out / a ~ burns (or: glows / goes out)
blaze [bleɪz]	Lichtschein (eines Feuers);	see the ~ of a fire
	loderndes Feuer	burst into a ~ / a **blazing** ['-ɪŋ] fire
burn (burnt, burnt) [bɜːn, bɜːnt, –]	(ver-)brennen,	~ wood (or: coal / gas) / ~ sth in the fire / ~ oneself (or: one's mouth)
	anbrennen (lassen)	~ the meat / **burnt** toast
flame [fleɪm]	Flamme,	bright (or: raging / roaring) ~s / light (or: blow out / put out) a ~ / burst into ~s / be in ~s
	(auf-)flammen	sth ~s up / a **flaming** ['-ɪŋ] fire
smoke [sməʊk]	Rauch	~ pouring from a chimney / the **smokeless** ['-lɪs] atmosphere of the countryside / the **smoky** ['-ɪ] atmosphere of an industrial town
fume [fjuːm]	Qualm, Gestank	smell ~s from a pipe / air thick with ~s of sth
ash [æʃ]	Asche	burn to ~es / remove the ~ (= ~es) from the stove / drop cigarette ~es on the carpet

Texture, surface – Struktur, Oberfläche (→ 18 Touch) 178

coarse [kɔːs]	rauh, grob	~ sand
harsh [hɑːʃ]	rauh	a ~ stone / sth feels ~ to the touch
rough [rʌf]	rauh	~ sand-paper (or: cloth / silk)
polish ['pɒlɪʃ]	polieren	~ shoes (or: furniture) / ~ sth up
smooth [smuːθ]	glatt, weich	~ paper (or: metal) / ~ to the touch / on ~ ground
even ['iːvn]	glatt, eben	an ~ surface / sth is perfectly ~ / an ~ texture
blunt [blʌnt]	stumpf	a ~ knife
sharp [ʃɑːp]	scharf, spitz	a ~ knife (or: axe / pencil) / **sharpen** ['-ən] a knife (or: pencil)
pointed ['pɔɪntɪd]	spitz	a ~ needle

fine [faın]	fein, zart;	~ linen (or: silk) / **finely wrought** ['-lı rɔːt] (gewirkt)
	scharf, spitz	a pencil with a ~ point
scratch [skrætʃ]	Kratzer, Schramme	a ~ on the table

179 Temperature – Temperatur

(→ 172 Sky, weather, climate)

thermometer [θə'mɒmıtə*]	Thermometer	The ~ shows a temperature of 21° C.
temperature ['temprətʃə*]	Temperatur	measure the ~ / the ~ rises (or: falls) / high (or: low) ~s / at a ~ of 21° C
degree [dı'griː]	Grad	at 21 ~s / have ten ~s of frost
Fahrenheit ['færənhaıt] = **F**	Fahrenheit	Water freezes at 32° F (read: thirty-two degrees Fahrenheit)
Centigrade ['sentıgreıd] = **Celsius** ['selsjəs] = **C**	Celsius	at 10° C (read: at ten degrees Centigrade)

Existence – Existenz

180 Exist – sein

exist [ıg'zıst]	sein, existieren	Does life ~ on Mars? / believe in the **existence** [-əns] of ... / come into **existence** / This is the only **existent** [-ənt] (= **extant** [ek'stænt] [noch vorhanden] / **existing** [-ıŋ]) copy of his last poem.
existing [ıg'zıstıŋ]	gegenwärtig, bestehend	under ~ conditions
current ['kʌrənt]	aktuell	sth is ~ in music and art
there [ðeə*] + **be**	geben, da sein	Undoubtedly, **there is** ['ðeər‿ız] a God. / **There have** always **been** wars. / **Is there** anyone coming to dinner? / **There are** ['ðeər‿ɑː] (= **There's** ['ðeəz]) two patients in the waiting room. / **There's** plenty of work to do.
depend [dı'pend]	abhängen	~ on / be **dependent** [-ənt] on / **dependance** [-əns]

have (had, had) [hæv, hæd, –] = **have got** [həv 'gɒt] (*BE inform.*)	haben	I ~ (= ~ ~) two buttons missing on my jacket. / We ~ (= ~ ~) a brother in the navy. / He **had** his wife working for him. / The car **had** its roof damaged.
available [ə'veɪləbl]	vorhanden, verfügbar	There were no tickets ~ for Friday's performance.
real ['rɪəl]	wirklich	a story of ~ life / in **reality** [rɪ'æləti]
genuine ['dʒenjʊɪn]	echt	~ pearls / a ~ signature / a ~ picture by Velasques [vɪ'læskwɪz]
fact [fækt]	Tatsache	in (+ actual) ~ / a well-known ~ / the bare (or: naked) ~s / know sth for a ~ / give a **factual** ['-jʊəl] account
essence ['esns]	Wesen, Kern	different in ~ / the ~ of a problem / It is **essential** [ɪ'senʃl] that ...
situation [ˌsɪtju'eɪʃn]	Situation	in the present ~ / be in a difficult ~
state [steɪt]	Zustand	the solid (or: liquid / gaseous) ~ of matter / the ~ of a patient / a ~ of happiness
condition [kən'dɪʃn]	Zustand; Bedingung	in good (or: poor) ~ / in a chaotic ~ on what ~? / accept (or: reject) sb's ~s / on ~ that ... / make it a ~ that ...
case [keɪs]	Fall	an interesting ~ / in such a ~ / in some ~s
circumstance ['sɜːkəmstəns]	Umstand	under (= in) no ~(s)
present ['preznt]	gegenwärtig, anwesend	be ~ at a meeting / in the ~ case / the ~ high prices
happen ['hæpən]	sich ereignen	What ~ed next? / sth ~s to sb / I ~ed to be (Zufällig war ich ...) out when he called. / It ~ed to be (Zufällig war es ...) a fine day.
occur [ə'kɜː*]	sich (unerwartet) ereignen, vorkommen	When did it ~? / It doesn't often ~ that ... / an everyday **occurrence** [ə'kʌrəns]
take (took, taken) **place** [teɪk, tʊk, 'teɪkən; – 'pleɪs]	stattfinden (wie geplant)	The game will ~ ~ this afternoon.
event [ɪ'vent]	Ereignis	current ~s / a(n) everyday (or: historical / tragic / unlikely) ~ / sth is quite an ~ / in the ~ of ... (für den Fall des ...)
incident ['ɪnsɪdent]	Begebenheit; Zwischenfall	a strange ~ frontier ~s

accident ['æksɪdənt]	Unglücksfall;	a serious (or: tragic / bad) ~ / be killed in an ~
	Zufall	meet by ~ / do sth by ~
misfortune [mɪs'fɔːtʃən]	Unglück(sfall)	suffer ~ / bear one's ~s bravely / have the ~ to …
unfortunate [ʌn'fɔːtʃnət]	unglücklich	an ~ expedition / an ~ remark / an ~ man with a broken leg
occasion [ə'keɪʒn]	Gelegenheit	an ~ for sth / on this (or: that) ~ / on one ~ / have met sb on several ~s / pay sb **occasional** [-l] visits
opportunity [ˌɒpə'tjuːnətɪ]	(günstige) Gelegenheit	find (or: get) an ~ / have no (or: little / not much) ~ of doing sth / take the ~ to do sth
chance [tʃɑːns]	Zufall;	leave nothing to ~ / meet sb by ~
	Möglichkeit, Chance	have a ~ to do (= of doing) sth / take a ~ / miss a ~ / There's a ~ that …
fate [feɪt]	Schicksal	the irony of ~ / a sad ~ / leave sb to his ~
fortune ['fɔːtʃuːn]	Schicksal, Zukunft;	tell sb his ~ / a **fortune-teller** [–ˌtelə*] / What will be our ~?
	Glück, Erfolg	F~ smiled on him. / seek one's ~ / have ~ on one's side
good fortune [ˌgʊd 'fɔːtʃuːn]	Glück	have the ~ ~ to find a good job
bad fortune [ˌbæd 'fɔːtʃuːn]	Pech	have the ~ ~ to break a leg
fortunate ['fɔːtʃnət]	glücklich	a ~ man / be ~ (Glück haben) / The weather was fine, **fortunately** [-lɪ]. / **Unfortunately** [ʌn-], it rained all the time we were there.
fortunes ['fɔːtʃuːnz]	Wechselfälle	the ~ of war
luck [lʌk]	(glücklicher) Zufall, Glück	by ~ / have good ~ / wish sb ~ / "Good ~!" / be in (or: out of) ~ / a **lucky** ['-ɪ] man / It's my **lucky** day. / **be lucky** (Glück haben) / a **luckless** ['-lɪs] day
bad luck [ˌbæd 'lʌk]	Pech	"B~ ~!" / have ~ ~ in one's affairs
seem [siːm]	scheinen	Things are not always what they ~. / ~ (+ to be) good (or: possible) / It ~s (+ to sb) that … / ~ to do sth
appear [ə'pɪə*]	(er-)scheinen	Things are not always as they ~. / ~ (+ to be) good (or: possible) / It ~s (+ to sb) that …
apparent [ə'pærənt]	offensichtlich	It was ~ to all of us … / sb's ~ indifference

appearance [ə'pɪərens]	Erscheinen, (An-)Schein	make an ~ / put in an ~ have the ~ of / have a slightly foreign ~ / to (= by / from) all ~
possible ['pɒsəbl]	möglich	as early as ~ / ~ for sb to do sth / believe in the **possibility** [ˌpɒsə'bɪlətɪ] of ... / sth is **impossible** [ɪm'pɒsəbl]
differ ['dɪfə*]	verschieden sein, sich unterscheiden	~ widely in sth / ~ from ... in ...
difference ['dɪfrəns]	Unterschied	the ~ between ... and ... / a great ~ / make a ~
resemble [rɪ'zembl]	ähneln	~ sb / ~ each other in shape (or: colour) / There's little **resemblance** [-əns] between ... and ...
refer [rɪ'fɜː*]	(sich) beziehen	~ to sb / ~ to a matter / Does this remark ~ to me?
probable ['prɒbəbl]	wahrscheinlich	sth seems ~ / a ~ result / **probably** [-ɪ] do sth
improbable [ɪm'prɒbəbl]	unwahrscheinlich	an ~ story (or: result)
inevitable [ɪn'evɪtəbl]	unvermeidlich	Death is ~. / an ~ argument
certain ['sɜːtn]	sicher;	It is ~ that ... / He is ~ to come. / be ~ of success
	gewiß (im Sinne von unbestimmt)	only on ~ days / a ~ George Miller
sure [ʃʊə*]	(ziemlich) sicher, zweifellos	I think so, but I'm not ~. / He's ~ to come. / Sure! [ʃɔː]
likely ['laɪklɪ]	wahrscheinlich, voraussichtlich	It is ~ he'll come. / He's ~ to come.
may [meɪ] = **could** [kʊd] = **might** [maɪt]	können (im Sinne von vielleicht)	The road ~ be blocked. (= perhaps it is blocked) / This ~ not be true.
can [kæn]	können (im Sinne von möglich)	The road ~ be blocked. (= it is possible to block it) / This **can't** [kɑːnt] (= **cannot** ['kænɒt]) be true. (= it is not possible that it is true)
perhaps [pə'hæps]	vielleicht	P~ it will rain. / ~ not / P~ I'll go to England next year.
maybe ['meɪbiː]	kann sein	'Will they come?' – 'M~ not.'
necessary ['nesəsərɪ]	nötig, notwendig	Food is ~ to life. / Hard work is ~ for success.
necessity [nɪ'sesətɪ]	Notwendigkeit	be driven by ~ / in case of ~ / the ~ties of life (= food, clothing and shelter)

important [ɪm'pɔːtnt]	wichtig	an ~ decision (or: person)
importance [ɪm'pɔːtns]	Wichtigkeit	sth is of great (or: little / not much / no) ~ to one / speak with an air of ~ (wichtigtuerisch)
must [mʌst]	müssen	I ~ see him. / He ~ be in London now.
have (had, had) (+ **got**) **to** [hæv, hæd, –; – ('gɒt) tə]	müssen	I **have** (+ **got**) **to** do this. / I **don't have** to (= **haven't got to**) do this.
need not ['niːd nɒt]	nicht brauchen	You ~ ~ help me.
ought to ['ɔːtə]	müssen (weil eine moralische Verpflichtung besteht),	She ~ ~ look after her children better. / We ~ ~ have done it.
	sollen (wenn man es annehmen kann)	They ~ ~ be here by now.

181 Cause – Ursache

cause [kɔːz]	Ursache, Anlaß, Grund,	the ~ of an accident / What was the ~ of it? / have (+ no) ~ for complaint / give (+ no) ~ for complaint
	verursachen, veranlassen	~ (+ sb) trouble / ~ damage (+ to sb / sth) / What ~d him to change his mind?
reason ['riːzn]	(logischer oder bekannter) Grund	For what ~? / have a ~ for doing sth / give the ~s for (or: against) (+ doing) sth
root [ruːt]	Wurzel, Ursprung	the ~ of a problem / "The love of money is the ~ of all evil." (1 Tim 6:10)
source [sɔːs]	Quelle, Ausgang, Ursprung	a fundamental ~
origin ['ɒrɪdʒɪn]	Ursprung, Herkunft	the ~ of a custom (or: rumour / quarrel)
because [bɪ'kɒz]	weil	~ the train was late …
because of [– əv] = **due to** ['djuː tə]	wegen	The train was late ~ ~ the fog.
out of ['aʊt‿əv]	aus … heraus	do sth ~ ~ pity (or: kindness / fear)
since [sɪns]	da, weil (bekanntlich oder offensichtlich)	S~ you can't answer the question, perhaps we'd better ask someone else.
as [æz], [əz]	da, weil	We left the party at eight o'clock, ~ it was raining.
for [fɔː*]	wegen, aus	~ many reasons / ~ fear of

by [baɪ]	von	written ~ Shakespeare
why [waɪ]	warum, weshalb	the reason ~ / Tell me ~ you were late this morning.
on account of [ɒn ə'kaʊnt‿əv]	wegen	The train was late ~ ~ ~ the fog.
need [ni:d]	Anlaß, Grund	There's no ~ to be angry.
lead (led, led) **to** [li:d, led, –; '– tə]	führen zu	~ ~ results
bring (brought, brought) **about** [brɪŋ, brɔ:t, –; ˌ– ə'baʊt]	zustande bringen, herbeiführen	~ ~ changes
excite [ɪk'saɪt]	erregen;	~ interest (or: attention / pity / envy / contempt / jealousy)
	aufreizen, anstacheln	~ sb to do sth
provoke [prə'vəʊk]	provozieren, heraufbeschwören	~ a fight / ~ sb to do sth / make a **provocative** [prə'vɒkətɪv] speach
inspire [ɪn'spaɪə*]	begeistern, anfeuern, erfüllen	~ sb to do sth / ~ sb with hope (or: courage / confidence)
encourage [ɪn'kʌrɪdʒ]	ermutigen	~ sb to do sth
urge [ɜ:dʒ]	nötigen	~ sb to do sth
force [fɔ:s]	zwingen	~ sb to do sth
influence ['ɪnflʊəns]	beeinflussen, Einfluß	~ sb's decision / ~ sb to do sth under the ~ of sb (or: sth) / ~ over (or: on) sb

Effect – Wirkung 182

effect [ɪ'fekt]	Wirkung	cause and ~ / have a deep (or: harmful) ~ on sb / Do you think this medicine will have any ~? / have no ~ / an **effective** [-ɪv] medicine / make an **effective** speech
after-effect ['ɑ:ftər‿ɪˌfekt]	(unangenehme, schlimme) Nachwirkung	the ~s of an atomic-bomb explosion
result [rɪ'zʌlt]	Folge, Ergebnis,	sth is the (or: a) ~ of ... / The ~ was that ... / without any ~ / with the ~ that ... / as a ~
	zur Folge haben	sth ~s from ... / sth ~s in ...
consequence ['kɒnsɪkwəns]	Konsequenz, Folge	sth is the ~ of ... / face (or: take) the ~s / inevitable (or: serious / far-reaching) ~s

react [rɪ'ækt]	reagieren	I touched his arm but he did not ~. / ~ to sth / ~ by doing sth / show no **reaction** [rɪ'ækʃn]
outcome ['aʊtkʌm]	Ergebnis	the ~ of the presidential election
affect [ə'fekt]	wirken auf	Smoking ~s the heart and lungs. / The Gulf Stream ~s our climate.
owing to ['əʊɪŋ tə]	infolge von, wegen, dank	We were late, ~ ~ the snow.
due to ['dju: tə]	zurückzuführen auf, infolge von	The accident was ~ ~ careless driving.
arise (arose, arisen) **from** [ə'raɪz, a'rəʊz, ə'rizn; – frɒm]	entstehen aus, entspringen aus	The problems ~ ~ …
grow (grew, grown) **from** [grəʊ, gru:, grəʊn; '– frɒm]	erwachsen aus, kommen von	The problems ~ ~ …
derive from [dɪ'raɪv frɒm]	ableiten von, seinen Ursprung haben in	a word ~s ~ Latin / The English word 'street' is ~d ~ the Old English word 'straet' which comes from Latin 'strata'.
come (came, come) **of** [kʌm, keɪm, kʌm; '– əv]	herauskommen, kommen von	I don't know if any good will ~ ~ your actions.

183 Begin, end – beginnen, enden

begin (began, begun) [bɪ'gɪn, bɪ'gæn, bɪ'gʌn]	beginnen	~ doing (= to do) sth / It ~s at three. / ~ the work (or: day / letter) / from **beginning** [-ɪŋ] to end / at the **beginning** / be a **beginner** [-ə*]
start [stɑ:t]	(etwas) anfangen (= beginnen), Anfang;	~ doing (= to do) sth / ~ work (or: dinner) / make a fresh ~
	(eine Reise) beginnen, aufbrechen;	~ for London
	(sich) in Gang setzen (lassen)	~ a car (or: fire) / The car won't ~.
set (set, set) **off** [set, –, –; –'ɒf] = **set out** [– 'aʊt]	aufbrechen	~ ~ on a trip across Europe
arise (arose, arisen) [ə'raɪz, ə'rəʊz, ə'rɪzn]	entstehen, sich ergeben	A new question (or: difficulty) has arisen. / If the need should ~.
emerge [ɪ'mɜ:dʒ]	auftauchen	No new ideas ~d.
birth [bɜ:θ]	Geburt	the ~ of a political party / the ~ of a nation

take (took, taken) **shape** [teɪk, tʊk, 'teɪkn; ˌ– 'ʃeɪp]	Gestalt annehmen	ideas ~ing ~ in one's mind
establish [ɪ'stæblɪʃ]	einrichten, gründen	~ a business (or: newspaper / shop / school)
found [faʊnd]	gründen	~ a colony (or: hospital / new city) / William Penn was the **founder** ['-ə*] of Pennsylvania.
create [kriː'eɪt]	erschaffen, machen, hervorrufen	God ~d the world. / ~ a theory / ~ trouble (or: difficulties / ~ a bad impression / a sensation)
introduce [ˌɪntrə'djuːs]	einführen	~ new ideas / ~ the idea that ... / a few **introductory** [ˌɪntrə'dʌktərɪ] remarks / Drake ~d potatoes into England. / an **introduction** [ˌɪntrə'dʌkʃn] (+ to sth)
arise (arose, arisen) [ə'raɪz, ə'rəʊz, ə'rɪzn]	entstehen, sich ergeben	difficulties (or: results / effects) ~ / a question (or: rumour) ~s / suspicion ~s
end [end]	enden, beendigen, Ende	How does the story ~? / ~ a speech (or: piece of work / quarrel) / the ~ of the day (or: year / century) / at the ~ of ... / towards the ~ of ... / from beginning to ~ / the ~ of a book / come to an ~
stop [stɒp]	aufhören, anhalten	~ doing sth / ~ a machine (or: clock) / ~ one's car / ~ the traffic / ~ to do sth (anhalten, stehen bleiben, um etwas zu tun) / The rain has ~ped.
finish ['fɪnɪʃ]	beenden	~ a speech (or: a journey) / ~ one's homework / When will you have ~ed? / ~ doing sth
cease [siːs] (*form.*)	aufhören, enden, zu Ende gehen, beenden, (Feuer) einstellen	~ to exist / ~ doing sth / ~ fire (*mil.*)
die out [daɪ 'aʊt]	aussterben	customs (or: families / races) ~ ~
abolish [ə'bɒlɪʃ]	abschaffen	~ slavery (or: customs / privileges) / ~ a law (or: tax) / ~ an office
disappear [ˌdɪsə'pɪə*]	verschwinden, aussterben	difficulties ~ / snow ~s / These beautiful birds are fast ~ing. / ~ gradually
vanish ['vænɪʃ]	(vollständig, oft plötzlich) verschwinden	prospects of success have ~ed / Many types of animals have now ~ed from the earth.
decay [dɪ'keɪ]	verfallen, verfaulen, Verfall	a ~ed tooth fall into ~

decline [dɪ'klaɪn]	abnehmen, Abnahme	sb's power (or: influence / health) ~s on the ~ / go into ~
extinct [ɪk'stɪŋkt]	ausgestorben,	The mammoth has been ~ for a long time.
	untergegangen, erloschen	an ~ language an ~ volcano
fade ['feɪd]	(langsam) verschwinden, verblassen	A custom is ~ing. / Cut flowers soon ~.
go (went, gone) [gəʊ, went, gɒn]	(ver-)gehen	The pain has gone. / All hope has gone.
pass [pɑːs]	vorbeigehen	The week has ~ed very quickly.
last [lɑːst]	letzt, zuletzt	my ~ dollar / be ~ in a race / The ~ house in a street. / When did you see him ~? / the ~ of the Stuarts
at last [ət 'lɑːst]	schließlich, endlich	A~ ~ he has done it. / A~ ~!
eventual [ɪ'ventʃʊəl]	schließlich, endlich	the ~ success of his efforts / He worked so hard that he **eventually** [-ɪ] became ill.
final ['faɪnl]	letzt, endgültig	a ~ remark (or: offer / decision) / ~ examinations / the ~ chapter of a book / **Finally** ['faɪnəlɪ], they decided not to go.

184 Remain, change – bleiben, ändern

remain [rɪ'meɪn]	bleiben	He ~ed a poor man. / ~ poor (or: calm)
same ['seɪm]	der-, die-, dasselbe; der, die, das gleiche	in the ~ way / at the ~ time / the ~ day
stay [steɪ]	bleiben	~ calm (or: clean) / The weather ~ed cold.
last [lɑːst]	andauern	~ long (or: ten days / until October) / His anger won't ~. / **lasting** ['-ɪŋ] peace / a **lasting** impression / **everlasting** [ˌevə'lɑːstɪŋ] love
go (went, gone) **on** [gəʊ, went, gɒn; ˌ– 'ɒn]	fortfahren, andauern	~ ~ doing sth / ~ ~ with sth / The work went ~ day after day.
continue [kən'tɪnjuː]	fortsetzen, fortfahren, bleiben	~ doing sth / ~ to do sth / ~ one's work (or: speech / journey) / ~ calm / The rain ~d all day.
keep (kept, kept) **on** [kiːp, kept, –; ˌ– 'ɒn	fortfahren	~ ~ doing sth

hold (held, held) **on** [həʊld, held, –; ˌ– 'ɒn]	dranbleiben (bes. am Telefon)	"H~ ~ there a minute."
endure [ɪn'djʊə*] (*form.*)	fortdauern	fame (or: books) that will ~ forever
carry on [ˌkærɪ 'ɒn]	(nach einer Unterbrechung, trotz Schwierigkeiten) weitermachen, fortsetzen	~ ~ doing sth / ~ ~ with one's work / ~ ~ a conversation / C~ ~, please!
maintain [meɪn'teɪn]	beibehalten, einhalten	~ friendly relations with ... / ~ law and order / ~ a speed of 60 miles an hour
persist [pə'sɪst]	beharren, (hartnäckig) fortfahren	~ in doing sth / ~ in one's opinions
equal ['i:kwəl]	gleich(-wertig)	~ pay for ~ work / be ~ in sth / divide sth into two ~ parts
alike [ə'laɪk] (*pred.*)	gleich	
change [tʃeɪndʒ]	(sich) ändern, Änderung	~ suddenly (or: gradually) / ~ one thing for another / sth ~s into ... / ~ from ... to ... / a ~ from ... to ... / make a ~ in the programme / for a ~ (zur Abwechslung) / **changeable** ['tʃeɪndʒəbl] (veränderlich) / remain **unchanged** [ˌʌn'tʃeɪndʒd]
grow (grew, grown) [grəʊ, gru:, grəʊn]	wachsen	~ quickly
develop [dɪ'veləp]	(sich) entwickeln	~ from ... / ~ into ... / ~ a business / ~ an idea
increase [ɪn'kri:s]	erhöhen, vergrößern, zunehmen,	~ prices (or: taxes / the production / one's efforts / one's knowledge)
['ɪnkri:s]	Zunahme	sth is on the ~
rise (rose, risen) [raɪz, rəʊz, 'rɪzn]	ansteigen, Anstieg, Aufstieg	Prices **have risen** (+ by 5 pence / to 30 pence). / "The R~ and Fall of the Roman Empire"
fall (fell, fallen) [fɔ:l, fel, 'fɔ:lən]	(ver-)fallen, werden	~ silent (or: asleep / ill) / ~ into disgrace (Schande) (or: bad habits / poverty / trouble / difficulties) / **fall in love** (+ with sb) (sich verlieben) / Prices **have fallen**.
tend [tend]	neigen	Prices are ~ing to climb (or: fall). / ~ to do sth / ~ towards sth / show a **tendency** ['-ənsɪ] to do sth / have a **tendency** to be ...
adapt [ə'dæpt]	anpassen	~ oneself to new manners (or: customs) / an **adaptable** [-əbl] man

adjust [ə'dʒʌst]	(sich) anpassen, einstellen	~ to changes / ~ oneself to new conditions / ~ a watch
adjustment [ə'dʒʌstmənt]	Anpassung	make ~s
turn [tɜ:n]	(ver-)wandeln, (etwas ganz anderes) werden	~ sth into ... / ~ Communist / sb's hair has ~ed grey
lessen ['lesn]	vermindern, geringer werden	~ a person's importance / ~ the effect of sth / The heat will ~ in the evening.
get (got, got) **worse** [get, gɒt, –; – 'wɜ:s]	schlechter werden	His condition has got (= grown) ~.
make (made, made) **worse** [meɪk, meɪd, –; ˌ– 'wɜ:s]	verschlimmern	~ ~ by the weather
get (got, got) **better** [get, gɒt, –; ˌ– 'betə*]	besser werden	He (or: the weather) is ~ting ~
better ['betə*]	bessern	~ oneself / ~ one's circumstances / ~ the conditions of ...
improve [ɪm'pru:v]	(sich) verbessern	~ one's abilities / ~ greatly / be **improving** [-ɪŋ] in sth / there has been a gradual (or: marked) **improvement** [-mənt]

185 Intensity – Intensität

extent [ɪk'stent]	Ausmaß	To what ~? / to some ~ / to a certain ~
degree [dɪ'gri:]	Grad, Umfang, Ausmaß	reach a high ~ of / by ~s / to a high ~ / To what ~?
actually ['æktʃʊəlɪ]	tatsächlich, eigentlich	He ~ sat next to her. / He says he likes the job but ~ he hates it.
certainly ['sɜ:tnlɪ]	sicher, natürlich	She's ~ very pretty. / 'Will you help me?' – 'C~ I will.'
clearly ['klɪəlɪ]	klar, natürlich	That's ~ a mistake. / C~, he's very stupid.
definitely ['defɪnɪtlɪ]	bestimmt, eindeutig	~ true / ~ yes / ~ no / 'Is he coming?' – 'D~!'
indeed [ɪn'deed]	tatsächlich, wirklich	very large ~ / 'Yes, it is ~ beautiful weather.' / like sth very much ~
obviously ['ɒbvɪəslɪ]	offensichtlich	He ~ works very hard.
plainly ['pleɪnlɪ]	offenbar, unverkennbar	The door is locked, so ~ they must be out.

really ['rɪəlɪ]	wirklich	'Did he ~ say that?' / It's ~ cold today. / 'R~?'
literally ['lɪtərəlɪ]	buchstäblich	do ~ nothing at all / ~ blue with cold
simply ['sɪmplɪ] (*inform.*)	einfach (nur)	It's ~ wonderful. / I don't like driving: I do it ~ to get to work.
fairly ['feəlɪ]	ziemlich	do sth ~ well / a ~ cold day / ~ cold weather / drive ~ fast
rather ['rɑːðə*]	ziemlich, fast zu ...	~ cold / ~ fast
just [dʒʌst]	genau; sehr; so eben noch	~ here / look ~ like sb else / ~ perfect / He ~ succeeded.
very ['verɪ]	sehr	~ high / ~ much
of course [əv 'kɔːs]	natürlich	'Yes, ~ ~!' / 'O~ ~ I love you.'
absolutely ['æbsəluːtlɪ]	absolut, auf jeden Fall	~ wrong / 'Do you think so?' 'A~!'
altogether [ɔːltə'geðə*]	ganz und gar	not ~ bad / different ~
completely [kəm'pliːtlɪ]	vollständig	~ forget sth / ~ successful
entirely [ɪn'taɪəlɪ]	vollständig, ganz	be ~ satisfied / an ~ different matter
fully ['fʊlɪ]	voll und ganz	~ understand / be ~ satisfied / It's ~ an hour since he left.
quite [kwaɪt]	ganz	~ ready / ~ right / not ~ enough / ~ good (= better than expected / ~ a lot of people
thoroughly ['θʌrəlɪ]	völlig, gründlich	feel ~ tired / be ~ amazed
utterly ['ʌtəlɪ]	völlig	~ mad (or: worthless)
in all respects [ɪn ˌɔːl riː'spekts]	in jeder Hinsicht	This room is fine ~ ~ ~.
extremely [ɪk'striːmlɪ]	äußerst	~ dangerous / ~ fast
badly ['bædlɪ]	dringend	~ need (or: want) sth
deeply ['diːplɪ]	tief	wound sb ~ / hurt sb's feelings ~ / be ~ offended (or: disturbed)
greatly ['greɪtlɪ]	sehr	admire sb (or: sth) ~ / enjoy sth ~ / sth (or: sb) surprises one ~
gradually ['grædʒʊəlɪ]	allmählich, stufenweise	change ~
highly ['haɪlɪ]	hoch-, besonders	~ paid ~ amusing / think (or: speak) ~ of sb
heartily ['hɑːtəlɪ] (*inform.*)	herzlich (im Sinne von sehr)	be ~ tired of / be ~ sick of sb's questions
much [mʌtʃ]	sehr	like sb (+ very) ~ / talk too ~
so [səʊ]	so	We're ~ glad you could come. / be ~ happy / be ~ very kind
well [wel]	gut	I can ~ understand you. / be ~ acquainted with sth

a great deal [ə greɪt 'di:l] = **a good deal** [ə gʊd 'di:l]	viel	~ ~ ~ faster / ~ ~ ~ of support
a lot [ə 'lɒt]	viel	~ ~ better / ~ ~ older
far [fɑ:*]	weit	~ better / ~ sooner / ~ more interesting / ~ easier
how [haʊ]	wie	H~ nice (+ of you to come).
how much [haʊ 'mʌtʃ]	wie sehr	I don't know ~ ~ he wants to come.
kind of ['kaɪnd‿əv] (*AE inform.*)	„so'n bißchen"	be ~ ~ tired / ~ ~ hope to ...
sort of ['sɔ:t‿əv] (*inform.*)	„so'n bißchen"	feel ~ ~ tired (or: ill)
more or less ['mɔ:r‿ə ˌles]	mehr oder weniger	The work is ~ ~ ~ done.
partly ['pɑ:tlɪ]	teilweise	~ true / be ~ to blame / be ~ responsible
slightly ['slaɪtlɪ]	ein bißchen, geringfügig	~ cold / feel ~ ill
somewhat ['sʌmwɒt]	ziemlich	~ higher than expected / suffer ~ from the heat
in part [ɪn 'pɑ:t]	zum Teil	The house belongs to him ~ ~.
extent [ɪk'stent]	Ausmaß	to some (or: a certain / a large) ~
a little [ə 'lɪtl]	ein wenig	be ~ ~ tired
a bit [ə 'bɪt]	ein bißchen	be ~ ~ tired
barely ['beəlɪ]	gerade, kaum	He had ~ arrived when he had to leave again. / have ~ enough to live on
at all [ət‿'ɔ:l]	überhaupt; keine Ursache	not ~ ~ / Do you go there ~ ~? 'I'm sorry to trouble you.' 'Not ~ ~.'
almost ['ɔ:lməʊst]	fast	~ all the boys / ~ every time / ~ always
practically ['præktɪkəlɪ]	praktisch	~ all the boys / ~ every time / ~ always
nearly ['nɪəlɪ]	beinah	~ all the boys / ~ every time / ~ always / not ~ / very ~ / pretty ~
hardly ['hɑ:dlɪ]	kaum	~ any ... / ~ ever / ~ notice sth / be ~ aware of sth
merely ['mɪəlɪ]	bloß	I wasn't serious, I was ~ joking. / I ~ asked his name.
only ['əʊnlɪ]	nur	

Action – Handeln (→ 43 Plans) 186

do (did, done) **nothing** [duː, dɪd, dʌn; ˌ– ˈnʌθɪŋ]	nichts tun	sit about ~ing ~
avoid [əˈvɔɪd]	vermeiden	~ doing sth
put (put, put) **off** [pʊt, –, –; – ˈɒf]	aufschieben	have to ~ ~ doing sth / ~ sth ~ (+ until / till) ...
delay [dɪˈleɪ]	verzögern, aufhalten, aufschieben,	~ a journey (or: one's holidays) (+ until / till ...) / ~ doing sth (+ until / till ...) / sth ~s one / Don't ~! / be ~ed by sth
	Aufschub, Verzögerung	after several ~s / do sth without ~
omit [əˈmɪt]	versäumen	~ doing sth / ~ to do sth
hesitate [ˈhesɪteɪt]	zögern	~ to do sth / be still **hesitating** [-ɪŋ] about doing sth (or: whether to do sth)
task [tɑːsk]	Aufgabe	be given the ~ of doing sth / set sb the ~ of doing sth / a difficult ~
try [traɪ]	versuchen; ausprobieren	~ to do sth / ~ doing sth / I'll ~. / ~ hard (or: very hard / very hard indeed) / ~ a hotel (or: the new soap)
attempt [əˈtempt]	versuchen, Versuch	~ to do sth / ~ doing sth / ~ an examination (or: a task) / make an (or: no) ~ to do sth (or: at doing sth)
experiment [ɪkˈsperɪmənt]	Versuch, Experiment;	do (or: perform / carry out) an ~ / learn sth by ~
	experimentieren	~ with new methods / **experimental** [ekˌsperɪˈmentl] methods
ready [ˈredɪ]	fertig, bereit	~ for work / ~ to start / get ~ for a journey
means [miːnz]	Mittel, Möglichkeit	a ~ to an end / try every ~ / **by means of** [baɪ ˈ–‿əv] (vermittels)
way [weɪ]	Art und Weise, Weg	know a ~ of doing sth / show sb the ~ to do sth / Is there another ~ of doing it? / **that way** (so)
method [ˈmeθəd]	Methode	introduce new ~s / show sb a ~ of doing sth
set (set, set) **about** [set, –, –; ˌ– əˈbaʊt]	sich an etwas begeben	~ ~ one's work
do (did, done) [duː, dɪd, dʌn]	machen, tun	~ sth / ~ repairs (or: a lesson / one's homework / science at school / one's hair) / What are you ~ing? / ~ the cooking (or: washing) / ~ one's best / ~ sb a kindness (or: favour) / That will ~. (Das genügt.)

make (made, made) [meɪk, meɪd, –]	machen, herstellen;	~ a car (or: hat / coat) / ~ a fire / ~ a hole (or: noise / mistake) / sth is **made of** ['meɪd‿əv] wood
	machen (zu etwas)	sth ~s one ill (or: better / worse) / ~ sth larger (or: better)
act [ækt]	handeln, tun,	~ wisely (or: foolishly / in a strange way) / ~ as if one were … / ~ as a manager
	Tat	a foolish (or: brave) ~ / commit an ~ of cruelty
deed [di:d]	(bedeutende) Tat	do (or: perform) a ~ of daring (Wagemut) / do a good (or: brave / heroic) ~ / commit an evil ~
action ['ækʃn]	Handeln, Tat	put sth into ~ / carry through (or: out) an ~ / perform an ~ / a good (or: cruel / kind / foolish) ~
perform [pə'fɔ:m]	machen, tun, leisten, bewerkstelligen	~ an operation (or: experiment) / ~ what one has promised / ~ very well / sb's **performance** [-əns] has been excellent
commit [kə'mɪt]	begehen (etwas negatives)	~ an error / ~ a crime
carry out [ˌkærɪ 'aʊt]	durchführen	~ ~ a plan (or: task / duty) / ~ ~ an order
manage ['mænɪdʒ]	leiten; umgehen mit etwas, mit etwas fertigwerden	~ a hotel / ~ a boat / Can you ~? / I can ~ (+ it). / I couldn't ~ to do sth.
take (took, taken) **great pains** [teɪk, tʊk, 'teɪkən; ˌ– 'greɪt ˌpeɪnz]	sich große Mühe geben	~ ~ ~ to do sth
take (took, taken) **the trouble** [teɪk, tʊk, 'teɪken; ˌ– ðə 'trʌbl]	die Mühe auf sich nehmen	~ ~ ~ to do sth
effort ['efət]	Mühe, Anstrengung	make an (or: every) ~ to do sth / do sth with (or: without) ~ / sth needs much (or: a / a lot of / little) ~
able ['eɪbl]	tüchtig	an ~ doctor
be able [bi: 'eɪbl]	können, fähig sein	~ ~ to do sth
ability [ə'bɪlətɪ]	Können, Fähigkeit	a man of great ~ / I'll do it to the best of my ~ties.
capable ['keɪpəbl]	tüchtig, geeignet (zu etwas), fähig	a ~ teacher / be ~ of any crime / That's ~ of being misunderstood.
competent ['kɒmpɪtənt]	kompetent, befähigt	be ~ as … / be ~ to do sth / be ~ in one's work / have a ~ knowledge of

busy ['bɪzɪ]	tätig, (eifrig) beschäftigt mit	a ~ man / be ~ doing sth
be busy [bi: 'bɪzɪ]	viel zu tun haben; belebt sein	She is ~ with her exams. The shop is very ~ today.
skill [skɪl]	Geschick, Fertigkeit	learn new ~s / be **skilful** ['skɪlfl]; (= **skillful**, *AE*) with sth (or: at doing sth)
skilled [skɪld]	geschickt, erfahren	a ~ workman / be ~ in doing sth
achieve [ə'tʃi:v]	erreichen	~ a goal / ~ success / ~ one's end (Ziel) / ~ nothing / ~ all that one wanted (+ to do) / sth is a great **achievement** [-mənt]
accomplish [ə'kʌmplɪʃ]	fertigbringen, erreichen	~ many remarkable things in one's life / ~ a task / ~ nothing / the **accomplishments** [-mənts] of science
purpose ['pɜ:pəs]	Ziel, Zweck, Absicht	What was your ~ in doing that? / do sth on ~ (absichtlich) / achieve one's ~
complete [kəm'pli:t]	beenden, vervollständigen	~ one's work (or: book) / This ought to be ~d before …
keep (kept, kept) **doing** [ki:p, kept, –; ˌ– 'du:ɪŋ]	fortfahren zu tun	

The order in our world – Die Ordnung in unserer Welt

Number – Anzahl

187 Calculating – Rechnen

arithmetic [ə'rɪθmətɪk]	Rechnen	be good at ~
figure ['fɪgə*]	Zahl, Ziffer	1, 2, 3: the second ~ is a 'two' / be good at ~s (gut rechnen können)
count [kaʊnt]	zählen	~ sth / ~ (+ up) to ten / ~ from one to ten / **countable** ['-əbl] (or: **uncountable** [ˌʌn'kaʊntəbl]) nouns (or: things)
calculate ['kælkjuleɪt]	(aus-)rechnen	~ the cost of sth / ~ the result / a (+ **pocket**) **calculator** [-ə*]
compute [kəm'pjuːt]	(be-)rechnen	~ a result (or: sum) / a **computer** [-ə*]
add [æd]	zusammenzählen, addieren	~ five and (= to) six / Five and six ~ up to eleven.
subtract [səb'trækt]	abziehen, subtrahieren	~ six from nine
divide [dɪ'vaɪd]	teilen, dividieren; sich teilen lassen	~ six into thirty / ~ thirty by six Thirty ~s (= is **divisable** [dɪ'vɪzəbl]) by six.
multiply ['mʌltɪplaɪ]	malnehmen, multiplizieren	~ five by eight
number ['nʌmbə*]	Zahl, Nummer,	a ~ between 1 and 10 / a high (or: low / whole) ~
	numerieren	~ the questions (+ from) 1 to 10
even ['iːvn]	gerade	2, 4, 6 are ~ numbers
odd [ɒd]	ungerade	3, 5, 7 are ~ numbers
no. ['nʌmbə*] = **No.** [–]	Nr.	~ 8 / ~s. 8 and 9
zero ['zɪərəʊ]	Null	ten degrees below ~ (= −10° C)
O [əʊ]	Null	My telephone number is 6012 (read: six-o-one-two).
nil [nɪl]	Null	reduce costs to almost ~ / The result of the game was 3–0 (read: three-nil).

Cardinal numbers – Grundzahlen

1	[wʌn]	one
2	[tuː]	two
3	[θriː]	three
4	[fɔː*]	four
5	[faɪv]	five
6	[sɪks]	six
7	['sevən]	seven
8	[eɪt]	eight
9	[naɪn]	nine
10	[ten]	ten
11	[ɪ'levn]	eleven
12	[twelv]	twelve
13	[ˌθɜː'tiːn]	thirteen
14	[ˌfɔː'tiːn]	fourteen
15	[ˌfɪf'tiːn]	fifteen
16	[ˌsɪks'tiːn]	sixteen
17	[ˌsevn'tiːn]	seventeen
18	[ˌeɪ'tiːn]	eighteen
19	[ˌnaɪn'tiːn]	nineteen
20	['twentɪ]	twenty
21	[ˌtwentɪ'wʌn]	twenty-one
22	[ˌtwentɪ'tuː]	twenty-two
23	[ˌtwentɪ'θriː]	twenty-three
30	['θɜːtɪ]	thirty
40	['fɔːtɪ]	forty
50	['fɪftɪ]	fifty
60	['sɪkstɪ]	sixty
70	['sevntɪ]	seventy
80	['eɪtɪ]	eighty
90	['naɪntɪ]	ninety
100	[ə 'hʌndred], [wʌn '–]	a (= one) hundred
200	[tuː 'hʌndred]	two hundred
220	[ˌtuː ˌhʌndred ənd 'twentɪ]	two hundred and twenty
1,000	[ə 'θaʊzənd], [wʌn '–]	a (= one) thousand
1,000,000	[ə 'mɪlɪən], [wʌn '–]	a (= one) million
2,320,000	[ˌtuː 'mɪlɪən ˌθriː hʌndred ənd twentɪ 'θaʊzənd]	two million three hundred and twenty thousand
1,000,000,000	[ə 'θaʊzənd 'mɪlɪənz], [wʌn '– '–]	a (= one) billion (*AE*) = a (= one) thousand million (*BE*)[1]
1,000,000,000,000	[ə 'bɪlɪən], [wʌn '–]	a (= one) billion (*BE*)

[1] The American version is gradually being accepted in British English.

Ordinal numbers – Ordnungszahlen

1st	[ðə 'fɜːst]	the first
2nd	[ðə 'sekənd]	the second
3rd	[ðə 'θɜːd]	the third
4th	[ðə 'fɔːθ]	the fourth
5th	[ðə 'fɪfθ]	the fifth
6th	[ðə 'sɪksθ]	the sixth
7th	[ðə 'sevənθ]	the seventh
8th	[ðɪ 'eɪtθ]	the eighth
9th	[ðə 'naɪnθ]	the ninth
10th	[ðə 'tenθ]	the tenth
11th	[ðɪ ɪ'levnθ]	the eleventh
12th	[ðə 'twelfθ]	the twelfth
13th	[ðə ˌθɜː'tiːnθ]	the thirteenth
14th	[ðə ˌfɔː'tiːnθ]	the fourteenth
15th	[ðə ˌfɪf'tiːnθ]	the fifteenth
16th	[ðə ˌsɪk'stiːnθ]	the sixteenth
17th	[ðə ˌsevn'tiːnθ]	the seventeenth
18th	[ðɪ ˌeɪ'tiːnθ]	the eighteenth
19th	[ðə ˌnaɪn'tiːnθ]	the nineteenth
20th	[ðə ˌtwentɪəθ]	the twentieth
21st	[ðə ˌtwentɪ'fɜːst]	the twenty-first
22nd	[ðə 'twentɪ'sekənd]	the twenty-second
23rd	[ðə ˌtwentɪ'θɜːd]	the twenty-third
30th	[ðə 'θɜːtɪəθ]	the thirtieth
40th	[ðə 'fɔːtɪəθ]	the fourtieth
50th	[ðə 'fɪftɪəθ]	the fiftieth
60th	[ðə 'sɪkstɪəθ]	the sixtieth
70th	[ðə 'sevntɪəθ]	the seventieth
80th	[ðɪ 'eɪtɪəθ]	the eightieth
90th	[ðə 'naɪntɪəθ]	the ninetieth
100th	[ðə wʌn 'hʌndredθ]	the (+ one) hundredth
1,000th	[ðə wʌn 'θaʊznθ]	the (+ one) thousandth
1,000,000th	[ðə wʌn 'mɪlɪənθ]	the (+ one) millionth
1,000,000,000th	[ðə wʌn 'bɪlɪənθ]	the (+ one) billionth (*AE*)
1,000,000,000,000th	[–]	the (+ one) billionth (*BE*)

Quantity – Menge 188

number ['nʌmbə*]	Anzahl	a ~ of (einige) / ~s of (sehr viele) / a large (or: great / small) ~ of
quantity ['kwɒntətɪ]	Menge	a large (or: small) ~ of
amount [ə'maʊnt]	Menge, Betrag,	I can give you any ~ as I have plenty. / pay (or: owe) the ~ of £50
	betragen	The bill ~s to 80p.
average ['ævərɪdʒ]	Durchschnitt	The ~ of 3 and 7 is 5. / on an (= the) ~ / be above (or: below) ~
double ['dʌbl]	doppelt, Doppelte	6 is the ~ of 3 / I'm ~ your age. / a ~ bed
	verdoppeln	~ a number
abundant [ə'bʌndənt]	reichlich	~ supplies of sth
numerous ['nju:mərəs]	zahlreich	happen ~ times / ~ books / become more ~
plenty ['plentɪ]	(über-)reichlich	have ~ to eat and drink / have ~ (+ of sth)
plentiful ['plentɪfl]	reichlich vorhanden	
a lot [ə 'lɒt]	jede Menge, viel	have ~ ~ of time (or: luck / friends) / ~ ~ of people / want ~ ~ (+ of sth)
lots [lɒts] (*inform.*)	jede Menge	have ~ (+ and ~) of friends
heap [hi:p] (*inform.*)	Haufen	have a ~ of trouble / have ~s of time
considerable [kən'sɪdərəbl]	beträchtlich	a ~ sum of money / a ~ quantity (or: amount)
many ['menɪ]	viele,	~ people (or: years / things) / ~ of the people / ~ of us / How ~ (+ books)? / too ~
	manche(-r, -s)	~ a young man (or: girl / thing)
much [mʌtʃ]	viel	not have ~ time (or: money) / How ~? / too ~
more [mɔ:*]	mehr, noch (mehr), weitere	Six is ~ than two. / ~ than one person / some ~ water / no ~ money / ten ~ miles (= ten miles ~)
most [məʊst]	meist, die meisten	Of the three brothers, Tom had the ~ money. / He has visited ~ (+ of the) countries in Europe.
increase [ɪn'kri:s]	vermehren	~ one's speed / ~ prices
reduce [rɪ'dju:s]	verringern	~ speed / ~ prices
some [sʌm]	einige;	~ people (or: apples) / ~ of us
	etwas	"May I give you ~ tea?" – "Yes, I'd like ~."
several ['sevrəl]	mehrere, einige	S~ people were standing at the bus stop. / ~ of them / need ~ more

enough [ɪ'nʌf]	genug	have more than ~ / We haven't (+ got) ~ time (= We haven't time ~). / There's ~. / That's ~.
sufficient [sə'fɪʃnt]	genügend, ausreichend	We have ~ coal for the winter.
plenty ['plentɪ]	im Überfluß	~ of money (or: friends)
odd [ɒd]	so ungefähr	5 pounds ~ / 20-~ years
about [ə'baʊt]	ungefähr	It will cost ~ £50.
couple ['kʌpl]	paar, einige;	have a ~ of drinks
	zwei (verwandte, aber nicht gleiche Dinge)	I found a ~ of socks, but they don't make a pair.
dozen ['dʌzn]	Dutzend	It's 60p a ~. / I want two ~ of these. / **dozens** [-z] of times (or: people)
few [fju:]	einige (wenige)	have only ~ friends / F~ people know that ... / very ~ / still **fewer** ['-ə*] / Who made the **fewest** ['-ɪst] mistakes?
a few [ə 'fju:]	ein paar, einige;	make ~ ~ mistakes / meet ~ ~ of one's friends
	eine Menge (*inform.*)	quite ~ ~
little ['lɪtl]	wenig	There's ~ hope. / have ~ money (or: time)
a little [ə 'lɪtl]	ein wenig, ein bißchen	There's still ~ ~ water. / have ~ ~ money / give sb ~ ~ / ~ ~ more (or: less)
less [les]	weniger	He has ~ money than ever. / Five is ~ than seven.
least [li:st]	geringst, kleinst, wenigst	A has little, B has less, C has (+ the) ~.
short [ʃɔ:t]	knapp	be ~ of sth / last year's **shortage** ['-ɪdʒ] of oil
scarce ['skeəs]	knapp;	sth is getting ~
	selten	a ~ book
nothing ['nʌθɪŋ]	nichts	There's ~ here. / hear ~ of sb
none [nʌn]	kein(-e, -r, -es)	I can't lend you money, I have ~. / N~ of the telephones is (or: are) working.

189 Part, whole – Teil, Ganzes

part [pɑ:t]	Teil	a large (or: small) ~ / a ~ of a country (or: book)
composed of [kəm'pəʊzd‿əv]	zusammengesetzt aus	Water is ~ ~ hydrogen and oxygen.
consist of [kən'sɪst‿əv]	bestehen aus	A fottball team ~s ~ eleven players.

comprise [kəm'praɪz]	umfassen	Japan ~s a great number of islands.
take apart [ˌteɪk‿ə'pɑːt]	auseinandernehmen	
partly ['pɑːtlɪ]	zum Teil	sth is made ~ of wood
portion ['pɔːʃn]	Anteil	a small (or: large) ~ / divide sth into three (+ equal) ~s
share [ʃeə*]	teilen,	~ a room with sb / ~ sth between two persons
	Anteil	do one's ~ of work / have an equal ~
fraction ['frækʃn]	Bruchteil,	It happened within a ~ of a second.
	Bruch	½, ⅓, ¼ are ~s
half [hɑːf]	halb,	~ a pound of sth / a ~ pound / ~ full / ~ as much
(*pl.* halves [hɑːvz])	Hälfte	cut sth into two ~ves / ~ of six is three
third [θɜːd]	Drittel	get one ~ of sth
quarter ['kwɔːtə*]	Viertel	15 minutes is a ~ of an hour
divide [dɪ'vaɪd]	teilen	~ sth in half / ~ one's time between reading and writing / ~ sth (+ up) between (or: among) two or more people

Vulgar fractions – Brüche

½	[ə 'hɑːf], [wʌn '–]	a (= one) half
⅓	[ə 'θɜːd], [wʌn '–]	a (= one) third
¼	[ə 'kwɔːtə*], [wʌn '–]	a (= one) quarter
⅔	[tuː 'θɜːdz]	two thirds
⅛	[ən 'eɪtθ], [wʌn '–]	an (= one) eighth
$4\frac{1}{7}$	[ˌfɔːr‿ənd wʌn 'sevenθ]	four and one seventh
$^{20}/_{83}$	[ˌtwentɪ ˌəʊvə(r) ˌeɪtɪ'θriː]	twenty over eighty-three

Decimal fractions – Dezimalbrüche

0·5	[(ˌnɔːt) pɔɪnt 'faɪv]	(+ o [əʊ]) point five
0·34	[(ˌnɔːt) pɔɪnt ˌθriː 'fɔː*]	(+ o [əʊ]) point three four
4·125	['fɔː pɔɪnt ˌwʌn ˌtuː 'faɪv]	four point one two five

piece [piːs]	Stück	a ~ of paper (or: cake) / a large (or: small / big / tiny) ~ of / break sth into ~s / two ~s of news (zwei Nachrichten)
bit [bɪt] (*inform.*)	Stück, ein bißchen	a ~ of cheese (or: money) / a ~ of information (eine Information)

add [æd]	hinzufügen	~ some sugar to one's tea
complete [kəm'pli:t]	vollständig,	have a ~ collection of sth / the ~ works of Shakespeare
	vervollständigen	~ one's work (or: a book)
put together [ˌpʊt tə'geðə*]	zusammensetzen	
whole [həʊl]	das Ganze,	the ~ of my money / the ~ of England
	ganz	the ~ world (or: truth) / the ~ lot (= alles)
all [ɔ:l]	alle,	~ (+ of the) students / ~ of them / The students ~ passed their exams.
	alles, ganz	take ~ there is / ~ England / ~ over the world
entire [ɪn'taɪə*]	vollständig	an ~ set of sth
total ['təʊtl]	gesamt,	the ~ number (or: amount / cost)
	Summe	If you add 4+5+6, the ~ is 15.
sum [sʌm]	Summe	a large (or: small) ~ / a ~ of money / The ~ of 4 and 6 is 10.
bulk [bʌlk]	(Haupt-)Masse	buy in ~ / the ~ of the books
mass [mæs]	Masse	a ~ of colour (or: flowers) / ~es of money (or: people) (*inform.*)
rest [rest]	Rest	the ~ of the book (or: people) / And all the ~ of it.

Time – Zeit

190 Clock – Uhr

clock [klɒk]	Uhr	put the ~ back (or: forward / on) / an **alarm-clock** [ə'lɑ:m –] / work round the ~
strike (struck, struck) [straɪk, strʌk, –]	schlagen	The clock has **struck** ten.
watch [wɒtʃ]	Armbanduhr	wear a ~ / It's five past two by my ~. / set one's ~ right / **wrist-watch** ['rɪst-] / **quartz watch** ['kwɔ:ts –]
wind (wound, wound) [waɪnd, waʊnd, –]	aufziehen	~ (+ up) one's watch
time [taɪm]	(Uhr-)Zeit	What ~ is it? / What's the ~? / What ~ do you make it? / at what ~? / ~ to go

o'clock [ə'klɒk]	Uhr (in Zeitangaben)	5 ~ / It's five ~ / the six ~ news / the five ~ train
past [pɑːst]	nach	It's twenty (+ minutes) ~ ten.
after ['æfter] (*AE*)	nach	five ~ one
clockwork ['klɒkwɜːk]	Uhrwerk(-)	~ toys / with ~ precision
clock-face ['klɒk feɪs]	Ziffer	
at [æt], [ət]	um	~ five o'clock
about [ə'baʊt]	ungefähr	at ~ five o'clock
quarter ['kwɔːtə*]	viertel	It's (+ a) ~ past (or: to) ten.
half [hɑːf]	halb	It's ~ past nine.

The twenty-four hour clock[1] *– die Uhrzeit*

07.00	read: seven hundred hours	[ˌsevn 'hʌndrəd ˌaʊəz]
07.15	read: seven fifteen	[ˌsevn ˌfɪf'tiːn]
07.27	read: seven twenty-seven	[ˌsevn ˌtwentɪ'sevn]
07.30	read: seven thirty	[ˌsevn 'θɜːtɪ]
07.45	read: seven forty-five	[ˌsevn ˌfɔːtɪ 'faɪv]
22.50	read: twenty-two fifty	[ˌtwentɪˌtuː 'fɪftɪ]
23.06	read: twenty-three-o-six	[ˌtwentɪˌθriː ˌəʊ 'sɪks]
24.00	read: twenty-four hundred hours	[ˌtwentɪˌfɔː 'hʌndred ˌaʊəz]

a.m. [ˌeɪ 'em]	vor 12 Uhr Mittag	It's 7 a.m. (= 07.00 Uhr)
p.m. [ˌpiː 'em]	nach 12 Uhr Mittag	It's 7 p.m. (= 19.00 Uhr)
second ['sekənd]	Sekunde, Moment	In ten ~s it was all over. / Please wait a ~. / at 5 o'clock to the nearest ~ (= Punkt 5 Uhr)
minute ['mɪnɪt]	Minute, Moment	ten ~s to twelve / Wait a ~, please. / I'll be there in a ~.
hour ['aʊə*]	Stunde	stay somewhere for three ~s / half an ~ / a quarter of an ~ / every two ~s / a two-~ journey / trains leave on the ~ (or: on the half ~)
hourly ['aʊəlɪ]	stündlich	an ~ bus service / This medicine is to be taken ~.

[1] Used most often in military orders etc.; sometimes used in travel timetables.

191 Day – Tag

day [deɪ]	Tag (von morgens bis abends),	~ and night / a fine (or: sunny) ~ / in the **daytime** ['-taɪm] / at **daybreak** ['-breɪk]
	Tag (24 Stunden)	What ~ of the week is it? / one ~ (= eines Tages) / some ~ (= eines Tages, in der Zukunft) / in these (or: those) ~s / the next ~ / ~ in ~ out (Tag für Tag)
daily ['deɪlɪ]	täglich	a ~ paper
dawn [dɔːn]	Morgendämmerung, dämmern	at ~ The day is ~ing.
sunrise ['sʌnraɪz]	Sonnenaufgang	get up at ~
morning ['mɔːnɪŋ]	Morgen, morgen	this (heute) ~ / in the ~ / one ~ / a fine ~ / "Good ~."
noon [nuːn]	Mittag, mittag	at ~ / it's 12 ~
midday ['mɪddeɪ]	Mittag(s-)	at ~ / the ~ sun (or: meal)
afternoon [ˌaːftə'nuːn]	Nachmittag, nachmittag	this (heute) ~ / in the ~ / "Good ~."
evening ['iːvnɪŋ]	Abend, abend	this (heute) ~ / in the ~ / "Good ~."
tonight [tə'naɪt]	heute abend; heute nacht	We're going to the cinema ~. I hope you sleep well ~.
sunset ['sʌnset] = **sundown** ['sʌndaʊn]	Sonnenuntergang	at ~
moonrise ['muːnraɪz]	Mondaufgang	at ~
dusk [dʌsk]	Abenddämmerung	at ~ / from dawn to ~
night [naɪt]	Nacht, Abend	in the ~ / at ~ / on Friday ~ / by ~ / last ~ / stay somewhere **overnight** [ˌəʊvə'-]
midnight ['mɪdnaɪt]	Mitternacht	at (or: before / after) ~
today [tə'deɪ]	heute	T~ is Monday. / ~ week (heute in einer Woche) / ~'s newspaper
tomorrow [tə'mɒrəʊ]	morgen	~ morning (or: afternoon) / the day after ~ (Übermorgen) / ~ week (in zahlenmäßig acht Tagen)
yesterday ['jestədɪ]	gestern	~ morning (or: afternoon) / the day before ~ (vorgestern) / ~'s newspaper
the other day [ðiː 'ʌðə ˌdeɪ]	neulich	I met him ~ ~ ~.

Week – Woche 192

week [wi:k]	Woche	this (or: last / next) ~ / in two ~s / a two ~s' holiday / a **weekly** ['-lɪ] paper
weekday ['wi:kdeɪ]	Werktag, werktäglich	I'm always busy on ~s. / the ~ train (or: bus) service

Sunday	['sʌndɪ]	Sonntag
Monday	['mʌndɪ]	Montag
Tuesday	['tju:zdɪ]	Dienstag
Wednesday	['wenzdɪ]	Mittwoch
Thursday	['θɜ:zdɪ]	Donnerstag
Friday	['fraɪdɪ]	Freitag
Saturday	['sætədɪ]	Samstag, Sonnabend

Sabbath ['sæbəθ]	Sabbat	hold (or: keep) the ~
weekend [ˌwi:k'end]	Wochenende	spend the ~ with sb (or: at the seaside) / invite sb for the ~ / at the ~
fortnight ['fɔ:tnaɪt]	vierzehn Tage	sb's birthday is on Monday ~ / once a ~ / every ~ / go away for a ~'s holiday

Year – Jahr 193

month [mʌnθ]	Monat	this (or: last / next) ~ / a ~ ago / on the third of this ~ / a baby of three ~s / a **three-month** old baby / a **monthly** ['-lɪ] magazine

January	['dʒænjuərɪ]	Januar
February	['febrʊərɪ]	Februar
March	[mɑ:tʃ]	März
April	['eɪprəl]	April
May	[meɪ]	Mai
June	[dʒu:n]	Juni
July	[dʒʊ'laɪ]	Juli
August	['ɔ:gəst]	August
September	[sep'tembə*]	September
October	[ɒk'təʊbə*]	Oktober
November	[nəʊ'vembə*]	November
December	[dɪ'sembə*]	Dezember

January ['dʒænjʊərɪ]	Januar	in ~ / last (or: next) ~
season ['si:zn]	Jahreszeit, -zeit	the four ~s of the year / the Christmas ~ / the holiday ~
spring [sprɪŋ]	Frühling	in ~ / ~ flowers (or: weather) / in the ~ of 1982
springtime ['sprɪŋtaɪm]	Frühling	I like ~ best of all.
summer ['sʌmə*]	Sommer	in ~ / in the ~ of 1982 / the ~ holidays / ~ weather
summertime ['sʌmətaɪm]	Sommerzeit	go swimming in the ~
autumn ['ɔ:təm (*BE*) = **fall** [fɔ:l] (*AE*)	Herbst	in (+ early / late) ~ / a mild (or: sunny) ~ / ~ weather
winter ['wɪntə*]	Winter	in ~ / a cold (or: hard) ~ / ~ sports / **wintertime** [-taɪm] / a **wintry** ['wɪntrɪ] day
year ['jɪə*]	Jahr	once a ~ / every ~ / ~ in ~ out / over the ~s / ~s ago / ~ by (= after) ~ / **New Year's Day** [ˌnju: jɪəz 'deɪ]
annual ['ænjʊəl]	jährlich	an ~ meeting (or: event / occasion)

194 When? – wann?

date [deɪt]	Datum, Zeitpunkt,	What's the ~ today? / What's today's ~? / to ~ (bis zum heutigen Zeitpunkt)
	datieren	receive a letter ~d 5th May / sth ~s back to 1245 / sth ~s from the 12th century
5 June 1980 = **5th June 1980 =** **5 Jun. '80 =** **5/6/1980 =** **5.6.1980 =**	5. Juni 1980	read: **the fifth of June nineteen eighty**
June 5, 1980 = **6. 5. 80** (*AE*)		read: **June fifth, nineteen eighty**
century ['sentʃʊrɪ]	Jahrhundert	in the 20th (or: last) ~ / at the beginning (or: end) of the ~
BC [bi:'si:] = **B.C.** [–]	vor Christus, v. Chr.	Caesar was murdered in 44 ~
AD [eɪ'di:] = **A.D.** [–]	nach Christus, n. Chr.	55 (= fifty-five) ~

Up to a certain point of time – bis zu einem bestimmten Zeitpunkt

until [ən'tɪl]	bis (vorangestellt)	~ now (or: then / about noon / ten o'clock / tomorrow) / U~ now we've been lucky.
not until ['nɒt ən'tɪl]	erst	He's ~ coming ~ Thursday.
till [tɪl]	bis (nachgestellt)	He will stay here ~ Saturday.
still [stɪl]	noch	Are you ~ in the bathroom? / He ~ comes to see us. / He was ~ asleep.
yet [jet]	schon	Has he gone ~?
not yet [nɒt 'jet]	noch nicht	He has ~ ~ gone. / He has ~ gone ~.
as yet [əz 'jet]	bis jetzt	Nothing unusual has happened ~ ~. / A~ ~ we haven't made any plans for our holidays.
so far ['səʊ 'fɑː*]	soweit, bis jetzt	Nothing has happened ~ ~.
by [baɪ]	bis (nicht später als)	Please be here ~ three o'clock.
not later than [nɒt 'leɪtə ðæn]	nicht später als	Christmas cards should be sent ~ ~ ~ 13th December.
up to ['ʌp tə]	bis	~ ~ now (or: the present / that day)
to (*BE*) [tuː], [tə]	bis	~ the end / from Monday ~ Friday
through [θruː] = **thru** [–] (*AE, inform.*)	bis einschließlich	(+ from) Monday ~ Friday
beyond [bɪ'jɒnd]	über ... hinaus	~ Christmas
already [ɔːl'redɪ]	schon (zu diesem Zeitpunkt)	I've ~ done my homework. / I've done my homework ~.

Before a certain point of time – vor einem bestimmten Zeitpunkt

before [bɪ'fɔː*]	vor, bevor, vorher	~ six o'clock / B~ he went home he bought a newspaper. / I've never seen that ~.
old [əʊld]	alt	~ customs (or: families / houses / clothes)
ancient ['eɪnʃənt]	alt (im Sinne von: aus alter Zeit)	~ Rome / ~civilizations (or: coins / rituals)
antique [æn'tiːk]	antik, alt, Antiquitäten	an ~ ring an ~ shop (or: dealer)
obsolete ['ɒbsəliːt]	veraltet	an ~ word
out-of-date [ˌaʊt‿əv 'deɪt] (= **outdated** [aʊt'deɪtɪd])	veraltet	sth is (or: becomes / seems rather) ~ / sth goes ~ / ~ methods

ago [ə'gəʊ]	vor, zuvor, ... her	a year ~ / How long ~ is that? / It is only a few days ~ that ...
earlier ['ɜ:lɪə*]	früher	in ~ times / two hours ~ / I couldn't come ~.
former ['fɔ:mə*]	früher	in ~ times / my ~ teacher
formerly ['fɔ:məlɪ]	früher, vormals	Mr Jones was ~ a policeman.
originally [ə'rɪdʒənlɪ]	ursprünglich	The school was ~ quite small.
previous ['pri:vjəs]	vorhergehend	on the ~ day (or: evening) / in ~ years.
previously ['pri:vjəslɪ]	früher, vorher	He had visited me two days ~. / P~ I went to a different school.
recent ['ri:snt]	neuest, jüngst	a ~ event / ~ news
recently ['ri:sntlɪ]	in letzter Zeit;	We haven't heard from him ~.
	vor kurzem	the man who died ~ ...
lately ['leɪtlɪ]	unlängst, in letzter Zeit	Have you been there ~? / until ~ / I haven't seen Bob ~.
then [ðen]	damals, damalig	We were ~ living in London. / the ~ Lord Mayor
over ['əʊvə*]	vorbei	It's all ~ now.
once [wʌns]	einst	She ~ lived in China.
Once upon a time ['wʌns‿əˌpɒn‿ə 'taɪm]	Es war einmal (in Märchen)	~ ~ ~ ~ there lived ...
past [pɑ:st]	Vergangenheit,	in the ~ / Grandfather told us stories of (= from) his ~.
	vergangen	in the ~ ten years / in years ~ / during the ~ week
just [dʒʌst]	gerade (vorbei)	We've ~ had dinner.
just now [dʒəst 'naʊ]	gerade eben;	Tom has come ~ ~.
	jetzt im Moment (*AE*)	He's having a bath ~ ~.
late [leɪt]	jüngst	the ~ agreement
last [lɑ:st]	letzt	the ~ train / ~ week / in the ~ two weeks
latest ['leɪtɪst]	neuest	the ~ news / his ~ novel
at one time [ət 'wʌn taɪm]	einst	A~ ~ ~ he was a soldier.
new [nju:]	neu	a ~ building / a ~ idea / sth is ~ to one
modern ['mɒdn]	modern	~ music
contemporary [kən'temprərɪ]	zeitgenössisch, zeitgemäß	in ~ style
up-to-date [ʌptə'deɪt]	modern	sth is ~ / bring sth ~ / ~ methods

At a certain point of time – zu einem bestimmten Zeitpunkt

at [æt], [ət]	um, am, an, zu, bei	~ ten o'clock (or: 6.30 p. m. / noon / the weekend) / ~ night / ~ Christmas / ~ first (or: last) / ~ that time / ~ the first opportunity
in [ɪn]	am, im, in, während	~ the morning (or: evening / afternoon / night) / at ten o'clock ~ the morning / ~ May (or: 1980 / the 20th century / the Middle Ages / the reign of Queen Elizabeth)
on [ɒn]	am, an, bei	~ Monday (or: the following day / the 1st of May) / ~ her birthday / ~ this occasion
when [wen]	wann;	W~ can you come? / till ~? / since ~?
	wenn, als	W~ the lights are red the traffic must stop. / It was raining ~ we arrived.
time [taɪm]	Zeit, Zeitpunkt;	this (or: next / that / another) ~ / at another ~ / one more ~ (noch einmal)
	Mal	for the first (or: last) ~
in time [ɪn 'taɪm]	pünktlich	He was there ~ ~.
on time [ɒn 'taɪm]	pünktlich, fahrplanmäßig	The bus came ~ ~.
instant ['ɪnstənt]	Augenblick	I'll be back in an ~. / Leave the room **instantly!** [-lɪ] / His death was **instantaneous** [ˌɪnstən'teɪnjəs].
moment ['məʊmənt]	Moment	at this (or: that) ~ / at the very (or: same) ~ / just (= only) this ~ (gerade eben) / I started the ~ your letter arrived.
on the spot [ɒn ðə 'spɒt] *(inform.)*	auf der Stelle	be killed ~ ~ ~ / fall dead ~ ~ ~
now [naʊ]	jetzt	I'm working in London ~. / not ~ / until ~ / ~ and again (von Zeit zu Zeit) / just ~ / ~ that he is twenty
nowadays ['naʊədeɪz]	heutzutage	A hundred years ago people used horses but ~ they use cars.
the other day [ði: ʌðə 'deɪ]	neulich	T~ ~ ~ I saw my teacher.
just [dʒʌst]	genau	It's ~ two o'clock. / ~ in time
this [ðɪs]	dies	~ week (or: month / year) / ~ time last year
these days [ði:z 'deɪz]	in diesen Tagen	~ ~ / one of ~ ~

while [waɪl]	während;	I met him often ~ (+ I was) in London.
	Weile	for a (+ little / long / short) ~
at the same time [ət ðə 'seɪm 'taɪm]	zur gleichen Zeit, gleichzeitig	Meet me ~ ~ ~ ~ tomorrow. read and eat ~ ~ ~ ~
about [ə'baʊt]	ungefähr	~ 2 o'clock / on or ~ the first of May
around [ə'raʊnd]	um ... herum	come ~ 10 o'clock
punctual ['pʌŋktʃʊəl]	pünktlich	be always ~ / arrive ~ly
at once [ət 'wʌns]	sofort	leave ~ ~ / all ~ ~ (ganz plötzlich)
sudden ['sʌdn]	plötzlich	a ~ noise / all of a ~ (ganz plötzlich) / **Suddenly** [-lɪ] a car came round the corner.
immediate [ɪ'mi:dɪət]	sofort, allernächst	an ~ reply / in the ~ future
immediately [ɪ'mi:dɪətlɪ]	sofort	come ~ / Stop that ~!
soon [su:n]	früh	How ~ can you come?
as soon as [əz 'su:n əz]	sobald als	A~ ~ ~ he heard this, he phoned the police.
no sooner ... than [nəʊ 'su:nə ... ðən]	kaum, daß ...	N~ ~ had we sat down ~ we found that it was time to go.
during ['djuːrɪŋ]	während	~ the day
by [baɪ]	während	~ day (or: night)
present ['preznt]	Gegenwart,	the past, the ~, and the future
	gegenwärtig	in the ~ case / the ~ government / **present-day** [-deɪ] problems
at present [ət 'preznt]	zur Zeit	He is with John ~ ~.
presently ['prezntlɪ]	zur Zeit;	He is ~ living in New York. (*AE*)
	bald, gleich	I'm busy now but I can help you ~. / He'll be here ~.
early ['ɜ:lɪ]	früh	come (or: go / leave) ~ / ~ in the summer / in the ~ summer / ~ in the morning / at an ~ hour
late [leɪt]	spät, zu spät	be (or: come / go / leave) ~ / very (or: too) ~ / get up ~ / a ~ visitor
of late [əv 'leɪt]	in letzter Zeit	He has been working very hard ~ ~.
contemporary [kən'temprərɪ]	zeitgenössisch,	in ~ style / ~ music
	Zeitgenosse	Byron was a ~ of Scott.
meantime ['mi:ntaɪm]	Zwischenzeit	in the ~
meanwhile ['mi:nwaɪl]	währenddessen	You pack the cases; ~ I'll get the car ready.
for the present [fə ðə 'preznt]	in der Zwischenzeit, für die nächste Zeit	We don't need any more ~ ~ ~.

After a certain point of time – nach einem bestimmten Zeitpunkt

after ['ɑːftə*]	nach,	~ two years / ~ two o'clock (or: that / then) / soon ~ that
	nachdem	He came ~ I had gone.
afterwards ['ɑːftəwədz]	danach, später	long ~
later ['leɪtə*]	später	much ~ / not ~ than / two days ~ / **sooner or later** [ˌsuːnər‿ɔː 'leɪtə*]
later on ['leɪtər‿ɒn]	später, danach	~ ~ in the evening (or: day) / Can we talk about it ~ ~?
then [ðen]	dann, danach	I had supper and ~ went to bed.
soon [suːn]	bald	He'll come ~. / ~ after (+ that)
following ['fɒləʊɪŋ]	folgend	on the ~ day / in the ~ year
next [nekst]	nächst,	the ~ day
	als nächstes	What happened ~?
again [ə'gen]	noch einmal	do sth ~
near ['nɪə*]	nah	Christmas is ~. / in the ~ future
before long [bɪˌfɔː 'lɒŋ]	binnen kurzem	Summer will be here ~ ~.
some day [səm 'deɪ]	eines Tages, irgendwann	He'll be a good doctor ~ ~.
one day [wʌn 'deɪ]	eines Tages	He'll be famous ~ ~.
one of these days ['wʌn əv ðiːz 'deɪz]	eines schönen Tages	O~ ~ ~ ~ I won't come back.
yet [jet]	noch	He may win the match ~. / He may surprise us all ~. / There's plenty of time ~.
in next to no time [ɪn ˌnekst tə 'nəʊ taɪm]	im Nu	The holidays will be upon us ~ ~ ~ ~ ~.
coming ['kʌmɪŋ]	kommend	the ~ generation / the ~ year
future ['fjuːtʃə*]	zukünftig,	in ~ years
	Zukunft	in the (+ near) ~

How often? – wie oft? 195

once [wʌns]	einmal	only ~ / more than ~ / ~ a day / ~ every week
twice [twaɪs]	zweimal	~ a day / I've been there ~.
times [taɪmz]	-mal	three ~ ['– –] / many ~ [– '–] / at all ~ [–'––] (immer) / at ~ [– '–] (manchmal)
every ['evrɪ]	alle;	~ two hours / ~ other day (alle zwei Tage)
	jede(-r, -s)	~ hour (or: day)

each [iːtʃ]	jede(-r, -s) (+ einzelne)	~ morning (or: day)
every now and again [ˌevrɪ naʊ ənd əˈgen] (*inform.*)	ab und zu	I see my parents ~ ~ ~ ~.
usually [ˈjuːʒʊəlɪ]	gewöhnlich	Where do you ~ go for your holidays?
as usual [əz ˈjuːʒʊəl]	wie gewöhnlich	He came late, ~ ~.
generally [ˈdʒenrəlɪ]	im allgemeinen	He is ~ at the office at this time.
constant [ˈkɒnstənt]	ständig	a ~ noise / It had been raining **constantly** [-lɪ].
continual [kənˈtɪnjʊəl]	ständig (mit Unterbrechungen)	~ rain / Except for a few sunny spells, it rained **continually** [-ɪ] during our holidays.
continuous [kənˈtɪnjʊəs]	ununterbrochen	a ~ performance / It had rained **continuously** [-lɪ].
regular [ˈregjʊlə*]	regelmäßig	a man of ~ habits / a ~ pulse / I get up at 6.30 **regularly** [-lɪ].
common [ˈkɒmən]	üblich	a ~ mistake
frequent [ˈfriːkwənt]	häufig	a ~ visitor (or: guest) / Hurricanes are ~ here in autumn. / I **frequently** [-lɪ] get up at seven. / His visits became more and more **infrequent** [ɪnˈ-].
often [ˈɒfn]	oft	I've ~ been here. / I have not been there very ~.
repeatedly [rɪˈpiːtɪdlɪ]	zum wiederholten Male	I asked him ~ not to do it again.
always [ˈɔːlweɪz]	immer	be ~ late / You ~ say that.
a lot [ə ˈlɒt]	viel, häufig	go to the cinema ~ ~
a good deal [ə gʊd ˈdiːl] = **a great deal** [ə greɪt ˈdiːl]	ziemlich viel	He has travelled ~ ~ ~.
sometimes [ˈsʌmtaɪmz]	manchmal	He ~ forgets his book.
a little [ə ˈlɪtl]	wenig	see sb only ~ ~
occasional [əˈkeɪʒənl]	gelegentlich	make an ~ visit / do sth **occasionally** [əˈkeiʒnəlɪ]
less [les]	weniger (oft)	People go out ~ in winter.
little [ˈlɪtl]	wenig	I go there very ~.
ever [ˈevə*]	jemals	Have you ~ been there? / If you ~ go to London, ...
hardly ever [ˈhɑːdlɪ ˈevə*] = **scarcely ever** [ˌskeəslɪ ˈevə*]	kaum jemals	I ~ ~ go to the cinema.
seldom [ˈseldəm]	selten	We ~ see him.

rarely ['reəlɪ]	kaum	He ~ comes now. / These animals are ~ found.
never ['nevə*]	niemals	I've ~ been there. / N~ in my life. / I ~ said such a thing.

How long? – wie lange? 196

time [taɪm]	Zeit	do sth for a long ~ / have no (or: a lot of) ~ / spend some ~ doing sth / in no ~ / all the ~ / ~ and again
space [speɪs]	Zeitraum	during the ~ of two years
age [eɪdʒ]	Zeitalter	the ~ of machinery / the stone (or: electronic / atomic) ~ / the **Middle Ages** [ˌmɪdl '-ɪz] (das Mittelalter) / **for ages** [fə'r‿'eɪdʒɪz] (*inform.*) (lange)
period ['pɪərɪəd]	Zeitabschnitt	a short ~ (+ of time) / a ~ of two hours / the ~ of the French Revolution
term [tɜːm]	(fester) Zeitabschnitt	~ of office (Amtszeit) / be elected for a ~ of four years
reign [reɪn]	Regierungszeit	during the ~ of George III
minute ['mɪnɪt]	Minute, Moment	Please wait a ~. / in a ~ / in a few ~s / just a ~ / for a ~
second ['sekənd]	Sekunde, Moment	Please wait a ~. / just a ~ / in a ~ / in a few ~s / for a ~
moment ['məʊmənt]	Moment	Please wait a ~. / just a ~ / in a few ~s / for a ~
last [lɑːst]	dauern	~ a long time / ~ two hours
pass [pɑːs]	verbringen;	~ the time (+ by doing sth)
	vergehen	The time ~ed pleasantly. / Six months ~ed.
spend (spent, spent) [spend, spent, –]	verbringen	~ one's time / ~ the summer holidays in ... / ~ (+ a lot of) time on sth (or: in doing sth) / ~ one's life doing sth
while [waɪl]	Weile	for a ~ / a ~ ago
eternity [ɪ'tɜːnətɪ]	Ewigkeit	from now until ~ / It seemed an ~. / **eternal** [ɪ'tɜːnl] life
endless ['endlɪs]	endlos	have ~ patience / ~ rain
always ['ɔːlweɪz]	immer	I've ~ lived here.
all [ɔːl]	ganz	~ day long / ~ the time / ~ the week
the whole [ðə 'həʊl]	der, die, das ganze	~ ~ week (or: evening / year)
forever [fə'revə*]	(für) immer	I'll love you ~ ~.
long [lɒŋ]	lang(-e)	two days ~ / be away (+ for) ~ / a ~ time

short [ʃɔːt]	kurz	a ~ speech (or: play)
brief [briːf] (*form.*)	kurz, knapp	have a ~ (look at / ~ and to the point
throughout [θruː'aʊt]	... hindurch	~ the summer (or: war)
over ['əʊvə*]	über, mehr als	(+ for) ~ an hour
more than ['mɔː ðən]	länger als	He was away for ~ ~ a year.
for [fə*]	für, ... lang	~ about a week / ~ a day or so / I haven't seen him ~ years.
since [sɪns]	seit; seitdem	~ 1978 / ~ the war I haven't seen him ~.

Space – Raum

197 Position, direction – Standort, Richtung

where [weə*]	wo, wohin	W~ are you? / W~ are you going? / Stay ~ you are. / Go ~ you like. / W~ are you from? / I can see it from ~ I am.
here [hɪə*]	hier, hierher	He is ~. / right ~ / ten miles from ~ / Come ~! / H~'s your tea. / H~ you are. (Hier, bitte.)
there [ðeə*]	da, dahin	Who's ~? / He's ~. / It's (+ up / over / under / down / through) ~. / T~ he is! / I'm on my way ~. / ~ and back
somewhere ['sʌmweə*]	irgendwo, irgendwohin	be (or: go) ~ / ~ nice / ~ where it's warm
anywhere ['enɪweə*]	irgendwo, irgendwohin; wo auch immer, wohin auch immer	Are you going ~ tomorrow? / No, I'm not going ~. / It could be ~. You can go ~ (+ you like).
everywhere ['evrɪweə*]	überall, überall hin	It was raining ~. / People are the same ~. / look ~ for sth / go ~ / E~ they went they kept meeting John.
elsewhere [ˌels'weə*]	anderswo, anderswohin	try (or: look / go) ~
nowhere ['nəʊweə*]	nirgends, nirgendwohin	He was ~ to be found. / be (or: go) ~ / have ~ to go
wherever [weə'revə*]	wo auch immer, wohin auch immer, wo denn nur, wohin denn nur?	W~ he is, we must find him. / You may go ~ you like. W~ could he be? / W~ will you go?

to [tʊ], [tə]	nach, zu, in, im	~ London / go (or: turn) ~ ... / the way ~ the station / the road ~ London / throw sth ~ the ground / ~ the west of ... / from north ~ south / a visit ~ London / I've never been ~ London.
towards [tə'wɔːdz]	auf ... zu, gegen, nach	turn one's eyes ~ sb (or: sth) / come ~ sb (or: sth) / look ~ the sun / with one's back ~ sb (or: sth) / The house faces ~ the South.
at [æt], [ət]	auf, an- (wohin?);	look (or: aim / shoot / laugh) ~ sb (or: sth) / point (+ one's finger) ~ sb (or: sth) / throw sth ~ sb (or: sth)
	an, in, im, bei, zu (wo?)	~ the door (or: office / station / grocer's) / ~ home / ~ Walton on the Naze / The plane didn't stop ~ London.
from [frɒm], [frəm]	von	travel ~ Glasgow to London / ~ one end to the other / not far ~ / a long way ~ / take sth ~ the table
up to ['ʌp tə]	auf ... zu	go ~ ~ sb (or: sth)
away from [ə'weɪ frəm]	von ... weg	take sth ~ ~ the child / five miles ~ ~ here
against [ə'genst]	gegen, an	lean (+ one's bicycle) ~ the wall
into ['ɪntə]	in, hinein, herein	go ~ the house / put sth ~ a box
in [ɪn]	in, an, am, auf, da (wo?),	~ London (or: England / the world / the street / Trafalgar Square / the field / the country / Cuba) / sth is ~ the box / Is anybody ~?
	hinein, herein	come (or: get / slip) ~ / look ~ at the window / dive ~ (or: into) the water
out [aʊt]	(aus ...) heraus;	come ~ (+ of the house) / look ~ (+ of the window) / go ~ for a walk / find one's way ~ / take sth ~ of one's pocket (or: bag / cupboard)
	draußen, aus-;	keep sb (or: sth) ~ / lock (or: shut) sb ~
	nicht da	The manager is ~.
off [ɒf]	von;	fall ~ (+ the roof) / roll ~ (+ the table) / take one's hat ~ / sth comes ~ (geht ab)
	weg, entfernt, weg-;	go (or: run) ~ / They're ~! / a house ~ the main road / five miles ~
	vor (Seemannssprache)	anchor five miles ~ Harwich

Position in the vertical sense – vertikale Lage

above [ə'bʌv]	über, oben	one ~ the other / ~ the clouds / from ~
overhead [ˌəʊvə'hed]	(unmittelbar) über, droben	the stars ~ (+ of us) / in the room ~
over [əʊvə*]	(genau, dicht) über	hang ~ / project (hervorragen) ~ / ~ one's head / hang ~ the door (or: desk)
on top [ɒn 'tɒp]	oben	The red book is ~ ~ (+ of the others). / ~ ~ of the roof
under ['ʌndə*]	(genau, dicht) unter	~ the table (or: tree) / ~ (+ the) water
below [bɪ'ləʊ]	unten, unterhalb	in the rooms ~ / from ~ / ~ the village / ~ sea level
upside down [ˌʌpsaɪd 'daʊn]	kopfüber, verkehrt herum	be (or: hang) ~ ~ / hold sth ~ ~
upstairs [ˌʌp'steəz]	oben (im Haus)	Are you ~?
downstairs [ˌdaʊn'steəz]	unten (im Haus)	He is ~ in the sitting-room.

Movement in the vertical sense – vertikale Bewegung

up [ʌp]	herauf, nach oben	go ~ the hill / hang ~ a picture / look (or: stand) ~ / get ~ (+ at seven / from the ground) / help sb ~
upward(s) ['ʌpwəd(z)]	aufwärts, nach oben	climb ~ / a path going ~ / The rocket shot ~.
uphill [ˌʌp'hɪl]	bergauf	walk ~ / a street going ~ / an ~ climb
upstairs [ˌʌp'steəz]	treppauf	go (or: walk / run) ~
down [daʊn]	herunter, nach unten; nieder, hin-	look (or: fall / put sth / come / go) ~ sit (or: lie / knock) ~
downward(s) ['daʊnwəd(z)]	abwärts, nach unten	climb (or: move) ~ / a path going ~ / hang head ~ from …
downhill [ˌdaʊn'hɪl]	bergab	run ~ / a street going ~ / a ~ climb
downstairs [ˌdaʊn'steəz]	(die Treppe, mit dem Lift) hinunter	go ~

Position in the horizontal sense – horizontale Lage

in front [ɪn 'frʌnt]	vorn, davor	a house with a tree ~ ~ / be ~ ~
in front of [ɪn 'frʌnt‿əv]	vor	a tree ~ ~ ~ the house
at the front [ət ðə 'frʌnt]	vorn	The cheapest seats at a cinema are ~ ~ ~.

ahead [ə'hed]	vor, vorn, voraus	the road ~
behind [bɪ'haɪnd]	hinter, hinten	walk (or: stay) ~ (+ sb) / a garden ~ the house / sit ~ sb / hide ~ a tree
at the back [ət ðə 'bæk]	hinter, hinten	There's a garden ~ ~ ~ (+ of the house).
beside [bɪ'saɪd]	neben, an	sit ~ sb / live ~ the sea
by [baɪ]	bei, (nahe) an	stand (or: sit) ~ sb (or: sth) / ~ the side of sb (or: sth) / side ~ side / spend a few days ~ the sea
with [wið]	bei	I left my keys ~ my wallet. / stay ~ sb
close [kləʊs]	nahe, dicht	come ~
near ['nɪə*]	nahe an	My house is ~ the river.
nearby ['nɪəbaɪ]	nahegelegen, nahe bei	a ~ town / There was a stream ~.
between [bɪ'twiːn]	zwischen	stand ~ A and B / ~ London and Manchester
among(st) [ə'mʌŋ(st)]	(mitten) unter, in	stand ~ the people / ~ the trees (or: hills)
inside [ˌɪn'saɪd]	drinnen, in	stay ~ / ~ the house / What's ~?
outside [ˌaʊt'saɪd]	draußen	stay (or: wait) ~ / It's cold ~.
on the right (+ **hand side**) [ɒn ðə 'raɪt (hænd 'saɪd)]	rechts	You'll see the post office ~ ~ ~ (+ ~ ~).
on one's right [ɒn wʌnz 'raɪt]	zu jemandes Rechten	It's ~ your ~.
to the right of [tə ðə 'raɪt əv]	rechts von	It's ~ ~ ~ ~ the post office.
on the left (+ **hand side**) [ɒn ðə 'left (hænd 'saɪd)]	links	O~ ~ ~ (+ ~ ~) you can see the White House.
on one's left [ɒn wʌnz 'left]	zu jemandes Linken	O~ your ~ you can see the Tower.
to the left of [tə ðə 'left‿əv]	links von	T~ ~ ~ ~ the President is his wife.
around [ə'raʊnd]	um ... (herum)	sit ~ the table / a wall ~ the castle
round [raʊnd]	rund ... um	stand ~ sb (or: sth)
beyond [bɪ'jɒnd]	jenseits	~ the lake (or: bridge)
along [ə'lɒŋ]	entlang	trees ~ the street
across [ə'krɒs]	drüben, auf der anderen Seite	My house is ~ the river.
over ['əʊvə*]	drüben	~ there (or: here) / ~ in America / **overseas** [ˌ-'siːz] countries
opposite ['ɒpəzɪt]	gegenüber	The town hall is ~ the church.
past [pɑːst]	nach, hinter	The post office is just ~ the cinema.
before [bɪ'fɔː*]	vor	just ~ the post office.

Movement in the horizontal sense – horizontale Bewegung

to the front [tə ðə 'frʌnt]	nach vorn	come ~ ~ ~
in front of [ɪn 'frʌnt əv]	vor ... her	run ~ ~ ~ a car
ahead [ə'hed]	nach vorn, voraus	go ~ / Full speed ~! / run on ~ / get ~ of
behind [bɪ'haɪnd]	hinter	run ~ a tree
to the back [tə ðə 'bæk]	nach hinten	go ~ ~ ~ of the room
backward ['bækwəd]	rückwärtig, nach hinten,	a ~ movement (or: look)
	Rück-	the ~ journey
backwards ['bækwədz]	rückwärts, zurück	look ~ / ~ and forwards
over ['əʊvə*]	über, um-, auf die andere Seite;	jump ~ (+ a wall) / fall ~ / roll ~ / climb ~ (+ a fence) / fly ~ (+ the Sahara)
	vorbei	Come ~ for a cup of tea.
through [θruː]	durch	go ~ the streets (or: grass) / let sb ~ / The train goes ~ to London. / ~ the tunnel
along [ə'lɒŋ]	entlang	walk ~ the river (or: street)
across [ə'krɒs]	hinüber, auf die andere Seite	go ~ (+ the road) / swim ~ (+ the river) / a bridge ~ the canal
past [pɑːst]	(an) ... vorbei	walk ~ sb (+ without stopping) / Would you let me get ~, please?
aside [ə'saɪd]	beiseite	lay (or: put) sth ~ / step ~
(+ to the) right [(tə ðə) 'raɪt]	(nach) rechts	keep (or: turn) (+ ~ ~) ~ / Take the first turning (+ ~ ~) ~.
(+ to the) left [(tə ðə) 'left]	(nach) links	keep (or: turn) / (+ ~ ~) ~ / Take the first turning (+ ~ ~) ~.
by [baɪ]	vorüber, an ... vorüber;	pass ~ (+ sb / sth)
	über	travel to Paris ~ Dover
via ['vaɪə]	über	travel to Paris ~ Dover
inside [ˌɪn'saɪd]	nach drinnen, nach innen, in... (herein)	go (or: look) ~ (+ the house)
outside [ˌaʊt'saɪd]	nach draußen, nach außen	go (or: look) ~ (+ the door)
up and down [ˌʌp‿ən 'daʊn]	auf und ab	go ~ ~ ~ the platform / run excitedly ~ ~ ~
upstream [ˌʌp'striːm]	stromauf	row a boat ~
downstream [ˌdaʊn'striːm]	stromab	sail ~
away [ə'weɪ]	weg	Go ~!
next door ['neks'dɔː]	nach nebenan	go ~ ~

The compass – die Himmelsrichtungen

north [nɔːθ]	Norden, Nord-; nach Norden	Which direction is ~? / a ~ wind travel ~ / a room facing ~
north of ['nɔːθ‿əv]	nördlich von, im Norden von	Luton is ~ ~ London. / Luton is to the ~ ~ London.
northern ['nɔːðn]	nördlich (gelegen)	the ~ hemisphere / the ~ wall of a building
northerly ['nɔːðəlɪ]	nördlich, aus nördlicher Richtung	the ~ shore of a lake / a ~ wind
northward ['nɔːθwəd]	nach Norden gehend	in a ~ direction
northwards ['nɔːθwədz]	nach Norden	travel ~
south [saʊθ]	Süden	Dover is to the ~ of London
east [iːst]	Osten	Los Angeles is on the ~ coast. / the Middle E~
west [west]	Westen	Boston is on the ~ coast.

We say:

the North Pole
[ðə ˌnɔːθ 'pəʊl]
Northern Europe
[ˌnɔːðn 'jʊərəp]
North Germany
[ˌnɔːθ 'dʒɜːmənɪ]
North America
[ˌnɔːθ ə'merɪkə]
the northern hemisphere
[ðə ˌnɔːðn 'hemɪˌsfɪə*]
East Germany
[ˌiːst 'dʒəːmənɪ]
Eastern countries
[iːstən 'kʌntriːz]
the East Side
[ðɪ 'iːst saɪd]

South Africa
[ˌsaʊθ 'æfrɪka]
Southern England
[ˌsʌðən 'ɪŋglənd]
South America
[ˌsaʊθ ə'merɪkə]
the Southern States (of the USA)
[ðə ˌsʌðən 'steɪts]
the West Indies
[ðə west 'ɪndiːz]
the Western world
[ðə ˌwestən 'wɜːld]

198 Line, distance – Linie, Entfernung

line [laɪn]	Linie, Strich	draw a ~
straight [streɪt]	gerade, geradeaus	draw a ~ line / The road goes ~ for five kilometres.
horizontal [ˌhɒrɪˈzɒntl]	waagerecht	move (or: extend) ~ly / in the ~ plane / Stand the table on its legs so that its top is ~.
vertical [ˈvɜːtɪkl]	senkrecht	draw a ~ line / move (or: rise / extend) ~ly
slant [slɑːnt]	sich neigen	sb's handwriting ~s to the right (or: left) / a **slanting** [ˈ-ɪŋ] roof
askew [əˈskjuː]	schief	hang a picture ~ / have one's hat on ~
parallel [ˈpærəlel]	parallel	draw ~ lines / The railway line runs ~ to (= with) the road.
zig-zag [ˈzɪgzæg]	zickzack	a ~ line (or: path)
angle [ˈæŋgl]	Winkel	draw an ~ / meet at right ~s
curve [kɜːv]	Kurve, Bogen	a ~ in the road / take ~s at high speed
wavy [ˈweɪvɪ]	wellenförmig	a ~ line
wind (wound, wound) [waɪnd, waʊnd, –]	sich winden	a river ~ing to the sea / a path ~ing up the hill / a ~ing road
spiral [ˈspaɪərəl]	Spirale, spiralförmig	go up in a ~ A snail's shell has a ~ form.
bend [bend]	Kurve	go round a ~ in the road
crooked [ˈkrʊkɪd]	krumm	a ~ line / The picture is ~.
distance [ˈdɪstəns]	Entfernung, Abstand	sth is some (or: a good) ~ away / see sth from (or: at) a ~ of 10 miles / What is the ~ from A to B (= between A and B)? / sth is within easy (+ walking / driving) ~
distant [ˈdɪstənt]	entfernt	~ lands / sth seen ~ly on the horizon
far [fɑː*]	weit	We did not go very ~. / How ~ did you go?
inch [ɪntʃ] = **in.** (1/12 of a foot)	Zoll (ca. 2,5 cm)	five ~es (= ins) long / He is 5 foot 8 ~es (= ins) tall.
foot [fʊt] = **ft** (1/3 of a yard)	Fuß (ca. 30,5 cm)	The building is 40 ~ high. / He is 5 ~ 8 inches tall. / a six-~ man
feet [fiːt] = **ft**		The building is 40 ~ high. / He is 6 ~ tall.
yard [jɑːd] = **yd**	ca. 91,5 cm	at a distance of 20 ~s (= yds)
mile [maɪl]	ca. 1,6 km	a 300 ~ (= ~s') journey / 30 ~s per (= an) hour (= 30 m.p.h.)

centimetre ['sentɪˌmiːtə*] (*BE*) = **centimeter** [-r] (*AE*) = **cm**	A ~ is less than an inch.
metre [miːtə*] (*BE*) = **meter** [-r] (*AE*) = **m**	There are more than three feet in a ~.

Plane, square measure – Fläche, Flächenmaß 199

plane [pleɪn]	Fläche, Ebene,	a vertical (or: horizontal) ~ / an inclined (geneigt) ~
	eben	a ~ surface
surface ['sɜːfɪs]	Oberfläche	have a plane (or: flat) ~ / have a rough (or: smooth) ~ / the earth's ~
side [saɪd]	Seite	the three ~s of a triangle / on the right (or: left) ~ / on both (or: all) ~s / carry sth **sideways** ['saɪdweɪz] (zur Seite)
triangle ['traɪæŋgl]	Dreieck	draw a ~ / be **triangular** [traɪ'æŋgjʊlə]
square [skweə*]	Quadrat,	the 64 ~s of a chessboard (Schachbrett) / have the shape of a ~ / 16 is the ~ of 4 / 3 is the **square root** [ˌskweə 'ruːt] of 9
	quadratisch	be ~ / a ~ measure
area ['eərɪə]	Fläche	a large ~ of land
rectangle ['rektæŋgl]	Rechteck	draw a ~ / be **rectangular** [rek'tæŋgjʊlə*]
circle ['sɜːkl]	Kreis	draw a ~ / stand in a ~ / a **circular** ['sɜːkjʊlə*] movement
centre ['sentə*] (*BE*) = **center** [-r] (*AE*)	Mittelpunkt	the ~ of a circle / **central** ['sentrəl]
diameter [daɪ'æmɪtə*]	Durchmesser	five inches in ~
radius ['reɪdjəs]	Halbmesser, Radius	within a ~ of five miles
circumference [sə'kʌmfərəns]	Umfang	measure (+ out) the ~
oval ['əʊvl]	Ellipse	have an **oval-shaped** [ˌəʊvl'ʃeɪpt] face
square measure [ˌskweə 'meʒə*]	Flächenmaß	
square inch [ˌskweər‿'ɪntʃ] = **in²**	ca. 645 mm^2	144 in^2 = 1 ft^2
square foot [ˌskweə 'fʊt] = **ft²**	ca. 0,09 m^2	9 ft^2 = 1 yd^2

square yard [ˌskweə 'jɑːd] = **yd^2**	ca. 0,8 m^2	4 840 yd^2 = 1 acre
acre ['eɪkə*]	ca. 4 047 m^2	640 acres = 1 square mile
square mile [ˌskweə 'maɪl]	ca. 2,59 km^2	

200 Solid figure, cubic measure, capacity – Körper, Raummaß, Rauminhalt

cube [kjuːb]	Würfel	
cylinder ['sɪlɪndə]	Zylinder	
cone [kəʊn]	Kegel	
prism ['prɪzəm]	Prisma	
sphere [sfɪə*]	Kugel	
pyramid ['pɪrəmɪd]	Pyramide	
top [tɒp]	Spitze, obere Seite	the ~ of a box / on (or: at) the ~ (+ of ...)
bottom ['bɒtəm]	Boden	the ~ of a box / sink to the ~ / on the ~
corner ['kɔːnə*]	Ecke	the eight ~s of a box
edge [edʒ]	Rand, Kante	the ~ of a plate / stand sth up on ~
side [saɪd]	Seite, Seitenfläche	the six ~s of a box
front [frʌnt]	Vorderseite	the ~ of a cupboard / the ~ of a building
back [bæk]	Rückseite	the ~ of a car
width [wɪdθ]	Breite, Weite	What is its ~ ? / sixty feet in ~ / have a ~ of ten feet / The ~ of the road is 20 feet.
wide [waɪd]	breit, weit	ten yards ~ / ~ enough
breadth [bredθ]	Breite	What is its ~? / The ~ is 12 yards. / It's 12 yards in ~.
broad [brɔːd]	breit	five metres ~ / a ~ river (or: road)
depth [depθ]	Tiefe	What is the ~ of this lake? / a ~ of 40 feet / in the ~s of the ocean
deep [diːp]	tief	a ~ hole / ~ snow (or: water) / a box three inches ~ / The river is 20 feet ~.
length [leŋθ]	Länge	What is its ~? / The ~ is 10 metres. / six feet in ~ / at full ~
long [lɒŋ]	lang	five feet ~ / a ~ river / How ~ is the Thames?
cubic measure [ˌkjuːbɪk 'meʒə*]	Raummaß	

cubic inch [ˌkjuːbɪk ˈɪntʃ] = **in^3**	ca. 16,39 cm^3	1 728 in^3 = 1 ft^3
cubic foot [ˌkjuːbɪk ˈfʊt] = **ft^3**	ca. 0,028 m^3	27 ft^3 = 1 yd^3
cubic yard [ˌkjuːbɪk ˈjɑːd] = **yd^3**	ca. 0,765 m^3	
volume [ˈvɒljuːm]	Inhalt, Volumen	The ~ of this container is 250 cubic metres.
capacity [kəˈpæsətɪ]	Rauminhalt, Fassungsvermögen	This bottle has half the ~ of that one.
empty [ˈemptɪ]	leer, leeren	an ~ room (or: bottle / cup) ~ a bottle / ~ out all one's pockets
full [fʊl]	voll	a ~ pot of coffee / a **potful** [ˈpɒtfʊl] of coffee / a **cupful** [ˈkʌpfʊl] of tea / ~ of people (or: water)
fill [fɪl]	(sich) füllen	~ sth with water
pint [paɪnt]	ca. 0,56 l	2 pints = 1 quart
quart [kwɔːt]	ca. 1,12 l	4 quarts are (= make) 1 gallon
gallon [ˈgælən] (*BE*)	ca. 4,5 l	
gallon [ˈgælən] (*AE*)	ca. 3,7 l	
litre [ˈliːtə*] (*BE*) = **liter** [-r] (*AE*)	ca. 1,76 pint, 0,22 UK gallon	

Size – Größe 201

big [bɪg]	groß, von großem Umfang	a ~ tree (or: box / house / book / man / stone / rat) / ~ clouds
large [lɑːdʒ]	groß, geräumig	a ~ house (or: town / boat / animal / tree / estate)
thick [θɪk]	dick, dicht	a ~ branch (or: wall / board / book) / two inches ~ / in the **thickest** [ˈ-ɪst] part of the forest / be **thickly** [ˈ-lɪ] covered with ...
vast [vɑːst]	weit, ausgedehnt	a ~ plain (or: forest / space / territory / city) / the **vastness** [ˈ-nɪs] of space (or: the skies / the sea)
huge [hjuːdʒ]	gewaltig	a ~ animal (or: man / mountain / castle / building / hall / tree)
giant [ˈdʒaɪənt]	riesenhaft, Riesen-	a ~ packet
gigantic [dʒaɪˈgæntɪk]	riesig	a ~ fish
immense [ɪˈmens]	unermeßlich	an ~ space (or: ocean) / the ~ universe
enormous [ɪˈnɔːməs]	enorm, über alle Maßen	an ~ amount (or: quantity) of sth

large-scale ['lɑːdʒ'skeɪl]	ausgedehnt	~ operations
spacious ['speɪʃəs]	weiträumig, geräumig	a ~ garden (or: room / apartment / library / hall)
small [smɔːl]	klein	a ~ man (or: child / dog / house / town / tree / box)
thin [θɪn]	dünn	~ grass (or: hair) / a ~ shirt / a ~ slice of bread
minute [maɪ'njuːt]	winzig	a ~ mark (Fleck) / a ~ portion of meat

Index

Der Index enthält alle Stichwörter und Ableitungen des Sachwörterbuchs in alphabetischer Reihenfolge. Die Ziffern beziehen sich auf die Nummer des jeweiligen Sachbereichs. Angaben in Klammern dienen lediglich der Orientierung.

A

B

C

A
B
C
D
E
F
G
H
I
J
K
L
M
N
O
P
Q
R
S
T
U
V
W
X
Y
Z

D

E

F

G

H

I

J

K

L

M

N

O

P

Q

R

S

T

U

V

W

X

Y

Z